Advanced Math
Test Masters

Test Solutions

About the Solutions

These solutions are designed to be representative of a student's work. Please keep in mind that many test problems will have more than one correct solution. We have attempted to stay as close as possible to the methods and procedures outlined in the textbook. The final answers have been set in bold type in order that they may be easily seen for grading purposes.

Below each problem number we have included a Lesson Reference Number. This number(s) refers to the lesson(s) in which the concepts for that problem type were taught. Some Lesson Reference Numbers are denoted as (*R*). This means "review problem," and students should know the concepts involved in solving these problems before entering *Advanced Mathematics*.

Test 1, Form A

1. (1)
$$2(90 - A) = (180 - A) - 40$$
$$180 - 2A = 140 - A$$
$$A = \mathbf{40°}$$

2. (R)
$$\frac{v}{p} = \frac{7}{3}$$
$$\frac{v}{1200} = \frac{7}{3}$$
$$3v = 8400$$
$$v = \mathbf{2800}$$

3. (R)
$$\frac{56}{100} = \frac{728}{T}$$
$$56T = 72{,}800$$
$$T = \mathbf{1300}$$

4. (4)

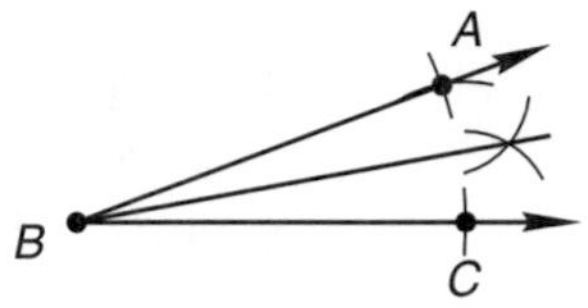

5. (4)

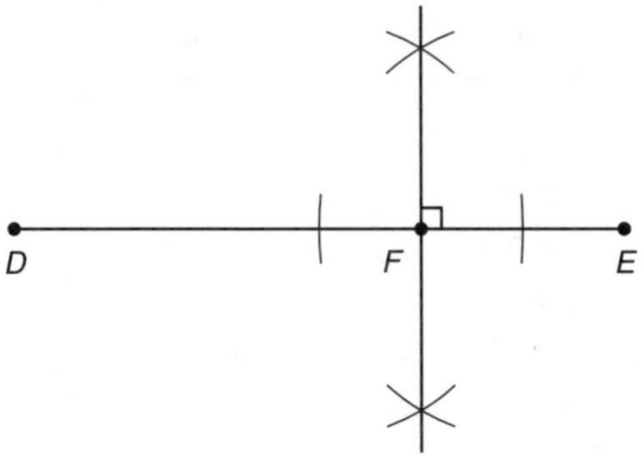

6. (4)

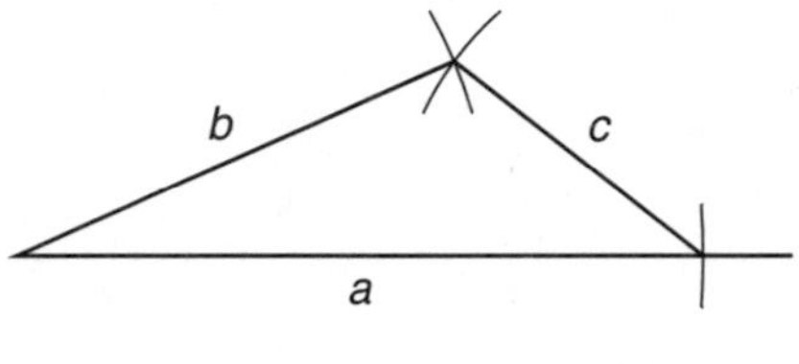

7. (R)
$$x - 2y = 0$$
$$x = 2y$$

$$3x + 5y = -22$$
$$3(2y) + 5y = -22$$
$$11y = -22$$
$$\mathbf{y = -2}$$

$$x = 2y$$
$$x = 2(-2)$$
$$\mathbf{x = -4}$$

8. (R)
$$2(x - x^0 + 1) = -4(2x - 5)$$
$$2x - 2 + 2 = -8x + 20$$
$$10x = 20$$
$$x = \mathbf{2}$$

9. (R)
$$\frac{4}{x} - \frac{2}{x - 1} + \frac{1}{x(x - 1)}$$
$$= \frac{4(x - 1) - 2x + 1}{x(x - 1)} = \mathbf{\frac{2x - 3}{x^2 - x}}$$

10. (R)
$$\frac{4^{-1}x^{-2}y^3}{2^2(xy)^{-4}} = \frac{(xy)^4 y^3}{(4)(2^2)x^2} = \mathbf{\frac{x^2 y^7}{16}}$$

11. (3)
$$c^2 \bigcirc a^2 + b^2$$
$$7^2 \bigcirc 5^2 + 5^2$$
$$49 \bigcirc 25 + 25$$
$$49 < 50$$

Since the square of the largest side is less than the sum of the squares of the other two sides, the triangle is an **acute triangle.**

12. (3)
$$4 \cdot \overleftarrow{SF} = 12$$
$$\overleftarrow{SF} = 3$$

$$x = 3 \cdot \overleftarrow{SF}$$
$$x = 3 \cdot (3)$$
$$\mathbf{x = 9}$$

$$y \cdot \overleftarrow{SF} = 8$$
$$y \cdot (3) = 8$$
$$\mathbf{y = \frac{8}{3}}$$

13. (3)
$$c^2 = 8^2 + 6^2$$
$$c = \sqrt{64 + 36}$$
$$\mathbf{c = 10}$$

$$\frac{6}{9} = \frac{8}{a + 8}$$
$$6a + 48 = 72$$
$$6a = 24$$
$$\mathbf{a = 4}$$

$$\frac{6}{9} = \frac{c}{b + c}$$
$$\frac{6}{9} = \frac{10}{b + 10}$$
$$6b + 60 = 90$$
$$6b = 30$$
$$\mathbf{b = 5}$$

14.
(1)
$$\frac{4}{5} = \frac{5}{d}$$
$$4d = 25$$
$$d = \frac{25}{4}$$

15.
(1)
$$x + 130 = 180$$
$$x = 50$$
$$y = 130$$

16.
(1)
$$B = \frac{30}{3} = 10$$
$$\text{Area} = \frac{1}{2}BH$$
$$H = \frac{(2)(\text{Area})}{B} = \frac{2(25\sqrt{3})}{10} = 5\sqrt{3} \text{ cm}$$

17.
(2)
$$V_{\text{sphere}} = \frac{4}{3}\pi r^3 = \frac{4}{3}\pi(3)^3 = 36\pi \text{ in.}^3$$
$$A_{\text{surface}} = 4\pi r^2 = 4\pi(3)^2 = 36\pi \text{ in.}^2$$

18.
(1)
$$A = 2\left[\frac{80}{360}\pi(\sqrt{7})^2\right] = \frac{28\pi}{9} \text{ m}^2$$

19.
(2)
$$V = \frac{1}{3}(A_{\text{base}})(h)$$
$$= \frac{1}{3}\left(\frac{2\cdot 3}{2} + (4 \cdot 3) + \frac{2 \cdot 3}{2}\right)(6)$$
$$= \frac{1}{3}(18)(6) = 36 \text{ cm}^3$$

20.
(R)
$$x^2 - 3y^2 + 2(x - y)(x^2 + 2xy + y^2)^0$$
$$= 2^2 - 3(1)^2 + 2(2 - 1)(1) = 4 - 3 + 2 = 3$$

Test 1, Form B

1.
(1)
$$3(90 - A) = (180 - A) + 50$$
$$270 - 3A = 230 - A$$
$$2A = 40$$
$$A = 20°$$

2.
(R)
$$\frac{c}{s} = \frac{8}{5}$$
$$\frac{c}{1500} = \frac{8}{5}$$
$$5c = 12,000$$
$$c = 2400$$

3.
(R)
$$\frac{38}{100} = \frac{874}{T}$$
$$38T = 87,400$$
$$T = 2300$$

4.
(4)
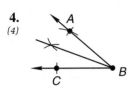

5.
(4)
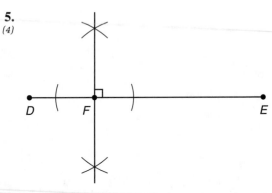

6.
(4)
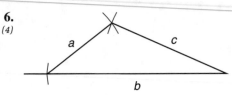

7.
(R)
$$2x - y = 0$$
$$y = 2x$$
$$2x + 5y = 24$$
$$2x + 5(2x) = 24$$
$$2x + 10x = 24$$
$$12x = 24$$
$$x = 2$$
$$y = 2x$$
$$y = 2(2)$$
$$y = 4$$

8.
(R)
$$4(x + x^0 + 2) = 3(3x - 1)$$
$$4x + 4(1) + 8 = 9x - 3$$
$$4x + 12 = 9x - 3$$
$$5x = 15$$
$$x = 3$$

9.
(R)
$$\frac{3}{x + 1} - \frac{2}{x} + \frac{1}{x(x + 1)}$$
$$= \frac{3x - 2(x + 1) + 1}{x(x + 1)} = \frac{x - 1}{x^2 + x}$$

10.
(R)
$$\frac{3^{-1}x^{-3}y^2}{2^3(xy)^{-1}} = \frac{y^2xy}{8(3)x^3} = \frac{y^3}{24x^2}$$

11. $c^2 \bigcirc a^2 + b^2$
(3)

$7^2 \bigcirc 6^2 + 6^2$

$49 \bigcirc 36 + 36$

$49 < 72$

Since the square of the largest side is less than the sum of the squares of the other two sides, the triangle is an **acute triangle.**

12. $22 \cdot \overleftrightarrow{SF} = 33$
(3)

$$\overleftrightarrow{SF} = \frac{3}{2}$$

$x = 20 \cdot \overleftrightarrow{SF}$

$x = 20 \cdot \dfrac{3}{2}$

$x = 30$

$y \cdot \overleftrightarrow{SF} = 27$

$y \cdot \dfrac{3}{2} = 27$

$y = 18$

13. $f^2 = 12^2 + 9^2$
(3)

$f = \sqrt{144 + 81}$

$f = 15$

$$\frac{12}{16} = \frac{9}{9 + e}$$

$108 + 12e = 144$

$12e = 36$

$e = 3$

$$\frac{12}{16} = \frac{f}{f + g}$$

$$\frac{3}{4} = \frac{15}{15 + g}$$

$45 + 3g = 60$

$3g = 15$

$g = 5$

14. $\dfrac{2}{3} = \dfrac{3}{x}$
(1)

$2x = 9$

$x = \dfrac{9}{2}$

15. $x + 160 = 180$
(1)

$x = 20$

$y = 160$

16. $B = \dfrac{6}{3} = 2$
(1)

Area $= \dfrac{1}{2}BH$

$H = \dfrac{(2)(\text{Area})}{B} = \dfrac{2(\sqrt{3})}{2} = \sqrt{3}$ **km**

17. $V_{\text{sphere}} = \dfrac{4}{3}\pi r^3 = \dfrac{4}{3}\pi(2)^3 = \dfrac{32\pi}{3}$ **mi³**
(2)

$A_{\text{surface}} = 4\pi r^2 = 4\pi(2)^2 = \mathbf{16\pi}$ **mi²**

18. $A = 2\left[\dfrac{62}{360}\pi(\sqrt{5})^2\right] = \dfrac{31\pi}{18}$ **cm²**
(1)

19. $V = \dfrac{1}{3}\left(A_{\text{base}}\right)(h)$
(2)

$= \dfrac{1}{3}\left[\dfrac{4 \cdot 6}{2} + (8 \cdot 6) + \dfrac{4 \cdot 6}{2}\right](9)$

$= \dfrac{1}{3}(72)(9) = \mathbf{216\ m^3}$

20. $x^3 - 2y^2 + 2(y - x)(6x^5 + 3xy^4 + x^2)^0$
(R)

$= 3^3 - 2(4)^2 + 2(4 - 3)(1)$

$= 27 - 32 + 2 = \mathbf{-3}$

Test 2, Form A

1. $\begin{cases} \dfrac{h}{s} = \dfrac{11}{2} \\ 5s = h - 3 \end{cases}$
(R)

$\dfrac{h}{s} = \dfrac{11}{2}$

$h = \dfrac{11s}{2}$

$5s = h - 3$

$5s = \dfrac{11s}{2} - 3$

$10s = 11s - 6$

$s = 6$

2.
(R)
$$\begin{cases} N_N + N_D = 25 \\ 5N_N + 10N_D = 175 \end{cases}$$

$$N_N + N_D = 25$$
$$N_N = 25 - N_D$$

$$5N_N + 10N_D = 175$$
$$5(25 - N_D) + 10N_D = 175$$
$$125 - 5N_D + 10N_D = 175$$
$$5N_D = 50$$
$$\mathbf{N_D = 10}$$

$$N_N + N_D = 25$$
$$N_N + 10 = 25$$
$$\mathbf{N_N = 15}$$

3. $N, N + 2, N + 4$
(7)
$$2(N + N + 2) = 3(N + 4) - 1$$
$$4N + 4 = 3N + 12 - 1$$
$$N = 7$$

7, 9, 11

4. **The argument is invalid.** The set described is the set
(7) of all parrots. For a valid argument the minor premise should have stated that she was a member of this set.

5. **If an animal is not a cat, then it is not furry.**
(7)

6. $\dfrac{1}{2} + \dfrac{2}{x + 1} = \dfrac{3}{4}$
(6)
$$\dfrac{2}{x + 1} = \dfrac{1}{4}$$
$$x + 1 = 8$$
$$x = 7$$

7. $\sqrt{3x - 2} - \sqrt{4} = 5$
(6)
$$\sqrt{3x - 2} = 7$$
$$3x - 2 = 49$$
$$3x = 51$$
$$x = 17$$

8. (a) $\begin{cases} x + y + z = 2 \\ 3x + 2y + z = 7 \\ 4x - y - 2z = 9 \end{cases}$
(6)
  (b)
  (c)

(a) $x + y + z = 2$
$$x = 2 - y - z$$

(b)
$$3x + 2y + z = 7$$
$$3(2 - y - z) + 2y + z = 7$$
$$6 - 3y - 3z + 2y + z = 7$$
(b′)
$$-y - 2z = 1$$

(c)
$$4x - y - 2z = 9$$
$$4(2 - y - z) - y - 2z = 9$$
$$8 - 4y - 4z - y - 2z = 9$$
(c′)
$$-5y - 6z = 1$$

-3(b′) $3y + 6z = -3$
(c′) $\dfrac{-5y - 6z = 1}{-2y \qquad = -2}$
$$y = 1$$

(b′) $-y - 2z = 1$
$$-(1) - 2z = 1$$
$$z = -1$$

(a) $x + y + z = 2$
$$x + (1) + (-1) = 2$$
$$\mathbf{x = 2}$$

9. $(\sqrt{5} - \sqrt{2})(\sqrt{5} + \sqrt{2})$
(5)
$$= (\sqrt{5})^2 - \sqrt{10} + \sqrt{10} - (\sqrt{2})^2 = 5 - 2 = \mathbf{3}$$

10. $\dfrac{\sqrt{x^4 y^2}\, xy^{-2}}{\sqrt[3]{x^3 y^6 (xy)^2}} = \dfrac{x^2 yx}{y^2 xy^2 (xy)^{2/3}} = \dfrac{x^3 y}{y^{14/3} x^{5/3}}$
(5)
$$= \mathbf{x^{4/3} y^{-11/3}}$$

11. $5i^2 - 7i^4 + 3i^3 - 1$
(5)
$$= 5(ii) - 7(ii)(ii) + 3(ii)i - 1$$
$$= 5(-1) - 7(-1)(-1) + 3(-1)i - 1$$
$$= -5 - 7 - 3i - 1 = \mathbf{-13 - 3i}$$

12. $(i - 2)(i - 3) = i^2 - 2i - 3i + 6$
(5)
$$= -1 - 5i + 6 = \mathbf{5 - 5i}$$

13.
(4)

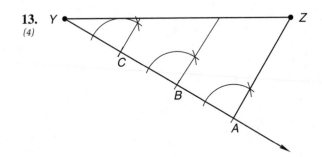

14. $(AB)^2 = 3^2 + d^2$
(5)

$AB = \sqrt{9 + d^2}$

$(AC)^2 = (AB)^2 + 4^2$

$(AC)^2 = (9 + d^2) + 16$

$AC = \sqrt{25 + d^2}$ **ft**

15. $A_{\text{shaded region}} = A_{\text{rectangle}} - A_{\text{circle}}$
(1)

$= 6(3 + 5) - \pi(3)^2$

$= (48 - 9\pi) \text{ cm}^2$

16. $\dfrac{2}{3x} = \dfrac{3}{4x + 1}$
(8)

$8x + 2 = 9x$

$x = 2$

17. $\dfrac{4}{6} = \dfrac{5}{c}$
(8)

$4c = 30$

$c = \dfrac{30}{4} = \dfrac{15}{2}$

18. $\dfrac{\text{Side}_1}{\text{Side}_2} = \dfrac{6}{1}$
(5)

$\dfrac{\text{Area}_1}{\text{Area}_2} = \left(\dfrac{\text{Side}_1}{\text{Side}_2}\right)^2 = \left(\dfrac{6}{1}\right)^2 = \dfrac{36}{1}$

19.
(8)

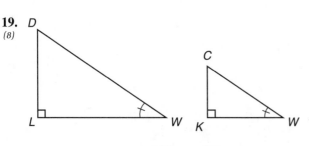

$\triangle DWL \sim \triangle CWK$ so $\dfrac{DW}{LW} = \dfrac{CW}{KW}$

20. $A_{\text{surface}} = \pi r^2 + \pi rl$
(2)

$= \pi(4)^2 + \pi(4)(8)$

$= 16\pi + 32\pi$

$= 48\pi \text{ in.}^2$

Test 2, Form B

1. $\begin{cases} \dfrac{d}{s} = \dfrac{3}{11} \\ 3d = s - 2 \end{cases}$
(R)

$\dfrac{d}{s} = \dfrac{3}{11}$

$s = \dfrac{11}{3}d$

$3d = s - 2$

$3d = \dfrac{11d}{3} - 2$

$9d = 11d - 6$

$2d = 6$

$d = 3$

2. $\begin{cases} N_N + N_D = 21 \\ 5N_N + 10N_D = 155 \end{cases}$
(R)

$N_N + N_D = 21$

$N_N = 21 - N_D$

$5N_N + 10N_D = 155$

$5(21 - N_D) + 10N_D = 155$

$105 - 5N_D + 10N_D = 155$

$5N_D = 50$

$N_D = 10$

$N_N + N_D = 21$

$N_N + 10 = 21$

$N_N = 11$

3. $N, N + 2, N + 4$
(7)

$2(N + N + 2) = 3(N + 4) + 8$

$4N + 4 = 3N + 12 + 8$

$N = 16$

16, 18, 20

4. **The argument is invalid.** The set described is the
(7) set of all poets. For a valid argument, the minor premise should have stated that Gogo was a member of this set.

5. **If a cat is not happy, then it is not purring.**
(7)

6. $\dfrac{1}{3} + \dfrac{4}{x + 2} = \dfrac{5}{6}$
(6)

$\dfrac{4}{x + 2} = \dfrac{1}{2}$

$x + 2 = 8$

$x = 6$

Test Solutions

7. $\sqrt{6x - 2} - \sqrt{9} = 5$
(6)

$$\sqrt{6x - 2} = 8$$
$$6x - 2 = 64$$
$$6x = 66$$
$$x = \mathbf{11}$$

8. (a) $\begin{cases} x + y + z = 2 \\ 2x + 3y + z = 6 \\ 2x + 4y - z = 7 \end{cases}$
(6) (b)
(c)

(a) $x + y + z = 2$
$$x = 2 - y - z$$

(b)
$$2x + 3y + z = 6$$
$$2(2 - y - z) + 3y + z = 6$$
$$4 - 2y - 2z + 3y + z = 6$$
(b′)
$$y - z = 2$$

(c)
$$2x + 4y - z = 7$$
$$2(2 - y - z) + 4y - z = 7$$
$$4 - 2y - 2z + 4y - z = 7$$
(c′)
$$2y - 3z = 3$$

–2(b′) $-2y + 2z = -4$
(c′) $\underline{2y - 3z = 3}$
$$-z = -1$$
$$z = \mathbf{1}$$

(b′) $y - z = 2$
$$y - 1 = 2$$
$$y = \mathbf{3}$$

(a) $x + y + z = 2$
$$x + 3 + 1 = 2$$
$$x = \mathbf{-2}$$

9. $(\sqrt{7} - \sqrt{3})(\sqrt{7} + \sqrt{3})$
(5)
$$= (\sqrt{7})^2 + \sqrt{21} - \sqrt{21} - (\sqrt{3})^2 = 7 - 3 = \mathbf{4}$$

10. $\dfrac{\sqrt[3]{x^6 y^3}\, x^{-1} y^2}{\sqrt{x^4 y^2 (xy)^3}} = \dfrac{x^2 y y^2}{x^2 y x^{3/2} y^{3/2} x} = \dfrac{y^2}{x^{5/2} y^{3/2}}$
(5)

$$= \mathbf{x^{-5/2} y^{1/2}}$$

11. $7i^3 - 6i^2 + 4i^3 + 1 = 11i^3 - 6i^2 + 1$
(5)
$$= 11(ii)i - 6(ii) + 1 = 11(-1)i - 6(-1) + 1$$
$$= -11i + 6 + 1 = \mathbf{7 - 11i}$$

12. $(4 - i)(2 - i) = 8 - 4i - 2i + i^2$
(5)
$$= 8 - 6i + (-1) = \mathbf{7 - 6i}$$

13.
(4)

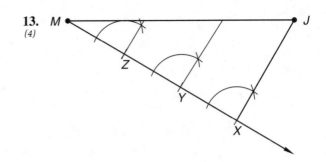

14. $(AB)^2 = 6^2 + d^2$
(5)
$$AB = \sqrt{36 + d^2}$$

$$(AC)^2 = (AB)^2 + 8^2$$
$$(AC)^2 = (36 + d^2) + 64$$
$$AC = \sqrt{100 + d^2}\ \mathbf{cm}$$

15. $A_{\text{shaded region}} = A_{\text{rectangle}} - A_{\text{circle}}$
(1)
$$= 4(5 + 3) - \pi(2)^2$$
$$= \mathbf{(32 - 4\pi)\ cm^2}$$

16. $\dfrac{4}{4x} = \dfrac{3}{2x + 2}$
(8)
$$8x + 8 = 12x$$
$$-4x = -8$$
$$x = \mathbf{2}$$

17. $\dfrac{z}{6} = \dfrac{12}{9}$
(8)
$$9z = 72$$
$$z = \mathbf{8}$$

18. $\dfrac{\text{Side}_1}{\text{Side}_2} = \dfrac{7}{1}$
(5)

$$\dfrac{\text{Area}_1}{\text{Area}_2} = \left(\dfrac{\text{Side}_1}{\text{Side}_2}\right)^2 = \left(\dfrac{7}{1}\right)^2 = \mathbf{\dfrac{49}{1}}$$

19.
(8)

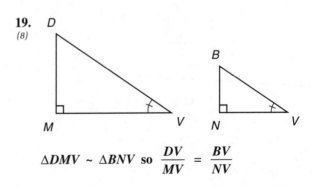

$\triangle DMV \sim \triangle BNV$ so $\dfrac{DV}{MV} = \dfrac{BV}{NV}$

20. $A_{\text{surface}} = \pi r^2 + \pi r l$
(2)

$\qquad = \pi(3)^2 + \pi(3)(9)$

$\qquad = 9\pi + 27\pi$

$\qquad = \mathbf{36\pi}$ **in.**^{2}

Test 3, Form A

1. R = Reisingers
(R)

C = Ochsenbeins

$\dfrac{C}{C + R} = \dfrac{2}{2 + 5}$

$\dfrac{C}{350} = \dfrac{2}{7}$

$7C = 700$

$C = \mathbf{100}$

2. Exterior = **360°**
(12)

Interior = $(N - 2)180° = (10 - 2)180° = \mathbf{1440°}$

3. $\begin{cases} N_D + N_C = 52 \\ 3N_D = N_C + 4 \end{cases}$
(R)

$3N_D = N_C + 4$

$N_C = 3N_D - 4$

$N_D + N_C = 52$

$N_D + \left(3N_D - 4\right) = 52$

$4N_D = 56$

$N_D = \mathbf{14}$

$N_D + N_C = 52$

$(14) + N_C = 52$

$N_C = \mathbf{38}$

4. $2y + 2x = 10$
(11)

$\dfrac{2y - 2x = 6}{4y = 16}$

$y = \mathbf{4}$

$2y + 2x = 10$

$2(4) + 2x = 10$

$2x = 2$

$x = \mathbf{1}$

5. $x = 2(70) = \mathbf{140}$
(11)

$y = 2(50) = \mathbf{100}$

$z = 360 - 100 - 140 = \mathbf{120}$

6. $ax^2 + bx + c = 0$
(11)

$x^2 + \dfrac{b}{a}x + \dfrac{c}{a} = 0$

$\left(x^2 + \dfrac{b}{a}x\right) = -\dfrac{c}{a}$

$\left(x^2 + \dfrac{b}{a}x + \dfrac{b^2}{4a^2}\right) = \dfrac{b^2}{4a^2} - \dfrac{c}{a}$

$\left(x + \dfrac{b}{2a}\right)^2 = \dfrac{b^2 - 4ac}{4a^2}$

$x + \dfrac{b}{2a} = \pm\sqrt{\dfrac{b^2 - 4ac}{4a^2}}$

$x = -\dfrac{b}{2a} \pm \sqrt{\dfrac{b^2 - 4ac}{4a^2}}$

$x = \dfrac{-b \pm \sqrt{b^2 - 4ac}}{2a}$

7. $2x^2 = 4x - 5$
(11)

$2x^2 - 4x + 5 = 0$

$a = 2, \; b = -4, \; c = 5$

$x = \dfrac{-(-4) \pm \sqrt{(-4)^2 - 4(2)(5)}}{2(2)}$

$x = \dfrac{4 \pm \sqrt{-24}}{4}$

$x = \dfrac{4}{4} \pm \dfrac{2\sqrt{6}i}{4}$

$x = \mathbf{1 \pm \dfrac{\sqrt{6}}{2}i}$

8. $5 + 2x^2 = -6x$
(10)

$2x^2 + 6x = -5$

$\left(x^2 + 3x\right) = -\dfrac{5}{2}$

$\left(x^2 + 3x + \dfrac{9}{4}\right) = \dfrac{9}{4} - \dfrac{5}{2}$

$\left(x + \dfrac{3}{2}\right)^2 = -\dfrac{1}{4}$

$x + \dfrac{3}{2} = \pm\sqrt{-\dfrac{1}{4}}$

$x = \mathbf{-\dfrac{3}{2} \pm \dfrac{1}{2}i}$

9.
(6)

$$\sqrt{3m + 7} + \sqrt{3m} = 7$$
$$\sqrt{3m + 7} = 7 - \sqrt{3m}$$
$$3m + 7 = 49 - 14\sqrt{3m} + 3m$$
$$14\sqrt{3m} = 42$$
$$\sqrt{3m} = 3$$
$$3m = 9$$
$$m = 3$$

10.
(5)

$$\sqrt{2}\sqrt{-8} - \sqrt{2}\sqrt{-2}\sqrt{-2} + 2\sqrt{-2}\sqrt{-2}\sqrt{-2}$$
$$= \sqrt{2}(2\sqrt{2}i) - \sqrt{2}(\sqrt{2}i)^2 + 2(\sqrt{2}i)^3$$
$$= 4i - 2\sqrt{2}i^2 + 4\sqrt{2}i^3$$
$$= 4i - 2\sqrt{2}(-1) + 4\sqrt{2}(-1)i$$
$$= 2\sqrt{2} + (4 - 4\sqrt{2})i$$

11. The argument is **valid** because the major premise
(7) identified a property of the set of all math teachers
and the minor premise identified Jim as a member of
this set.

12. $c = \sqrt{3^2 + 4^2}$
(3)

$$c = \sqrt{25}$$
$$c = 5$$

$$\frac{3}{12} = \frac{4}{4 + a}$$
$$3(4 + a) = 4(12)$$
$$3a = 36$$
$$a = 12$$

$$\frac{c}{b} = \frac{4}{a}$$
$$\frac{5}{b} = \frac{4}{12}$$
$$4b = 60$$
$$b = 15$$

13. $\dfrac{a^{-2} + m^{-3}}{a^{-3}m^2} = \dfrac{a^{-2}}{a^{-3}m^2} + \dfrac{m^{-3}}{a^{-3}m^2}$
(5)

$$= \frac{a}{m^2} + \frac{a^3}{m^5} = \frac{am^3 + a^3}{m^5}$$

14. $\dfrac{\sqrt{a^2b^4}\left(a^3b^{-2}\right)^3}{\sqrt[3]{a^6b^{-9}}\left(\sqrt{a}\right)^{-1}} = \dfrac{ab^2a^9b^{-6}}{a^2b^{-3}a^{-1/2}}$
(5)

$$= \frac{aa^9a^{1/2}b^2b^3}{a^2b^6} = \frac{a^{21/2}b^5}{a^2b^6} = \frac{a^{17/2}}{b}$$

15.
(10)

$$\frac{3 - 2i + 3i^3}{1 - i} = \frac{3 - 2i + 3i(-1)}{1 - i}$$
$$= \frac{3 - 5i}{1 - i} \cdot \frac{1 + i}{1 + i} = \frac{3 + 3i - 5i - 5i^2}{1 + i - i - i^2}$$
$$= \frac{3 - 2i - 5(-1)}{1 - (-1)} = \frac{8 - 2i}{2} = \mathbf{4 - i}$$

16. $V_{\text{sphere}} = \dfrac{4}{3}\pi r^3 = \dfrac{4}{3}\pi\,(12)^3 = \mathbf{2304\pi\ in.^3}$
(2)

$$A_{\text{surface}} = 4\pi r^2 = 4\pi(12)^2 = \mathbf{576\pi\ in.^2}$$

17.
(9)

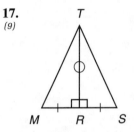

$\triangle TMR \cong \triangle TSR$ **by** *SAS* **congruency postulate**
$\overline{TM} \cong \overline{TS}$ **by** *CPCTC*

18. *SAS* **congruency postulate**
(9)

19.
(4)

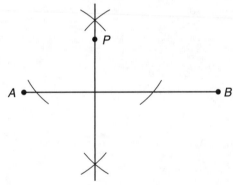

20.
(4)

Test 3, Form B

1. $\dfrac{P}{P + A} = \dfrac{2}{2 + 3}$
(R)

$$\frac{P}{85} = \frac{2}{5}$$
$$5P = 170$$
$$P = \mathbf{34}$$

2.
(12)
Exterior = **360°**

Interior = $(N - 2)180° = (9 - 2)180° = \mathbf{1260°}$

3.
(R)
$\begin{cases} N_B + N_R = 128 \\ N_B = 3N_R + 4 \end{cases}$

$N_B + N_R = 128$

$(3N_R + 4) + N_R = 128$

$4N_R = 124$

$\mathbf{N_R = 31}$

$N_B + N_R = 128$

$N_B + (31) = 128$

$\mathbf{N_B = 97}$

4.
(11)
$3x + 4y = 10$

$\underline{4x - 4y = 4}$

$7x \qquad = 14$

$\mathbf{x = 2}$

$3x + 4y = 10$

$3(2) + 4y = 10$

$4y = 4$

$\mathbf{y = 1}$

5.
(11)
$y = 2(80) = \mathbf{160}$

$z = 2(70) = \mathbf{140}$

$x = 360 - 140 - 160 = \mathbf{60}$

6.
(11)
$ax^2 + bx + c = 0$

$x^2 + \dfrac{b}{a}x + \dfrac{c}{a} = 0$

$\left(x^2 + \dfrac{b}{a}x\right) = -\dfrac{c}{a}$

$\left(x^2 + \dfrac{b}{a}x + \dfrac{b^2}{4a^2}\right) = \dfrac{b^2}{4a^2} - \dfrac{c}{a}$

$\left(x + \dfrac{b}{2a}\right)^2 = \dfrac{b^2 - 4ac}{4a^2}$

$x + \dfrac{b}{2a} = \pm\sqrt{\dfrac{b^2 - 4ac}{4a^2}}$

$x = -\dfrac{b}{2a} \pm \sqrt{\dfrac{b^2 - 4ac}{4a^2}}$

$x = \dfrac{-b \pm \sqrt{b^2 - 4ac}}{2a}$

7.
(11)
$3x^2 = 2x - 4$

$3x^2 - 2x + 4 = 0$

$a = 3, \ b = -2, \ c = 4$

$x = \dfrac{-(-2) \pm \sqrt{(-2)^2 - 4(3)(4)}}{2(3)}$

$x = \dfrac{2 \pm \sqrt{-44}}{6} = \dfrac{2}{6} \pm \dfrac{2\sqrt{11}i}{6}$

$x = \dfrac{1}{3} \pm \dfrac{\sqrt{11}}{3}i$

8.
(10)
$-7 + 2x^2 = 4x$

$2x^2 - 4x = 7$

$(x^2 - 2x) = \dfrac{7}{2}$

$(x^2 - 2x + 1) = \dfrac{7}{2} + 1$

$(x - 1)^2 = \dfrac{9}{2}$

$x - 1 = \pm\sqrt{\dfrac{9}{2}}$

$x = \dfrac{\pm 3\sqrt{2} + 2}{2}$

9.
(6)
$\sqrt{5y - 9} + \sqrt{5y} = 9$

$\sqrt{5y - 9} = 9 - \sqrt{5y}$

$5y - 9 = 81 - 18\sqrt{5y} + 5y$

$18\sqrt{5y} = 90$

$\sqrt{5y} = 5$

$5y = 25$

$\mathbf{y = 5}$

10.
(5)
$\sqrt{3}\sqrt{-3} + \sqrt{-9}\sqrt{9}\sqrt{3} - 3i\sqrt{-3}\sqrt{-3}$

$= \sqrt{3}(\sqrt{3}i) + \sqrt{9}i(3)\sqrt{3} - 3i(\sqrt{3}i)^2$

$= 3i + (3)(3)\sqrt{3}i - (3)(3)i^3$

$= 3i + 9\sqrt{3}i - 9(-1)i = \mathbf{(12 + 9\sqrt{3})i}$

11.
(7)
The argument is **valid** because the major premise identified a property of the set of all english teachers and the minor premise identified Mrs. Backer as a member of this set.

12.
(3)

$$a = \sqrt{5^2 + 12^2}$$

$$a = \sqrt{169}$$

$$a = \mathbf{13}$$

$$\frac{15}{5} = \frac{c + 12}{12}$$

$$5c + 60 = 180$$

$$5c = 120$$

$$c = \mathbf{24}$$

$$\frac{15}{5} = \frac{b + a}{a}$$

$$3 = \frac{b + 13}{13}$$

$$b + 13 = 39$$

$$b = \mathbf{26}$$

13.
(5)

$$\frac{x^{-1} + y^{-3}}{x^2 y^{-4}} = \frac{x^{-1}}{x^2 y^{-4}} + \frac{y^{-3}}{x^2 y^{-4}}$$

$$= \frac{y^4}{x^3} + \frac{y}{x^2} = \frac{y^4 + xy}{x^3}$$

14.
(5)

$$\frac{\sqrt{a^4 b^2}\left(a^3 b^{-2}\right)^2}{\sqrt[3]{a^3 b^{-6}}\left(\sqrt{b}\right)^{-1}} = \frac{a^2 b a^6 b^{-4}}{ab^{-2} b^{-1/2}} = \frac{a^2 a^6 b b^{1/2} b^2}{ab^4}$$

$$= \frac{a^8 b^{7/2}}{ab^4} = \frac{a^7}{b^{1/2}}$$

15.
(10)

$$\frac{i^3 + 3 - (-3i)}{2 - i} = \frac{i(-1) + 3 + 3i}{2 - i}$$

$$= \frac{3 + 2i}{2 - i} \cdot \frac{2 + i}{2 + i} = \frac{6 + 3i + 4i + 2i^2}{4 + 2i - 2i - i^2}$$

$$= \frac{6 + 7i + 2(-1)}{4 - (-1)} = \frac{4 + 7i}{5} = \frac{4}{5} + \frac{7}{5}i$$

16.
(2)

$$V_{\text{sphere}} = \frac{4}{3}\pi r^3 = \frac{4}{3}\pi(9 \text{ cm})^3 = \mathbf{972\pi \text{ cm}^3}$$

$$A_{\text{surface}} = 4\pi r^2 = 4\pi(9 \text{ cm})^2 = \mathbf{324\pi \text{ cm}^2}$$

17.
(9)

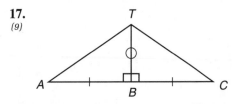

$\Delta TAB \cong \Delta TCB$ **by** *SAS* **congruency postulate**

$\overline{TA} \cong \overline{TC}$ **by** *CPCTC*

18. *SAS* **congruency postulate**
(9)

19.
(4)

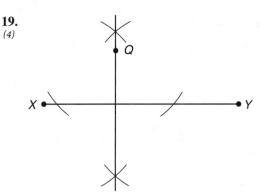

20.
(4)

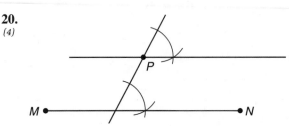

Test 4, Form A

1. $S_1 = 900 - 420 = 480$
(R)

$$\frac{S_2}{2100} = \frac{S_1}{900}$$

$$\frac{S_2}{2100} = \frac{480}{900}$$

$$900 S_2 = 1{,}008{,}000$$

$$S_2 = \mathbf{1120 \text{ ounces}}$$

2.
(14)

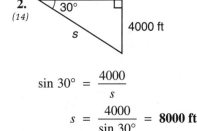

$$\sin 30° = \frac{4000}{s}$$

$$s = \frac{4000}{\sin 30°} = \mathbf{8000 \text{ ft}}$$

3.
(10)

$$2x = 5 - 3y$$

$$-3y = 2x - 5$$

$$y = -\frac{2}{3}x + \frac{5}{3}$$

Perpendicular lines have slopes that are negative reciprocals of each other.

$$y = \frac{3}{2}x + b$$

$$(5) = \left(\frac{3}{2}\right)(-2) + b$$

$$b = 5 + 3 = 8$$

$$y = \frac{3}{2}x + 8$$

4. $-4.5\hat{i} + 3.7\hat{j}$
(14)

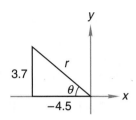

$r = \sqrt{(-4.5)^2 + (3.7)^2} = \sqrt{33.94} = 5.83$

$\tan\theta = \dfrac{3.7}{4.5}$

$\theta = 39.43°$ in second quadrant

$180° - \theta = 180° - 39.43° = 140.57°$

5.83$\underline{/140.57°}$ **5.83$\underline{/-219.43°}$**

–5.83$\underline{/-39.43°}$ **–5.83$\underline{/320.57°}$**

5. $-5\underline{/-342°}$
(14)

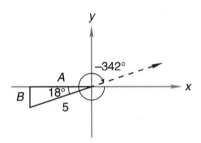

$A = 5\cos 18° = 4.76$

$B = 5\sin 18° = 1.55$

$-4.76\hat{i} - 1.55\hat{j}$

6. $\left(3x^{5/2} - 7y^{7/2}\right)\left(3x^{5/2} + 7y^{7/2}\right)$
(5)
$= \left(3x^{5/2}\right)^2 - \left(7y^{7/2}\right)^2 = \mathbf{9x^5 - 49y^7}$

7. (a) $\begin{cases}\dfrac{1}{2}x - \dfrac{1}{4}y = \dfrac{1}{2}\\[2mm] (b) \quad 0.2y - 0.2z = 1 \\[2mm] (c) \quad -\dfrac{1}{8}x + \dfrac{1}{4}z = -\dfrac{1}{4}\end{cases}$
(6)

$\begin{array}{r} 10(b) \quad 2y - 2z = 10 \\ 8(c) \quad -x \quad\;\; + 2z = -2 \\ \hline (d) \quad -x + 2y \quad\;\; = 8 \end{array}$

$\begin{array}{r} 2(d) \quad -2x + 4y = 16 \\ 4(a) \quad 2x - y = 2 \\ \hline 3y = 18 \\ \mathbf{y = 6} \end{array}$

$\begin{array}{r} 4(a) \quad 2x - (6) = 2 \\ 2x = 8 \\ \mathbf{x = 4} \end{array}$

$\begin{array}{r} 8(c) \quad -(4) + 2z = -2 \\ 2z = 2 \\ \mathbf{z = 1} \end{array}$

8. $y = v\left(\dfrac{ax}{b} + \dfrac{m}{c}\right)$
(16)

$y = \dfrac{vax}{b} + \dfrac{mv}{c}$

$bcy = cvax + bmv$

$bcy - cvax = bmv$

$c(by - vax) = bmv$

$c = \dfrac{bmv}{by - vax}$

9. $\dfrac{1 + 5\sqrt{3}}{3\sqrt{3} - 5} = \dfrac{1 + 5\sqrt{3}}{3\sqrt{3} - 5} \cdot \dfrac{3\sqrt{3} + 5}{3\sqrt{3} + 5}$
(10)

$= \dfrac{3\sqrt{3} + 5 + 15(3) + 25\sqrt{3}}{9(3) + 15\sqrt{3} - 15\sqrt{3} - 25}$

$= \dfrac{50 + 28\sqrt{3}}{2} = \mathbf{25 + 14\sqrt{3}}$

10. $\dfrac{a^{-7}b^5 + b^3a^{-3}}{a^{-2}b^4} = \dfrac{a^{-7}b^5}{a^{-2}b^4} + \dfrac{b^3a^{-3}}{a^{-2}b^4}$
(5)

$= \dfrac{b}{a^5} + \dfrac{1}{ab} = \dfrac{b^2 + a^4}{a^5b}$

11.
(15)

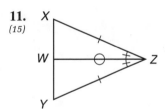

Statements	Reasons
1. $\overline{XZ} \cong \overline{YZ}$	1. Given
2. $\overline{ZW}$ bisects $\angle XZY$	2. Given
3. $\angle XZW \cong \angle YZW$	3. A bisector divides an angle into two congruent angles.
4. $\overline{ZW} \cong \overline{ZW}$	4. Reflexive axiom
5. $\triangle XZW \cong \triangle YZW$	5. *SAS* congruency postulate
6. $\overline{XW} \cong \overline{YW}$	6. CPCTC

12. $\dfrac{7}{3} = \dfrac{x}{6}$
(8)

$3x = 42$

$x = \mathbf{14}$

13.
(3)

(1) 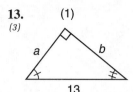   (2) 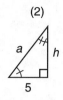   (3)

Triangles (1) and (2): $\dfrac{a}{13} = \dfrac{5}{a}$

$$a^2 = 65$$
$$a = \sqrt{65}$$

Triangle (1): $a^2 + b^2 = 13^2$
$$(\sqrt{65})^2 + b^2 = 13^2$$
$$b^2 = 169 - 65$$
$$b = \sqrt{104}$$
$$b = 2\sqrt{26}$$

Triangle (2): $5^2 + h^2 = a^2$
$$5^2 + h^2 = (\sqrt{65})^2$$
$$h^2 = 65 - 25$$
$$h = \sqrt{40}$$
$$h = 2\sqrt{10}$$

14.
(5)
$\sqrt{5}\sqrt{2}\sqrt{-5}\sqrt{-2} - \sqrt{5}\sqrt{2}i\sqrt{5}\sqrt{2}i^3 - \sqrt{-25}$
$= \sqrt{5}\sqrt{2}\sqrt{5}i\sqrt{2}i - \sqrt{5}\sqrt{5}\sqrt{2}\sqrt{2}i^4 - 5i$
$= 5(2)(-1) - 5(2)(1) - 5i = -20 - 5i$

15. $x = \dfrac{85 + 95}{2} = 90$
(13)

16. $x = \dfrac{110 - 40}{2} = 35$
(13)

17. $12 \cdot x = 15 \cdot 8$
(11)
$$12x = 120$$
$$x = 10$$

18. $6(6 + x) = 5(5 + 10)$
(13)
$$36 + 6x = 25 + 50$$
$$6x = 39$$
$$x = \dfrac{13}{2}$$

19. **If a student is with it then the student is an algebra**
(7) **student.** The argument is **valid.** Eric belongs to the
set identified by the contrapositive.

20. $\dfrac{88 + 100 + 95 + 84 + x}{5} = 90$
(R)
$$\dfrac{367 + x}{5} = 90$$
$$367 + x = 450$$
$$x = 83$$

Test 4, Form B

1. $Z_1 = 1010 - 700 = 310$
(R)
$$\dfrac{Z_1}{1010} = \dfrac{Z_2}{1818}$$
$$\dfrac{310}{1010} = \dfrac{Z_2}{1818}$$
$$1010Z_2 = 563{,}580$$
$$Z_2 = \textbf{558 tons}$$

2.
(14)

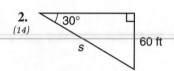

$$\sin 30° = \dfrac{60}{s}$$
$$s = \dfrac{60}{\sin 30°} = \textbf{120 ft}$$

3. $2x = \dfrac{1}{2}y - 3$
(10)
$$4x = y - 6$$
$$y = 4x + 6$$

Perpendicular lines have slopes that are negative
reciprocals of each other.

$$y = -\dfrac{1}{4}x + b$$
$$(6) = -\dfrac{1}{4}(-4) + b$$
$$b = 6 - 1 = 5$$
$$y = -\dfrac{1}{4}x + 5$$

4. $-2.5\,\hat{i} + 3.1\,\hat{j}$
(14)

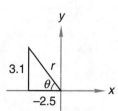

$$r = \sqrt{(-2.5)^2 + (3.1)^2} = \sqrt{15.86} = 3.98$$

$\tan \theta = \dfrac{3.1}{2.5}$

$\theta = 51.12°$ in second quadrant

$180° - \theta = 180° - 51.12° = 128.88°$

3.98/128.88°   **–3.98/308.88°**

3.98/–231.12°   **–3.98/–51.12°**

5. $-4/-330°$
(14)

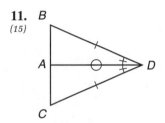

$A = 4 \cos 30° = 4 \cdot \dfrac{\sqrt{3}}{2} = 2\sqrt{3}$

$B = 4 \sin 30° = 4 \cdot \dfrac{1}{2} = 2$

$-2\sqrt{3}\,\hat{i} - 2\,\hat{j}$

6. $(2x^{3/2} - 3y^{5/2})(2x^{3/2} + 3y^{5/2})$
(5)
$= (2x^{3/2})^2 - (3y^{5/2})^2 = 4x^3 - 9y^5$

7. (a) $\begin{cases} \dfrac{1}{4}y - \dfrac{2}{5}z = \dfrac{1}{10} \\ \end{cases}$
(6)
  (b) $\begin{cases} 0.5x + 0.5z = 2.5 \\ \end{cases}$

  (c) $\begin{cases} \dfrac{3}{4}x + \dfrac{5}{2}y = 8 \end{cases}$

$\begin{array}{ll} 40(a) & 10y - 16z = 4 \\ -4(c) & -3x - 10y = -32 \\ \hline (d) & -3x - 16z = -28 \end{array}$

$\begin{array}{ll} 30(b) & 15x + 15z = 75 \\ 5(d) & -15x - 80z = -140 \\ \hline & -65z = -65 \\ & z = 1 \end{array}$

$\begin{array}{l} 10(b) \quad 5x + 5(1) = 25 \\ 5x = 20 \\ x = 4 \end{array}$

$\begin{array}{l} 4(c) \quad 3(4) + 10y = 32 \\ 10y = 20 \\ y = 2 \end{array}$

8. $y = r\left(\dfrac{bx}{c} + \dfrac{a}{d}\right)$
(16)

$y = \dfrac{bxr}{c} + \dfrac{ar}{d}$

$dcy = bxrd + car$

$dcy - bxrd = car$

$d(cy - bxr) = car$

$d = \dfrac{car}{cy - bxr}$

9. $\dfrac{1 + 3\sqrt{2}}{4\sqrt{2} - 3} = \dfrac{1 + 3\sqrt{2}}{4\sqrt{2} - 3} \cdot \dfrac{4\sqrt{2} + 3}{4\sqrt{2} + 3}$
(10)

$= \dfrac{4\sqrt{2} + 3 + 12(2) + 9\sqrt{2}}{16(2) + 12\sqrt{2} - 12\sqrt{2} - 9} = \dfrac{27 + 13\sqrt{2}}{23}$

10. $\dfrac{h^5 r^{-7} + r^{-2}h^3}{h^6 r^{-4}} = \dfrac{h^5 r^{-7}}{h^6 r^{-4}} + \dfrac{r^{-2}h^3}{h^6 r^{-4}}$
(5)

$= \dfrac{1}{hr^3} + \dfrac{r^2}{h^3} = \dfrac{h^2 + r^5}{h^3 r^3}$

11.
(15)

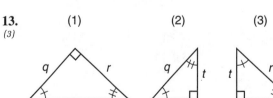

STATEMENTS	REASONS
1. $\overline{BD} \cong \overline{CD}$	1. Given
2. $\overline{DA}$ bisects $\angle BDC$	2. Given
3. $\angle ADB \cong \angle ADC$	3. A bisector divides an angle into two congruent angles.
4. $\overline{AD} \cong \overline{AD}$	4. Reflexive axiom
5. $\triangle ADB \cong \triangle ADC$	5. *SAS* congruency postulate
6. $\overline{BA} \cong \overline{CA}$	6. *CPCTC*

12. $\dfrac{9}{5} = \dfrac{k}{7}$
(8)

$5k = 63$

$k = \dfrac{63}{5}$

13.   (1)   (2)   (3)
(3)

Triangles (1) and (2): $\dfrac{13}{q} = \dfrac{q}{6}$

$q^2 = 78$

$q = \sqrt{78}$

Triangle (2): $6^2 + t^2 = (\sqrt{78})^2$

$$t^2 = 42$$
$$t = \sqrt{42}$$

Triangle (3): $t^2 + 7^2 = r^2$

$$(\sqrt{42})^2 + 49 = r^2$$
$$r = \sqrt{91}$$

14. $\sqrt{6}\sqrt{3}\sqrt{-6}\sqrt{-3} - \sqrt{6}\sqrt{3}i\sqrt{6}\sqrt{3}i^3 - \sqrt{-36}$
(5)

$= \sqrt{6}\sqrt{3}\sqrt{6}i\sqrt{3}i - \sqrt{6}\sqrt{6}\sqrt{3}\sqrt{3}i^4 - 6i$

$= (6)(3)(-1) - (6)(3)(1) - 6i = \mathbf{-36 - 6i}$

15. $x = \dfrac{120 + 70}{2} = \mathbf{95}$
(13)

16. $x = \dfrac{120 - 30}{2} = \mathbf{45}$
(13)

17. $8 \cdot x = 6 \cdot 4$
(11)
$$8 \cdot x = 24$$
$$x = \mathbf{3}$$

18. $10(10 + x) = 9(9 + 11)$
(13)
$$100 + 10x = 81 + 99$$
$$10x = 80$$
$$x = \mathbf{8}$$

19. **All emancipated are egalitarian.** The argument is
(7) **valid.** Sven belongs to the set identified by the contrapositive.

20. $\dfrac{87 + 99 + 93 + 81 + x}{5} = 90$
(R)

$$\dfrac{360 + x}{5} = 90$$
$$360 + x = 450$$
$$x = \mathbf{90}$$

Test 5, Form A

1. (a)
(20)

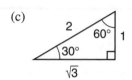

$$\sin 30° = \frac{1}{2}$$

$$\frac{\sqrt{3}}{2} \sin 30° = \frac{\sqrt{3}}{2}\left(\frac{1}{2}\right) = \frac{\sqrt{3}}{4}$$

(b)

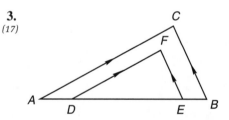

$$\cos 45° = \frac{1}{\sqrt{2}} = \frac{\sqrt{2}}{2}$$

$$4 \cos 45° = 4\left(\frac{\sqrt{2}}{2}\right) = \mathbf{2\sqrt{2}}$$

(c)

$$\tan 60° = \frac{\sqrt{3}}{1} = \sqrt{3}$$

$$\frac{\sqrt{3}}{3} \tan 60° = \frac{\sqrt{3}}{3}(\sqrt{3}) = \mathbf{1}$$

2. $\text{Glycol}_1 + \text{glycol}_2 = \text{total glycol}$
(18)
$$0.74(P_N) + 0.31(67) = 0.59(P_N + 67)$$
$$0.74P_N + 20.77 = 0.59P_N + 39.53$$
$$0.15P_N = 18.76$$
$$P_N = \mathbf{125.07 \text{ liters}}$$

3.
(17)

STATEMENTS	REASONS
1. $\overline{AC} \parallel \overline{DF}$	1. Given
2. $\angle A \cong \angle EDF$	2. If two parallel lines are cut by a transversal, then each pair of corresponding angles is congruent.
3. $\overline{BC} \parallel \overline{EF}$	3. Given
4. $\angle B \cong \angle DEF$	4. If two parallel lines are cut by a transversal, then each pair of corresponding angles is congruent.
5. $\angle C \cong \angle F$	5. $AA \rightarrow AAA$
6. $\triangle ABC \sim \triangle DEF$	6. AAA

4. $\begin{cases} x^2 + y^2 = 16 \\ y - x = 2 \end{cases}$
(19)

$$y - x = 2$$
$$y = x + 2$$

$$x^2 + y^2 = 16$$
$$x^2 + (x + 2)^2 = 16$$
$$x^2 + x^2 + 4x + 4 = 16$$
$$2x^2 + 4x - 12 = 0$$
$$x^2 + 2x - 6 = 0$$

$$x = \frac{-2 \pm \sqrt{2^2 - 4(1)(-6)}}{2(1)}$$

$$= \frac{-2 \pm \sqrt{28}}{2} = -1 \pm \sqrt{7}$$

For $x = -1 + \sqrt{7}$

$$y - x = 2$$
$$y - (-1 + \sqrt{7}) = 2$$
$$y = 1 + \sqrt{7}$$

For $x = -1 - \sqrt{7}$

$$y - x = 2$$
$$y - (-1 - \sqrt{7}) = 2$$
$$y = 1 - \sqrt{7}$$

$$(-1 + \sqrt{7},\ 1 + \sqrt{7}),\ (-1 - \sqrt{7},\ 1 - \sqrt{7})$$

5.
(16)

$$
\begin{array}{r}
x^2 + 3x + 14 \\
x - 3\overline{\smash{)}x^3 + 0x^2 + 5x - 6} \\
\underline{x^3 - 3x^2} \\
3x^2 + 5x \\
\underline{3x^2 - 9x} \\
14x - 6 \\
\underline{14x - 42} \\
36
\end{array}
$$

$$\frac{x^3 + 5x - 6}{x - 3} = x^2 + 3x + 14 + \frac{36}{x - 3}$$

6.
(19)
$$27x^3y^9 - 8z^{12} = (3xy^3)^3 - (2z^4)^3$$
$$= (3xy^3 - 2z^4)(9x^2y^6 + 6xy^3z^4 + 4z^8)$$

7.
(19)
$$8x^{4n+1} - 12x^{7n+3} = 2^3x^{4n}x - 3(2^2x^{7n}x^3)$$
$$= 2^2x^{4n}x(2 - 3x^{3n}x^2) = 4x^{4n+1}(2 - 3x^{3n+2})$$

8.
(10)
$$\frac{2i^3 - 4i^4 + i^2}{3 + 3i + \sqrt{-16}} = \frac{-2i - 4 - 1}{3 + 3i + 4i}$$

$$= \frac{-5 - 2i}{3 + 7i} \cdot \frac{3 - 7i}{3 - 7i} = \frac{-15 - 6i + 35i + 14i^2}{9 - 49i^2}$$

$$= \frac{-29 + 29i}{58} = -\frac{1}{2} + \frac{1}{2}i$$

9.
(18)
$$R = \frac{kB^2}{G}$$

$$160 = \frac{k(4)^2}{2}$$

$$k = 20$$

$$R = \frac{20B^2}{G} = \frac{20(7)^2}{10} = \textbf{98 reds}$$

10.
(16)
$$\frac{a}{a + \dfrac{a}{c + \dfrac{a}{b}}} = \frac{a}{a + \dfrac{a}{bc + a}} = \frac{a}{a + \dfrac{ab}{bc + a}}$$

$$= \frac{a}{\dfrac{a(bc + a) + ab}{bc + a}} = \frac{a(bc + a)}{abc + a^2 + ab}$$

$$= \frac{a(bc + a)}{a(bc + a + b)} = \frac{bc + a}{bc + a + b}$$

11.
(16)
$$\frac{\dfrac{3x}{y^2} + \dfrac{2z}{xy}}{\dfrac{x}{y} - \dfrac{z}{x}} \cdot \frac{\dfrac{xy^2}{1}}{\dfrac{xy^2}{1}} = \frac{3x^2 + 2zy}{x^2y - zy^2}$$

12.
(5)
$$(3x^4y)^{-2}\left(\frac{3x^2y}{xy}\right)^2 = \frac{9x^4y^2}{9x^8y^2x^2y^2} = \frac{1}{x^4x^2y^2}$$

$$= \frac{1}{x^6y^2}$$

13.
(18)
$$\begin{cases} T + U = 6 \\ 10U + T = (10T + U) + 18 \end{cases}$$

$$10U + T = (10T + U) + 18$$
$$9U - 9T = 18$$
$$U - T = 2$$
$$U = T + 2$$

$$T + U = 6$$
$$T + (T + 2) = 6$$
$$2T = 4$$
$$T = 2$$

$$T + U = 6$$
$$2 + U = 6$$
$$U = 4$$

The original number was **24**.

14.
(14)

$$\sin 70° = \frac{h}{300}$$
$$h = 300 \sin 70° = \textbf{281.91 ft}$$

15. $MX = OM = 7$
(3)

$$r = OX = \sqrt{7^2 + 7^2} = 7\sqrt{2}$$

$$A_{\text{shaded region}} = A_{\text{circle}} - A_{\text{square}}$$

$$= \pi r^2 - lw$$

$$= \pi(7\sqrt{2})^2 - (14)(14)$$

$$= 98\pi - 196 = \textbf{111.88}$$

16.
(15, 17)

STATEMENTS	REASONS
1. $\overline{LM} \parallel \overline{ON}$	1. Given
2. $\angle L \cong \angle O$ and $\angle M \cong \angle N$	2. If two parallel lines are cut by a transversal, each pair of alternate interior angles is congruent.
3. $\angle LPM \cong \angle OPN$	3. Vertical angles are congruent.
4. $\overline{LM} \cong \overline{ON}$	4. Given
5. $\triangle LPM \cong \triangle OPN$	5. *AAAS* congruency postulate

17.
(19)

$$\frac{x^{4a} - y^{4a}}{x^{2a} + y^{2a}} = \frac{(x^{2a})^2 - (y^{2a})^2}{x^{2a} + y^{2a}}$$

$$= \frac{(x^{2a} + y^{2a})(x^{2a} - y^{2a})}{(x^{2a} + y^{2a})} = x^{2a} - y^{2a}$$

18. $x + 4y = 3$
(10)

$$4y = -x + 3$$

$$y = -\frac{1}{4}x + \frac{3}{4}$$

Parallel lines have identical slopes.

$$y = -\frac{1}{4}x + b$$

$$(-1) = -\frac{1}{4}(4) + b$$

$$b = 0$$

$$y = -\frac{1}{4}x$$

19.
(13)

$$\frac{130 - x}{2} = 40$$

$$130 - x = 80$$

$$x = \textbf{50}$$

20. $5(x) = 8(10)$
(11)

$$5x = 80$$

$$x = \textbf{16}$$

Test 5, Form B

1. (a)
(20)

$$\cos 60° = \frac{1}{2}$$

$$\frac{1}{2} \cos 60° = \frac{1}{2}\left(\frac{1}{2}\right) = \frac{1}{4}$$

(b)

$$\tan 30° = \frac{1}{\sqrt{3}} = \frac{\sqrt{3}}{3}$$

$$\sqrt{3} \tan 30° = \sqrt{3}\left(\frac{\sqrt{3}}{3}\right) = \textbf{1}$$

(c)

$$\sin 45° = \frac{1}{\sqrt{2}} = \frac{\sqrt{2}}{2}$$

$$6 \sin 45° = 6\left(\frac{\sqrt{2}}{2}\right) = \textbf{3}\sqrt{\textbf{2}}$$

2. Glycol$_1$ + glycol$_2$ = total glycol
(18)

$$0.76(P_N) + 0.33(69) = 0.61(P_N + 69)$$

$$0.76P_N + 22.77 = 0.61P_N + 42.09$$

$$0.15P_N = 19.32$$

$$P_N = \textbf{128.80 liters}$$

3.
(17)

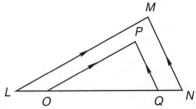

STATEMENTS	REASONS
1. $\overline{LM} \parallel \overline{OP}$	1. Given
2. $\angle L \cong \angle POQ$	2. If two parallel lines are cut by a transversal, then each pair of corresponding angles is congruent.
3. $\overline{MN} \parallel \overline{PQ}$	3. Given
4. $\angle N \cong \angle PQO$	4. If two parallel lines are cut by a transversal, then each pair of corresponding angles is congruent.
5. $\angle M \cong \angle P$	5. $AA \rightarrow AAA$
6. $\triangle LMN \sim \triangle OPQ$	6. AAA

4.
(19)
$$\begin{cases} y - x = 3 \\ x^2 + y^2 = 17 \end{cases}$$

$$y - x = 3$$
$$y = x + 3$$

$$x^2 + y^2 = 17$$
$$x^2 + (x + 3)^2 = 17$$
$$x^2 + x^2 + 6x + 9 = 17$$
$$2x^2 + 6x - 8 = 0$$
$$x^2 + 3x - 4 = 0$$
$$(x + 4)(x - 1) = 0$$
$$x = -4, 1$$

For $x = -4$
$$y - x = 3$$
$$y - (-4) = 3$$
$$y = -1$$

For $x = 1$
$$y - x = 3$$
$$y - (1) = 3$$
$$y = 4$$

$(-4, -1), (1, 4)$

5.
(16)

$$x + 3 \overline{\smash{\big)}\, x^3 + 4x^2 + 0x + 10} \quad \frac{x^2 + x - 3}{}$$
$$\underline{x^3 + 3x^2}$$
$$x^2 + 0x$$
$$\underline{x^2 + 3x}$$
$$-3x + 10$$
$$\underline{-3x - 9}$$
$$19$$

$$\frac{x^3 + 4x^2 + 10}{x + 3} = x^2 + x - 3 + \frac{19}{x + 3}$$

6.
(19)
$$64y^{12} - 8x^9z^3 = 8\left[(2y^4)^3 - (x^3z)^3\right]$$
$$= 8(2y^4 - x^3z)(4y^8 + 2x^3y^4z + x^6z^2)$$

7.
(19)
$$3x^{8n+2} - 9x^{5n+3} = 3x^{8n}x^2 - 3^2x^{5n}x^3$$
$$= 3x^{5n}x^2(x^{3n} - 3x) = 3x^{5n+2}(x^{3n} - 3x)$$

8.
(10)
$$\frac{3i^2 - 4i^3 - 2i^4}{2 + \sqrt{-9} + 4i} = \frac{-3 + 4i - 2}{2 + 3i + 4i}$$

$$= \frac{-5 + 4i}{2 + 7i} \cdot \frac{2 - 7i}{2 - 7i}$$

$$= \frac{-10 + 35i + 8i - 28i^2}{4 - 49i^2} = \frac{18}{53} + \frac{43}{53}i$$

9.
(18)
$$Y = \frac{ky}{j^2}$$

$$15 = \frac{k(90)}{6^2}$$

$$k = 6$$

$$Y = \frac{6y}{j^2} = \frac{6(64)}{(4)^2} = 24 \text{ yins}$$

10.
(16)
$$\frac{n}{n + \dfrac{n}{x + \dfrac{n}{y}}} = \frac{n}{n + \dfrac{n}{\dfrac{xy + n}{y}}} = \frac{n}{n + \dfrac{ny}{xy + n}}$$

$$= \frac{n}{\dfrac{n(xy + n) + ny}{xy + n}} = \frac{n(xy + n)}{nxy + n^2 + ny}$$

$$= \frac{n(xy + n)}{n(xy + n + y)} = \frac{xy + n}{xy + n + y}$$

11.
(16)
$$\frac{\dfrac{3x}{yz} + \dfrac{2z}{x}}{\dfrac{y}{x} - \dfrac{x}{z}} \cdot \frac{\dfrac{xyz}{1}}{\dfrac{xyz}{1}} = \frac{3x^2 + 2yz^2}{y^2z - x^2y}$$

12.
(5)
$$(2xy^3)^{-3} \left(\frac{2xy^2}{xy}\right)^2 = \frac{4x^2y^4}{8x^3y^9x^2y^2}$$

$$= \frac{1}{2xy^5x^2y^2} = \frac{1}{2x^3y^7}$$

13.
(18)
$\begin{cases} T + U = 9 \\ 10U + T = (10T + U) + 45 \end{cases}$

$10U + T = (10T + U) + 45$

$9U - 9T = 45$

$U - T = 5$

$U = T + 5$

$T + U = 9$

$T + (T + 5) = 9$

$2T = 4$

$T = 2$

$T + U = 9$

$2 + U = 9$

$U = 7$

The original number was **27**.

14.
(14)

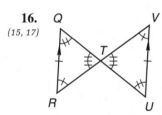

$\sin 50° = \dfrac{h}{150}$

$h = 150 \sin 50° = \textbf{114.91 ft}$

15. $BM = OM = 5$
(3)

$r = OB = \sqrt{5^2 + 5^2} = 5\sqrt{2}$

$A_{\text{shaded region}} = A_{\text{circle}} - A_{\text{square}}$

$= \pi r^2 - lw$

$= \pi(5\sqrt{2})^2 - (10)(10)$

$= 50\pi - 100 = \textbf{57.08}$

16.
$(15, 17)$

STATEMENTS	REASONS
1. $\overline{QR} \parallel \overline{UV}$	1. Given
2. $\angle R \cong \angle V$ and $\angle Q \cong \angle U$	2. If two parallel lines are cut by a transversal, each pair of alternate interior angles is congruent.
3. $\angle QTR \cong \angle UTV$	3. Vertical angles are congruent.
4. $\overline{QR} \cong \overline{UV}$	4. Given
5. $\triangle QRT \cong \triangle UVT$	5. *AAAS* congruency postulate

17.
(19)
$\dfrac{x^{4m} - y^{4n}}{x^{2m} + y^{2n}} = \dfrac{(x^{2m})^2 - (y^{2n})^2}{x^{2m} + y^{2n}}$

$= \dfrac{(x^{2m} - y^{2n})(x^{2m} + y^{2n})}{x^{2m} + y^{2n}} = x^{2m} - y^{2n}$

18. $x + 3y = 4$
(10)

$3y = -x + 4$

$y = -\dfrac{1}{3}x + \dfrac{4}{3}$

Parallel lines have identical slopes.

$y = -\dfrac{1}{3}x + b$

$(-2) = -\dfrac{1}{3}(2) + b$

$b = -\dfrac{4}{3}$

$y = -\dfrac{1}{3}x - \dfrac{4}{3}$

19.
(13)
$\dfrac{160 - x}{2} = 50$

$160 - x = 100$

$x = \textbf{60}$

20. $3(x) = 5(6)$
(11)

$3x = 30$

$x = \textbf{10}$

Test 6, Form A

1.
(18)
$\begin{cases} T + U = 11 \\ 10U + T = 10T + U + 27 \end{cases}$

$10U + T = 10T + U + 27$

$9U = 9T + 27$

$U = T + 3$

$T + U = 11$

$T + (T + 3) = 11$

$2T = 8$

$T = 4$

$T + U = 11$

$(4) + U = 11$

$U = 7$

The original number was **47**.

2. (a) **Not a function**
(21) (b) **Function**
    (c) **Function**
    (d) **Not a function**

3. (a)
(22)

    (b)

4. $3\hat{i} + 16\hat{j}$
(14)

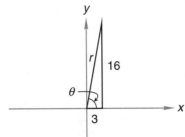

$r = \sqrt{3^2 + 16^2} = 16.28$

$\tan\theta = \dfrac{16}{3}$

$\theta = 79.38°$

16.28$\underline{/79.38°}$ **16.28$\underline{/-280.62°}$**
–16.28$\underline{/259.38°}$ **–16.28$\underline{/-100.62°}$**

5. $f(x) = x^2 - x + 3$
(21)

   (a) $f(-2) = (-2)^2 - (-2) + 3 = 4 + 2 + 3 =$ **9**

   (b) $f(10) = 10^2 - 10 + 3$

             $= 100 - 10 + 3 =$ **93**

6. (a) $64a^3b^9 - 125p^6$
(19)

    $= \left(4ab^3\right)^3 - \left(5p^2\right)^3$

    $= (4ab^3 - 5p^2)(16a^2b^6 + 20ab^3p^2 + 25p^4)$

   (b) $x^{4m} - y^{4n}$

    $= \left(x^{2m}\right)^2 - \left(y^{2n}\right)^2$

    $= \left(x^{2m} + y^{2n}\right)\left(x^{2m} - y^{2n}\right)$

    $= \left(x^{2m} + y^{2n}\right)\left(x^m + y^n\right)\left(x^m - y^n\right)$

7. $H_{\text{cone}} = \sqrt{\left(6\sqrt{2}\right)^2 - 6^2} = 6$
(2)

  $V_{\text{solid}} = V_{\text{cone}} + V_{\text{cylinder}} + V_{\text{hemisphere}}$

      $= \dfrac{1}{3}\pi(6)^2(6) + \pi(6)^2(9) + \dfrac{1}{2}\left(\dfrac{4}{3}\pi(6)^3\right)$

      $= 72\pi + 324\pi + 144\pi$

      $=$ **540π cm^3**

8. (a) $f(x) = \sqrt{x + 2}$
(21)

    $x + 2 \geq 0$

    $x \geq -2$

   Domain of $f = \left\{x \in \mathbb{R} \mid x \geq -2\right\}$

   (b) $g(x) = \dfrac{1}{x^2 - 4}$

$x^2 - 4 \neq 0$

$(x + 2)(x - 2) \neq 0$

$x \neq 2, -2$

Domain of $g = \left\{x \in \mathbb{R} \mid x \neq 2, -2\right\}$

9. $5\underline{/-138°}$
(14)

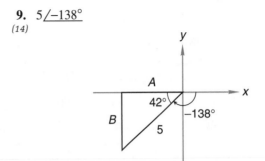

$A = 5\cos 42° = 3.72$

$B = 5\sin 42° = 3.35$

$-3.72\hat{i} - 3.35\hat{j}$

10. $4x^{5n+2} - 8x^{8n+1} = 2^2x^{5n}x^2 - 2^3x^{8n}x$
(19)

    $= 2^2x^{5n}x\left(x - 2x^{3n}\right) = \mathbf{4x^{5n+1}\left(x - 2x^{3n}\right)}$

11.
(23)

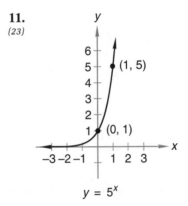

$y = 5^x$

12.
(23)

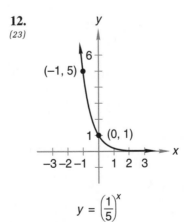

$y = \left(\dfrac{1}{5}\right)^x$

13. (a) **Function, not 1 to 1**
(21) (b) **Function, not 1 to 1**
   (c) **Not a function**
   (d) **Function, 1 to 1**

14.
(18)
$$\begin{cases} N_N + N_D + N_Q = 40 \\ 5N_N + 10N_D + 25N_Q = 560 \\ N_Q = N_N \end{cases}$$

$$N_N + N_D + N_Q = 40$$
$$N_N + N_D + (N_N) = 40$$
$$N_D = 40 - 2N_N$$

$$5N_N + 10N_D + 25N_Q = 560$$
$$5N_N + 10(40 - 2N_N) + 25(N_N) = 560$$
$$400 - 20N_N + 30N_N = 560$$
$$10N_N = 160$$
$$N_N = 16$$

$$N_Q = N_N$$
$$N_Q = 16$$

$$N_N + N_D + N_Q = 40$$
$$(16) + N_D + (16) = 40$$
$$N_D = 8$$

15.
(15, 17)

STATEMENTS	REASONS
1. $\overline{WF} \cong \overline{ZF}$	1. Given
2. $\overline{XF} \cong \overline{YF}$	2. Given
3. $\angle XFW \cong \angle YFZ$	3. Vertical angles are congruent.
4. $\triangle XFW \cong \triangle YFZ$	4. *SAS* congruency postulate

16.
(19)
$$x^2 + y^2 = 9$$
$$\underline{x^2 - y^2 = 5}$$
$$2x^2 \qquad = 14$$
$$x^2 = 7$$
$$x = \pm\sqrt{7}$$

For $x = \sqrt{7}$

$$x^2 + y^2 = 9$$
$$(\sqrt{7})^2 + y^2 = 9$$
$$y^2 = 2$$
$$y = \pm\sqrt{2}$$

$$(\sqrt{7}, \sqrt{2}), \ (\sqrt{7}, -\sqrt{2})$$

For $x = -\sqrt{7}$

$$x^2 + y^2 = 9$$
$$(-\sqrt{7})^2 + y^2 = 9$$
$$y^2 = 2$$
$$y = \pm\sqrt{2}$$

$$(-\sqrt{7}, \sqrt{2}), \ (-\sqrt{7}, -\sqrt{2})$$

17.
(5)
$$(x + y)(xy^{-1} - x^{-1}y)^{-1} = \frac{x + y}{\left(\dfrac{x}{y} - \dfrac{y}{x}\right)}$$

$$= \frac{x + y}{\dfrac{x^2 - y^2}{xy}} = \frac{(x + y)(xy)}{x^2 - y^2} = \frac{(x + y)(xy)}{(x + y)(x - y)}$$

$$= \frac{xy}{x - y}$$

18.
(24)

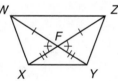

$$\tan 60° = \frac{\sqrt{3}}{1} = \sqrt{3}$$

$$\sin 45° = \frac{1}{\sqrt{2}} = \frac{\sqrt{2}}{2}$$

$$\cos 30° = \frac{\sqrt{3}}{2}$$

$$\frac{1}{2}\tan 60° - \frac{1}{\sqrt{2}}\sin 45° + \sqrt{3}\cos 30°$$

$$= \frac{1}{2}\sqrt{3} - \frac{1}{\sqrt{2}}\left(\frac{\sqrt{2}}{2}\right) + \sqrt{3}\left(\frac{\sqrt{3}}{2}\right)$$

$$= \frac{\sqrt{3}}{2} - \frac{1}{2} + \frac{3}{2} = \frac{2 + \sqrt{3}}{2}$$

19.
(2)
$$V = \frac{4}{3}\pi r^3$$
$$972\pi = \frac{4}{3}\pi r^3$$
$$r^3 = 729$$
$$r = 9 \text{ in.}$$

$$A_{\text{surface}} = 4\pi r^2$$
$$= 4\pi(9)^2$$
$$= 324\pi \text{ in.}^2$$
$$= 1017.88 \text{ in.}^2$$

20. $0.37(77) = 0.3(P_N + 77)$
(18)

$\qquad 28.49 = 0.3P_N + 23.10$

$\qquad 0.3P_N = 5.39$

$\qquad P_N = \textbf{17.97 gal}$

Test 6, Form B

1. $\begin{cases} T + U = 11 \\ 10U + T = 10T + U + 9 \end{cases}$
(18)

$\qquad 10U + T = 10T + U + 9$

$\qquad 9U = 9T + 9$

$\qquad U = T + 1$

$\qquad T + U = 11$

$\qquad T + (T + 1) = 11$

$\qquad 2T = 10$

$\qquad T = 5$

$\qquad U = T + 1$

$\qquad U = (5) + 1$

$\qquad U = 6$

The original number was **56.**

2. (a) **Function**
(21) (b) **Not a function**
(c) **Not a function**
(d) **Not a function**

3. (a)
(22)

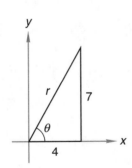

(b)

4. $4\hat{i} + 7\hat{j}$
(14)

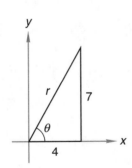

$r = \sqrt{4^2 + 7^2} = \sqrt{65}$

$\tan \theta = \dfrac{7}{4}$

$\qquad \theta = 60.25°$

$\underline{\sqrt{65}/60.25°} \qquad \underline{-\sqrt{65}/-119.75°}$

$\underline{\sqrt{65}/-299.75°} \qquad \underline{-\sqrt{65}/240.25°}$

5. $f(x) = x^2 - 2x + 3$
(21)

$\quad$ (a) $f(2) = 2^2 - 2(2) + 3$

$\qquad = 4 - 4 + 3$

$\qquad = \textbf{3}$

$\quad$ (b) $f(-3) = (-3)^2 - 2(-3) + 3$

$\qquad = 9 + 6 + 3$

$\qquad = \textbf{18}$

6. (a) $27x^3y^6 - 8d^9$
(19)

$\qquad = \left(3xy^2\right)^3 - \left(2d^3\right)^3$

$\qquad = \left(3xy^2 - 2d^3\right)\left(9x^2y^4 + 6xy^2d^3 + 4d^6\right)$

$\quad$ (b) $x^{4a} - y^{4b}$

$\qquad = \left(x^{2a} - y^{2b}\right)\left(x^{2a} + y^{2b}\right)$

$\qquad = \left(x^a - y^b\right)\left(x^a + y^b\right)\left(x^{2a} + y^{2b}\right)$

7. $H_{\text{cone}} = \sqrt{\left(3\sqrt{2}\right)^2 - 3^2} = 3$
(2)

$\quad V_{\text{solid}} = V_{\text{cone}} + V_{\text{cylinder}} + V_{\text{hemisphere}}$

$\qquad = \dfrac{1}{3}\pi(3)^2(3) + \pi(3)^2(5) + \dfrac{1}{2}\left(\dfrac{4}{3}\pi(3)^3\right)$

$\qquad = 9\pi + 45\pi + 18\pi = \textbf{72}\boldsymbol{\pi}\ \textbf{cm}^3$

8. (a) $f(x) = \sqrt{x + 3}$
(21)

$\qquad x + 3 \geq 0$

$\qquad x \geq -3$

$\qquad$ Domain of $f = \left\{x \in \mathbb{R} \mid x \geq \textbf{-3}\right\}$

$\quad$ (b) $g(x) = \dfrac{1}{x^2 - 16}$

$\qquad x^2 - 16 \neq 0$

$\qquad (x + 4)(x - 4) \neq 0$

$\qquad x \neq 4, -4$

$\qquad$ Domain of $g = \left\{x \in \mathbb{R} \mid x \neq \textbf{4, -4}\right\}$

9. $\underline{3/-125°}$
(14)

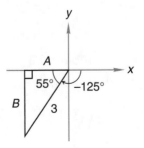

$A = 3\cos 55° = 1.72$

$B = 3\sin 55° = 2.46$

$\textbf{-1.72}\hat{i} - \textbf{2.46}\hat{j}$

10. $3x^{6n+2} - 6x^{7n+1} = 3x^{6n}x^2 - (3)(2)x^{7n}x$
(19)
$= 3x^{6n}x(x - 2x^n) = 3x^{6n+1}(x - 2x^n)$

$N_N + N_D + N_Q = 43$

$(22) + (16) + N_Q = 43$

$N_Q = 5$

11.
(23)

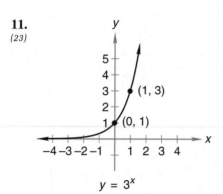

$y = 3^x$

15.
(15, 17)

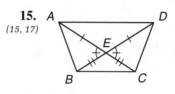

STATEMENTS	REASONS
1. $\overline{AE} \cong \overline{DE}$	1. Given
2. $\overline{BE} \cong \overline{CE}$	2. Given
3. $\angle AEB \cong \angle DEC$	3. Vertical angles are congruent.
4. $\triangle AEB \cong \triangle DEC$	4. *SAS* congruency postulate

12.
(23)

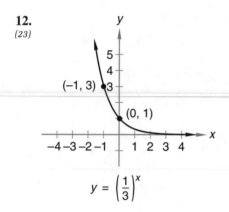

$y = \left(\frac{1}{3}\right)^x$

13. (a) **Function, 1 to 1**
(21) (b) **Function, not 1 to 1**
(c) **Function, 1 to 1**
(d) **Function, not 1 to 1**

14.
(18)

$$\begin{cases} N_N + N_D + N_Q = 43 \\ 5N_N + 10N_D + 25N_Q = 395 \\ N_N = N_D + 6 \end{cases}$$

$N_N + N_D + N_Q = 43$

$(N_D + 6) + N_D + N_Q = 43$

$N_Q = 37 - 2N_D$

$5N_N + 10N_D + 25N_Q = 395$

$5(N_D + 6) + 10N_D + 25(37 - 2N_D) = 395$

$5N_D + 30 + 10N_D + 925 - 50N_D = 395$

$35N_D = 560$

$N_D = 16$

$N_N = N_D + 6$

$N_N = (16) + 6$

$N_N = 22$

16. $x^2 + y^2 = 4$
(19)
$\underline{x^2 - y^2 = 2}$

$2x^2 \qquad = 6$

$x^2 = 3$

$x = \pm\sqrt{3}$

For $x = \sqrt{3}$

$x^2 + y^2 = 4$

$(\sqrt{3})^2 + y^2 = 4$

$y^2 = 1$

$y = \pm 1$

$(\sqrt{3}, 1), (\sqrt{3}, -1)$

For $x = -\sqrt{3}$

$x^2 + y^2 = 4$

$(-\sqrt{3})^2 + y^2 = 4$

$y^2 = 1$

$y = \pm 1$

$(-\sqrt{3}, 1), (-\sqrt{3}, -1)$

17. $(x - y)(xy^{-1} + x^{-1}y)^{-1} = \dfrac{(x - y)}{\dfrac{x}{y} + \dfrac{y}{x}}$
(5)

$= \dfrac{(x - y)}{\dfrac{x^2 + y^2}{xy}} = \dfrac{(x - y)xy}{x^2 + y^2}$

18.
(24)

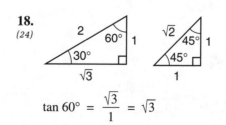

$\tan 60° = \dfrac{\sqrt{3}}{1} = \sqrt{3}$

$$\cos 45° = \frac{1}{\sqrt{2}} = \frac{\sqrt{2}}{2}$$

$$\tan 30° = \frac{1}{\sqrt{3}} = \frac{\sqrt{3}}{3}$$

$$\sqrt{3} \tan 60° + \sqrt{2} \cos 45° - 2\sqrt{3} \tan 30°$$

$$= \sqrt{3}(\sqrt{3}) + \sqrt{2}\left(\frac{\sqrt{2}}{2}\right) - 2\sqrt{3}\left(\frac{\sqrt{3}}{3}\right)$$

$$= 3 + 1 - 2 = \mathbf{2}$$

19.
(2)

$$V = \frac{4}{3}\pi r^3$$

$$2304\pi = \frac{4}{3}\pi r^3$$

$$r^3 = 1728$$

$$r = 12 \text{ mi}$$

$$A_{\text{surface}} = 4\pi r^2$$

$$= 4\pi(12)^2$$

$$= \mathbf{576\pi \ mi^2}$$

$$= \mathbf{1809.56 \ mi^2}$$

20.
(18)

$$414(0.21) = 0.18(P_N + 414)$$

$$86.94 = 0.18P_N + 74.52$$

$$0.18P_N = 12.42$$

$$P_N = \mathbf{69 \ oz}$$

Test 7, Form A

1.
(24)

$$\sin 30° = \frac{1}{2}$$

$$\cos 60° = \frac{1}{2}$$

$$\tan 45° = \frac{1}{1} = 1$$

$$2 \sin 30° + 3 \cos 60° - 2 \tan 45°$$

$$= 2\left(\frac{1}{2}\right) + 3\left(\frac{1}{2}\right) - 2(1)$$

$$= \frac{2}{2} + \frac{3}{2} - 2 = \mathbf{\frac{1}{2}}$$

2.
(21)

$$f(x) = \frac{\sqrt{x-20}}{x^2 - 3x - 4} = \frac{\sqrt{x-20}}{(x+1)(x-4)}$$

$$(x+1)(x-4) \neq 0$$

$$x \neq -1, 4$$

$$x - 20 \geq 0$$

$$x \geq 20$$

Domain of $f = \left\{x \in \mathbb{R} \mid x \geq 20\right\}$

3.
(21)

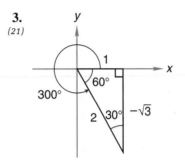

$$f(300°) = 4 \cos(300°) = 4\left(\frac{1}{2}\right) = \mathbf{2}$$

4.
(28)

$$\frac{9!}{3!6!} = \frac{9 \cdot 8 \cdot 7 \cdot 6!}{3 \cdot 2 \cdot 1 \cdot 6!} = \mathbf{84}$$

5. $f(x) = x^2 - x$
(21)

$$f(x+h) = (x+h)^2 - (x+h)$$

$$= \mathbf{x^2 + 2xh + h^2 - x - h}$$

6. $A_N - 10 =$ Anne 10 years ago
(25)

$A_N + 5 =$ Anne 5 years from now

$S_N - 5 =$ Sylvia 5 years ago

$S_N - 10 =$ Sylvia 10 years ago

$$\begin{cases} A_N - 10 = \frac{1}{2}(S_N - 10) \\ A_N + 5 = S_N - 5 \end{cases}$$

$$A_N + 5 = S_N - 5$$

$$A_N = S_N - 10$$

$$A_N - 10 = \frac{1}{2}(S_N - 10)$$

$$(S_N - 10) - 10 = \frac{1}{2}S_N - 5$$

$$\frac{1}{2}S_N = 15$$

$$S_N = \mathbf{30}$$

7. (a) $\log_x 3 = \dfrac{1}{2}$
(26)

$\qquad x^{1/2} = 3$

$\qquad x = \mathbf{9}$

(b) $\log_2 \dfrac{1}{16} = x$

$\qquad 2^x = \dfrac{1}{16}$

$\qquad 2^x = \dfrac{1}{2^4}$

$\qquad 2^x = 2^{-4}$

$\qquad x = \mathbf{-4}$

(c) $\log_4 x = 2$

$\qquad x = 4^2 = \mathbf{16}$

8. $\qquad 3s = \dfrac{2}{3p}\left(\dfrac{6z}{t} - \dfrac{5q}{r}\right)$
(16)

$\qquad 3s = \dfrac{4z}{pt} - \dfrac{10q}{3pr}$

$\qquad 3s = \dfrac{12zr - 10tq}{3ptr}$

$\qquad 9prts = 12zr - 10tq$

$\qquad t(9prs + 10q) = 12zr$

$\qquad t = \dfrac{12zr}{9prs + 10q}$

9. $\dfrac{\sqrt{-3}\sqrt{-3} - \sqrt{-25} + \sqrt{4}\sqrt{-4}\sqrt{4}}{2 + 3i^3}$
(5, 10)

$= \dfrac{3i^2 - 5i + 8i}{2 + 3(-1)i} = \dfrac{-3 + 3i}{2 - 3i}$

$= \dfrac{-3 + 3i}{2 - 3i} \cdot \dfrac{2 + 3i}{2 + 3i} = \dfrac{-6 - 3i + 9i^2}{4 - 9i^2}$

$= \dfrac{-15 - 3i}{13} = -\dfrac{15}{13} - \dfrac{3}{13}i$

10.
(22)

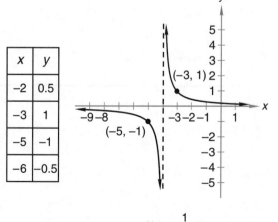

x	y
−2	0.5
−3	1
−5	−1
−6	−0.5

$y = \dfrac{1}{x + 4}$

11. $\qquad R_C T_C + R_M T_M = 1 \text{ lawn}$
(25)

$\left(\dfrac{1 \text{ lawn}}{20 \text{ min}}\right)(T + 10 \text{ min}) + \left(\dfrac{1 \text{ lawn}}{30 \text{ min}}\right)T = 1 \text{ lawn}$

$\left(\dfrac{1 \text{ lawn}}{20 \text{ min}}\right)T + \dfrac{1}{2} \text{ lawn} + \left(\dfrac{1 \text{ lawn}}{30 \text{ min}}\right)T = 1 \text{ lawn}$

$\left(\dfrac{1}{12}\dfrac{\text{lawn}}{\text{min}}\right)T = \dfrac{1}{2} \text{ lawn}$

$T = \mathbf{6 \ min}$

12.
(15, 17)

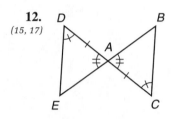

STATEMENTS	REASONS
1. A is the midpoint of $\overline{DC}$	1. Given
2. $\overline{DA} \cong \overline{CA}$	2. A midpoint divides a segment into two congruent segments.
3. $\angle D \cong \angle C$	3. Given
4. $\angle DAE \cong \angle CAB$	4. Vertical angles are congruent.
5. $\angle E \cong \angle B$	5. If two angles in one triangle are congruent to two angles in a second triangle, then the third angles are congruent.
6. $\triangle EDA \cong \triangle BCA$	6. AAAS congruency postulate
7. $\overline{ED} \cong \overline{BC}$	7. CPCTC

13. $\qquad RWT = J$
(25)

$R(5 \text{ men})(6 \text{ hours}) = 4 \text{ rooms}$

$\qquad R = \dfrac{2 \text{ rooms}}{15 \text{ men-hours}}$

$RWT = J$

$\qquad T = \dfrac{J}{RW}$

$\qquad T = \dfrac{28 \text{ rooms}}{\dfrac{2 \text{ rooms}}{15 \text{ men-hours}}(5 + 9) \text{ men}}$

$\qquad T = \mathbf{15 \ hours}$

14. $\quad d = \dfrac{kt}{s^2}$
(18)

$\quad 50 = \dfrac{k(125)}{(5)^2}$

$\quad k = 10$

$\quad d = \dfrac{10t}{s^2} = \dfrac{10(16)}{(2)^2} = \mathbf{40 \ dolphins}$

15. $9x^{2n+3} + 18x^{5n+1}$
(19)

$= 3^2 x^{2n} x^3 + (2)3^2 x^{5n} x^1$

$= 9x^{2n+1}(x^2 + 2x^{3n})$

16. $125a^9 b^3 - 8c^3 d^6$
(19)

$= 5^3 (a^3)^3 b^3 - 2^3 c^3 (d^2)^3$

$= (5a^3 b)^3 - (2cd^2)^3$

$= (5a^3 b - 2cd^2)(25a^6 b^2 + 10a^3 bcd^2 + 4c^2 d^4)$

17. (a) **Function, not 1 to 1**
(21) (b) **Not a function**
(c) **Function, not 1 to 1**
(d) **Not a function**

18. $\dfrac{x^{a+3}(\sqrt{y^4})^{2a}}{y^{2a-2}} = \dfrac{x^{a+3}(y^2)^{2a}}{y^{2a-2}}$
(5)

$= x^{a+3} y^{4a} y^{-2a+2} = x^{a+3} y^{2a+2}$

19. (a) $(fg)(x) = 2x(1 - x^2) = 2x - 2x^3$
(24)

$(fg)(4) = 2(4) - 2(4)^3 = 8 - 128 = \mathbf{-120}$

(b) $(f/g)(x) = \dfrac{2x}{1 - x^2}$

$(f/g)(4) = \dfrac{2(4)}{1 - (4)^2} = -\dfrac{8}{15}$

(c) $(f \circ g)(x) = 2(1 - x^2) = 2 - 2x^2$

$(f \circ g)(4) = 2 - 2(4)^2 = 2 - 32 = \mathbf{-30}$

20. Distance $= l$ m
(28)

Rate $= v \dfrac{m}{s}$

Time $= \dfrac{\text{distance}}{\text{rate}} = \dfrac{lm}{v\dfrac{m}{s}} = \dfrac{l}{v}$ s

New distance $= l$ m

New time $= \left(\dfrac{l}{v} - 5\right)$ s $= \dfrac{l - 5v}{v}$ s

New rate $= \dfrac{\text{new distance}}{\text{new time}}$

$= \dfrac{l \, m}{\dfrac{l - 5v}{v} \, s} = \dfrac{lv}{l - 5v} \dfrac{m}{s}$

Test 7, Form B

1.
(24)

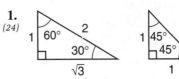

$\cos 60° = \dfrac{1}{2}$

$\tan 45° = \dfrac{1}{1} = 1$

$\sin 30° = \dfrac{1}{2}$

$3 \cos 60° - \dfrac{1}{2} \tan 45° + 2 \sin 30°$

$= 3\left(\dfrac{1}{2}\right) - \dfrac{1}{2}(1) + 2\left(\dfrac{1}{2}\right) = \dfrac{3}{2} - \dfrac{1}{2} + \dfrac{2}{2} = \mathbf{2}$

2. $f(x) = \dfrac{\sqrt{x + 5}}{x^2 + x - 6} = \dfrac{\sqrt{x + 5}}{(x + 3)(x - 2)}$
(21)

$(x + 3)(x - 2) \neq 0$

$x \neq -3, 2$

$x + 5 \geq 0$

$x \geq -5$

Domain of $f = \{x \in \mathbb{R} \mid x \geq -5, \ x \neq -3, 2\}$

3.
(21)

$f(330°) = 4 \sin(330°) = 4\left(-\dfrac{1}{2}\right) = \mathbf{-2}$

4. $\dfrac{8!}{4! \, 4!} = \dfrac{8 \cdot 7 \cdot 6 \cdot 5 \cdot 4!}{4 \cdot 3 \cdot 2 \cdot 1 \cdot 4!} = \mathbf{70}$
(28)

5. $f(x) = x^2 + x$
(21)

$f(x + h) = (x + h)^2 + (x + h)$

$= x^2 + 2xh + h^2 + x + h$

6. $P_N - 15$ = Phil 15 years ago
(25)
$P_N - 4$ = Phil 4 years ago
$D_N - 15$ = Darell 15 years ago
$D_N + 3$ = Darell 3 years from now

$$\begin{cases} P_N - 15 = 2(D_N - 15) \\ P_N - 4 = D_N + 3 \end{cases}$$

$P_N - 4 = D_N + 3$
$\quad D_N = P_N - 7$

$P_N - 15 = 2(D_N - 15)$
$P_N - 15 = 2D_N - 30$
$P_N - 15 = 2(P_N - 7) - 30$
$P_N - 15 = 2P_N - 44$
$\quad\quad P_N = \mathbf{29}$

7. (a) $\log_x 2 = \dfrac{1}{2}$
(26)
$\quad x^{1/2} = 2$
$\quad\quad x = \mathbf{4}$

(b) $\log_3 \dfrac{1}{3} = x$
$\quad 3^x = \dfrac{1}{3}$
$\quad 3^x = 3^{-1}$
$\quad\quad x = \mathbf{-1}$

(c) $\log_2 x = -3$
$\quad x = 2^{-3}$
$\quad x = \dfrac{1}{2^3} = \mathbf{\dfrac{1}{8}}$

8. $\quad 3s = \dfrac{3}{2t}\left(\dfrac{8d}{l} - \dfrac{3m}{d}\right)$
(16)
$\quad 2st = \dfrac{8d}{l} - \dfrac{3m}{d}$

$\quad 2std = \dfrac{8d^2}{l} - 3m$

$\quad 2std + 3m = \dfrac{8d^2}{l}$

$\quad\quad l = \dfrac{8d^2}{2std + 3m}$

9. $\dfrac{\sqrt{-16} + \sqrt{9}\sqrt{-9}\sqrt{-9} - \sqrt{-5}\sqrt{5}}{2 - 3i^3}$
(5, 10)

$= \dfrac{4i + 27i^2 - 5i}{2 - 3(-1)i} = \dfrac{-27 - i}{2 + 3i}$

$= \dfrac{-27 - i}{2 + 3i} \cdot \dfrac{2 - 3i}{2 - 3i} = \dfrac{-54 + 79i + 3i^2}{4 - 9i^2}$

$= \dfrac{-57 + 79i}{13} = \mathbf{-\dfrac{57}{13} + \dfrac{79}{13}i}$

10.
(22)

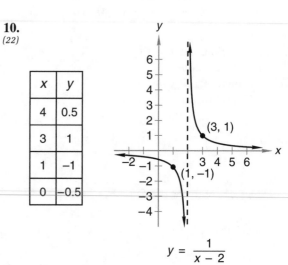

x	y
4	0.5
3	1
1	−1
0	−0.5

$$y = \dfrac{1}{x - 2}$$

11. $\quad R_M T_M + R_K T_K = 1 \text{ lawn}$
(25)

$\left(\dfrac{1 \text{ lawn}}{30 \text{ min}}\right)(T + 10 \text{ min}) + \left(\dfrac{1 \text{ lawn}}{20 \text{ min}}\right)T = 1 \text{ lawn}$

$\left(\dfrac{1 \text{ lawn}}{30 \text{ min}}\right)T + \dfrac{1}{3} \text{ lawn} + \left(\dfrac{1 \text{ lawn}}{20 \text{ min}}\right)T = 1 \text{ lawn}$

$\left(\dfrac{1}{12}\dfrac{\text{lawn}}{\text{min}}\right)T = \dfrac{2}{3} \text{ lawn}$

$T = \mathbf{8 \text{ min}}$

12.
(15, 17)

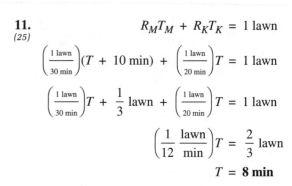

STATEMENTS	REASONS
1. N is the midpoint of $\overline{MO}$	1. Given
2. $\overline{MN} \cong \overline{ON}$	2. A midpoint divides a segment into two congruent segments.
3. $\angle M \cong \angle O$	3. Given
4. $\angle MNL \cong \angle ONP$	4. Vertical angles are congruent.
5. $\angle L \cong \angle P$	5. If two angles in one triangle are congruent to two angles in a second triangle, then the third angles are congruent.
6. $\triangle MNL \cong \triangle ONP$	6. AAAS congruency postulate
7. $\overline{LM} \cong \overline{PO}$	7. CPCTC

13.
(25)

$$RMT = A$$

$$R(12 \text{ men})(4 \text{ hours}) = 3 \text{ acres}$$

$$R = \frac{1 \text{ acre}}{16 \text{ man-hours}}$$

$$RMT = A$$

$$T = \frac{A}{RM}$$

$$T = \frac{18 \text{ acres}}{\dfrac{1 \text{ acre}}{16 \text{ man-hours}}(12 + 12) \text{ men}}$$

$$T = \textbf{12 hours}$$

14.
(18)

$$d = \frac{km^2}{c}$$

$$250 = \frac{k(10)^2}{2}$$

$$k = 5$$

$$d = \frac{5(3)^2}{15} = \textbf{3 dancers}$$

15. $13x^{5n+2} - 26x^{3n+1} = 13x^{5n}x^2 - 2(13)x^{3n}x^1$
(19)

$$= \textbf{13}x^{\textbf{3}n+\textbf{1}}\left(x^{\textbf{2}n+\textbf{1}} - \textbf{2}\right)$$

16. $64x^3y^6 - 27z^9w^3$
(19)

$$= 4^3x^3\left(y^2\right)^3 - (3)^3\left(z^3\right)^3w^3$$

$$= \left(4xy^2\right)^3 - \left(3z^3w\right)^3$$

$$= \left(\textbf{4}xy^{\textbf{2}} - \textbf{3}z^{\textbf{3}}w\right)\left(\textbf{16}x^{\textbf{2}}y^{\textbf{4}} + \textbf{12}xy^{\textbf{2}}z^{\textbf{3}}w + \textbf{9}z^{\textbf{6}}w^{\textbf{2}}\right)$$

17. (a) **Function, not 1 to 1**
(21) (b) **Function, not 1 to 1**
(c) **Not a function**
(d) **Not a function**

18.
(5)

$$\frac{y^{b+2}\left(\sqrt{x^6}\right)^{2b}}{x^{3b-1}} = \frac{y^{b+2}\left(x^3\right)^{2b}}{x^{3b-1}} = y^{b+2}x^{6b}x^{-3b+1}$$

$$= x^{\textbf{3}b+\textbf{1}}y^{b+\textbf{2}}$$

19. (a) $(fg)(x) = (2 - x)\left(3x^2\right) = 6x^2 - 3x^3$
(24)

$$(fg)(3) = 6(3)^2 - 3(3)^3 = 54 - 81 = \textbf{-27}$$

(b) $(f/g)(x) = \dfrac{2 - x}{3x^2}$

$$(f/g)(3) = \frac{2 - 3}{3(3)^2} = -\frac{\textbf{1}}{\textbf{27}}$$

(c) $(f \circ g)(x) = 2 - 3x^2$

$$(f \circ g)(3) = 2 - 3(3)^2 = 2 - 27 = \textbf{-25}$$

20. Distance $= d$ km
(28)

$$\text{Rate} = m \frac{\text{km}}{\text{min}}$$

$$\text{Time} = \frac{\text{distance}}{\text{rate}} = \frac{d \text{ km}}{m \dfrac{\text{km}}{\text{min}}} = \frac{d}{m} \text{ min}$$

New distance $= d$ km

$$\text{New time} = \left(\frac{d}{m} - 7\right) \text{min} = \frac{d - 7m}{m} \text{ min}$$

$$\text{New rate} = \frac{\text{new distance}}{\text{new time}}$$

$$= \frac{d \text{ km}}{\dfrac{d - 7m}{m} \text{ min}} = \frac{dm}{d - 7m} \frac{\textbf{km}}{\textbf{min}}$$

Test 8, Form A

1. Rate $= k \dfrac{\text{mi}}{\text{hr}}$
(28)

Time $= t$ hr

$$\text{Distance} = (\text{rate})(\text{time}) = \left(k \frac{\text{mi}}{\text{hr}}\right)(t \text{ hr}) = kt \text{ mi}$$

New distance $= (kt + 40)$ mi

$$\text{New rate} = (k + 10) \frac{\text{mi}}{\text{hr}}$$

$$\text{New time} = \frac{\text{new distance}}{\text{new rate}}$$

$$= \frac{(kt + 40) \text{ mi}}{(k + 10) \dfrac{\text{mi}}{\text{hr}}} = \frac{kt + 40}{k + 10} \textbf{ hr}$$

2. $\dfrac{9!}{5!4!} = \dfrac{9 \cdot 8 \cdot 7 \cdot 6 \cdot 5!}{4 \cdot 3 \cdot 2 \cdot 1 \cdot 5!} = \textbf{126}$
(28)

3. $f(x) = \dfrac{\sqrt{x - 10}}{x^2 - 4x - 5} = \dfrac{\sqrt{x - 10}}{(x + 1)(x - 5)}$
(21)

$$(x + 1)(x - 5) \neq 0$$

$$x \neq -1, 5$$

$$x - 10 \geq 0$$

$$x \geq 10$$

Domain of $f = \left\{x \in \mathbb{R} \mid x \geq \textbf{10}\right\}$

4.
(20, 29)

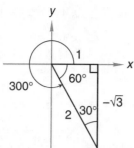

$$\sin 30° = \frac{1}{2}, \quad \cos 300° = \frac{1}{2}$$

$$\sin 30° - \cos 300° + \cos 180° + \sin 90°$$

$$= \left(\frac{1}{2}\right) - \left(\frac{1}{2}\right) + (-1) + (1) = \mathbf{0}$$

5.
(30)

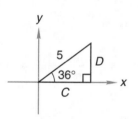

$$A = 7\cos 20° = 6.578$$
$$B = 7\sin 20° = 2.394$$

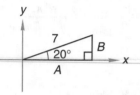

$$C = 5\cos 36° = 4.045$$
$$D = 5\sin 36° = 2.939$$

$$(6.578 + 4.045)\hat{i} + (2.394 + 2.939)\hat{j}$$
$$= 10.623\hat{i} + 5.333\hat{j}$$

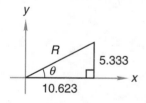

$$R = \sqrt{(10.623)^2 + (5.333)^2} = 11.89$$

$$\theta = \tan^{-1}\frac{5.333}{10.623} = 26.66°$$

11.89 /26.66°

6. $N, N + 1, N + 2, N + 3$
(7)

$$(N)(N + 1) = 3(N + 3) + 6$$
$$N^2 + N = 3N + 15$$
$$N^2 - 2N - 15 = 0$$
$$(N + 3)(N - 5) = 0$$
$$N = 5, -3$$

5, 6, 7, 8

7. (a)
(22)

x	y
-2	-4
-1	-1
$-\frac{1}{2}$	$-\frac{1}{4}$
$\frac{1}{2}$	$-\frac{1}{4}$
1	-1
2	-4

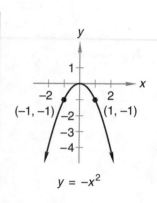

$$y = -x^2$$

(b)

x	y
-2	$-\frac{1}{4}$
-1	-1
$-\frac{1}{2}$	-4
$\frac{1}{2}$	-4
1	-1
2	$-\frac{1}{4}$

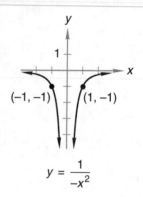

$$y = \frac{1}{-x^2}$$

8. (a)
(32)

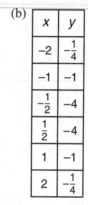

$$\text{Arcsin }\frac{1}{2} = \mathbf{30°}$$

(b)

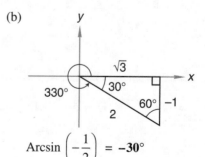

$$\text{Arcsin }\left(-\frac{1}{2}\right) = \mathbf{-30°}$$

9. $g(x) = -\sqrt{x}$
(31)

10. $49a^{4n+3} - 7a^{6n+5} = 7^2a^{4n}a^3 - 7a^{6n}a^5$
(19)

$= 7a^{4n}a^3\left(7 - a^{2n}a^2\right) = 7a^{4n+3}\left(7 - a^{2n+2}\right)$

11. $\dfrac{1}{b + \dfrac{2x}{1 + \dfrac{3}{c}}} = \dfrac{1}{b + \dfrac{2x}{\dfrac{c+3}{c}}} = \dfrac{1}{b + \dfrac{2xc}{c+3}}$
(16)

$= \dfrac{1}{\dfrac{bc + 3b + 2xc}{c+3}} = \dfrac{c+3}{bc + 3b + 2xc}$

12. (a) $\log_x 49 = 2$
(26)

$x^2 = 49$

$x^2 = 7^2$

$x = \mathbf{7}$

(b) $\log_5 \dfrac{1}{125} = x$

$5^x = \dfrac{1}{125}$

$5^x = 5^{-3}$

$x = \mathbf{-3}$

(c) $\log_{1/4} x = 3$

$x = \left(\dfrac{1}{4}\right)^3$

$x = \dfrac{1}{64}$

13. J_N = Jim's age now
(25)

D_N = Dot's age now

$D_N - 20$ = Dot's age 20 years ago

$\begin{cases} J_N = D_N + 5 \\ \dfrac{1}{2}J_N = D_N - 20 \end{cases}$

$J_N = D_N + 5$

$D_N = J_N - 5$

$\dfrac{1}{2}J_N = D_N - 20$

$\dfrac{1}{2}J_N = (J_N - 5) - 20$

$\dfrac{1}{2}J_N = 25$

$J_N = \mathbf{50}$

14.
(15, 17)

STATEMENTS	REASONS
1. $\overline{CD} \perp \overline{AB}$	1. Given
2. $\angle CDA$ and $\angle CDB$ are right angles.	2. Perpendicular lines intersect to form right angles.
3. $\triangle CDA$ and $\triangle CDB$ are right triangles.	3. A triangle which contains a right angle is a right triangle.
4. $\overline{AC} \cong \overline{BC}$	4. Given
5. $\overline{CD} \cong \overline{CD}$	5. Reflexive axiom
6. $\triangle CDA \cong \triangle CDB$	6. HL congruency postulate

15. $\dfrac{z^{3+b}\left(\sqrt{z^3}\right)^{b+2}}{z^{2b-1}} = \dfrac{z^{3+b}\left(z^{3/2}\right)^{b+2}}{z^{2b-1}}$
(5)

$= \dfrac{z^{3+b}z^{\frac{3}{2}(b+2)}}{z^{2b-1}} = z^{3+b}z^{-2b+1}z^{\frac{3}{2}b+3} = z^{\frac{1}{2}b+7}$

16. $y = 7x + 3$
(32)

$7x = y - 3$

$x = \dfrac{1}{7}y - \dfrac{3}{7}$

$y = \dfrac{1}{7}x - \dfrac{3}{7}$

17. $\begin{cases} y^2 - x^2 = 4 \\ y + 3x = 2 \end{cases}$
(19)

$y + 3x = 2$

$y = -3x + 2$

$y^2 - x^2 = 4$

$(-3x + 2)^2 - x^2 = 4$

$9x^2 - 12x + 4 - x^2 = 4$

$8x^2 - 12x = 0$

$x^2 - \dfrac{3}{2}x = 0$

$x\left(x - \dfrac{3}{2}\right) = 0$

$x = 0, \dfrac{3}{2}$

For $x = 0$

$$y + 3x = 2$$
$$y + 3(0) = 2$$
$$y = 2$$

(0, 2)

For $x = \dfrac{3}{2}$

$$y + 3\left(\dfrac{3}{2}\right) = 2$$
$$y = -\dfrac{5}{2}$$

$$\left(\dfrac{3}{2}, -\dfrac{5}{2}\right)$$

18.
(5, 10)
$$\dfrac{\sqrt{3}\sqrt{-3}\sqrt{2}\sqrt{-2} - \sqrt{-16} + \sqrt{-5}\sqrt{5}}{1 + \sqrt{-16}\,i^3}$$

$$= \dfrac{\sqrt{3}\sqrt{3}i\sqrt{2}\sqrt{2}i - 4i + \sqrt{5}i\sqrt{5}}{1 + 4i\left(i^3\right)}$$

$$= \dfrac{(3)(2)i^2 - 4i + 5i}{1 + 4i^2 i^2} = \dfrac{6(-1) + i}{1 + 4(-1)(-1)}$$

$$= \dfrac{-6 + i}{5} = -\dfrac{6}{5} + \dfrac{1}{5}i$$

19. $f(x) = 2x^2 - x + 3$
(21)
$$f(x + h) - f(x)$$
$$= 2(x + h)^2 - (x + h) + 3 - \left(2x^2 - x + 3\right)$$
$$= 2\left(x^2 + 2xh + h^2\right) - x - h + 3 - 2x^2 + x - 3$$
$$= 2x^2 + 4xh + 2h^2 - h - 2x^2$$
$$= \mathbf{2h^2 + 4xh - h}$$

20.
(18)
$$\begin{cases} 0.70(P_N) + 0.30(D_N) = 0.50(5) \\ P_N + D_N = 5 \end{cases}$$

$$P_N + D_N = 5$$
$$D_N = 5 - P_N$$

$$0.70(P_N) + 0.30(D_N) = 0.50(5)$$
$$7P_N + 3D_N = 25$$
$$7P_N + 3(5 - P_N) = 25$$
$$7P_N + 15 - 3P_N = 25$$
$$4P_N = 10$$
$$P_N = \textbf{2.5 liters of 70\% alcohol}$$

$$P_N + D_N = 5$$
$$(2.5) + D_N = 5$$
$$D_N = \textbf{2.5 liters of 30\% alcohol}$$

Test 8, Form B

1. Rate $= k\,\dfrac{\text{mi}}{\text{hr}}$
(28)

Time $= a$ hr

Distance $=$ (rate)(time) $= \left(k\,\dfrac{\text{mi}}{\text{hr}}\right)(a\text{ hr}) = ka$ mi

New distance $= (ka + 20)$ mi

New rate $= (k + 35)\,\dfrac{\text{mi}}{\text{hr}}$

New time $= \dfrac{\text{new distance}}{\text{new rate}}$

$$= \dfrac{(ka + 20)\text{ mi}}{(k + 35)\,\dfrac{\text{mi}}{\text{hr}}} = \dfrac{ka + 20}{k + 35}\text{ hr}$$

2. $\dfrac{8!}{6!\,2!} = \dfrac{8 \cdot 7 \cdot 6!}{2 \cdot 1 \cdot 6!} = \mathbf{28}$
(28)

3. $f(x) = \dfrac{\sqrt{x - 5}}{x^2 - 6x - 7} = \dfrac{\sqrt{x - 5}}{(x - 7)(x + 1)}$
(21)

$$(x - 7)(x + 1) \neq 0$$
$$x \neq -1, 7$$

$$x - 5 \geq 0$$
$$x \geq 5$$

Domain of $f = \left\{x \in \mathbb{R} \mid x \geq 5, x \neq 7\right\}$

4.
(20, 29)

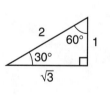 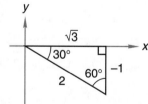

$\cos 60° = \dfrac{1}{2}$, $\sin 330° = -\dfrac{1}{2}$

$\cos 60° - \sin 270° + \sin 330° + \cos 90°$

$$= \left(\dfrac{1}{2}\right) - (-1) + \left(-\dfrac{1}{2}\right) + 0 = \mathbf{1}$$

5.
(30)

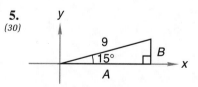

$A = 9 \cos 15° = 8.693$

$B = 9 \sin 15° = 2.329$

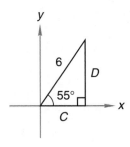

$C = 6 \cos 55° = 3.441$

$D = 6 \sin 55° = 4.915$

$(8.693 + 3.441)\hat{i} + (2.329 + 4.915)\hat{j}$

$= 12.135\hat{i} + 7.244\hat{j}$

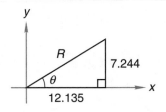

$R = \sqrt{(12.135)^2 + (7.244)^2} = 14.132$

$\theta = \tan^{-1} \dfrac{7.244}{12.135} = 30.84°$

14.13/30.84°

6. $N, N + 1, N + 2$
(7)

$N(N + 1) - 26 = (N + 2)^2$

$N^2 + N - 26 = N^2 + 4N + 4$

$3N = -30$

$N = -10$

−10, −9, −8

7. (a)
(22)

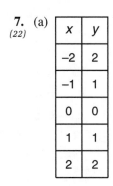

x	y
−2	2
−1	1
0	0
1	1
2	2

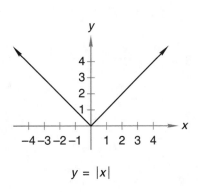

$y = |x|$

(b)

x	y
−2	$\frac{1}{2}$
−1	1
$-\frac{1}{2}$	2
$\frac{1}{2}$	2
1	1
2	$\frac{1}{2}$

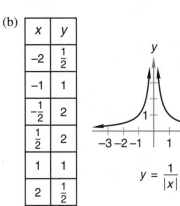

$y = \dfrac{1}{|x|}$

8. (a)
(32)

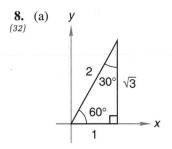

$\text{Arcsin } \dfrac{\sqrt{3}}{2} = \mathbf{60°}$

(b)

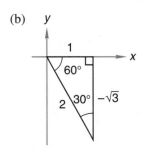

$\text{Arcsin } \left(-\dfrac{\sqrt{3}}{2}\right) = \mathbf{-60°}$

9. $g(x) = \sqrt{-x}$
(31)

10. $6a^{3n+1} - 42a^{5n+4} = 6a^{3n}a - (6)(7)a^{5n}a^4$
(19)
$= 6a^{3n}a\left(1 - 7a^{2n}a^3\right) = \mathbf{6a^{3n+1}\left(1 - 7a^{2n+3}\right)}$

11.
(16)
$$\dfrac{1}{a + \dfrac{3b}{2 + \dfrac{4}{x}}} = \dfrac{1}{a + \dfrac{3b}{\dfrac{2x + 4}{x}}} = \dfrac{1}{a + \dfrac{3bx}{2x + 4}}$$

$$= \dfrac{1}{\dfrac{2xa + 4a + 3bx}{2x + 4}} = \mathbf{\dfrac{2x + 4}{2xa + 3xb + 4a}}$$

12. (a) $\log_x 27 = 3$
(26)

$$x^3 = 27$$
$$x^3 = 3^3$$
$$x = \mathbf{3}$$

(b) $\log_6 \dfrac{1}{36} = x$

$$6^x = \dfrac{1}{36}$$
$$6^x = 6^{-2}$$
$$x = \mathbf{-2}$$

(c) $\log_{1/7} x = -2$

$$x = \left(\dfrac{1}{7}\right)^{-2}$$
$$x = 7^2$$
$$x = \mathbf{49}$$

13. $G_N = $ Greg's age now
(25)

$G_N - 6 = $ Greg's age 6 years ago

$M_N = $ Marsha's age now

$$\begin{cases} G_N + 8 = M_N \\ G_N - 6 = \dfrac{1}{2}M_N \end{cases}$$

$$G_N + 8 = M_N$$
$$G_N = M_N - 8$$

$$G_N - 6 = \dfrac{1}{2}M_N$$

$$\left(M_N - 8\right) - 6 = \dfrac{1}{2}M_N$$

$$\dfrac{1}{2}M_N = 14$$
$$M_N = \mathbf{28}$$

14.
(15, 17)

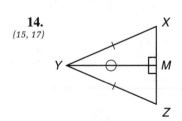

STATEMENTS	REASONS
1. $\overline{MY} \perp \overline{XZ}$	1. Given
2. $\angle YMX$ and $\angle YMZ$ are right angles.	2. Perpendicular lines intersect to form right angles.
3. $\triangle YMX$ and $\triangle YMZ$ are right triangles.	3. A triangle which contains a right angle is a right triangle.
4. $\overline{XY} \cong \overline{ZY}$	4. Given
5. $\overline{MY} \cong \overline{MY}$	5. Reflexive axiom
6. $\triangle YMX \cong \triangle YMZ$	6. HL congruency postulate

15. $\dfrac{y^{2-b}\left(y^3\right)^{b+1}}{\sqrt[3]{y^{4b}}} = \dfrac{y^{-b+2}y^{3b+3}}{y^{(4b)\frac{1}{3}}} = \dfrac{y^{2b+5}}{y^{\frac{4}{3}b}}$
(5)

$$= y^{2b+5-\frac{4}{3}b} = \mathbf{y^{\frac{2}{3}b+5}}$$

16. $y = 5x - 2$
(32)

$$5x = y + 2$$

$$x = \dfrac{1}{5}y + \dfrac{2}{5}$$

$$y = \dfrac{1}{5}x + \dfrac{2}{5}$$

17. $\begin{cases} y^2 - x^2 = 9 \\ y + 3 = 2x \end{cases}$
(19)

$$y + 3 = 2x$$
$$y = 2x - 3$$

$$y^2 - x^2 = 9$$
$$(2x - 3)^2 - x^2 = 9$$
$$4x^2 - 12x + 9 - x^2 = 9$$
$$3x^2 - 12x = 0$$
$$x^2 - 4x = 0$$
$$x(x - 4) = 0$$
$$x = 0, 4$$

For $x = 0$

$$y + 3 = 2x$$
$$y + 3 = 2(0)$$
$$y = -3$$

$(\mathbf{0, -3})$

For $x = 4$

$$y + 3 = 2x$$
$$y + 3 = 2(4)$$
$$y = 5$$

$(\mathbf{4, 5})$

18. $\dfrac{\sqrt{4}\sqrt{-4}\sqrt{-4} + \sqrt{-25} + \sqrt{-3}\sqrt{3}}{1 + \sqrt{-4}\,i^3}$
(5, 10)

$$= \dfrac{(2)(2i)(2i) + 5i + \sqrt{3}i\sqrt{3}}{1 + 2i(i)^3} = \dfrac{8i^2 + 5i + 3i}{1 + 2i^2 i^2}$$

$$= \dfrac{8(-1) + 8i}{1 + 2(-1)(-1)} = \dfrac{-8 + 8i}{3} = \mathbf{-\dfrac{8}{3} + \dfrac{8}{3}i}$$

19. $f(x) = x^2 - 6x + 1$
(21)

$$f(x + h) - f(x)$$

$$= (x + h)^2 - 6(x + h) + 1 - \left(x^2 - 6x + 1\right)$$

$$= x^2 + 2xh + h^2 - 6x - 6h + 1 - x^2 + 6x - 1$$

$$= \mathbf{h^2 + 2xh - 6h}$$

20.
(18)
$$\begin{cases} 0.10(P_N) + 0.40(D_N) = 0.25(1) \\ P_N + D_N = 1 \end{cases}$$

$$P_N + D_N = 1$$

$$D_N = 1 - P_N$$

$$0.10(P_N) + 0.40(D_N) = 0.25(1)$$

$$10P_N + 40D_N = 25$$

$$10P_N + 40(1 - P_N) = 25$$

$$10P_N + 40 - 40P_N = 25$$

$$30P_N = 15$$

$$P_N = \frac{1}{2} \text{ liter of 10\% alcohol}$$

$$P_N + D_N = 1$$

$$\left(\frac{1}{2}\right) + D_N = 1$$

$$D_N = \frac{1}{2} \text{ liter of 40\% alcohol}$$

Test 9, Form A

1.
(36)
$$\begin{cases} (A + W)T_D = D_D \\ (A - W)T_U = D_U \end{cases}$$

$$A = 6W, \ T_U = T_D + 3$$

$$(A + W)T_D = D_D$$

$$(6W + W)T_D = 560$$

$$7WT_D = 560$$

$$WT_D = 80$$

$$(A - W)T_U = D_U$$

$$(6W - W)(T_D + 3) = 700$$

$$(5W)(T_D + 3) = 700$$

$$5WT_D + 15W = 700$$

$$5(80) + 15W = 700$$

$$15W = 300$$

$$W = 20$$

$$A = 6W = 6(20) = \textbf{120 mph}$$

2. Number $= -3\frac{2}{5} + \frac{2}{5}(\Delta C)$
(35)

$$= -3\frac{2}{5} + \frac{2}{5}\left(C_F - C_I\right)$$

$$= -3\frac{2}{5} + \frac{2}{5}\left[5\frac{3}{5} - \left(-3\frac{2}{5}\right)\right]$$

$$= -3\frac{2}{5} + \frac{2}{5}(9) = -\frac{17}{5} + \frac{18}{5} = \frac{1}{5}$$

3.
(30)

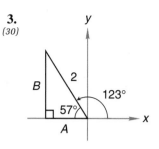

$$A = 2 \cos 57° = 1.0893$$

$$B = 2 \sin 57° = 1.6773$$

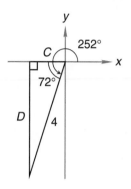

$$C = 4 \cos 72° = 1.2361$$

$$D = 4 \sin 72° = 3.8042$$

$$(-1.089 - 1.236)\hat{i} + (1.677 - 3.804)\hat{j}$$

$$= -2.325\hat{i} - 2.127\hat{j}$$

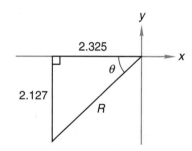

$$R = \sqrt{(2.325)^2 + (2.127)^2} = 3.15$$

$$\theta = \tan^{-1}\frac{2.127}{2.325} = 42.45°$$

Resultant $= 3.15\underline{/222.45°}$

Equilibrant $= \textbf{−3.15}\underline{\textbf{/222.45°}}$

4. $A_1 = L \times W$
(5)

$$A_2 = (L + 0.3L)(W - 0.3W)$$

$$= LW - 0.3LW + 0.3LW - 0.09LW$$

$$= LW - 0.09LW$$

It decreases by 9%.

5.
(28)
$$\frac{10!}{3!7!} = \frac{10 \cdot 9 \cdot 8 \cdot 7!}{3 \cdot 2 \cdot 1 \cdot 7!} = \textbf{120}$$

6.
(34)
$$\sum_{j=1}^{3} \frac{2^j}{2 + j} = \frac{2^1}{2 + 1} + \frac{2^2}{2 + 2} + \frac{2^3}{2 + 3}$$

$$= \frac{2}{3} + \frac{4}{4} + \frac{8}{5} = \frac{40 + 60 + 96}{60} = \frac{196}{60} = \frac{49}{15}$$

7. $f(x) = \dfrac{1}{x}$
(21)

$$f(x + h) - f(x) = \frac{1}{x + h} - \frac{1}{x}$$

$$= \frac{x - (x + h)}{x(x + h)} = -\frac{h}{x(x + h)}$$

8. $8x^6y^9 - 64a^3b^{12} = 8(x^6y^9 - 8a^3b^{12})$
(19)

$$= 8\left[(x^2y^3)^3 - (2ab^4)^3\right]$$

$$= 8(x^2y^3 - 2ab^4)(x^4y^6 + 2x^2y^3ab^4 + 4a^2b^8)$$

9. $f(\theta) = \cos \theta, \; g(\theta) = \tan \theta$
$(24, 36)$

$$f(540°) + g(225°) = f(180°) + g(225°)$$

$$= \cos 180° + \tan 225° = -1 + 1 = 0$$

10. (a)
(32)

$$c = \sqrt{1^2 + 1^2} = \sqrt{2}$$

$$\sin (\text{Arctan } 1) = \frac{1}{\sqrt{2}} = \frac{\sqrt{2}}{2}$$

(b)

$$b = \sqrt{2^2 - 1^2} = \sqrt{3}$$

$$\tan \left(\text{Arccos } \frac{1}{2}\right) = \frac{\sqrt{3}}{1} = \sqrt{3}$$

11. Two points $(40, 5), (160, 15)$
(34)

$$m = \frac{15 - 5}{160 - 40} = \frac{10}{120} = \frac{1}{12}$$

$$S = \frac{1}{12}C + b$$

$$5 = \frac{1}{12}(40) + b$$

$$b = \frac{5}{3}$$

$$S = \frac{1}{12}C + \frac{5}{3}$$

12. Distance $= m$ ft, rate $= z \dfrac{\text{ft}}{\text{min}}$
(28)

$$\text{Time} = \frac{\text{distance}}{\text{rate}} = \frac{m \text{ ft}}{z \dfrac{\text{ft}}{\text{min}}} = \frac{m}{z} \text{ min}$$

New distance $= m$ ft

$$\text{New time} = \left(\frac{m}{z} - 3\right) \text{min} = \frac{m - 3z}{z} \text{ min}$$

$$\text{New rate} = \frac{\text{new distance}}{\text{new time}}$$

$$= \frac{m \text{ ft}}{\dfrac{m - 3z}{z} \text{ min}} = \frac{mz}{m - 3z} \frac{\text{ft}}{\text{min}}$$

13.
(25)
$$RST = P$$

$$R(5 \text{ students})(2 \text{ hr}) = 100 \text{ problems}$$

$$R = 10 \frac{\text{problems}}{\text{student-hr}}$$

$$RST = P$$

$$T = \frac{P}{RS}$$

$$T = \frac{1000 \text{ problems}}{10 \dfrac{\text{problems}}{\text{student-hr}} (10 \text{ students})}$$

$$T = \textbf{10 hr}$$

14.
(25)
$$R_ET_E + R_PT_P = 30 \text{ problems}$$

$$\left(\frac{1}{2} \frac{\text{problem}}{\text{min}}\right)T + \left(\frac{3}{5} \frac{\text{problem}}{\text{min}}\right)T = 30 \text{ problems}$$

$$\left(\frac{11}{10} \frac{\text{problems}}{\text{min}}\right)T = 30 \text{ problems}$$

$$T = \frac{300}{11} \text{ min}$$

15. $f(x) = \dfrac{\sqrt{x - 3}}{x^2 - 5x + 6} = \dfrac{\sqrt{x - 3}}{(x - 3)(x - 2)}$
(21)

$$(x - 3)(x - 2) \neq 0$$

$$x \neq 3, 2$$

$$x - 3 \geq 0$$
$$x \geq 3$$
Domain of $f = \left\{ x \in \mathbb{R} \mid x > 3 \right\}$

16.
(32)
$$y = \frac{7}{8}x - \frac{1}{4}$$

$$\frac{7}{8}x = y + \frac{1}{4}$$

$$x = \frac{8}{7}y + \frac{2}{7}$$

$$y = \frac{8}{7}x + \frac{2}{7}$$

17.
(30)

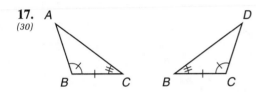

STATEMENTS	REASONS
1. $\angle ABC \cong \angle DCB$	1. Given
2. $\angle BCA \cong \angle CBD$	2. Given
3. $\overline{BC} \cong \overline{BC}$	3. Reflexive axiom
4. $\angle BAC \cong \angle CDB$	4. If two angles in one triangle are congruent to two angles in a second triangle, then the third angles are congruent.
5. $\triangle ABC \cong \triangle DCB$	5. *AAAS* congruency postulate
6. $\overline{AC} \cong \overline{DB}$	6. *CPCTC*

18. (a) $\log_x \dfrac{27}{64} = 3$
(26)

$$x^3 = \frac{27}{64}$$

$$x^3 = \frac{3^3}{4^3}$$

$$x^3 = \left(\frac{3}{4}\right)^3$$

$$x = \frac{3}{4}$$

(b) $\log_3 \dfrac{1}{27} = x$

$$3^x = \frac{1}{27}$$

$$3^x = \frac{1}{3^3}$$

$$3^x = 3^{-3}$$

$$x = -3$$

(c) $\log_{1/3} x = -4$

$$x = \left(\frac{1}{3}\right)^{-4}$$

$$x = 3^4$$

$$x = \mathbf{81}$$

19. $g(x) = \sqrt{-x}$
(31)

20.
(33)
$$EF = \frac{1}{2}\left(\text{base}_1 + \text{base}_2\right)$$

$$3x + 5 = \frac{1}{2}(2x - 1 + 6x - 9)$$

$$3x + 5 = 4x - 5$$

$$x = \mathbf{10}$$

Test 9, Form B

1.
(36)
$$\begin{cases} (G + W)T_D = D_D \\ (G - W)T_U = D_U \end{cases}$$

$$G = 3W, \ T_D = T_U + 1$$

$$(G - W)T_U = D_U$$

$$(3W - W)T_U = 138$$

$$2WT_U = 138$$

$$WT_U = 69$$

$$(G + W)T_D = D_D$$

$$(3W + W)(T_U + 1) = 368$$

$$(4W)(T_U + 1) = 368$$

$$4WT_U + 4W = 368$$

$$4(69) + 4W = 368$$

$$4W = 92$$

$$W = 23$$

$$G = 3W = 3(23) = \mathbf{69 \ mph}$$

2. Number $= -5\dfrac{1}{3} + \dfrac{2}{3}(\Delta C)$
(35)

$$= -5\frac{1}{3} + \frac{2}{3}\left(C_F - C_I\right)$$

$$= -5\frac{1}{3} + \frac{2}{3}\left[9\frac{2}{3} - \left(-5\frac{1}{3}\right)\right]$$

$$= -5\frac{1}{3} + \frac{2}{3}(15)$$

$$= -\frac{16}{3} + \frac{30}{3} = \mathbf{\frac{14}{3}}$$

3.
(30)

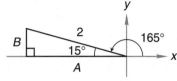

$A = 2 \cos 15° = 1.9318$

$B = 2 \sin 15° = 0.5176$

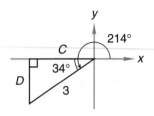

$C = 3 \cos 34° = 2.4871$

$D = 3 \sin 34° = 1.6776$

$(-1.9318 - 2.4871)\,\hat{i} + (0.5176 - 1.6776)\,\hat{j}$

$= -4.4189\,\hat{i} + (-1.160)\,\hat{j}$

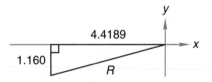

$R = \sqrt{(-4.4189)^2 + (-1.160)^2} = 4.5686$

$\theta = \tan^{-1}\left(\dfrac{-1.160}{-4.4189}\right) = 194.71°$

Resultant $= 4.57\underline{/194.71°}$

Equilibrant $= -\mathbf{4.57}\underline{/\mathbf{194.71°}}$

4. $A_1 = L \times W$
(5)

$A_2 = (L + 0.5L)(W - 0.7W)$

$= LW - 0.7LW + 0.5LW - 0.35LW$

$= LW - 0.55LW$

It decreases by 55%.

5. $\dfrac{9!}{3!\,6!} = \dfrac{9 \cdot 8 \cdot 7 \cdot 6!}{3 \cdot 2 \cdot 1 \cdot 6!} = \mathbf{84}$
(28)

6. $\displaystyle\sum_{q=1}^{3} \dfrac{3^q}{3 + q} = \dfrac{3}{3 + 1} + \dfrac{3^2}{3 + 2} + \dfrac{3^3}{3 + 3}$
(34)

$= \dfrac{3}{4} + \dfrac{9}{5} + \dfrac{27}{6} = \dfrac{3}{4} + \dfrac{9}{5} + \dfrac{9}{2}$

$= \dfrac{15 + 36 + 90}{20} = \dfrac{\mathbf{141}}{\mathbf{20}}$

7. $f(x) = \dfrac{1}{x}$
(21)

$f(x + h) - f(x) = \dfrac{1}{x + h} - \dfrac{1}{x}$

$= \dfrac{x - (x + h)}{x(x + h)} = -\dfrac{h}{x(x + h)}$

8. $27x^3y^9 - 8q^6z^{12} = \left(3xy^3\right)^3 - \left(2q^2z^4\right)^3$
(19)

$= \left(3xy^3 - 2q^2z^4\right)\left(9x^2y^6 + 6xy^3q^2z^4 + 4q^4z^8\right)$

9. $h(\theta) = \tan \theta,\ k(\theta) = \cos \theta$
(24, 36)

$h(315°) + k(420°) = h(-45°) + k(60°)$

$= \tan(-45°) + \cos 60° = -1 + \dfrac{1}{2} = -\dfrac{1}{2}$

10. (a)
(32)

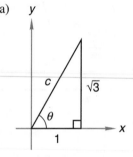

$c = \sqrt{\left(\sqrt{3}\right)^2 + 1^2} = 2$

$\cos\left(\text{Arctan } \sqrt{3}\right) = \dfrac{1}{2}$

(b)

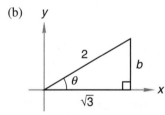

$b = \sqrt{2^2 - \left(\sqrt{3}\right)^2} = 1$

$\sin\left(\text{Arccos } \dfrac{\sqrt{3}}{2}\right) = \dfrac{1}{2}$

11. Two points $(160, 1500),\ (40, 500)$
(34)

$m = \dfrac{1500 - 500}{160 - 40} = \dfrac{1000}{120} = \dfrac{25}{3}$

$T = \dfrac{25}{3}B + c$

$1500 = \dfrac{25}{3}(160) + c$

$c = 166.67$

$T = \dfrac{25}{3}B + 166.67$

12. Distance $= d$ ft, Rate $= r \dfrac{\text{ft}}{\text{min}}$
(28)

Time $= \dfrac{\text{distance}}{\text{rate}} = \dfrac{d \text{ ft}}{r \dfrac{\text{ft}}{\text{min}}} = \dfrac{d}{r}$ min

New distance $= d$ ft

New time $= \left(\dfrac{d}{r} - 7\right)$min $= \dfrac{d - 7r}{r}$ min

New rate $= \dfrac{\text{new distance}}{\text{new time}}$

$= \dfrac{d \text{ ft}}{\dfrac{d - 7r}{r} \text{ min}} = \dfrac{dr}{d - 7r} \dfrac{\text{ft}}{\text{min}}$

13. $RPT = H$
(25)

$R(6 \text{ players})(15 \text{ min}) = 60 \text{ hot dogs}$

$R = \dfrac{2}{3} \dfrac{\text{hot dogs}}{\text{player-min}}$

$RPT = H$

$T = \dfrac{H}{RP}$

$T = \dfrac{96 \text{ hot dogs}}{\dfrac{2}{3} \dfrac{\text{hot dogs}}{\text{player-min}} (12 \text{ players})} = \textbf{12 min}$

14. $R_B T_B + R_F T_F = 49 \text{ rocks}$
(25)

$\left(\dfrac{1}{2} \dfrac{\text{rock}}{\text{min}}\right)T + \left(\dfrac{3}{8} \dfrac{\text{rock}}{\text{min}}\right)T = 49 \text{ rocks}$

$\left(\dfrac{7}{8} \dfrac{\text{rock}}{\text{min}}\right)T = 49 \text{ rocks}$

$T = \textbf{56 min}$

15. $f(x) = \dfrac{\sqrt{x + 2}}{x^2 - 5x - 14} = \dfrac{\sqrt{x + 2}}{(x - 7)(x + 2)}$
(21)

$(x - 7)(x + 2) \neq 0$

$x \neq 7, -2$

$x + 2 \geq 0$

$x \geq -2$

Domain of $f = \left\{x \in \mathbb{R} \mid x > -2, x \neq 7\right\}$

16. $y = \dfrac{10}{11}x + \dfrac{1}{22}$
(32)

$22y = 20x + 1$

$-20x = -22y + 1$

$x = \dfrac{22}{20}y - \dfrac{1}{20}$

$y = \dfrac{11}{10}x - \dfrac{1}{20}$

17.
(30)

STATEMENTS	REASONS
1. $\angle XYZ \cong \angle VZY$	1. Given
2. $\angle XZY \cong \angle VYZ$	2. Given
3. $\overline{YZ} \cong \overline{YZ}$	3. Reflexive axiom
4. $\angle YXZ \cong \angle ZVY$	4. If two angles in one triangle are congruent to two angles in a second triangle, then the third angles are congruent.
5. $\triangle XYZ \cong \triangle VZY$	5. *AAAS* congruency postulate
6. $\overline{XZ} \cong \overline{VY}$	6. *CPCTC*

18. (a) $\log_x \dfrac{8}{125} = 3$
(26)

$x^3 = \dfrac{8}{125}$

$x^3 = \dfrac{2^3}{5^3}$

$x^3 = \left(\dfrac{2}{5}\right)^3$

$x = \dfrac{2}{5}$

(b) $\log_6 \dfrac{1}{36} = x$

$6^x = \dfrac{1}{36}$

$6^x = \dfrac{1}{6^2}$

$6^x = 6^{-2}$

$x = -2$

(c) $\log_{1/4} x = -2$

$x = \left(\dfrac{1}{4}\right)^{-2}$

$x = 4^2$

$x = \textbf{16}$

19. $g(x) = -\sqrt{-x}$
(31)

20. $EF = \dfrac{1}{2}\left(\text{base}_1 + \text{base}_2\right)$
(33)

$(3x + 8) = \dfrac{1}{2}(4x + 1 + 7x - 5)$

$6x + 16 = 11x - 4$

$5x = 20$

$x = \textbf{4}$

Test 10, Form A

1. Overall average rate = $\dfrac{\text{overall distance}}{\text{overall time}}$
(38)

$$4\,\frac{\text{mi}}{\text{hr}} = \frac{10\text{ mi} + 6\text{ mi} + 8\text{ mi}}{\text{overall time}}$$

$$4\,\frac{\text{mi}}{\text{hr}} = \frac{24\text{ mi}}{\text{overall time}}$$

Overall time = 6 hr

$$\text{Time}_1 = \frac{10\text{ mi}}{5\,\frac{\text{mi}}{\text{hr}}} = 2\text{ hr}$$

$$\text{Time}_2 = \frac{6\text{ mi}}{2\,\frac{\text{mi}}{\text{hr}}} = 3\text{ hr}$$

$$\text{Time}_3 = 6\text{ hr} - 2\text{ hr} - 3\text{ hr} = 1\text{ hr}$$

$$\text{Rate}_3 = \frac{\text{distance}_3}{\text{time}_3} = \frac{8\text{ mi}}{1\text{ hr}} = \mathbf{8\,\frac{mi}{hr}}$$

2. Two points (48, 150), (112, 50)
(34)
$$m = \frac{150 - 50}{48 - 112} = -\frac{100}{64} = -\frac{25}{16}$$

$$S = -\frac{25}{16}P + b$$

$$50 = -\frac{25}{16}(112) + b$$

$$b = 225$$

$$S = -\frac{25}{16}P + 225$$

3. $\sqrt{(x-5)^2 + (y-2)^2} = \sqrt{(x)^2 + (y+4)^2}$
(37)
$$(x-5)^2 + (y-2)^2 = x^2 + (y+4)^2$$
$$x^2 + y^2 - 10x - 4y + 29 = x^2 + y^2 + 8y + 16$$
$$12y = -10x + 13$$
$$y = -\frac{5}{6}x + \frac{13}{12}$$

4. $4 \cdot 4 \cdot 4 \cdot 4 \cdot 4 = \mathbf{1024}$
(38)

5. $(x - 3)(x - 2) = 0$
(38)
$$x^2 - 5x + 6 = 0$$

6. $f(x) = 2x^2 - 3$
(21)
$$\frac{f(x+h) - f(x)}{h} = \frac{2(x+h)^2 - 3 - (2x^2 - 3)}{h}$$
$$= \frac{2x^2 + 4xh + 2h^2 - 2x^2}{h} = \frac{4xh + 2h^2}{h}$$
$$= \mathbf{4x + 2h}$$

7. $\displaystyle\sum_{k=2}^{5}\left(\frac{k^2}{3} - k\right)$
(34)

$$= \left(\frac{2^2}{3} - 2\right) + \left(\frac{3^2}{3} - 3\right)$$

$$+ \left(\frac{4^2}{3} - 4\right) + \left(\frac{5^2}{3} - 5\right)$$

$$= \frac{4}{3} - 2 + \frac{9}{3} - 3 + \frac{16}{3} - 4 + \frac{25}{3} - 5$$

$$= \frac{54}{3} - 14 = \mathbf{4}$$

8. $40° \times \dfrac{\pi\,\text{rad}}{180°} = \dfrac{2\pi}{9}\text{ rad}$
(39)

$$\text{Distance} = \frac{2\pi}{9}(7\text{ in.}) = \mathbf{4.89\ in.}$$

9. $x = \dfrac{x_1 + x_2}{2} = \dfrac{-2 + 6}{2} = 2$
(37)

$$y = \frac{y_1 + y_2}{2} = \frac{6 + (-4)}{2} = 1$$

$$\text{Midpoint} = \mathbf{(2, 1)}$$

10. $\log_{96} 3 + \log_{96} 5 = \log_{96}(5 + x)$
(40)
$$\log_{96}(3 \cdot 5) = \log_{96}(5 + x)$$
$$15 = 5 + x$$
$$x = \mathbf{10}$$

11. $\log_{20}(2x + 6) - \log_{20} 2 = \log_{20} 8$
(40)
$$\log_{20}\left(\frac{2x + 6}{2}\right) = \log_{20} 8$$
$$\frac{2x + 6}{2} = 8$$
$$x + 3 = 8$$
$$x = \mathbf{5}$$

12. $4\log_b x = \log_b 16$
(40)
$$\log_b x^4 = \log_b 16$$
$$x^4 = 16$$
$$x^4 = 2^4$$
$$x = \mathbf{2}$$

13. $\log_3 \dfrac{1}{81} = x$
(26)

$$3^x = \frac{1}{81}$$

$$3^x = \frac{1}{3^4}$$

$$3^x = 3^{-4}$$

$$x = \mathbf{-4}$$

14.
(36, 39)

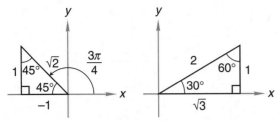

$$\sin \frac{\pi}{2} - \cos \frac{3\pi}{4} - \tan \frac{\pi}{6}$$

$$= \sin 90° - \cos 135° - \tan 30°$$

$$= 1 - \left(-\frac{1}{\sqrt{2}}\right) - \frac{1}{\sqrt{3}} = 1 + \frac{\sqrt{2}}{2} - \frac{\sqrt{3}}{3}$$

$$= \frac{6 + 3\sqrt{2} - 2\sqrt{3}}{6}$$

15.
(32)

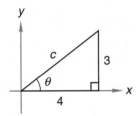

$$c = \sqrt{3^2 + 4^2} = 5$$

$$\sin \left(\text{Arctan} \frac{3}{4}\right) = \frac{3}{5}$$

16.
(39)

$$y - y_1 = m(x - x_1)$$

$$y - 7 = -3(x + 1)$$

$$y - 7 = -3x - 3$$

$$3x + y - 4 = 0$$

$$3x + y = 4$$

$$\frac{3x}{4} + \frac{y}{4} = 1$$

$$\frac{x}{\frac{4}{3}} + \frac{y}{4} = 1$$

17.
(28) Distance $= m$ mi, rate $= r \dfrac{\text{mi}}{\text{hr}}$

$$\text{Time} = \frac{\text{distance}}{\text{rate}} = \frac{m \text{ mi}}{r \dfrac{\text{mi}}{\text{hr}}} = \frac{m}{r} \text{ hr}$$

New distance $= m$ mi

$$\text{New time} = \left(\frac{m}{r} - 2\right) \text{hr} = \frac{m - 2r}{r} \text{ hr}$$

$$\text{New rate} = \frac{m \text{ mi}}{\dfrac{m - 2r}{r} \text{ hr}} = \frac{mr}{m - 2r} \frac{\text{mi}}{\text{hr}}$$

18.
(25)

$$R_T T_T + R_A T_A = 22 \text{ shelves}$$

$$3 \frac{\text{shelves}}{\text{day}} (T) + 2 \frac{\text{shelves}}{\text{day}} (T + 1 \text{ day}) = 22 \text{ shelves}$$

$$5 \frac{\text{shelves}}{\text{day}} T + 2 \text{ shelves} = 22 \text{ shelves}$$

$$5 \frac{\text{shelves}}{\text{day}} T = 20 \text{ shelves}$$

$$T = \textbf{4 days}$$

19.
(31) $g(x) = \dfrac{1}{x} + 1$

20.
(15)

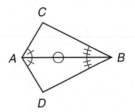

STATEMENTS	REASONS
1. $\overline{AB}$ bisects $\angle CAD$	1. Given
2. $\overline{AB}$ bisects $\angle CBD$	2. Given
3. $\angle CAB \cong \angle DAB$ and $\angle CBA \cong \angle DBA$	3. An angle bisector divides an angle into two congruent angles.
4. $\overline{AB} \cong \overline{AB}$	4. Reflexive axiom
5. $\angle C \cong \angle D$	5. If two angles in one triangle are congruent to two angles in another triangle, then the third angles are congruent.
6. $\triangle ACB \cong \triangle ADB$	6. *AAAS* congruency postulate

Test 10, Form B

1.
(38) Overall average rate $= \dfrac{\text{overall distance}}{\text{overall time}}$

$$3 \frac{\text{mi}}{\text{hr}} = \frac{8 \text{ mi} + 4 \text{ mi} + 6 \text{ mi}}{\text{overall time}}$$

$$3 \frac{\text{mi}}{\text{hr}} = \frac{18 \text{ mi}}{\text{overall time}}$$

Overall time $= 6$ hr

$$\text{Time}_1 = \frac{8 \text{ mi}}{4 \dfrac{\text{mi}}{\text{hr}}} = 2 \text{ hr}$$

$$\text{Time}_2 = \frac{4 \text{ mi}}{2 \dfrac{\text{mi}}{\text{hr}}} = 2 \text{ hr}$$

$$\text{Time}_3 = 6 \text{ hr} - 2 \text{ hr} - 2 \text{ hr} = 2 \text{ hr}$$

$$\text{Rate}_3 = \frac{\text{distance}_3}{\text{time}_3} = \frac{6 \text{ mi}}{2 \text{ hr}} = \textbf{3} \frac{\textbf{mi}}{\textbf{hr}}$$

Test Solutions

2. Two points $(24, 150)$, $(56, 50)$
(34)

$$m = \frac{150 - 50}{24 - 56} = -\frac{100}{32} = -\frac{25}{8}$$

$$S = -\frac{25}{8}P + b$$

$$50 = -\frac{25}{8}(56) + b$$

$$b = 225$$

$$S = -\frac{25}{8}P + 225$$

3.
(37)

$$\sqrt{(x - 4)^2 + (y - 3)^2} = \sqrt{(x)^2 + (y + 2)^2}$$

$$(x - 4)^2 + (y - 3)^2 = x^2 + (y + 2)^2$$

$$x^2 - 8x + y^2 - 6y + 25 = x^2 + y^2 + 4y + 4$$

$$10y = -8x + 21$$

$$y = -\frac{4}{5}x + \frac{21}{10}$$

4. $3 \cdot 3 \cdot 3 \cdot 3 \cdot 3 \cdot 3 \cdot 3 = \mathbf{2187}$
(38)

5. $(x + 3)(x - 5) = 0$
(38)

$$x^2 - 2x - 15 = 0$$

6. $f(x) = 3x^2 - 4$
(21)

$$\frac{f(x + h) - f(x)}{h} = \frac{3(x + h)^2 - 4 - (3x^2 - 4)}{h}$$

$$= \frac{3x^2 + 6xh + 3h^2 - 3x^2}{h} = \frac{6xh + 3h^2}{h}$$

$$= 6x + 3h$$

7. $\displaystyle\sum_{k=3}^{6} \frac{k^2}{2} - 2k$
(34)

$$= \left(\frac{3^2}{2} - 2(3)\right) + \left(\frac{4^2}{2} - 2(4)\right)$$

$$+ \left(\frac{5^2}{2} - 2(5)\right) + \left(\frac{6^2}{2} - 2(6)\right)$$

$$= \frac{9}{2} - 6 + \frac{16}{2} - 8 + \frac{25}{2} - 10 + \frac{36}{2} - 12$$

$$= -36 + \frac{86}{2} = 7$$

8. $60° \times \dfrac{\pi \, \text{rad}}{180°} = \dfrac{\pi}{3}$ rad
(39)

$$\text{Distance} = \frac{\pi}{3}(100 \text{ mm}) = \mathbf{104.72 \text{ mm}}$$

9. $x = \dfrac{x_1 + x_2}{2} = \dfrac{-8 + 14}{2} = 3$
(37)

$$y = \frac{y_1 + y_2}{2} = \frac{-15 + 7}{2} = -4$$

$$\text{Midpoint} = \mathbf{(3, -4)}$$

10. $\log_{87} 4 + \log_{87} 3 = \log_{87}(4 + x)$
(40)

$$\log_{87}(4 \cdot 3) = \log_{87}(4 + x)$$

$$12 = 4 + x$$

$$x = \mathbf{8}$$

11. $\log_{20}(3x + 9) - \log_{20} 2 = \log_{20} 12$
(40)

$$\log_{20}\left(\frac{3x + 9}{2}\right) = \log_{20} 12$$

$$\frac{3x + 9}{2} = 12$$

$$3x + 9 = 24$$

$$3x = 15$$

$$x = \mathbf{5}$$

12. $5 \log_b x = \log_b 32$
(40)

$$\log_b x^5 = \log_b 32$$

$$x^5 = 32$$

$$x^5 = 2^5$$

$$x = \mathbf{2}$$

13. $\log_4 \dfrac{1}{64} = x$
(26)

$$4^x = \frac{1}{64}$$

$$4^x = \frac{1}{4^3}$$

$$4^x = 4^{-3}$$

$$x = \mathbf{-3}$$

14.
(36, 39)

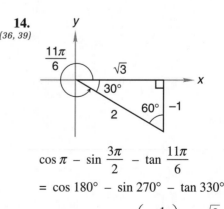

$$\cos \pi - \sin \frac{3\pi}{2} - \tan \frac{11\pi}{6}$$

$$= \cos 180° - \sin 270° - \tan 330°$$

$$= (-1) - (-1) - \left(-\frac{1}{\sqrt{3}}\right) = \frac{\sqrt{3}}{3}$$

15.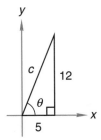
(32)

$$c = \sqrt{12^2 + 5^2} = 13$$

$$\sin\left(\text{Arctan}\,\frac{12}{5}\right) = \frac{12}{13}$$

16.
(39)
$$y - y_1 = m(x - x_1)$$
$$y + 1 = -2(x - 2)$$
$$y + 1 = -2x + 4$$
$$\mathbf{2x + y - 3 = 0}$$
$$2x + y = 3$$
$$\frac{2x}{3} + \frac{y}{3} = 1$$
$$\frac{x}{\frac{3}{2}} + \frac{y}{3} = 1$$

17. Distance $= k$ km, rate $= s\,\dfrac{\text{km}}{\text{day}}$
(28)

$$\text{Time} = \frac{\text{distance}}{\text{rate}} = \frac{k\,\text{km}}{s\,\dfrac{\text{km}}{\text{day}}} = \frac{k}{s}\,\text{day}$$

New distance $= k$ km

$$\text{New time} = \left(\frac{k}{s} - 2\right)\text{day} = \frac{k - 2s}{s}\,\text{day}$$

$$\text{New rate} = \frac{k\,\text{km}}{\dfrac{k - 2s}{s}\,\text{day}} = \frac{ks}{k - 2s}\,\frac{\text{km}}{\text{day}}$$

18.
(25)
$$R_C T_C + R_F T_F = 20\ \text{loads}$$

$$2\,\frac{\text{loads}}{\text{day}}(T + 1\ \text{day}) + \frac{5}{2}\,\frac{\text{loads}}{\text{day}}(T) = 20\ \text{loads}$$

$$\frac{9}{2}\,\frac{\text{loads}}{\text{day}}T + 2\ \text{loads} = 20\ \text{loads}$$

$$\frac{9}{2}\,\frac{\text{loads}}{\text{day}}T = 18\ \text{loads}$$

$$T = \mathbf{4\ days}$$

19. $g(x) - 2 = -\dfrac{1}{x - (-2)}$
(31)

$$g(x) = -\frac{1}{x + 2} + 2$$

20.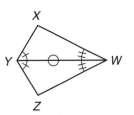
(15)

STATEMENTS	REASONS
1. $\overline{YW}$ bisects $\angle XYZ$	1. Given
2. $\overline{YW}$ bisects $\angle XWZ$	2. Given
3. $\angle XYW \cong \angle ZYW$ and $\angle XWY \cong \angle ZWY$	3. An angle bisector divides an angle into two congruent angles.
4. $\overline{YW} \cong \overline{YW}$	4. Reflexive axiom
5. $\angle X \cong \angle Z$	5. If two angles in one triangle are congruent to two angles in another triangle, then the third angles are congruent.
6. $\triangle YXW \cong \triangle YZW$	6. *AAAS* congruency postulate

Test 11, Form A

1. Rate $\times$ turkeys = price or $RT = P$
(44)

Turkeys $= t$

Price $= d$ dollars

$$\text{Rate} = \frac{d}{t}\,\frac{\text{dollars}}{\text{turkey}}$$

$$\text{New rate} = \left(\frac{d}{t} - 2\right)\frac{\text{dollars}}{\text{turkey}} = \frac{d - 2t}{t}\,\frac{\text{dollars}}{\text{turkey}}$$

New price $= 1000$ dollars

$$RT = P$$

$$\left(\frac{d - 2t}{t}\,\frac{\text{dollars}}{\text{turkey}}\right)T = 1000\ \text{dollars}$$

$$T = \frac{1000\ \text{dollars}}{\dfrac{d - 2t}{t}\,\dfrac{\text{dollars}}{\text{turkey}}}$$

$$T = \frac{\mathbf{1000}t}{d - 2t}\ \textbf{turkeys}$$

2.
(39)
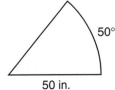

$$50° \times \frac{\pi\,\text{rad}}{180°} = \frac{5\pi}{18}\,\text{rad}$$

$$\text{Distance} = \frac{5\pi}{18}(50) = \mathbf{43.63\ in.}$$

Test Solutions

3. $y = \left(\dfrac{1}{2}\right)^{-2x} = \left(\left(\dfrac{1}{2}\right)^{-2}\right)^x = 4^x$
(23)

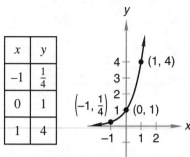

x	y
-1	$\dfrac{1}{4}$
0	1
1	4

4. $_nP_r = \dfrac{n!}{(n-r)!}$
(41)

$_6P_4 = \dfrac{6!}{(6-4)!} = \dfrac{6!}{2!} = 360$

$_6P_2 = \dfrac{6!}{(6-2)!} = \dfrac{6!}{4!} = 30$

$360 - 30 = \mathbf{330}$

5. (a) $3\log_2 x = 2\log_2 8$
(26, 40)

$\log_2 x^3 = \log_2 8^2$

$x^3 = 64$

$x^3 = 4^3$

$x = \mathbf{4}$

(b) $\log_9 \dfrac{1}{81} = x$

$9^x = \dfrac{1}{81}$

$9^x = \dfrac{1}{9^2}$

$9^x = 9^{-2}$

$x = \mathbf{-2}$

(c) $\log_x 81 = 4$

$x^4 = 81$

$x^4 = 3^4$

$x = \mathbf{3}$

6. (a)
(32)

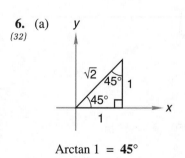

Arctan $1 = \mathbf{45°}$

(b) Arccos $(-1) = \mathbf{180°}$

(c)

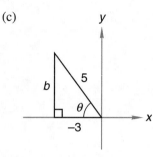

$b = \sqrt{5^2 - (-3)^2} = \sqrt{16} = 4$

$\sin\left(\text{Arccos}\left(-\dfrac{3}{5}\right)\right) = \dfrac{\mathbf{4}}{\mathbf{5}}$

7. $\log_2 2^3 + \log_3 3^2 - \log_5 5^2 = 3 + 2 - 2 = \mathbf{3}$
(40)

8. $\log_7 (x+8) - \log_7 (x-1) = \log_7 10$
(40)

$\log_7 \dfrac{(x+8)}{(x-1)} = \log_7 10$

$\dfrac{(x+8)}{(x-1)} = 10$

$x + 8 = 10x - 10$

$9x = 18$

$x = \mathbf{2}$

9. (a)
(22)

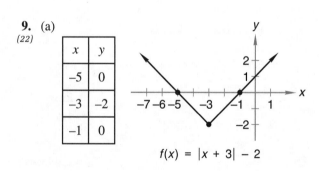

x	y
-5	0
-3	-2
-1	0

$f(x) = |x+3| - 2$

(b)

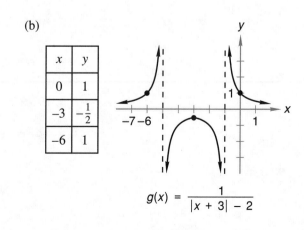

x	y
0	1
-3	$-\dfrac{1}{2}$
-6	1

$g(x) = \dfrac{1}{|x+3| - 2}$

10. $\sqrt{(x-3)^2 + (y+2)^2}$
(37)

$$= \sqrt{(x+3)^2 + (y-4)^2}$$

$$x^2 - 6x + 9 + y^2 + 4y + 4$$

$$= x^2 + 6x + 9 + y^2 - 8y + 16$$

$$12y = 12x + 12$$

$$y = x + 1$$

11. $f(x) = \dfrac{\sqrt{-x}}{x^3 + 2x^2 - 3x}$
(21)

$$= \dfrac{\sqrt{-x}}{x(x^2 + 2x - 3)}$$

$$= \dfrac{\sqrt{-x}}{x(x+3)(x-1)}$$

$$x(x+3)(x-1) \neq 0$$

$$x \neq 0, -3, 1$$

$$-x \geq 0$$

$$x \leq 0$$

Domain of $f = \{x \in \mathbb{R} \mid x < 0, x \neq -3\}$

12. $\displaystyle\sum_{j=2}^{4} (3j - j^2)$
(34)

$$= \left[3(2) - (2)^2\right] + \left[3(3) - (3)^2\right] + \left[3(4) - (4)^2\right]$$

$$= 2 + 0 + (-4) = -2$$

13. $f(x) = \dfrac{1}{x-2}$ and $g(x) = \dfrac{2x+1}{x}$
(40)

$$f(g(x)) = \dfrac{1}{\dfrac{2x+1}{x} - 2} = \dfrac{1}{\dfrac{2x+1-2x}{x}}$$

$$= \dfrac{1}{\dfrac{1}{x}} = x$$

$$g(f(x)) = \dfrac{2\left(\dfrac{1}{x-2}\right) + 1}{\dfrac{1}{x-2}} = \dfrac{\dfrac{2 + x - 2}{x-2}}{\dfrac{1}{x-2}}$$

$$= \dfrac{x(x-2)}{x-2} = x$$

$$f(g(x)) = g(f(x)) = x$$

Yes, f and g are inverse functions.

14. $(x-h)^2 + (y-k)^2 = r^2$
(42)

$$(x-2)^2 + (y-5)^2 = 4^2$$

15.
(15, 17)

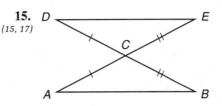

STATEMENTS	REASONS
1. $\overline{AC} \cong \overline{DC}$	1. Given
2. $\overline{BC} \cong \overline{EC}$	2. Given
3. $\angle ACB \cong \angle DCE$	3. Vertical angles are congruent.
4. $\triangle ACB \cong \triangle DCE$	4. *SAS* congruency postulate
5. $\angle A \cong \angle D$	5. *CPCTC*

16.
(41)

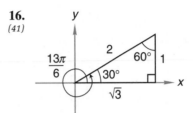

$$\dfrac{13\pi}{6} = 390°$$

$$\cos 390° = \cos 30° = \dfrac{\sqrt{3}}{2}$$

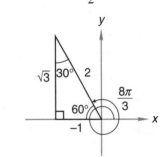

$$\dfrac{8\pi}{3} = 480°$$

$$\tan 480° = -\tan 60° = -\dfrac{\sqrt{3}}{1} = -\sqrt{3}$$

$$\cos \dfrac{13\pi}{6} - \tan \dfrac{8\pi}{3} = \dfrac{\sqrt{3}}{2} + \sqrt{3} = \dfrac{3\sqrt{3}}{2}$$

17. Rate × students × time = problems or $RST = P$
(44)

$$R(33 \text{ students})(x \text{ hours}) = n \text{ problems}$$

$$R = \dfrac{n}{33x} \dfrac{\text{problems}}{\text{student-hr}}$$

$$RST = P$$

$$T = \dfrac{P}{RS}$$

$$T = \dfrac{100 \text{ problems}}{\dfrac{n}{33x} \dfrac{\text{problems}}{\text{student-hr}} (33 - 3) \text{ students}}$$

$$T = \dfrac{100(33x)}{30n} \text{ hr} = \dfrac{110x}{n} \text{ hr}$$

18. $x = \dfrac{x_1 + x_2}{2} = \dfrac{2 + 12}{2} = \dfrac{14}{2} = 7$
(37)

$y = \dfrac{y_1 + y_2}{2} = \dfrac{4 + (-2)}{2} = \dfrac{2}{2} = 1$

(7, 1)

19.
(41)

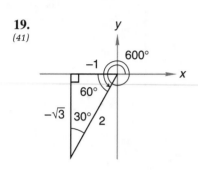

$\sec 600° = \sec 240° = -\sec 60° = -2$

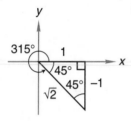

$\cot 315° = -\cot 45° = -1$

$\sec 600° + \cot 315° = -2 - 1 = \mathbf{-3}$

20. Function $= \cos x$
(43)

Amplitude $= 7$

$y = \mathbf{7 \cos x}$

Test 11, Form B

1. Rate $\times$ amps $=$ price or $RA = P$
(44)

Amps $= t$

Price $= m$ dollars

Rate $= \dfrac{m}{t} \dfrac{\text{dollars}}{\text{amp}}$

New rate $= \left(\dfrac{m}{t} - 15\right)\dfrac{\text{dollars}}{\text{amp}} = \dfrac{m - 15t}{t} \dfrac{\text{dollars}}{\text{amp}}$

New price $= 3000$ dollars

$$RA = P$$

$$\left(\dfrac{m - 15t}{t} \dfrac{\text{dollars}}{\text{amp}}\right)A = 3000 \text{ dollars}$$

$$A = \dfrac{3000 \text{ dollars}}{\dfrac{m - 15t}{t} \dfrac{\text{dollars}}{\text{amp}}}$$

$$A = \dfrac{\mathbf{3000}t}{m - 15t} \textbf{ amps}$$

2.
(39)

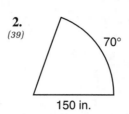

$70° \times \dfrac{\pi \, \text{rad}}{180°} = \dfrac{7\pi}{18} \text{ rad}$

Distance $= \dfrac{7\pi}{18}(150) = \mathbf{183.26 \text{ in.}}$

3. $y = \left(\dfrac{1}{3}\right)^{-2x} = \left(\left(\dfrac{1}{3}\right)^{-2}\right)^{x} = 9^x$
(23)

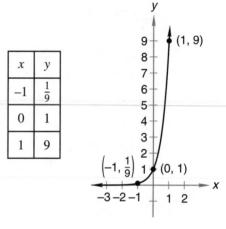

4. $_nP_r = \dfrac{n!}{(n - r)!}$
(41)

$_5P_4 = \dfrac{5!}{(5 - 4)!} = \dfrac{5!}{1!} = 120$

$_5P_2 = \dfrac{5!}{(5 - 2)!} = \dfrac{5!}{3!} = 20$

$120 - 20 = \mathbf{100}$

5. (a) $4 \log_3 x = 2 \log_3 9$
(26, 40)

$\log_3 x^4 = \log_3 9^2$

$x^4 = 81$

$x^4 = 3^4$

$x = \mathbf{3}$

(b) $\log_4 \dfrac{1}{64} = x$

$4^x = \dfrac{1}{64}$

$4^x = \dfrac{1}{4^3}$

$4^x = 4^{-3}$

$x = \mathbf{-3}$

(c) $\log_x 32 = 5$

$$x^5 = 32$$
$$x^5 = 2^5$$
$$x = \mathbf{2}$$

6. (a) Arcsin 1 = **90°**
(32)

(b)

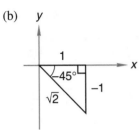

Arctan (−1) = **−45°**

(c)

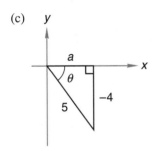

$$a = \sqrt{(5)^2 - (-4)^2} = \sqrt{9} = 3$$

$$\cos\left(\text{Arcsin}\left(-\frac{4}{5}\right)\right) = \frac{3}{5}$$

7. $\log_3 3^4 + \log_5 5^3 - \log_2 2^4 = 4 + 3 - 4 = \mathbf{3}$
(40)

8. $\log_9 (x + 2) - \log_9 (x - 3) = \log_9 6$
(40)

$$\log_9 \frac{(x + 2)}{(x - 3)} = \log_9 6$$

$$\frac{(x + 2)}{(x - 3)} = 6$$

$$x + 2 = 6x - 18$$

$$5x = 20$$

$$x = \mathbf{4}$$

9. (a)
(22)

x	y
1	−2
2	−3
3	−2

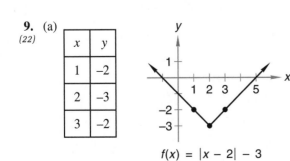

$f(x) = |x - 2| - 3$

(b)

x	y
−2	1
0	−1
2	$-\frac{1}{3}$
4	−1
6	1

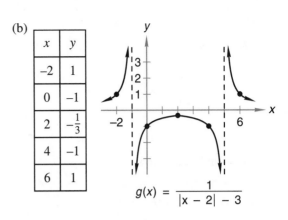

$$g(x) = \frac{1}{|x - 2| - 3}$$

10. $\sqrt{[x - (-3)]^2 + (y - 3)^2}$
(37)

$$= \sqrt{(x - 5)^2 + [y - (-1)]^2}$$

$$x^2 + 6x + 9 + y^2 - 6y + 9$$

$$= x^2 - 10x + 25 + y^2 + 2y + 1$$

$$-8y = -16x + 8$$

$$y = \mathbf{2x - 1}$$

11. $f(x) = \dfrac{\sqrt{2 - x}}{x^3 + 3x^2 - 4x}$
(21)

$$= \frac{\sqrt{2 - x}}{x(x^2 + 3x - 4)}$$

$$= \frac{\sqrt{2 - x}}{x(x + 4)(x - 1)}$$

$$x(x + 4)(x - 1) \neq 0$$

$$x \neq 0, -4, 1$$

$$2 - x \geq 0$$

$$-x \geq -2$$

$$x \leq 2$$

Domain of $f = \{x \in \mathbb{R} \mid x \leq 2, x \neq 0, -4, 1\}$

12. $\displaystyle\sum_{i=1}^{3} \left(4i - 2i^2\right)$
(34)

$$= \left[4(1) - 2(1)^2\right] + \left[4(2) - 2(2)^2\right] + \left[4(3) - 2(3)^2\right]$$

$$= 2 + 0 + (-6) = \mathbf{-4}$$

13. $f(x) = \dfrac{1}{2x + 1}$ and $g(x) = \dfrac{1 - x}{2x}$
(40)

$$f(g(x)) = \frac{1}{2\left(\dfrac{1 - x}{2x}\right) + 1} = \frac{1}{\dfrac{1 - x}{x} + 1}$$

$$= \frac{1}{\dfrac{1 - x + x}{x}} = \frac{1}{\dfrac{1}{x}} = x$$

$$g(f(x)) = \frac{1 - \left(\dfrac{1}{2x+1}\right)}{2\left(\dfrac{1}{2x+1}\right)} = \frac{\dfrac{2x+1-1}{2x+1}}{\dfrac{2}{2x+1}}$$

$$= \frac{2x}{2} = x$$

$$f(g(x)) = g(f(x)) = x$$

Yes, f and g are inverse functions.

14. $(x - h)^2 + (y - k)^2 = r^2$
(42)

$$(x + 3)^2 + (y - 2)^2 = 5^2$$

15.
(15, 17)

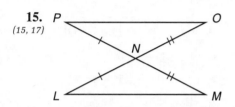

STATEMENTS	REASONS
1. $\overline{LN} \cong \overline{PN}$	1. Given
2. $\overline{MN} \cong \overline{ON}$	2. Given
3. $\angle PNO \cong \angle LNM$	3. Vertical angles are congruent.
4. $\triangle PNO \cong \triangle LNM$	4. *SAS* congruency postulate
5. $\angle L \cong \angle P$	5. *CPCTC*

16.
(41)

$$\frac{13\pi}{6} = 390°$$

$$\sin 390° = \sin 30° = \frac{1}{2}$$

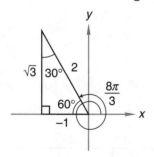

$$\frac{8\pi}{3} = 480°$$

$$\tan 480° = -\tan 60° = -\frac{\sqrt{3}}{1} = -\sqrt{3}$$

$$\sin \frac{13\pi}{6} + \tan \frac{8\pi}{3} = \frac{1}{2} + (-\sqrt{3}) = \frac{1 - 2\sqrt{3}}{2}$$

17. Rate $\times$ students $\times$ time = vases or $RST = V$
(44)

$$R(22 \text{ students})(9 \text{ hours}) = b \text{ vases}$$

$$R = \frac{b}{198} \frac{\text{vases}}{\text{student-hr}}$$

$$RST = V$$

$$T = \frac{V}{RS}$$

$$T = \frac{30 \text{ vases}}{\dfrac{b}{198} \dfrac{\text{vases}}{\text{student-hr}} (22 - 2) \text{ students}}$$

$$T = \frac{30(198)}{20b} \text{ hr} = \frac{297}{b} \text{ hr}$$

18.
(37)

$$x = \frac{x_1 + x_2}{2} = \frac{4 + 2}{2} = \frac{6}{2} = 3$$

$$y = \frac{y_1 + y_2}{2} = \frac{12 + 2}{2} = \frac{14}{2} = 7$$

(3, 7)

19.
(41)

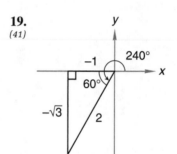

$$\sec 240° = -\sec 60° = -\frac{1}{\cos 60°} = -\frac{1}{\dfrac{1}{2}} = -2$$

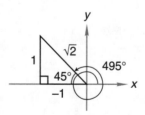

$$\cot 495° = \cot 135° = -\cot 45° = -1$$

$$\sec 240° + \cot 495° = -2 - 1 = -3$$

20. Function $= \sin x$
(43)

Amplitude $= 5$

$$y = 5 \sin x$$

Test 12, Form A

1.
$(39, 48)$ $x_m = \dfrac{x_1 + x_2}{2} = \dfrac{-2 + (-6)}{2} = -4$

$y_m = \dfrac{y_1 + y_2}{2} = \dfrac{3 + 1}{2} = 2$

$(-4, 2)$

$m = \dfrac{-1}{\left(\dfrac{y_2 - y_1}{x_2 - x_1}\right)} = \dfrac{-1}{\left(\dfrac{1 - 3}{-6 - (-2)}\right)} = \dfrac{-1}{\dfrac{1}{2}} = -2$

$y = -2x + b$

$(2) = -2(-4) + b$

$b = -6$

$y = -2x - 6$

$2x + y = -6$

$\dfrac{x}{-3} + \dfrac{y}{-6} = 1$

2.
(45)

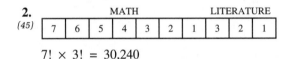

MATH · LITERATURE

7	6	5	4	3	2	1	3	2	1

$7! \times 3! = 30{,}240$

LITERATURE · MATH

3	2	1	7	6	5	4	3	2	1

$3! \times 7! = 30{,}240$

$30{,}240 + 30{,}240 = \mathbf{60{,}480}$

3.
(25)

$$R_S T_S + R_T T_T = \text{words}$$

$$\left(\frac{24}{6}\,\frac{\text{words}}{\text{min}}\right)(T + 2\text{ min}) + \left(\frac{18}{3}\,\frac{\text{words}}{\text{min}}\right)T = 88\text{ words}$$

$$\left(4\,\frac{\text{words}}{\text{min}}\right)T + 8\text{ words} + \left(6\,\frac{\text{words}}{\text{min}}\right)T = 88\text{ words}$$

$$\left(10\,\frac{\text{words}}{\text{min}}\right)T = 80\text{ words}$$

$$T = \mathbf{8\text{ min}}$$

4.
(18) $\text{Alcohol}_1 - \text{Alcohol}_{\text{extracted}} = \text{Alcohol}_2$

$$0.6(1000) - A_e = 0.45\left(1000 - A_e\right)$$

$$600 - A_e = 450 - 0.45A_e$$

$$0.55A_e = 150$$

$$A_e = \mathbf{272.73\text{ L}}$$

5. (a)
(31) **x axis, no**

   y axis, yes

   origin, no

(b) **x axis, yes**

   y axis, no

   origin, no

6. (a)
(32)

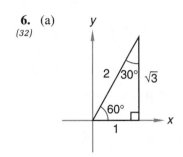

$\text{Arctan }\sqrt{3} = \mathbf{60°}$

(b)

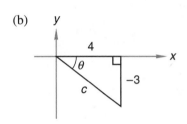

$c = \sqrt{(-3)^2 + (4)^2} = \sqrt{25} = 5$

$\sin\left(\text{Arctan}\left(-\dfrac{3}{4}\right)\right) = -\dfrac{3}{5}$

7.
(40) $\dfrac{1}{2}\log_{15} 9 + \log_{15}(x + 1) = \log_{15} 12$

$\log_{15}\left[9^{1/2}(x + 1)\right] = \log_{15} 12$

$3x + 3 = 12$

$3x = 9$

$x = \mathbf{3}$

8.
(40) $\log_7 1 = 2\log_7 (x - 7)$

$\log_7 1 = \log_7 (x - 7)^2$

$1 = x^2 - 14x + 49$

$x^2 - 14x + 48 = 0$

$(x - 6)(x - 8) = 0$

$x = 6, 8$

$x = \mathbf{8}$

9. $\sec 780° + \cos(-540°) + \sin 630°$
$(29, 41)$

$= \sec 60° + \cos 180° + \sin 270°$

$= 2 + (-1) + (-1) = \mathbf{0}$

10.
(48)

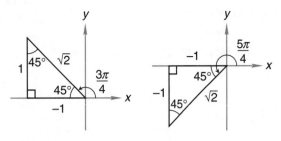

$$\csc^2 \frac{3\pi}{4} - \tan^3 \frac{5\pi}{4} + \sin^3 \frac{\pi}{2}$$

$$= \left(\frac{\sqrt{2}}{1}\right)^2 - \left(\frac{-1}{-1}\right)^3 + (1)^3 = \mathbf{2}$$

11. (a) $(f - g)(x) = 4x^2 - x + \dfrac{3}{x}$
(24)

$$(f - g)(3) = 4(3)^2 - 3 + \frac{3}{3} = \mathbf{34}$$

(b) $(f/g)(x) = \dfrac{4x^2}{x - \dfrac{3}{x}}$

$$(f/g)(3) = \frac{4(3)^2}{3 - \dfrac{3}{3}} = \mathbf{18}$$

(c) $(f \circ g)(x) = 4\left(x - \dfrac{3}{x}\right)^2$

$$(f \circ g)(3) = 4\left(3 - \frac{3}{3}\right)^2 = 4(2)^2 = \mathbf{16}$$

12. $(x + 2)^2 + (y - 3)^2 = 5^2$
(42)

13. $f(x) = \left(\dfrac{1}{2}\right)^{-x-2} = \left[\left(\dfrac{1}{2}\right)^{-1}\right]^x \left(\dfrac{1}{2}\right)^{-2} = 4 \cdot 2^x$
(42)

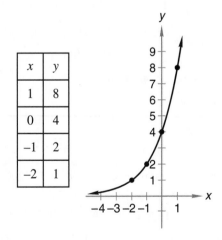

x	y
1	8
0	4
-1	2
-2	1

14. (a)
(22)

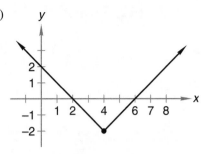

$$g(x) = |x - 4| - 2$$

(b)

x	1	4	7
y	1	$-\frac{1}{2}$	1

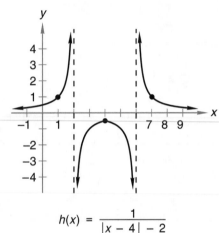

$$h(x) = \frac{1}{|x - 4| - 2}$$

15.
(45)

| 2 | 5 | 5 | $\rightarrow$ $2 \times 5 \times 5 = \mathbf{50}$

16. Rate × students × time = cookies or $RST = C$
(44)

$$R(s \text{ students})(10 \text{ days}) = c \text{ cookies}$$

$$R = \frac{c}{10s} \frac{\text{cookies}}{\text{student-days}}$$

$$RST = C$$

$$T = \frac{C}{RS}$$

$$T = \frac{c \text{ cookies}}{\dfrac{c}{10s} \dfrac{\text{cookies}}{\text{student-days}} (s + m) \text{ students}}$$

$$T = \frac{10s}{s + m} \text{ days}$$

17. Function: $\sin x$
(47)
Centerline: 1

Amplitude: $6 - 1 = 5$

$$y = 1 + 5 \sin x$$

18. Function: $-\cos\theta$
(43)

Centerline: 0

Amplitude: 5

$y = -5\cos\theta$

19. $x^2 - 4x + 6 = 0$
(46)

$$x = \frac{4 \pm \sqrt{(-4)^2 - 4(1)(6)}}{2(1)}$$

$$= \frac{4 \pm \sqrt{-8}}{2} = 2 \pm \sqrt{2}\,i$$

$$\left(x - 2 - \sqrt{2}\,i\right)\left(x - 2 + \sqrt{2}\,i\right)$$

20. $[x - (1 - 2i)][x - (1 + 2i)]$
(46)

$= (x - 1 + 2i)(x - 1 - 2i)$

$= x^2 - x - 2xi - x + 1 + 2i + 2xi - 2i - 4i^2$

$= x^2 - 2x + 5$

Test 12, Form B

1. $x_m = \dfrac{x_1 + x_2}{2} = \dfrac{2 + 6}{2} = 4$
(39, 48)

$y_m = \dfrac{y_1 + y_2}{2} = \dfrac{-3 - 1}{2} = -2$

$(4, -2)$

$m = \dfrac{-1}{\left(\dfrac{y_2 - y_1}{x_2 - x_1}\right)} = \dfrac{-1}{\left(\dfrac{-1 + 3}{6 - 2}\right)} = \dfrac{-1}{\dfrac{1}{2}} = -2$

$y = -2x + b$

$(-2) = -2(4) + b$

$b = 6$

$y = -2x + 6$

$2x + y = 6$

$\dfrac{x}{3} + \dfrac{y}{6} = 1$

2.
(45)

PHONICS				PHILOSOPHY				
4	3	2	1	5	4	3	2	1

$4! \times 5! = 2880$

PHILOSOPHY					PHONICS			
5	4	3	2	1	4	3	2	1

$5! \times 4! = 2880$

$2880 + 2880 = \mathbf{5760}$

3.
(25)

$$R_M T_M + R_L T_L = \text{cords}$$

$$\left(2\,\frac{\text{cords}}{\text{day}}\right)T + \left(\frac{2}{3}\,\frac{\text{cords}}{\text{day}}\right)(T + 2\text{ days}) = 12\text{ cords}$$

$$\left(2\,\frac{\text{cords}}{\text{day}}\right)T + \left(\frac{2}{3}\,\frac{\text{cords}}{\text{day}}\right)T + \frac{4}{3}\text{ cords} = 12\text{ cords}$$

$$\left(\frac{8}{3}\,\frac{\text{cords}}{\text{day}}\right)T = \frac{32}{3}\text{ cords}$$

$$T = \mathbf{4\ days}$$

4. $\text{Alcohol}_1 - \text{Alcohol}_{\text{extracted}} = \text{Alcohol}_2$
(18)

$$0.75(500) - A_e = 0.30\left(500 - A_e\right)$$

$$375 - A_e = 150 - 0.30A_e$$

$$0.70A_e = 225$$

$$A_e = \mathbf{321.43\ L}$$

5. (a) **x axis, no**
(31)

y axis, yes

origin, no

(b) **x axis, yes**

y axis, no

origin, no

6. (a)
(32)

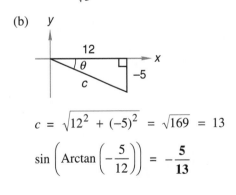

$\text{Arctan}\,\dfrac{1}{\sqrt{3}} = \mathbf{30°}$

(b)

$c = \sqrt{12^2 + (-5)^2} = \sqrt{169} = 13$

$\sin\left(\text{Arctan}\left(-\dfrac{5}{12}\right)\right) = -\dfrac{5}{13}$

7. $\dfrac{1}{2}\log 16 + \log(x + 2) = 5\log 2$
(40)

$$\log\left[16^{1/2}(x + 2)\right] = \log 2^5$$

$$4x + 8 = 32$$

$$4x = 24$$

$$x = \mathbf{6}$$

8.
(40)

$$3 \log_8 1 = 2 \log_8 (x - 5)$$
$$\log_8 1^3 = \log_8 (x - 5)^2$$
$$1 = x^2 - 10x + 25$$
$$x^2 - 10x + 24 = 0$$
$$(x - 6)(x - 4) = 0$$
$$x = 4, 6$$
$$x = \mathbf{6}$$

9.
(29, 41)

$$\csc^2 (-750°) + \tan 495° + \cos 630°$$
$$= \csc^2 (-30°) + \tan 135° + \cos 270°$$
$$= (-2)^2 + (-1) + 0 = 4 - 1 + 0 = \mathbf{3}$$

10.
(48)

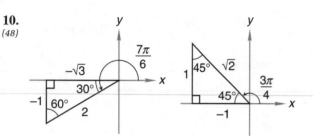

$$\csc^2 \frac{7\pi}{6} - \cot^3 \frac{3\pi}{4} + \sin^3 \left(-\frac{\pi}{2}\right)$$

$$= \left(\frac{2}{-1}\right)^2 - \left(\frac{-1}{1}\right)^3 + (-1)^3 = \mathbf{4}$$

11. (a) $(f - g)(x) = 3x^2 - x + \dfrac{2}{x}$
(24)

$$(f - g)(2) = 3(2)^2 - 2 + \frac{2}{2} = \mathbf{11}$$

(b) $(f/g)(x) = \dfrac{3x^2}{x - \dfrac{2}{x}}$

$$(f/g)(2) = \frac{3(2)^2}{2 - \dfrac{2}{2}} = \frac{12}{1} = \mathbf{12}$$

(c) $(f \circ g)(x) = 3\left(x - \dfrac{2}{x}\right)^2$

$$(f \circ g)(2) = 3\left(2 - \frac{2}{2}\right)^2 = 3(1)^2 = \mathbf{3}$$

12. $(x - 4)^2 + (y + 4)^2 = 6^2$
(42)

13. $f(x) = \left[\left(\dfrac{1}{3}\right)^{-1}\right]^x \left(\dfrac{1}{3}\right)^{-1} = 3 \cdot 3^x$
(42)

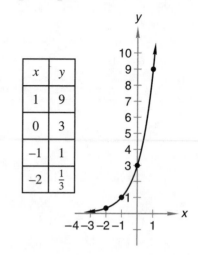

x	y
1	9
0	3
−1	1
−2	$\frac{1}{3}$

14. (a)
(22)

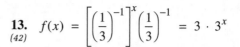

$$g(x) = |x + 2| - 3$$

(b)

x	−6	−2	2
y	1	$-\frac{1}{3}$	1

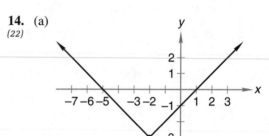

$$h(x) = \frac{1}{|x + 2| - 3}$$

15.
(45)

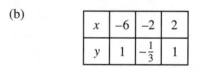

| 3 | 5 | 5 | $\rightarrow 3 \times 5 \times 5 = \mathbf{75}$

16. Rate × workers × time = products or $RWT = P$
(44)

$$R(w \text{ workers})(8 \text{ days}) = p \text{ products}$$

$$R = \frac{p}{8w} \frac{\text{products}}{\text{worker-days}}$$

$$RWT = P$$

$$T = \frac{P}{RW}$$

$$T = \frac{p \text{ products}}{\dfrac{p}{8w} \dfrac{\text{products}}{\text{worker-days}} (w + x) \text{ workers}}$$

$$T = \frac{8w}{w + x} \text{ days}$$

17. Function: $-\sin x$
(47)

Centerline: -1

Amplitude: $2 - (-1) = 3$

$$y = -1 - 3 \sin x$$

18. Function: $\cos \theta$
(43)

Centerline: 0

Amplitude: 10

$$y = 10 \cos \theta$$

19. $x^2 + 5x + 8 = 0$
(46)

$$x = \frac{-5 \pm \sqrt{5^2 - 4(1)(8)}}{2(1)}$$

$$= \frac{-5 \pm \sqrt{-7}}{2} = -\frac{5}{2} \pm \frac{\sqrt{7}}{2}i$$

$$\left(x + \frac{5}{2} + \frac{\sqrt{7}}{2}i \right)\left(x + \frac{5}{2} - \frac{\sqrt{7}}{2}i \right)$$

20. $[x - (2 - 3i)][x - (2 + 3i)]$
(46)

$$= (x - 2 + 3i)(x - 2 - 3i)$$

$$= x^2 - 2x - 3xi - 2x + 4 + 6i + 3xi - 6i - 9i^2$$

$$= x^2 - 4x + 13$$

Test 13, Form A

1. $x_m = \dfrac{x_1 + x_2}{2} = \dfrac{4 + -2}{2} = 1$
(39, 48)

$$y_m = \frac{y_1 + y_2}{2} = \frac{-3 + -5}{2} = -4$$

$$(1, -4)$$

$$m = \frac{-1}{\dfrac{y_2 - y_1}{x_2 - x_1}} = \frac{-1}{\dfrac{-5 - (-3)}{-2 - 4}} = \frac{-1}{\dfrac{-2}{-6}} = -3$$

$$y = -3x + b$$

$$(-4) = -3(1) + b$$

$$b = -1$$

$$y = -3x - 1$$

$$3x + y + 1 = 0$$

2. Rate $\times$ infants $\times$ time $=$ milk or $RIT = M$
(44)

$$R(s \text{ infants})(12 \text{ days}) = g \text{ gallons}$$

$$R = \frac{g}{12s} \frac{\text{gallons}}{\text{infant-days}}$$

$$RIT = M$$

$$T = \frac{M}{RI}$$

$$T = \frac{m \text{ gallons}}{\dfrac{g}{12s} \dfrac{\text{gallons}}{\text{infant-days}} (s + 15) \text{ infants}}$$

$$T = \frac{12sm}{g(s + 15)} \text{ days}$$

3. $\sqrt{(x - 3)^2 + (4 - y)^2} = \sqrt{(-2 - x)^2 + (y + 5)^2}$
(37)

$$x^2 - 6x + 9 + 16 - 8y + y^2$$

$$= 4 + 4x + x^2 + y^2 + 10y + 25$$

$$-18y = 10x + 4$$

$$y = -\frac{5}{9}x - \frac{2}{9}$$

4. $R_C T_C + R_S T_S = \text{jobs}$
(25)

$$\left(\frac{2}{3} \frac{\text{job}}{\text{day}} \right)(T + 3 \text{ days}) + \left(\frac{5}{6} \frac{\text{job}}{\text{day}} \right)T = 74 \text{ jobs}$$

$$\left(\frac{2}{3} \frac{\text{job}}{\text{day}} \right)T + 2 \text{ jobs} + \left(\frac{5}{6} \frac{\text{job}}{\text{day}} \right)T = 74 \text{ jobs}$$

$$\left(\frac{3}{2} \frac{\text{jobs}}{\text{day}} \right)T = 72 \text{ jobs}$$

$$T = 48 \text{ days}$$

5. $[x - (1 + 4i)][x - (1 - 4i)] = 0$
(46)

$$(x - 1 - 4i)(x - 1 + 4i) = 0$$

$$x^2 - x + 4xi - x + 1 - 4i - 4xi + 4i - 16i^2 = 0$$

$$x^2 - 2x + 17 = 0$$

6. Distance $= d$ mi
(28)

Time $= h$ hr

$$\text{Rate} = \frac{\text{distance}}{\text{time}} = \frac{d}{h} \frac{\text{mi}}{\text{hr}}$$

New time $= (h - 3)$ hr

$$\text{New rate} = \frac{\text{new distance}}{\text{new time}} = \frac{d}{h - 3} \frac{\text{mi}}{\text{hr}}$$

7. $f(x) = |x|$
(31)

$g(x) - (-4) = |x - (-3)|$

$g(x) = |x + 3| - 4$

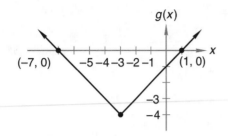

8. (a)
(50)

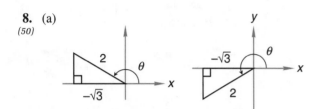

$\cos \theta = -\dfrac{\sqrt{3}}{2}$

$\theta = \cos^{-1}\left(-\dfrac{\sqrt{3}}{2}\right)$

$\theta = 150°, 210°$

(b)

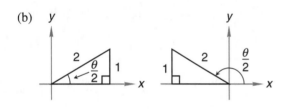

$\sin \dfrac{\theta}{2} - \dfrac{1}{2} = 0$

$\sin \dfrac{\theta}{2} = \dfrac{1}{2}$

$\dfrac{\theta}{2} = \sin^{-1}\left(\dfrac{1}{2}\right)$

$\dfrac{\theta}{2} = 30°, 150°$

$\theta = 60°, 300°$

9. Function $= \cos x$
(47)

Amplitude $= 15 - 4 = 11$

Centerline $= 4$

$y = 4 + 11 \cos x$

10. $C = m\text{H} + b$
(45)

$m = 0.11047$

$b = -2.4757$

$r = 0.9114$

$C = (0.11)\text{H} - 2.48$

Since $r > 0.9$, the line is a good model for the data.

11.
(48)

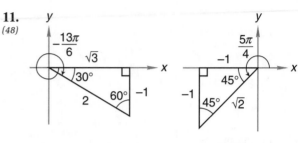

$-\dfrac{13\pi}{6} \cdot \dfrac{180°}{\pi} = -390° = -30°$

$\dfrac{5\pi}{4} \cdot \dfrac{180°}{\pi} = 225°$

$\sec^2\left(-\dfrac{13\pi}{6}\right) - \csc^2 \dfrac{5\pi}{4} = \sec^2(-30°) - \csc^2 225°$

$= \left(\dfrac{2}{\sqrt{3}}\right)^2 - (-\sqrt{2})^2 = \dfrac{4}{3} - 2 = -\dfrac{2}{3}$

12. $\ln 4500 = 8.4118$
(51)

$4500 = e^{8.4118}$

13. $f(x) = \left(\dfrac{1}{3}\right)^{x-2} = \left(\dfrac{1}{3}\right)^x\left(\dfrac{1}{3}\right)^{-2} = 9 \cdot \left(\dfrac{1}{3}\right)^x$
(42)

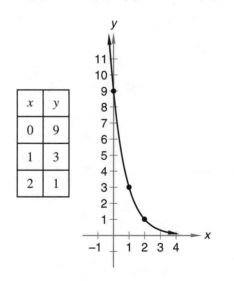

x	y
0	9
1	3
2	1

14. $f(x) = \sqrt{x}$
(31)

$g(x) = \sqrt{-(x - 2)}$

$g(x) = \sqrt{-x + 2}$

15.
(33)

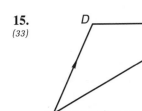

STATEMENTS	REASONS
1. $\overline{AD} \parallel \overline{BC}$	1. Given
2. $\angle ACB \cong \angle CAD$	2. If two parallel lines are cut by a transversal, then each pair of alternate interior angles is congruent.
3. $\overline{DC} \parallel \overline{AB}$	3. Given
4. $\angle DCA \cong \angle BAC$	4. If two parallel lines are cut by a transversal, then each pair of alternate interior angles is congruent.
5. $\angle D \cong \angle B$	5. If two angles in one triangle are congruent to two angles in a second triangle, then the third angles are congruent.
6. $\overline{AC} \cong \overline{AC}$	6. Reflexive axiom
7. $\triangle ADC \cong \triangle CBA$	7. *AAAS* congruency postulate
8. $\overline{AD} \cong \overline{BC}$	8. *CPCTC*

16.
(47)

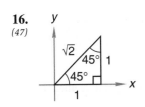

Arctan $(\sin 90°)$ = Arctan 1 = **45°**

17. $\log 5.6 = \mathbf{0.7482}$
(51)

18. $\ln 5.6 = \mathbf{1.7228}$
(51)

19.
(45)

4	5	5
	5	5
		5

$\rightarrow \quad 4 \times 5 \times 5 = 100$

$\rightarrow \quad 5 \times 5 = 25$

$\rightarrow \quad 5$

$100 + 25 + 5 = \mathbf{130}$

20.
(45)

6	4	1	6

$6 \times 4 \times 1 \times 6 = \mathbf{144}$

Test 13, Form B

1.
(39, 48)

$x_m = \dfrac{x_1 + x_2}{2} = \dfrac{3 + 5}{2} = \dfrac{8}{2} = 4$

$y_m = \dfrac{y_1 + y_2}{2} = \dfrac{-2 + 4}{2} = \dfrac{2}{2} = 1$

$(4, 1)$

$m = \dfrac{-1}{\dfrac{y_2 - y_1}{x_2 - x_1}} = \dfrac{-1}{\dfrac{4 - (-2)}{5 - 3}} = \dfrac{-1}{\dfrac{6}{2}} = -\dfrac{1}{3}$

$y = -\dfrac{1}{3}x + b$

$(1) = -\dfrac{1}{3}(4) + b$

$b = 1 + \dfrac{4}{3} = \dfrac{7}{3}$

$y = -\dfrac{1}{3}x + \dfrac{7}{3}$

$\dfrac{1}{3}x + y - \dfrac{7}{3} = 0$

$\mathbf{x + 3y - 7 = 0}$

2. Rate $\times$ bands $\times$ time $=$ dollars or $RBT = D$
(44)

$R(j \text{ bands})(7 \text{ days}) = d \text{ dollars}$

$R = \dfrac{d}{7j} \dfrac{\text{dollars}}{\text{band-days}}$

$RBT = D$

$T = \dfrac{D}{RB}$

$T = \dfrac{n \text{ dollars}}{\dfrac{d}{7j} \dfrac{\text{dollars}}{\text{band-days}} (j + 3) \text{ bands}}$

$T = \mathbf{\dfrac{7jn}{d(j + 3)}} \textbf{ days}$

3. $\sqrt{(x - 5)^2 + (-3 - y)^2} = \sqrt{(x - 3)^2 + (y - 2)^2}$
(37)

$x^2 - 10x + 25 + 9 + 6y + y^2$

$\qquad = x^2 - 6x + 9 + y^2 - 4y + 4$

$10y = 4x - 21$

$y = \dfrac{2}{5}x - \dfrac{21}{10}$

4.
(25)

$$R_H T_H + R_L T_L = \text{jobs}$$

$$\left(\frac{5}{8}\frac{\text{job}}{\text{day}}\right)T + \left(\frac{1}{2}\frac{\text{job}}{\text{day}}\right)(T + 4 \text{ days}) = 74 \text{ jobs}$$

$$\left(\frac{5}{8}\frac{\text{job}}{\text{day}}\right)T + \left(\frac{1}{2}\frac{\text{job}}{\text{day}}\right)T + 2 \text{ jobs} = 74 \text{ jobs}$$

$$\left(\frac{9}{8}\frac{\text{jobs}}{\text{day}}\right)T = 72 \text{ jobs}$$

$$T = \mathbf{64\ days}$$

5.
(46)

$$[x - (1 + 2i)][x - (1 - 2i)] = 0$$
$$(x - 1 - 2i)(x - 1 + 2i) = 0$$
$$x^2 - x + 2xi - x + 1 - 2i - 2xi + 2i - 4i^2 = 0$$
$$\mathbf{x^2 - 2x + 5 = 0}$$

6. Distance $= x$ km
(28)

Time $= t$ hr

$$\text{Rate} = \frac{\text{distance}}{\text{time}} = \frac{x}{t}\frac{\text{km}}{\text{hr}}$$

New time $= (t - 1)$ hr

$$\text{New rate} = \frac{\text{new distance}}{\text{new time}} = \frac{x}{t - 1}\frac{\text{km}}{\text{hr}}$$

7. $f(x) = |x|$
(31)

$$g(x) - (-3) = |x - 2|$$
$$g(x) = |x - 2| - 3$$

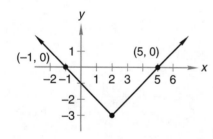

8. (a)
(50)

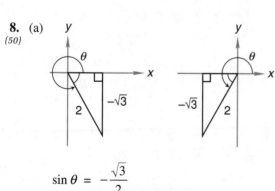

$$\sin \theta = -\frac{\sqrt{3}}{2}$$

$$\theta = \sin^{-1}\left(-\frac{\sqrt{3}}{2}\right)$$

$$\theta = \mathbf{240°,\ 300°}$$

(b)

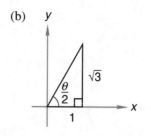

$$\tan \frac{\theta}{2} - \sqrt{3} = 0$$

$$\tan \frac{\theta}{2} = \sqrt{3}$$

$$\frac{\theta}{2} = \tan^{-1}\sqrt{3}$$

$$\frac{\theta}{2} = 60°$$

$$\theta = \mathbf{120°}$$

9. Function $= -\cos x$
(47)

Amplitude $= 13 - 2 = 11$

Centerline $= 13$

$$y = \mathbf{13 - 11\cos x}$$

10. C $= m$A $+ b$
(45)

$m = 3.4351$

$b = -4.9280$

$r = 0.9104$

C = (3.44)A − 4.93

Since $r > 0.9$, the line is a good model for the data.

11.
(48)

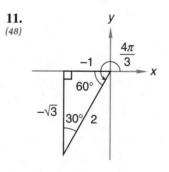

$$\frac{4\pi}{3} \cdot \frac{180°}{\pi} = 240°$$

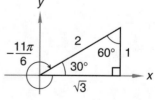

$$-\frac{11\pi}{6} \cdot \frac{180°}{\pi} = -330° = 30°$$

$$\tan^2 \frac{4\pi}{3} - \sec^2\left(-\frac{11\pi}{6}\right) = \tan^2 240° - \sec^2 30°$$

$$= \left(\frac{-\sqrt{3}}{-1}\right)^2 - \left(\frac{2}{\sqrt{3}}\right)^2 = 3 - \frac{4}{3} = \frac{5}{3}$$

12. $\ln 4900 = 8.4970$
(51)
$$4900 = e^{8.4970}$$

13. $f(x) = \left(\frac{1}{2}\right)^{x-2} = \left(\frac{1}{2}\right)^x \left(\frac{1}{2}\right)^{-2} = 4 \cdot \left(\frac{1}{2}\right)^x$
(42)

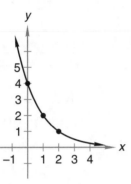

x	y
0	4
1	2
2	1

14. $f(x) = \sqrt{-x}$
(31)
$$-g(x) = \sqrt{-[x - (-3)]}$$
$$g(x) = -\sqrt{-x - 3}$$

15.
(33)

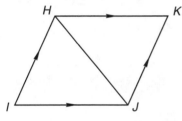

STATEMENTS	REASONS
1. $\overline{HK} \parallel \overline{IJ}$	1. Given
2. $\angle IJH \cong \angle KHJ$	2. If two parallel lines are cut by a transversal, then each pair of alternate interior angles is congruent.
3. $\overline{HI} \parallel \overline{KJ}$	3. Given
4. $\angle IHJ \cong \angle KJH$	4. If two parallel lines are cut by a transversal, then each pair of alternate interior angles is congruent.
5. $\angle I \cong \angle K$	5. If two angles in one triangle are congruent to two angles in a second triangle, then the third angles are congruent.
6. $\overline{HJ} \cong \overline{HJ}$	6. Reflexive axiom
7. $\triangle HIJ \cong \triangle JKH$	7. AAAS congruency postulate
8. $\overline{IJ} \cong \overline{HK}$	8. CPCTC

16.
(47)

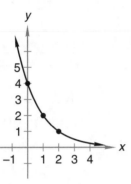

$\text{Arccos}(\tan 45°) = \text{Arccos } 1 = \mathbf{0°}$

17. $\log 6.3 = \mathbf{0.7993}$
(51)

18. $\ln 6.3 = \mathbf{1.8405}$
(51)

19.
(45)

3	5	5	$\rightarrow$ $3 \times 5 \times 5 = 75$
	4	5	$\rightarrow$ $4 \times 5 = 20$
		4	$\rightarrow$ 4

$75 + 20 + 4 = \mathbf{99}$

20.
(45)

5	5	1	6	6

$5 \times 5 \times 1 \times 6 \times 6 = \mathbf{900}$

Test 14, Form A

1. Distance $= x$ mi
(28)

$$\text{Rate} = m \, \frac{\text{mi}}{\text{hr}}$$

$$\text{Time} = \frac{\text{distance}}{\text{rate}} = \frac{x}{m} \text{ hr}$$

$$\text{New time} = \left(\frac{x}{m} - 2\right) \text{hr} = \frac{x - 2m}{m} \text{ hr}$$

$$\text{New rate} = \frac{\text{new distance}}{\text{new time}}$$

$$= \frac{x \text{ mi}}{\dfrac{x - 2m}{m} \text{ hr}} = \frac{xm}{x - 2m} \frac{\text{mi}}{\text{hr}}$$

2. $(N - 1)! = (8 - 1)! = 7! = \mathbf{5040}$
(55)

3.
(25)
$\begin{cases} R_1 T_1 = 450 \text{ mi} \\ R_2 T_2 = 450 \text{ mi} \end{cases}$

$R_2 = 3R_1$

$T_1 + T_2 = 8 \text{ hr}$

$T_2 = 8 \text{ hr} - T_1$

$R_2 T_2 = 450 \text{ mi}$

$3R_1(8 \text{ hr} - T_1) = 450 \text{ mi}$

$(24 \text{ hr})R_1 - 3R_1 T_1 = 450 \text{ mi}$

$(8 \text{ hr})R_1 - R_1 T_1 = 150 \text{ mi}$

$(8 \text{ hr})R_1 - (450 \text{ mi}) = 150 \text{ mi}$

$(8 \text{ hr})R_1 = 600 \text{ mi}$

$R_1 = 75 \text{ mph}$

$R_2 = 3R_1$

$R_2 = 3(75)$

$R_2 = \mathbf{225 \text{ mph}}$

4.
(55)
$\dfrac{N!}{a!\,b!} = \dfrac{7!}{3!\,2!} = \mathbf{420}$

5.
(54)
$y = x^2 - 2x + 4$

$y = (x^2 - 2x + 1) - 1 + 4$

$y = (x - 1)^2 + 3$

Opens upward

Axis of symmetry is $x = 1$

y coordinate of vertex is 3

x	y
0	4
1	3
2	4

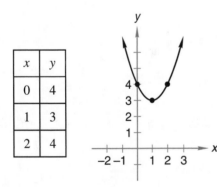

6.
(51, 59)
$2 \ln 2 + 2 \ln 3 = 2 \ln (x + 4)$

$\ln 2^2 + \ln 3^2 = \ln (x + 4)^2$

$\ln (2^2 \cdot 3^2) = \ln (x + 4)^2$

$36 = x^2 + 8x + 16$

$x^2 + 8x - 20 = 0$

$(x - 2)(x + 10) = 0$

$x = 2, -10$

$x = \mathbf{2}$

7.
(59)
$\log_9 12x - 3 \log_9 2 = 1$

$\log_9 12x - \log_9 2^3 = 1$

$\log_9 \dfrac{12x}{2^3} = 1$

$\dfrac{12x}{8} = 9^1$

$12x = 72$

$x = \mathbf{6}$

8.
(53)
$v = \omega r$

$v = \left(60 \,\dfrac{\text{rad}}{\text{s}}\right)\left(\dfrac{2 \text{ in.}}{2}\right)\left(\dfrac{1 \text{ ft}}{12 \text{ in.}}\right)\left(\dfrac{60 \text{ s}}{1 \text{ min}}\right)$

$v = \dfrac{(60)(2)(1)(60)}{(2)(12)} \,\dfrac{\text{ft}}{\text{min}} = \mathbf{300} \,\dfrac{\textbf{ft}}{\textbf{min}}$

9.
(51)
(a) $\log 6300 = 3.799341$

$6300 = 10^{3.7993}$

(b) $\ln 6300 = 8.748305$

$6300 = e^{8.7483}$

10. A.
(31)

11.
(44)
Rate × elves × time = dolls or $RET = D$

$R(e \text{ elves})(h \text{ hr}) = d \text{ dolls}$

$R = \dfrac{d}{he} \,\dfrac{\text{dolls}}{\text{elf-hr}}$

$RET = D$

$T = \dfrac{D}{RE} = \dfrac{s \text{ dolls}}{\dfrac{d}{he} \dfrac{\text{dolls}}{\text{elf-hr}} \times (e - n) \text{ elves}}$

$T = \dfrac{\textbf{she}}{\textbf{d(e - n)}} \textbf{ hr}$

12.
(44)
Rate × cards = price

Cards = c

Price = t cents

Rate = $\dfrac{t}{c} \,\dfrac{\text{cents}}{\text{card}}$

New rate = $\left(\dfrac{t}{c} - 20\right)\dfrac{\text{cents}}{\text{card}} = \dfrac{t - 20c}{c} \,\dfrac{\text{cents}}{\text{card}}$

Rate × N = price

$\dfrac{t - 20c}{c} \,\dfrac{\text{cents}}{\text{card}} \times N = 500 \text{ cents}$

$N = \dfrac{\mathbf{500c}}{\mathbf{t - 20c}} \textbf{ cards}$

13. Function $= \sin\theta$
(47)

Amplitude $= 0 - (-9) = 9$

Centerline is $y = -9$

$y = -9 + 9\sin\theta$

14.
(56)

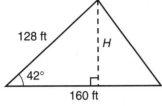

$H = 128\sin 42° = 85.65$ ft

$\text{Area} = \dfrac{B \times H}{2} = \dfrac{(160)(85.65)}{2} = \mathbf{6851.90\ ft^2}$

15.
(56)

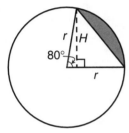

$r = 10$ ft

$H = r\sin 80° = 10\sin 80° = 9.848$ ft

$\text{Area} = \pi r^2\left(\dfrac{80°}{360°}\right) - \dfrac{r \times H}{2}$

$\qquad = \pi(10)^2\left(\dfrac{80°}{360°}\right) - \dfrac{10 \times 9.848}{2}$

$\qquad = 69.81 - 49.24 = \mathbf{20.57\ ft^2}$

16.
(39)

$39° \times \dfrac{\pi\,\text{rad}}{180°} = \dfrac{13\pi}{60}$ rad

$\text{Distance} = \dfrac{13\pi}{60}(3960\ \text{mi}) = \mathbf{2695.49\ mi}$

17. $x^2 - 5x + 8 = 0$
(46)

$x = \dfrac{-(-5) \pm \sqrt{(-5)^2 - 4(8)}}{2}$

$x = \dfrac{5 \pm \sqrt{-7}}{2} = \dfrac{5}{2} \pm \dfrac{\sqrt{7}}{2}i$

$\left(x - \dfrac{5}{2} - \dfrac{\sqrt{7}}{2}i\right)\left(x - \dfrac{5}{2} + \dfrac{\sqrt{7}}{2}i\right)$

18. $3\tan 3\theta - \sqrt{3} = 0$
(52)

$3\tan 3\theta = \sqrt{3}$

$\tan 3\theta = \dfrac{\sqrt{3}}{3}$

$\tan 3\theta = \dfrac{1}{\sqrt{3}}$

$\tan 3\theta = 30°, 210°, 390°, 570°, 750°, 930°$

$\theta = \mathbf{10°, 70°, 130°, 190°, 250°, 310°}$

19. $3\csc\dfrac{\theta}{2} - 2\sqrt{3} = 0$
(41, 52)

$3\csc\dfrac{\theta}{2} = 2\sqrt{3}$

$\csc\dfrac{\theta}{2} = \dfrac{2\sqrt{3}}{3}$

$\sin\dfrac{\theta}{2} = \dfrac{\sqrt{3}}{2}$

$\dfrac{\theta}{2} = 60°, 120°$

$\theta = \mathbf{120°, 240°}$

20. $\sqrt{(x-2)^2 + (y-4)^2}$
(37, 39)

$\qquad = \sqrt{[x-(-4)]^2 + [y-(-4)]^2}$

$x^2 - 4x + 4 + y^2 - 8y + 16$

$\qquad = x^2 + 8x + 16 + y^2 + 8y + 16$

$-12x - 16y = 12$

$-x - \dfrac{16}{12}y = 1$

$\dfrac{x}{-1} + \dfrac{y}{-\dfrac{3}{4}} = 1$

Test 14, Form B

1. Distance $= m$ mi
(28)

$\text{Rate} = v\ \dfrac{\text{mi}}{\text{hr}}$

$\text{Time} = \dfrac{\text{distance}}{\text{rate}} = \dfrac{m}{v}$ hr

$\text{New time} = \left(\dfrac{m}{v} - 3\right)\text{hr} = \dfrac{m - 3v}{v}$ hr

$\text{New rate} = \dfrac{\text{new distance}}{\text{new time}}$

$\qquad = \dfrac{m\ \text{mi}}{\dfrac{m - 3v}{v}\ \text{hr}} = \dfrac{mv}{m - 3v}\ \dfrac{\text{mi}}{\text{hr}}$

2. $(N - 1)! = (11 - 1)! = 10! = \mathbf{3{,}628{,}800}$
(55)

3. $\begin{cases} R_1T_1 = 480 \text{ mi} \\ R_2T_2 = 480 \text{ mi} \end{cases}$
(25)

$R_2 = 2R_1$

$T_1 + T_2 = 6 \text{ hr}$

$\quad T_2 = 6 \text{ hr} - T_1$

$R_2T_2 = 480 \text{ mi}$

$2R_1(6 \text{ hr} - T_1) = 480 \text{ mi}$

$(12 \text{ hr})R_1 - 2R_1T_1 = 480 \text{ mi}$

$(6 \text{ hr})R_1 - R_1T_1 = 240 \text{ mi}$

$(6 \text{ hr})R_1 - (480 \text{ mi}) = 240 \text{ mi}$

$(6 \text{ hr})R_1 = 720 \text{ mi}$

$R_1 = 120 \text{ mph}$

$R_2 = 2R_1$

$R_2 = 2(120)$

$R_2 = \mathbf{240 \text{ mph}}$

4. $\dfrac{N!}{a!} = \dfrac{5!}{3!} = \mathbf{20}$
(55)

5. $y = x^2 - 4x + 2$
(54)

$y = (x^2 - 4x + 4) - 4 + 2$

$y = (x - 2)^2 - 2$

Opens upward

Axis of symmetry is $x = 2$

y coordinate of vertex is -2

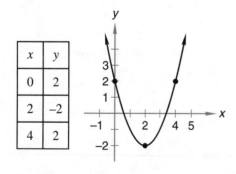

x	y
0	2
2	-2
4	2

6. $2 \ln 3 + 2 \ln 2 = 2 \ln (x + 2)$
(51, 59)

$\ln 3^2 + \ln 2^2 = \ln (x + 2)^2$

$\ln (3^2 \cdot 2^2) = \ln (x + 2)^2$

$36 = x^2 + 4x + 4$

$x^2 + 4x - 32 = 0$

$(x + 8)(x - 4) = 0$

$x = -8, 4$

$x = \mathbf{4}$

7. $\log_6 9x - 2 \log_6 3 = 1$
(59)

$\log_6 9x - \log_6 3^2 = 1$

$\log_6 \dfrac{9x}{9} = 1$

$\dfrac{9x}{9} = 6^1$

$x = \mathbf{6}$

8. $v = \omega r$
(53)

$v = \left(2000 \dfrac{\text{rad}}{\text{min}}\right)\left(\dfrac{2 \text{ ft}}{2}\right)\left(\dfrac{12 \text{ in.}}{1 \text{ ft}}\right)\left(\dfrac{1 \text{ min}}{60 \text{ s}}\right)$

$v = \dfrac{(2000)(2)(12)}{(2)(60)} \dfrac{\text{in.}}{\text{s}} = \mathbf{400} \dfrac{\text{in.}}{\text{s}}$

9. (a) $\log 6900 = 3.8389$
(51)

$6900 = 10^{\mathbf{3.8389}}$

(b) $\ln 6900 = 8.8393$

$6900 = e^{\mathbf{8.8393}}$

10. C.
(31)

11. Rate $\times$ kindred $\times$ time $=$ drums or $RKT = D$
(44)

$\quad R(d \text{ kindred})(t \text{ hr}) = m \text{ drums}$

$\quad R = \dfrac{m}{dt} \dfrac{\text{drums}}{\text{kindred-hr}}$

$RKT = D$

$T = \dfrac{D}{RK}$

$T = \dfrac{r \text{ drums}}{\dfrac{m}{dt} \dfrac{\text{drums}}{\text{kindred-hr}} (d - k) \text{ kindred}}$

$T = \dfrac{rdt}{m(d - k)} \mathbf{hr}$

12. Rate $\times$ tapes $=$ price
(44)

Tapes $= p$

Price $= c$ cents

Rate $= \dfrac{c}{p} \dfrac{\text{cents}}{\text{tape}}$

New rate $= \left(\dfrac{c}{p} - 10\right) \dfrac{\text{cents}}{\text{tape}}$

$= \dfrac{c - 10p}{p} \dfrac{\text{cents}}{\text{tape}}$

Rate $\times N =$ price

$\dfrac{c - 10p}{p} \dfrac{\text{cents}}{\text{tape}} \times N = 600 \text{ cents}$

$N = \dfrac{600p}{c - 10p} \text{ tapes}$

13. Function $= -\sin \theta$
(47)

Amplitude $= 1 - (-3) = 4$

Centerline is $y = -3$

$y = -3 - 4 \sin \theta$

14.
(56)

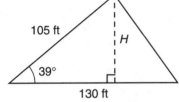

105 ft

39°

H

130 ft

$H = 105 \sin 39° = 66.08 \text{ ft}$

$\text{Area} = \dfrac{B \times H}{2} = \dfrac{(130)(66.08)}{2} = \mathbf{4295.11 \ ft^2}$

15.
(56)

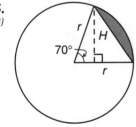

r

H

70°

r

$r = 12 \text{ ft}$

$H = r \sin 70° = 12 \sin 70° = 11.28 \text{ ft}$

$\text{Area} = \pi r^2 \left(\dfrac{70°}{360°}\right) - \dfrac{r \times H}{2}$

$= \pi(12)^2 \left(\dfrac{70°}{360°}\right) - \dfrac{12 \times 11.28}{2}$

$= 87.96 - 67.66 = \mathbf{20.31 \ ft^2}$

16.
(39)

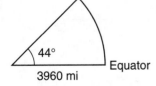

44°

3960 mi

Equator

$44° \times \dfrac{\pi \text{ rad}}{180°} = \dfrac{11\pi}{45} \text{ rad}$

$\text{Distance} = \dfrac{11\pi}{45}(3960 \text{ mi}) = \mathbf{3041.06 \ mi}$

17. $x^2 + 2x + 9 = 0$
(46)

$x = \dfrac{-2 \pm \sqrt{2^2 - 4(9)}}{2}$

$x = \dfrac{-2 \pm \sqrt{-32}}{2} = -1 \pm 2\sqrt{2}\,i$

$(x + 1 - 2\sqrt{2}\,i)(x + 1 + 2\sqrt{2}\,i)$

18. $3 \sec 2\theta - 2\sqrt{3} = 0$
(52)

$3 \sec 2\theta = 2\sqrt{3}$

$\sec 2\theta = \dfrac{2\sqrt{3}}{3}$

$\sec 2\theta = \dfrac{2}{\sqrt{3}}$

$2\theta = 30°, 330°, 390°, 690°$

$\theta = \mathbf{15°, 165°, 195°, 345°}$

19. $2 \sin \dfrac{\theta}{3} - \sqrt{2} = 0$
(52)

$2 \sin \dfrac{\theta}{3} = \sqrt{2}$

$\sin \dfrac{\theta}{3} = \dfrac{\sqrt{2}}{2}$

$\sin \dfrac{\theta}{3} = \dfrac{1}{\sqrt{2}}$

$\dfrac{\theta}{3} = 45°$

$\theta = \mathbf{135°}$

20. $\sqrt{(x - 7)^2 + (y - 1)^2}$
(37, 39)

$= \sqrt{[x - (-1)]^2 + [y - (-5)]^2}$

$x^2 - 14x + 49 + y^2 - 2y + 1$

$= x^2 + 2x + 1 + y^2 + 10y + 25$

$-16x - 12y = -24$

$\dfrac{2}{3}x + \dfrac{1}{2}y = 1$

$\dfrac{x}{\frac{3}{2}} + \dfrac{y}{2} = 1$

Test 15, Form A

1. $v = rw$
(53)

$$v = \left(\frac{400 \text{ rad}}{1 \text{ min}}\right)\left(\frac{20 \text{ m}}{1}\right)\left(\frac{100 \text{ cm}}{1 \text{ m}}\right)\left(\frac{1 \text{ in.}}{2.54 \text{ cm}}\right)$$

$$\times \left(\frac{1 \text{ ft}}{12 \text{ in.}}\right)\left(\frac{1 \text{ mi}}{5280 \text{ ft}}\right)\left(\frac{60 \text{ min}}{\text{hr}}\right)$$

$$v = \frac{(400)(20)(100)(60)}{(2.54)(12)(5280)} \frac{\text{mi}}{\text{hr}} = \textbf{298.26} \frac{\textbf{mi}}{\textbf{hr}}$$

2. $\dfrac{N!}{a!b!c!} = \dfrac{10!}{3!2!5!} = \textbf{2520}$
(55)

3. Function $= \cos x$
(47)

Amplitude $= 3 - (-3) = 6$

Centerline is $y = -3$

$y = \textbf{-3 + 6 cos } x$

4. $H = 7 \sin 50°$
(56)

$$A = \frac{1}{2}H(B_1 + B_2)$$

$$A = \frac{1}{2}(7 \sin 50°)(6 + 10) = \textbf{42.90 cm}^2$$

5. $A = \left(\dfrac{1.2 \text{ rad}}{2\pi \text{ rad}}\right)\pi r^2 = \left(\dfrac{1.2}{2\pi}\right)\pi(4)^2$
(56)

$$= \frac{(1.2)(16)}{2} = \textbf{9.6 m}^2$$

6. (a) $\log 41{,}000 = 4.6128$
(51)

$$41{,}000 = \textbf{10}^{\textbf{4.6128}}$$

(b) $\ln 41{,}000 = 10.6213$

$$41{,}000 = \textbf{\textit{e}}^{\textbf{10.6213}}$$

7. $\begin{cases} y \geq x^2 - 4x + 2 \\ y \leq -x + 4 \end{cases}$
(56)

$$y \geq (x^2 - 4x + 4) - 4 + 2$$

$$y \geq (x - 2)^2 - 2$$

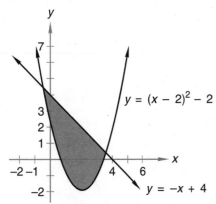

8. $(x - h)^2 + (y - k)^2 = r^2$
(42)

$$(x - 4)^2 + (y + 5)^2 = 7^2$$

9. $\cos^2 \theta - 1 = 0$
(60)

$$(\cos \theta - 1)(\cos \theta + 1) = 0$$

$$\cos \theta = 1 \qquad \cos \theta = -1$$

$$\theta = \textbf{0°} \qquad\qquad \theta = \textbf{180°}$$

10. $2 \sin \theta \cos \theta = \cos \theta$
(60)

$$2 \sin \theta \cos \theta - \cos \theta = 0$$

$$\cos \theta (2 \sin \theta - 1) = 0$$

$$\cos \theta = 0 \qquad\qquad 2 \sin \theta - 1 = 0$$

$$\theta = \textbf{90°, 270°} \qquad\qquad \sin \theta = \frac{1}{2}$$

$$\theta = \textbf{30°, 150°}$$

11. $\log_{20}(x + 2) + \log_{20}(x + 3) = 1$
(59)

$$\log_{20}(x + 2)(x + 3) = 1$$

$$(x + 2)(x + 3) = 20^1$$

$$x^2 + 5x + 6 = 20$$

$$x^2 + 5x - 14 = 0$$

$$(x + 7)(x - 2) = 0$$

$$x = -7, 2$$

$$x = \textbf{2}$$

12. $\dfrac{4}{5}\log_8 32 - \log_8(x + 2) = \log_8 2$
(59)

$$\log_8 32^{4/5} - \log_8(x + 2) = \log_8 2$$

$$\log_8 \frac{16}{(x + 2)} = \log_8 2$$

$$16 = 2(x + 2)$$

$$16 = 2x + 4$$

$$2x = 12$$

$$x = \textbf{6}$$

13. $4^{\log_4 \sqrt{2} + \log_4 \sqrt{6}} = 4^{\log_4 \sqrt{12}} = \sqrt{12} = \textbf{2}\sqrt{\textbf{3}}$
(59)

14.
(39, 48)

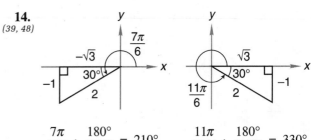

$$\frac{7\pi}{6} \cdot \frac{180°}{\pi} = 210° \qquad \frac{11\pi}{6} \cdot \frac{180°}{\pi} = 330°$$

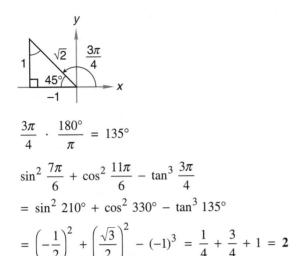

$$\frac{3\pi}{4} \cdot \frac{180°}{\pi} = 135°$$

$$\sin^2 \frac{7\pi}{6} + \cos^2 \frac{11\pi}{6} - \tan^3 \frac{3\pi}{4}$$

$$= \sin^2 210° + \cos^2 330° - \tan^3 135°$$

$$= \left(-\frac{1}{2}\right)^2 + \left(\frac{\sqrt{3}}{2}\right)^2 - (-1)^3 = \frac{1}{4} + \frac{3}{4} + 1 = \mathbf{2}$$

15. The line perpendicular to the given line has a slope
(58) of −1, so

$$y = -x + b$$
$$(1) = -(3) + b$$
$$b = 4$$

$$y = -x + 4$$
$$(x - 4) = -x + 4$$
$$2x = 8$$
$$x = 4$$

$$y = -(4) + 4 = 0$$

$$(3, 1), (4, 0)$$

$$D = \sqrt{(3 - 4)^2 + (1 - 0)^2} = \mathbf{\sqrt{2}}$$

16. $x^2 - 3x + 3 = 0$
(46)

$$x = \frac{-(-3) \pm \sqrt{(-3)^2 - 4(3)}}{2}$$

$$x = \frac{3 \pm \sqrt{-3}}{2} = \frac{3}{2} \pm \frac{\sqrt{3}}{2}i$$

$$\left(x - \frac{3}{2} - \frac{\sqrt{3}}{2}i\right)\left(x - \frac{3}{2} + \frac{\sqrt{3}}{2}i\right)$$

17.
(25) $$R_D T_D + R_K T_K = \text{jobs}$$

$$\left(\frac{2}{3}\frac{\text{job}}{\text{day}}\right)T + \left(\frac{4}{7}\frac{\text{job}}{\text{day}}\right)(T + 3 \text{ days}) = 8 \text{ jobs}$$

$$\left(\frac{2}{3}\frac{\text{job}}{\text{day}}\right)T + \left(\frac{4}{7}\frac{\text{job}}{\text{day}}\right)T + \frac{12}{7} \text{ jobs} = 8 \text{ jobs}$$

$$\left(\frac{26}{21}\frac{\text{jobs}}{\text{day}}\right)T = \frac{44}{7} \text{ jobs}$$

$$T = \frac{66}{13} \text{ days}$$

18. $H = 4W$
(36)

Upwind:
$$(H - W)T_U = 300$$
$$3WT_U = 300$$
$$WT_U = 100$$

Downwind:
$$(H + W)T_D = 600$$
$$5W(T_U + 1) = 600$$
$$5WT_U + 5W = 600$$
$$5(100) + 5W = 600$$
$$5W = 100$$
$$W = 20$$

$$H = 4W = \mathbf{80 \text{ mph}}$$

19. Domain = $\{x \in \mathbb{R} \mid -4 < x \le 6\}$
(21)
Range = $\{y \in \mathbb{R} \mid -4 \le y \le 4\}$

20. Domain = $\{x \in \mathbb{R} \mid x \le 4\}$
(21)
Range = $\{y \in \mathbb{R} \mid y \le 4\}$

Test 15, Form B

1. $v = rw$
(53)

$$v = \left(\frac{20 \text{ rad}}{1 \text{ s}}\right)\left(\frac{2 \text{ m}}{1}\right)\left(\frac{100 \text{ cm}}{1 \text{ m}}\right)\left(\frac{1 \text{ in.}}{2.54 \text{ cm}}\right)$$

$$\times \left(\frac{1 \text{ ft}}{12 \text{ in.}}\right)\left(\frac{1 \text{ mi}}{5280 \text{ ft}}\right)\left(\frac{60 \text{ s}}{1 \text{ min}}\right)\left(\frac{60 \text{ min}}{\text{hr}}\right)$$

$$v = \frac{(20)(2)(100)(60)(60)}{(2.54)(12)(5280)} \frac{\text{mi}}{\text{hr}} = \mathbf{89.48} \frac{\text{mi}}{\text{hr}}$$

2. $\frac{N!}{a!b!c!} = \frac{9!}{4!2!3!} = \mathbf{1260}$
(55)

3. Function = $\cos x$
(47)
Amplitude = $9 - 5 = 4$
Centerline is $y = 5$
$$y = \mathbf{5 + 4\cos x}$$

4. $H = 6 \sin 40°$
(56)
$$A = \frac{1}{2}H(B_1 + B_2)$$
$$A = \frac{1}{2}(6 \sin 40°)(10 + 12) = \mathbf{42.42 \text{ km}^2}$$

5. $A = \left(\dfrac{3.4 \text{ rad}}{2\pi \text{ rad}}\right)\pi r^2 = \left(\dfrac{3.4}{2\pi}\right)\pi(3)^2$
(56)

$\quad = \dfrac{(3.4)(9)}{2} = \mathbf{15.3 \text{ cm}^2}$

6. (a) $\log 3{,}800 = 3.5798$
(51)

$\qquad 3{,}800 = 10^{3.5798}$

$\quad$ (b) $\ln 3{,}800 = 8.2428$

$\qquad 3{,}800 = e^{8.2428}$

7. $\begin{cases} y \geq x^2 - 2x - 2 \\ y \leq \dfrac{1}{2}x - 1 \end{cases}$
(56)

$\quad y \geq \left(x^2 - 2x + 1\right) - 1 - 2$

$\quad y \geq (x - 1)^2 - 3$

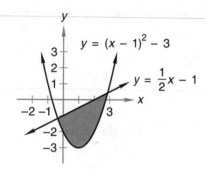

8. $(x - h)^2 + (y - k)^2 = r^2$
(42)

$\quad (x - 2)^2 + (y + 3)^2 = 4^2$

9. $\qquad \sin^2 \theta - 1 = 0$
(60)

$\quad (\sin \theta + 1)(\sin \theta - 1) = 0$

$\quad \sin \theta = -1 \qquad \sin \theta = 1$

$\qquad \theta = \mathbf{270°} \qquad\quad \theta = \mathbf{90°}$

10. $\qquad 2 \sin \theta \cos \theta = \sin \theta$
(60)

$\quad 2 \sin \theta \cos \theta - \sin \theta = 0$

$\qquad \sin \theta(2 \cos \theta - 1) = 0$

$\quad \sin \theta = 0 \qquad\qquad 2 \cos \theta - 1 = 0$

$\qquad \theta = \mathbf{0°, 180°} \qquad\qquad \cos \theta = \dfrac{1}{2}$

$\qquad\qquad\qquad\qquad\qquad \theta = \mathbf{60°, 300°}$

11. $\log_{14} (2x + 3) + \log_{14} (x + 3) = 1$
(59)

$\qquad \log_{14} (2x + 3)(x + 3) = 1$

$\qquad (2x + 3)(x + 3) = 14^1$

$\qquad 2x^2 + 9x + 9 = 14$

$\qquad 2x^2 + 9x - 5 = 0$

$\qquad (2x - 1)(x + 5) = 0$

$\qquad\qquad\qquad x = \dfrac{1}{2}, -5$

$\qquad\qquad\qquad x = \dfrac{1}{2}$

12. $\dfrac{4}{3} \log_3 8 - \log_3 (x + 3) = \log_3 2$
(59)

$\quad \log_3 8^{4/3} - \log_3 (x + 3) = \log_3 2$

$\qquad \log_3 \left(\dfrac{16}{x + 3}\right) = \log_3 2$

$\qquad\qquad 16 = 2(x + 3)$

$\qquad\qquad 16 = 2x + 6$

$\qquad\qquad 2x = 10$

$\qquad\qquad\; x = \mathbf{5}$

13. $9^{\log_9 \sqrt{3} + \log_9 \sqrt{6}} = 9^{\log_9 \sqrt{18}} = \sqrt{18} = \mathbf{3\sqrt{2}}$
(59)

14.
(39, 48)

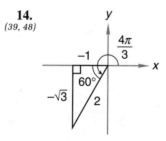

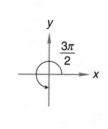

$\dfrac{4\pi}{3} \cdot \dfrac{180°}{\pi} = 240° \qquad \dfrac{3\pi}{2} \cdot \dfrac{180°}{\pi} = 270°$

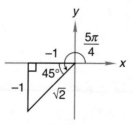

$\dfrac{5\pi}{4} \cdot \dfrac{180°}{\pi} = 225°$

$$\sin^2 \frac{4\pi}{3} - \cos^3 \frac{3\pi}{2} + \tan^2 \frac{5\pi}{4}$$

$$= \sin^2 240° - \cos^3 270° + \tan^2 225°$$

$$= \left(-\frac{\sqrt{3}}{2}\right)^2 - (0)^3 + \left(\frac{-1}{-1}\right)^2$$

$$= \frac{3}{4} - 0 + 1 = \frac{7}{4}$$

15. The line perpendicular to the given line has a slope
(58) of 1, so

$$y = x + b$$
$$(1) = (-3) + b$$
$$b = 4$$

$$y = x + 4$$
$$(-x + 4) = x + 4$$
$$2x = 0$$
$$x = 0$$

$$y = (0) + 4 = 4$$

$$(-3, 1), (0, 4)$$

$$D = \sqrt{(4-1)^2 + [0-(-3)]^2} = \sqrt{18} = 3\sqrt{2}$$

16. $x^2 - x + 6 = 0$
(46)
$$x = \frac{-(-1) \pm \sqrt{(-1)^2 - 4(1)(6)}}{2}$$

$$x = \frac{1 \pm \sqrt{-23}}{2} = \frac{1}{2} \pm \frac{\sqrt{23}}{2}i$$

$$\left(x - \frac{1}{2} - \frac{\sqrt{23}}{2}i\right)\left(x - \frac{1}{2} + \frac{\sqrt{23}}{2}i\right)$$

17.
(25)
$$R_R T_R + R_C T_C = \text{patients}$$

$$\left(\frac{7}{2}\frac{\text{pat.}}{\text{day}}\right)(T + 3 \text{ days}) + \left(\frac{3}{1}\frac{\text{pat.}}{\text{day}}\right)T = 50 \text{ patients}$$

$$\left(\frac{7}{2}\frac{\text{pat.}}{\text{day}}\right)T + \frac{21}{2} \text{ patients} + \left(3\frac{\text{pat.}}{\text{day}}\right)T = 50 \text{ patients}$$

$$\left(\frac{13}{2}\frac{\text{patients}}{\text{day}}\right)T = \frac{79}{2} \text{ pat.}$$

$$T = \frac{79}{13} \text{ days}$$

18. $P = 5W$
(36)

Upstream:
$$(P - W)T_U = 160$$
$$4WT_U = 160$$
$$WT_U = 40$$

Downstream:
$$(P + W)T_D = 180$$
$$6W(T_U - 1) = 180$$
$$6WT_U - 6W = 180$$
$$6(40) - 6W = 180$$
$$6W = 60$$
$$W = 10$$

$$P = 5W = \textbf{50 mph}$$

19. Domain $= \{x \in \mathbb{R} \mid -3 \le x \le 4\}$
(21)
Range $= \{y \in \mathbb{R} \mid -5 \le y \le 2\}$

20. Domain $= \{\theta \in \mathbb{R} \mid \theta \le 5\}$
(21)
Range $= \{y \in \mathbb{R} \mid y \le 3\}$

Test 16, Form A

1.
(56)

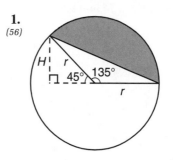

$$H = r \sin 45° = 2 \sin 45° = 1.414 \text{ cm}$$

$$\text{Area} = \left(\frac{135°}{360°}\right)\pi r^2 - \frac{r \times H}{2}$$

$$= \left(\frac{135°}{360°}\right)\pi(2)^2 - \frac{2 \times 1.414}{2}$$

$$= 4.712 - 1.414 = \textbf{3.30 cm}^2$$

2. $v = r\omega = 170 \text{ cm} \times 500 \dfrac{\text{rad}}{\text{min}}$
(53)

$= \dfrac{(170)(500) \text{ cm·rad}}{\text{min}} \times \dfrac{1 \text{ m}}{100 \text{ cm}} \times \dfrac{1 \text{ km}}{1000 \text{ m}}$

$\times \dfrac{60 \text{ min}}{1 \text{ hr}}$

$= \dfrac{(170)(500)(60)}{(100)(1000)} \dfrac{\text{km}}{\text{hr}} = \mathbf{51} \dfrac{\mathbf{km}}{\mathbf{hr}}$

3. $C = mN + b$
(62)

(a) $\begin{cases} 450 = m20 + b \\ (b) \quad 650 = m30 + b \end{cases}$

(−a) $\quad -450 = -m20 - b$

(b) $\quad \dfrac{650 = m30 + b}{200 = m10}$

$\quad\quad m = 20$

(a) $450 = 20(20) + b$

$\quad\quad b = 50$

$C = \mathbf{20N + 50}$

$C = 20(100) + 50 = \mathbf{\$2050}$

4. $\mu \pm \sigma = 83 \pm 3 = 80 \text{ to } 86$
(61) **68% of the data lie between 80 and 86**

$\mu \pm 2\sigma = 83 \pm 2(3) = 77 \text{ to } 89$
95% of the data lie between 77 and 89

$\mu \pm 3\sigma = 83 \pm 3(3) = 74 \text{ to } 92$
99% of the data lie between 74 and 92

5. $\begin{cases} cx + by = d \\ px + qy = f \end{cases}$
(62)

$cqx + bqy = dq$

$\dfrac{-pbx - bqy = -fb}{(cq - pb)x = dq - fb}$

$\quad\quad x = \dfrac{dq - fb}{cq - pb}$

6. $(\sqrt{3} \text{ cis } 15°)(2 \text{ cis } 45°) = (\sqrt{3})(2) \text{ cis } (15° + 45°)$
(64)

$= 2\sqrt{3} \text{ cis } 60° = 2\sqrt{3}(\cos 60° + i \sin 60°)$

$= 2\sqrt{3}\left[\dfrac{1}{2} + i\left(\dfrac{\sqrt{3}}{2}\right) \right] = \mathbf{\sqrt{3} + 3i}$

7. Overall average rate $= \dfrac{\text{overall distance}}{\text{overall time}}$
(38)

$= \dfrac{(t + m) \text{ mi}}{(s + z) \text{ hr}}$

Time $= \dfrac{\text{distance}}{\text{rate}}$

$= \dfrac{150 \text{ mi}}{\dfrac{(t + m) \text{ mi}}{(s + z) \text{ hr}}} = \dfrac{150(s + z)}{t + m} \text{ hr}$

8. $\quad\quad x^2 + y^2 - 2x + 8y + 8 = 0$
(63)

$\left(x^2 - 2x \quad\right) + \left(y^2 + 8y \quad\right) = -8$

$\left(x^2 - 2x + 1\right) + \left(y^2 + 8y + 16\right) = 9$

$\quad\quad (x - 1)^2 + (y + 4)^2 = 3^2$

Center = (1, −4); Radius = 3

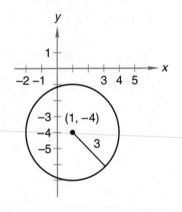

9. $\sin \theta \cos 2\theta - \cos 2\theta = 0$
(60)

$\cos 2\theta(\sin \theta - 1) = 0$

$\cos 2\theta = 0$

$2\theta = 90°, 270°, 450°, 630°$

$\theta = \mathbf{45°, 135°, 225°, 315°}$

$\sin \theta - 1 = 0$

$\sin \theta = 1$

$\theta = \mathbf{90°}$

10.
(61)

STEM	LEAF	In order:	STEM	LEAF
7	1		7	1
6	4		6	4
5	7, 9, 5, 4		5	4, 5, 7, 9
4	2, 6, 4, 9		4	2, 4, 6, 9
3	3, 2		3	2, 3

11. Mean = 555.5
(61)
Standard deviation = 88.99

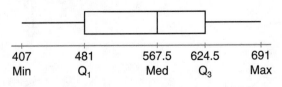

407	481	567.5	624.5	691
Min	Q_1	Med	Q_3	Max

12.
(47)

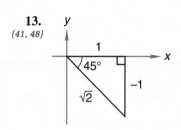

$$c = \sqrt{4^2 + 1^2} = \sqrt{17}$$

$$\sin\left(\text{Arctan } \frac{1}{4}\right) = \frac{1}{\sqrt{17}} = \frac{\sqrt{17}}{17}$$

13.
(41, 48)

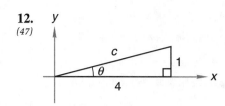

$$\tan^2(-405°) - \sec^2(-405°) + \cos 900°$$

$$= \tan^2(-45°) - \sec^2(-45°) + \cos 180°$$

$$= (-1)^2 - \left(\sqrt{2}\right)^2 + (-1) = -2$$

14.
(56)

0.5 m

0.4 m

H

30°

0.9 m

$$H = 0.4 \sin 30° = 0.2 \text{ m}$$

$$\text{Area} = \frac{1}{2} H\left(B_1 + B_2\right)$$

$$= \frac{1}{2}(0.2)(0.5 + 0.9) = 0.14 \text{ m}^2$$

$$0.14 \text{ m}^2\left(\frac{(100)(100) \text{ cm}^2}{1 \text{ m}^2}\right) = 1400 \text{ cm}^2$$

15.
(57)

Function $= \sin x$

Amplitude $= 15 - 5 = 10$

Centerline $= 5$

$$\text{Period} = \frac{9\pi}{8} - \left(-\frac{7\pi}{8}\right) = 2\pi$$

$$\text{Coefficient} = \frac{2\pi}{2\pi} = 1$$

$$\text{Phase angle} = \frac{\pi}{8}$$

$$y = 5 + 10 \sin\left(x - \frac{\pi}{8}\right)$$

16.
(59)

$$\log_7(x + 3) - \log_7 x = \log_7 4$$

$$\log_7\left(\frac{x + 3}{x}\right) = \log_7 4$$

$$\frac{x + 3}{x} = 4$$

$$x + 3 = 4x$$

$$3x = 3$$

$$x = 1$$

17.
(59)

$$\log x + \log(x - 3) = 1$$

$$\log[x(x - 3)] = 1$$

$$x(x - 3) = 10^1$$

$$x^2 - 3x = 10$$

$$x^2 - 3x - 10 = 0$$

$$(x - 5)(x + 2) = 0$$

$$x = 5, -2$$

$$x = 5$$

18.
(56)

$$\begin{cases} y \leq -(x - 1)^2 + 5 \\ y \leq x + 2 \end{cases}$$

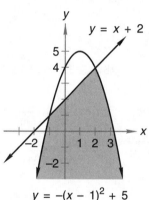

19.
(61)

$$\text{Range} = 15 - 7 = 8$$

$$\text{Mean} = \frac{12 + 7 + 8 + 9 + 11 + 8 + 15}{7}$$

$$= \frac{70}{7} = 10$$

Median $= 9$

Mode $= 8$

Variance $=$

$$\frac{2^2 + 3^2 + 2^2 + 1^2 + 1^2 + 2^2 + 5^2}{7}$$

$$= \frac{48}{7} = 6.86$$

$$\text{Standard deviation} = \sqrt{\frac{48}{7}} = 2.62$$

20. $f(x) = x(x + 2)$
(21)

$f(x + h) = (x + h)[(x + h) + 2]$

$= x^2 + 2xh + h^2 + 2x + 2h$

$f(x - h) = (x - h)[(x - h) + 2]$

$= x^2 - 2xh + h^2 + 2x - 2h$

$\dfrac{f(x + h) - f(x - h)}{2h} = \dfrac{4xh + 4h}{2h} = 2x + 2$

Test 16, Form B

1.
(56)

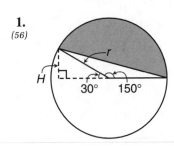

$H = r \sin 30° = 3 \sin 30° = 1.5 \text{ km}$

$\text{Area} = \left(\dfrac{150°}{360°}\right)\pi r^2 - \dfrac{r \times H}{2}$

$= \left(\dfrac{150°}{360°}\right)\pi (3)^2 - \dfrac{3 \times 1.5}{2}$

$= 11.78 - 2.25 = \mathbf{9.53 \text{ km}^2}$

2. $v = r\omega = 50 \text{ cm} \times 300 \dfrac{\text{rad}}{\text{min}}$
(53)

$= \dfrac{(50)(300) \text{ cm·rad}}{\text{min}} \times \dfrac{1 \text{ m}}{100 \text{ cm}} \times \dfrac{1 \text{ km}}{1000 \text{ m}}$

$\times \dfrac{60 \text{ min}}{1 \text{ hr}}$

$= \dfrac{(50)(300)(60)}{(100)(1000)} \dfrac{\text{km}}{\text{hr}} = \mathbf{9} \dfrac{\text{km}}{\text{hr}}$

3. $C = mN + b$
(62)

(a) $\begin{cases} 172 = m10 + b \\ \text{(b)} \ \ 412 = m25 + b \end{cases}$

$\begin{array}{l} (-a) \ -172 = -m10 - b \\ \text{(b)} \ \ \underline{\ \ \ 412 = \ \ \ m25 + b} \\ \ \ \ \ \ \ \ \ \ 240 = \ \ \ m15 \\ \ \ \ \ \ \ \ \ \ \ \ \ m = 16 \end{array}$

(a) $172 = 16(10) + b$

$b = 12$

$\mathbf{C = 16N + 12}$

$C = 16(20) + 12 = \mathbf{\$332}$

4. $\mu \pm \sigma = 92 \pm 2 = 90 \text{ to } 94$
(61)

68% of the data lie between 90 and 94

$\mu \pm 2\sigma = 92 \pm 2(2) = 88 \text{ to } 96$

95% of the data lie between 88 and 96

$\mu \pm 3\sigma = 92 \pm 3(2) = 86 \text{ to } 98$

99% of the data lie between 86 and 98

5. $\begin{cases} cx + dy = f \\ wx + zy = t \end{cases}$
(62)

$czx + dzy = fz$

$\underline{-wdx - dzy = -td}$

$(cz - wd)x = fz - td$

$x = \dfrac{fz - td}{cz - wd}$

6. $(2 \text{ cis } 75°)(\sqrt{3} \text{ cis } (-15°))$
(64)

$= (2)(\sqrt{3}) \text{ cis } (75° - 15°)$

$= 2\sqrt{3} \text{ cis } 60° = 2\sqrt{3}(\cos 60° + i \sin 60°)$

$= 2\sqrt{3}\left[\dfrac{1}{2} + i\left(\dfrac{\sqrt{3}}{2}\right)\right] = \mathbf{\sqrt{3} + 3i}$

7. Overall average rate $= \dfrac{\text{overall distance}}{\text{overall time}}$
(38)

$= \dfrac{(t + r) \text{ mi}}{(h + m) \text{ hr}}$

Time $= \dfrac{\text{distance}}{\text{rate}}$

$= \dfrac{26 \text{ mi}}{\dfrac{(t + r) \text{ mi}}{(h + m) \text{ hr}}} = \dfrac{26(h + m)}{t + r} \text{ hr}$

8. $x^2 + y^2 + 2x - 4y - 4 = 0$
(63)

$\left(x^2 + 2x \ \ \ \ \right) + \left(y^2 - 4y \ \ \ \ \right) = 4$

$\left(x^2 + 2x + 1\right) + \left(y^2 - 4y + 4\right) = 9$

$(x + 1)^2 + (y - 2)^2 = 3^2$

Center = (-1, 2); Radius = 3

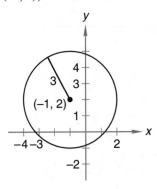

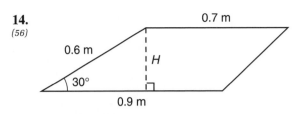

9. $\tan\theta\sin 2\theta + \sin 2\theta = 0$
(60)
$\qquad \sin 2\theta(\tan\theta + 1) = 0$

$\sin 2\theta = 0$

$\qquad 2\theta = 0°, 180°, 360°, 540°$

$\qquad \boldsymbol{\theta = 0°, 90°, 180°, 270°}$

$\tan\theta + 1 = 0$

$\qquad \tan\theta = -1$

$\qquad \boldsymbol{\theta = 135°, 315°}$

10.
(61)

STEM	LEAF	In order:	STEM	LEAF
6	3, 8		6	3, 8
5	6, 7, 6, 3		5	3, 6, 6, 7
4	3, 8, 7, 9		4	3, 7, 8, 9
3	4, 2		3	2, 4

11. Mean = 555.75
(61)
Standard deviation = 89.41

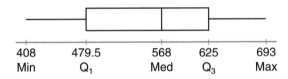

408	479.5	568	625	693
Min	Q_1	Med	Q_3	Max

12.
(47)

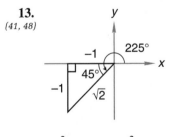

$c = \sqrt{5^2 + 2^2} = \sqrt{29}$

$\sin\left(\text{Arctan}\ \dfrac{2}{5}\right) = \dfrac{2}{\sqrt{29}} = \boldsymbol{\dfrac{2\sqrt{29}}{29}}$

13.
(41, 48)

$\tan^2 225° - \sec^2 225° + \cos(-540°)$

$= \tan^2 225° - \sec^2 225° + \cos 180°$

$= \left(\dfrac{-1}{-1}\right)^2 - \left(\dfrac{\sqrt{2}}{-1}\right)^2 + (-1) = \boldsymbol{-2}$

14.
(56)

$H = 0.6\sin 30° = 0.3$ m

$\text{Area} = \dfrac{1}{2}H(B_1 + B_2)$

$\qquad = \dfrac{1}{2}(0.3)(0.7 + 0.9) = 0.24$ m^2

$0.24\ \text{m}^2\ \dfrac{(100)(100)\ \text{cm}^2}{1\ \text{m}^2} = \boldsymbol{2400\ \text{cm}^2}$

15. Function = $\sin x$
(57)
Amplitude = $10 - 5 = 5$

Centerline = 5

Period = $\dfrac{3\pi}{4} - \left(-\dfrac{\pi}{4}\right) = \pi$

Coefficient = $\dfrac{2\pi}{\pi} = 2$

Phase angle = $\dfrac{\pi}{4}$

$\boldsymbol{y = 5 + 5\sin 2\left(x - \dfrac{\pi}{4}\right)}$

16. $\log_5(x + 2) - \log_5 x = \log_5 3$
(59)
$\qquad \log_5\left(\dfrac{x + 2}{x}\right) = \log_5 3$

$\qquad \dfrac{x + 2}{x} = 3$

$\qquad x + 2 = 3x$

$\qquad 2x = 2$

$\qquad \boldsymbol{x = 1}$

17. $\log x + \log(x + 3) = 1$
(59)
$\qquad \log[x(x + 3)] = 1$

$\qquad x(x + 3) = 10^1$

$\qquad x^2 + 3x = 10$

$\qquad x^2 + 3x - 10 = 0$

$\qquad (x + 5)(x - 2) = 0$

$\qquad x = -5, 2$

$\qquad \boldsymbol{x = 2}$

18.
(56)
$$\begin{cases} y \ge (x - 1)^2 - 5 \\ y \le -x - 2 \end{cases}$$

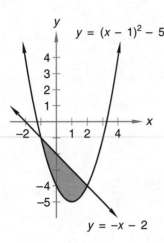

19. Range = $13 - 6 = \mathbf{7}$
(61)

Mean = $\dfrac{13 + 8 + 7 + 11 + 8 + 10 + 6}{7}$

$= \dfrac{63}{7} = \mathbf{9}$

Median = **8**

Mode = **8**

Variance =

$\dfrac{(-4)^2 + 1^2 + 2^2 + (-2)^2 + 1^2 + (-1)^2 + 3^2}{7}$

$= \dfrac{36}{7} = \mathbf{5.14}$

Standard deviation = $\sqrt{\dfrac{36}{7}} = \mathbf{2.27}$

20. $f(x) = x(x + 1)$
(21)

$f(x + h) = (x + h)[(x + h) + 1]$
$= x^2 + 2xh + h^2 + x + h$

$f(x - h) = (x - h)[(x - h) + 1]$
$= x^2 - 2xh + h^2 + x - h$

$\dfrac{f(x + h) - f(x - h)}{2h} = \dfrac{4xh + 2h}{2h} = \mathbf{2x + 1}$

Test 17, Form A

1. C = mN + b
(62)

  (a) $\begin{cases} 7.80 = m6 + b \\ 2.60 = m2 + b \end{cases}$

  (a) $\quad 7.80 = m6 + b$
  (−b) $\underline{-2.60 = -m2 - b}$
        $5.20 = m4$
          $m = 1.30$

  (b) $2.60 = (1.30)(2) + b$
        $b = 0$

  C = 1.30N = $1.30(10) = \mathbf{\$13.00}$

2. Overall average rate $= \dfrac{\text{overall distance}}{\text{overall time}}$
(38)

$= \dfrac{(m + n)\text{ mi}}{(h + 2h - 1)\text{ hr}}$

$= \dfrac{m + n}{3h - 1}\dfrac{\text{mi}}{\text{hr}}$

Time $= \dfrac{\text{distance}}{\text{rate}}$

$= \dfrac{50\text{ mi}}{\dfrac{m + n}{3h - 1}\dfrac{\text{mi}}{\text{hr}}} = \dfrac{150h - 50}{m + n}\textbf{ hr}$

3. (a) $\text{antilog}_6 3 = 6^3 = \mathbf{216}$
(67)
  (b) $\text{antilog}_3 2 = 3^2 = \mathbf{9}$

4. $\begin{cases} ax + by = c \\ dx + fy = g \end{cases}$
(62)

$-adx - bdy = -cd$
$\underline{adx + afy = ag}$
$(af - bd)y = ag - cd$

$y = \dfrac{ag - cd}{af - bd}$

5. $\begin{cases} 2x + y = 7 \\ 5x + 8y = 1 \end{cases}$
(62, 66)

$\begin{cases} ax + by = c \\ dx + fy = g \end{cases}$

$y = \dfrac{ag - cd}{af - bd} = \dfrac{2(1) - 7(5)}{2(8) - 1(5)} = \dfrac{2 - 35}{16 - 5}$

$= \dfrac{-33}{11} = \mathbf{-3}$

6. $y = \log_3 x$
(65)

$3^y = x$

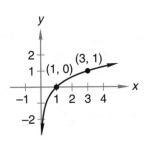

7. (a) $3 - 4i$
(64)

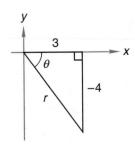

$r = \sqrt{3^2 + (-4)^2} = 5$

$\theta = \tan^{-1}\left(\dfrac{-4}{3}\right) = -53.13°$

5 cis (–53.13°)

(b)

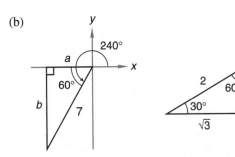

$7 \text{ cis } 240° = 7(\cos 240° + i \sin 240°)$

$= 7\left[\left(-\dfrac{1}{2}\right) + i\left(-\dfrac{\sqrt{3}}{2}\right)\right] = -\dfrac{7}{2} - \dfrac{7\sqrt{3}}{2}\, i$

8. $\omega = \dfrac{v}{r} = \dfrac{26 \dfrac{\text{mi}}{\text{hr}}}{15 \text{ in.}} = \dfrac{26}{15} \dfrac{\text{mi}}{\text{hr-in.}}$
(53)

$= \dfrac{26}{15} \dfrac{\text{mi}}{\text{hr-in.}} \times \dfrac{5280 \text{ ft}}{1 \text{ mi}} \times \dfrac{12 \text{ in.}}{1 \text{ ft}} \times \dfrac{1 \text{ hr}}{60 \text{ min}}$

$= \dfrac{(26)(5280)(12)}{(15)(60)} \dfrac{\text{rad}}{\text{min}} = \textbf{1830.4} \dfrac{\textbf{rad}}{\textbf{min}}$

9. Range $= 12 - 3 = \textbf{9}$
(61)

Mean $= \dfrac{5 + 4 + 12 + 3 + 5 + 7}{6} = \dfrac{36}{6} = \textbf{6}$

Median $= \dfrac{5 + 5}{2} = \textbf{5}$

Mode $= \textbf{5}$

Variance $=$

$\dfrac{(-1)^2 + (-2)^2 + 6^2 + (-3)^2 + (-1)^2 + 1^2}{6}$

$= \dfrac{52}{6} = \textbf{8.67}$

Standard deviation $= \sqrt{\dfrac{52}{6}} = \textbf{2.94}$

10. (a) Function $= -\sin \theta$
(66)

Amplitude $= 19 - (-2) = 21$

Centerline $= -2$

Period $= 120°$

Coefficient $= \dfrac{360°}{120°} = 3$

Phase angle $= 0$

$y = -2 - 21 \sin 3\theta$

(b) Function $= -\cos \theta$

Amplitude $= 10 - 8 = 2$

Centerline $= 8$

Period $= 60° - (-20°) = 80°$

Coefficient $= \dfrac{360°}{80°} = \dfrac{9}{2}$

Phase angle $= 0$

$y = 8 - 2 \cos \dfrac{9}{2}\theta$

11. $9 \ln e^2 + 4^{\log_4 6 - \log_4 2} - 7^{\log_7 21 + \log_7 1}$
(51, 59)

$= 9(2) \ln e + 4^{\log_4 (6/2)} - 7^{\log_7 21(1)}$

$= 18 + 3 - 21 = \textbf{0}$

12.
(64)

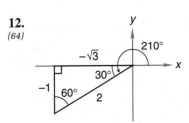

$[5 \text{ cis } (-70°)](3 \text{ cis } 280°)$

$= (5)(3) \text{ cis } [(-70°) + 280°]$

$= 15 \text{ cis } (210°) = 15(\cos 210° + i \sin 210°)$

$= 15\left[-\dfrac{\sqrt{3}}{2} + i\left(-\dfrac{1}{2}\right)\right] = -\dfrac{15\sqrt{3}}{2} - \dfrac{15}{2}i$

13.
(56)
$$\begin{cases} y \geq (x + 3)^2 - 2 \\ y \leq x + 3 \end{cases}$$

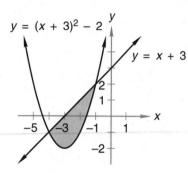

$y = (x + 3)^2 - 2$

$y = x + 3$

14.
(63)
$$x^2 + y^2 - 6x - 8y + 21 = 0$$
$$\left(x^2 - 6x \quad\right) + \left(y^2 - 8y \quad\right) = -21$$
$$\left(x^2 - 6x + 9\right) + \left(y^2 - 8y + 16\right) = 4$$
$$(x - 3)^2 + (y - 4)^2 = 2^2$$

Center = (3, 4); Radius = 2

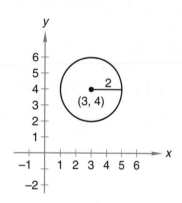

15. **Mean = 335.25**
(61)
Standard deviation = 52.50

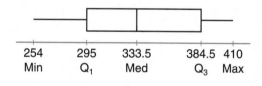

254	295	333.5	384.5	410
Min	Q₁	Med	Q₃	Max

16. (a) $\mu = 43, \sigma = 3$
(61)
$\mu \pm \sigma = 43 \pm 3 = 40$ to 46

About **68%** of the data points lie within one standard deviation of the mean.

(b) $\mu + \sigma = 43 + 3 = 46$

About **34%** of the data points lie on one side of the mean within one standard deviation of the mean.

17. $\ln (x + 3) = \ln 4 + \ln (x - 3)$
(51, 59)
$\ln (x + 3) = \ln 4(x - 3)$
$x + 3 = 4x - 12$
$3x = 15$
$x = \mathbf{5}$

18. Directrix: $y = -2 = k - p$
(68)
Focus: $(h, k + p) = (0, 2)$

$$k + p = 2$$
$$\underline{k - p = -2}$$
$$2k \quad = 0$$
$$k = 0$$

$$k + p = 2$$
$$0 + p = 2$$
$$p = 2$$

Vertex: $(h, k) = \mathbf{(0, 0)}$

$$y - k = \frac{1}{4p}(x - h)^2$$
$$y - 0 = \frac{1}{4(2)}(x - 0)^2$$
$$\boldsymbol{y = \frac{1}{8}x^2}$$

19. (a) $\cos 2x + \dfrac{1}{2} = 0$
(50, 52)
$$\cos 2x = -\frac{1}{2}$$
$$2x = \frac{2\pi}{3}, \frac{4\pi}{3}, \frac{8\pi}{3}, \frac{10\pi}{3}$$
$$x = \frac{\pi}{3}, \frac{2\pi}{3}, \frac{4\pi}{3}, \frac{5\pi}{3}$$

(b) $\left(\sqrt{3} \tan x + 1\right)\left(2 \sin x - \sqrt{3}\right) = 0$

$$\sqrt{3} \tan x + 1 = 0$$
$$\sqrt{3} \tan x = -1$$
$$\tan x = -\frac{1}{\sqrt{3}}$$
$$x = \frac{5\pi}{6}, \frac{11\pi}{6}$$

$$2 \sin x - \sqrt{3} = 0$$
$$2 \sin x = \sqrt{3}$$
$$\sin x = \frac{\sqrt{3}}{2}$$
$$x = \frac{\pi}{3}, \frac{2\pi}{3}$$

20.
(56)

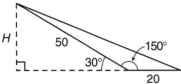

$H = 50 \sin 30° = 25$ in.

$$\text{Area} = \frac{B \times H}{2} = \frac{20 \times 25}{2} = \textbf{250 in.}^2$$

Test 17, Form B

1. $C = mN + b$
(62)

(a) $\begin{cases} 8.45 = m5 + b \\ 3.38 = m2 + b \end{cases}$
(b)

$$\begin{array}{rl}
\text{(a)} & 8.45 = m5 + b \\
\text{(–b)} & -3.38 = -m2 - b \\
\hline
& 5.07 = m3 \\
& m = 1.69
\end{array}$$

(b) $3.38 = (1.69)(2) + b$

$\qquad b = 0$

$C = 1.69N = 1.69(10) = \textbf{\$16.90}$

2. Overall average rate $= \dfrac{\text{overall distance}}{\text{overall time}}$
(38)

$\qquad = \dfrac{(j + k) \text{ in.}}{(t + 4t - 2) \text{ s}}$

$\qquad = \dfrac{j + k}{5t - 2} \dfrac{\text{in.}}{\text{s}}$

$\text{Time} = \dfrac{\text{distance}}{\text{rate}}$

$\qquad = \dfrac{10 \text{ in.}}{\dfrac{j + k}{5t - 2} \dfrac{\text{in.}}{\text{s}}} = \dfrac{50t - 20}{j + k} \text{ s}$

3. (a) $\text{antilog}_5 2 = 5^2 = \textbf{25}$
(67)

(b) $\text{antilog}_9 3 = 9^3 = \textbf{729}$

4. $\begin{cases} dx + cy = f \\ gx + hy = j \end{cases}$
(62)

$\qquad -dgx - cgy = -fg$

$\qquad \dfrac{dgx + dhy = dj}{(dh - cg)y = dj - fg}$

$\qquad\qquad y = \dfrac{dj - fg}{dh - cg}$

5. $\begin{cases} 9x + y = 6 \\ x + y = 10 \end{cases}$
(62, 66)

$\begin{cases} dx + cy = f \\ gx + hy = j \end{cases}$

$y = \dfrac{dj - fg}{dh - cg} = \dfrac{9(10) - 6(1)}{9(1) - 1(1)} = \dfrac{90 - 6}{9 - 1}$

$\quad = \dfrac{84}{8} = \dfrac{\textbf{21}}{\textbf{2}}$

6. $y = \log_2 x$
(65)

$2^y = x$

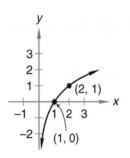

7. (a) $4 - 3i$
(64)

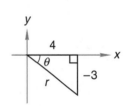

$r = \sqrt{(-3)^2 + 4^2} = 5$

$\theta = \tan^{-1}\left(\dfrac{-3}{4}\right) = -36.87°$

$\textbf{5 cis (–36.87°)}$

(b)

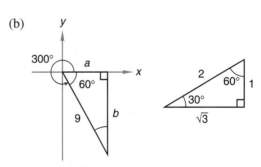

$9 \text{ cis } 300° = 9(\cos 300° + i \sin 300°)$

$= 9\left[\left(\dfrac{1}{2}\right) + i\left(-\dfrac{\sqrt{3}}{2}\right)\right] = \dfrac{\textbf{9}}{\textbf{2}} - \dfrac{\textbf{9}\sqrt{\textbf{3}}}{\textbf{2}}i$

8. $\omega = \dfrac{v}{r} = \dfrac{40 \, \frac{\text{mi}}{\text{hr}}}{18 \text{ in.}} = 40 \, \dfrac{\text{mi}}{18 \text{ hr-in.}}$
(53)

$= \dfrac{40}{18} \, \dfrac{\text{mi}}{\text{hr-in.}} \times \dfrac{12 \text{ in.}}{1 \text{ ft}} \times \dfrac{5280 \text{ ft}}{1 \text{ mi}} \times \dfrac{1 \text{ hr}}{60 \text{ min}}$

$= \dfrac{(40)(12)(5280)}{(18)(60)} \, \dfrac{\text{rad}}{\text{min}} = \mathbf{2346.67 \, \dfrac{\text{rad}}{\text{min}}}$

9. Range $= 14 - 5 = \mathbf{9}$
(61)

$\text{Mean} = \dfrac{5 + 10 + 14 + 9 + 10 + 6}{6} = \dfrac{54}{6} = \mathbf{9}$

$\text{Median} = \dfrac{9 + 10}{2} = \mathbf{9.5}$

$\text{Mode} = \mathbf{10}$

$\text{Variance} = \dfrac{4^2 + (-1)^2 + (-5)^2 + (-1)^2 + 3^2}{6}$

$= \dfrac{52}{6} = \mathbf{8.67}$

$\text{Standard deviation} = \sqrt{\dfrac{52}{6}} = \mathbf{2.94}$

10. (a) Function $= -\sin \theta$
(66)
Amplitude $= 6 - (-1) = 7$
Centerline $= -1$
Period $= 180°$
Coefficient $= \dfrac{360°}{180°} = 2$
Phase angle $= 0$
$\mathbf{y = -1 - 7 \sin 2\theta}$

(b) Function $= -\cos \theta$
Amplitude $= 20 - 11 = 9$
Centerline $= 11$
Period $= 120°$
Coefficient $= \dfrac{360°}{120°} = 3$
Phase angle $= 0$
$\mathbf{y = 11 - 9 \cos 3\theta}$

11. $7^{\log_7 4 - 2 \log_7 2} + 3^{\log_3 5 + \log_3 2} - 2 \ln e^3$
(51, 59)
$= 7^{\log_7 (4/4)} + 3^{\log_3 5(2)} - 2(3) \ln e$
$= 1 + 10 - 6 = \mathbf{5}$

12.
(64)

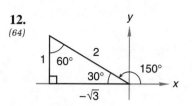

$[4 \text{ cis } (-20°)](5 \text{ cis } 170°)$
$= (4)(5) \text{ cis } [(-20°) + 170°]$
$= 20 \text{ cis } (150°) = 20(\cos 150° + i \sin 150°)$
$= 20 \left[-\dfrac{\sqrt{3}}{2} + i\left(\dfrac{1}{2}\right) \right] = \mathbf{-10\sqrt{3} + 10i}$

13. $\begin{cases} y \geq (x-1)^2 + 3 \\ y \leq x + 4 \end{cases}$
(56)

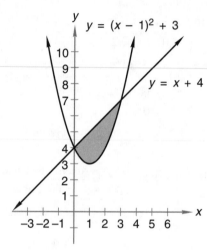

14. $x^2 + y^2 - 8x + 6y + 16 = 0$
(63)
$\left(x^2 - 8x \quad\right) + \left(y^2 + 6y \quad\right) = -16$
$\left(x^2 - 8x + 16\right) + \left(y^2 + 6y + 9\right) = 9$
$\qquad\qquad (x - 4)^2 + (y + 3)^2 = 3^2$

Center $= (4, -3)$; Radius $= 3$

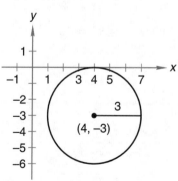

15. Mean = **357.25**
(61)

Standard deviation = **108.29**

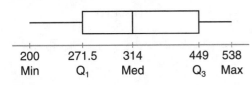

200	271.5	314	449	538
Min	Q_1	Med	Q_3	Max

16. (a) $\mu = 68, \sigma = 4$
(61)

$\mu \pm \sigma = 68 \pm 4 = 64$ to 72

About **68%** of the data points lie within one standard deviation of the mean.

(b) $\mu + \sigma = 68 + 4 = 72$

About **34%** of the data points lie on one side of the mean within one standard deviation of the mean.

17. $\ln(x + 5) = \ln 3 + \ln(x - 5)$
(51, 59)

$\ln(x + 5) = \ln 3(x - 5)$

$x + 5 = 3x - 15$

$2x = 20$

$x = \mathbf{10}$

18. Directrix: $y = -5 = k - p$
(68)

Focus: $(h, k + p) = (0, 5)$

$k + p = 5$

$\underline{k - p = -5}$

$2k \quad\quad = 0$

$k = 0$

$k + p = 5$

$0 + p = 5$

$p = 5$

Vertex: $(h, k) = \mathbf{(0, 0)}$

$y - k = \dfrac{1}{4p}(x - h)^2$

$y - 0 = \dfrac{1}{4(5)}(x - 0)^2$

$y = \dfrac{1}{20}x^2$

19. (a) $\sin 2x + \dfrac{\sqrt{3}}{2} = 0$
(50, 52)

$\sin 2x = -\dfrac{\sqrt{3}}{2}$

$2x = \dfrac{4\pi}{3}, \dfrac{5\pi}{3}, \dfrac{10\pi}{3}, \dfrac{11\pi}{3}$

$x = \dfrac{2\pi}{3}, \dfrac{5\pi}{6}, \dfrac{5\pi}{3}, \dfrac{11\pi}{6}$

(b) $(2 \sin x - 1)(2 \cos x - \sqrt{2}) = 0$

$2 \sin x - 1 = 0$

$2 \sin x = 1$

$\sin x = \dfrac{1}{2}$

$x = \dfrac{\pi}{6}, \dfrac{5\pi}{6}$

$2 \cos x - \sqrt{2} = 0$

$2 \cos x = \sqrt{2}$

$\cos x = \dfrac{\sqrt{2}}{2}$

$x = \dfrac{\pi}{4}, \dfrac{7\pi}{4}$

20.
(56)

$H = 12 \sin 60° = 6\sqrt{3}$ cm

$\text{Area} = \dfrac{B \times H}{2} = \dfrac{15 \times 6\sqrt{3}}{2} = \mathbf{77.94 \text{ cm}^2}$

Test 18, Form A

1. $ax^2 = \dfrac{1}{36}x^2$
(68)

$a = \dfrac{1}{36}$

$\dfrac{1}{4p} = \dfrac{1}{36}$

$p = \mathbf{9 \text{ ft}}$

2. Focus: $(h, k + p) = (-2, -1)$
(68)

Vertex: $(h, k) = (-2, 1)$

$k + p = -1$

$\qquad p = -1 - k$

$\qquad p = -1 - 1$

$\qquad p = -2$

$y - k = \dfrac{1}{4p}(x - h)^2$

$y - 1 = \dfrac{1}{4(-2)}(x - (-2))^2$

$\qquad y = -\dfrac{1}{8}(x + 2)^2 + 1$

Directrix: $y = k - p$

$\qquad\qquad y = 1 - (-2)$

$\qquad\qquad y = 3$

Axis of symmetry: $x = h$

$\qquad\qquad\qquad x = -2$

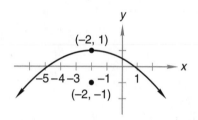

3. (a) $\text{antilog}_7 2 = 7^2 = \mathbf{49}$
(67)

(b) $\text{antilog}_8 (-2) = 8^{-2} = \dfrac{1}{8^2} = \dfrac{1}{\mathbf{64}}$

4.
(69)
$\begin{vmatrix} x + 2 & -2 \\ 1 & x \end{vmatrix} = 5$

$x(x + 2) - (1)(-2) = 5$

$\qquad x^2 + 2x + 2 = 5$

$\qquad x^2 + 2x - 3 = 0$

$\qquad (x + 3)(x - 1) = 0$

$\qquad\qquad\qquad x = \mathbf{-3, 1}$

5. $m = \dfrac{ky}{p^2 \sqrt{n}}$
(18)

$\dfrac{k(2y)}{(3p)^2 \sqrt{4n}} = \dfrac{2ky}{9p^2\, 2\sqrt{n}} = \dfrac{1}{9} \dfrac{ky}{p^2 \sqrt{n}} = \dfrac{1}{9} m$

m is divided by 9

6. $(6 \text{ cis } 72°)(-3 \text{ cis } 48°)$
(64)

$= (6)(-3) \text{ cis } (72° + 48°) = -18 \text{ cis } 120°$

$= -18(\cos 120° + i \sin 120°)$

$= -18\left(-\dfrac{1}{2} + i\,\dfrac{\sqrt{3}}{2}\right) = \mathbf{9 - 9\sqrt{3}\, i}$

7. $\dfrac{N!}{a!b!} = \dfrac{7!}{5!2!} = \mathbf{21}$
(55)

8. $\qquad R_M T_M + R_K T_K = \text{jobs}$
(25)

$\left(\dfrac{2}{3} \dfrac{\text{job}}{\text{hr}}\right)(3 \text{ hr}) + R_K(3 \text{ hr}) = 8 \text{ jobs}$

$\qquad 2 \text{ jobs} + R_K(3 \text{ hr}) = 8 \text{ jobs}$

$\qquad\qquad\qquad R_K(3 \text{ hr}) = 6 \text{ jobs}$

$\qquad\qquad\qquad\qquad R_K = 2\,\dfrac{\text{jobs}}{\text{hr}}$

$\qquad R_K T_K = 1 \text{ job}$

$\left(2\,\dfrac{\text{jobs}}{\text{hr}}\right) T_K = 1 \text{ job}$

$\qquad\qquad T_K = \dfrac{1}{2} \text{ hr}$

9. $\dfrac{x^2}{9} + \dfrac{y^2}{4} = 1$
(71)

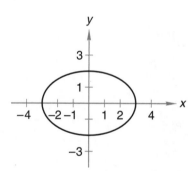

10. $\qquad \cos\theta + 2\cos^2\theta = 1$
(60)

$\qquad 2\cos^2\theta + \cos\theta - 1 = 0$

$\qquad (2\cos\theta - 1)(\cos\theta + 1) = 0$

$2\cos\theta - 1 = 0 \qquad\qquad \cos\theta + 1 = 0$

$\quad 2\cos\theta = 1 \qquad\qquad\qquad \cos\theta = -1$

$\qquad\qquad\qquad\qquad\qquad\qquad\qquad \theta = \mathbf{180°}$

$\quad \cos\theta = \dfrac{1}{2}$

$\qquad \theta = \mathbf{60°, 300°}$

11. Range $= 7 - 1 = $ **6**
(61)

Mean $= \dfrac{5 + 1 + 7 + 2 + 5 + 4}{6} = \dfrac{24}{6} = $ **4**

Median $= \dfrac{4 + 5}{2} = $ **4.5**

Mode $= $ **5**

Variance $= \dfrac{(-1)^2 + 3^2 + (-3)^2 + 2^2 + (-1)^2}{6}$

$= \dfrac{24}{6} = $ **4**

Standard deviation $= \sqrt{\dfrac{24}{6}} = $ **2**

12. $2(180 - A) = 5(90 - A) + 126$
(1)
$360 - 2A = 450 - 5A + 126$
$3A = 216$
$A = $ **72°**

13.
(72)

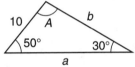

$A = 180° - 30° - 50°$
$A = $ **100°**

$\dfrac{b}{\sin 50°} = \dfrac{10}{\sin 30°}$

$b = \dfrac{10 \sin 50°}{\sin 30°}$

$b = $ **15.32**

$\dfrac{a}{\sin 100°} = \dfrac{10}{\sin 30°}$

$a = \dfrac{10 \sin 100°}{\sin 30°}$

$a = $ **19.70**

14.
(56)

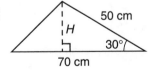

$H = 50 \sin 30° = 25$ cm

Area $= \dfrac{1}{2}BH = \dfrac{1}{2}(70)(25) = $ **875 cm²**

15. $\begin{cases} (x - 4)^2 + y^2 \geq 4^2 \\ y \geq (x - 4)^2 \end{cases}$
(56)

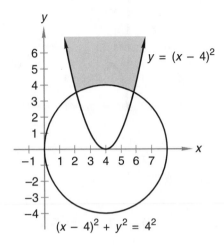

16. (a) $\log 10 - \ln e = 1 - 1 = $ **0**
(51, 59)

(b) $\log 10^3 + \log 10^{1/3} = 3 + \dfrac{1}{3} = \dfrac{10}{3}$

(c) $\log_3 9 + 3^{\log_3 7} = 2 + 7 = $ **9**

17. $\dfrac{2}{3}\log_4 8 - 3 \log_4 x = \log_4 4$
(59)
$\log_4 8^{2/3} - \log_4 x^3 = \log_4 4$

$\log_4 \dfrac{8^{2/3}}{x^3} = \log_4 4$

$\dfrac{4}{x^3} = 4$

$4x^3 = 4$

$x^3 = 1$

$x = $ **1**

18. $\ln x + \ln (x + 2) = \ln 3$
(51, 59)
$\ln [x(x + 2)] = \ln 3$
$x(x + 2) = 3$
$x^2 + 2x - 3 = 0$
$(x + 3)(x - 1) = 0$
$x = 1, -3$
$x = $ **1**

19. $y = \log_4 x$
(65)

$4^y = x$

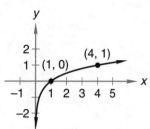

20. z score $= \dfrac{x - \mu}{\sigma} = \dfrac{2.7 - 3.2}{0.5} = -1.0$
(70)

$.1587 = \mathbf{15.87\%}$

3. (a) $\text{antilog}_3 3 = 3^3 = \mathbf{27}$
(67)

(b) $\text{antilog}_5 (-2) = 5^{-2} = \dfrac{1}{5^2} = \mathbf{\dfrac{1}{25}}$

4.
(69)
$$\begin{vmatrix} x + 1 & -3 \\ 4 & x \end{vmatrix} = 18$$

$$x(x + 1) - (4)(-3) = 18$$

$$x^2 + x + 12 = 18$$

$$x^2 + x - 6 = 0$$

$$(x + 3)(x - 2) = 0$$

$$x = \mathbf{-3, 2}$$

Test 18, Form B

1. $ax^2 = \dfrac{1}{16}x^2$
(68)

$a = \dfrac{1}{16}$

$\dfrac{1}{4p} = \dfrac{1}{16}$

$p = \mathbf{4\ ft}$

2. Focus: $(h, k + p) = (2, 1)$
(68)

Vertex: $(h, k) = (2, -1)$

$k + p = 1$

$\quad p = 1 - k$

$\quad p = 1 - (-1)$

$\quad p = 2$

$$y - k = \dfrac{1}{4p}(x - h)^2$$

$$y - (-1) = \dfrac{1}{4(2)}(x - 2)^2$$

$$y = \mathbf{\dfrac{1}{8}(x - 2)^2 - 1}$$

Directrix: $y = k - p$

$\quad\quad\quad y = (-1) - 2$

$\quad\quad\quad y = \mathbf{-3}$

Axis of symmetry: $x = h$

$\quad\quad\quad\quad\quad\quad x = \mathbf{2}$

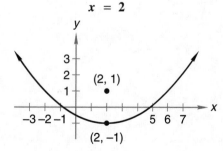

5. $t = \dfrac{km}{y^2 \sqrt{n}}$
(18)

$$\dfrac{k(3m)}{(5y)^2 \sqrt{9n}} = \dfrac{3km}{25y^2 3\sqrt{n}} = \dfrac{1}{25}\dfrac{km}{y^2 \sqrt{n}} = \dfrac{1}{25}t$$

t **is divided by 25**

6. $(2\ \text{cis}\ 84°)(-3\ \text{cis}\ 66°)$
(64)

$= 2(-3)\ \text{cis}\ (84° + 66°) = -6\ \text{cis}\ 150°$

$= -6(\cos 150° + i \sin 150°)$

$= -6\left(-\dfrac{\sqrt{3}}{2} + \dfrac{1}{2}i\right) = \mathbf{3\sqrt{3} - 3i}$

7. $\dfrac{N!}{a!b!} = \dfrac{7!}{4!3!} = \mathbf{35}$
(55)

8.
(25)
$$R_J T_J + R_B T_B = \text{jobs}$$

$$\left(\dfrac{3}{5}\dfrac{\text{job}}{\text{hr}}\right)(25\ \text{hr}) + R_B(25\ \text{hr}) = 65\ \text{jobs}$$

$$15\ \text{jobs} + R_B(25\ \text{hr}) = 65\ \text{jobs}$$

$$R_B(25\ \text{hr}) = 50\ \text{jobs}$$

$$R_B = 2\ \dfrac{\text{jobs}}{\text{hr}}$$

$$R_B T_B = 1\ \text{job}$$

$$\left(2\ \dfrac{\text{jobs}}{\text{hr}}\right)T_B = 1\ \text{job}$$

$$T_B = \mathbf{\dfrac{1}{2}\ hr}$$

9. $\dfrac{x^2}{16} + \dfrac{y^2}{1} = 1$
(71)

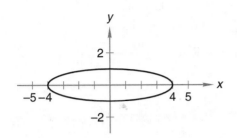

10. $\sin \theta + 2 \sin^2 \theta = 1$
(60)

$2 \sin^2 \theta + \sin \theta - 1 = 0$

$(2 \sin \theta - 1)(\sin \theta + 1) = 0$

$2 \sin \theta - 1 = 0 \qquad \qquad \sin \theta + 1 = 0$

$2 \sin \theta = 1 \qquad \qquad \sin \theta = -1$

$\sin \theta = \dfrac{1}{2} \qquad \qquad \boldsymbol{\theta = 270°}$

$\boldsymbol{\theta = 30°, 150°}$

11. Range $= 7 - 1 = \boldsymbol{6}$
(61)

Mean $= \dfrac{2 + 1 + 7 + 2 + 4 + 2}{6} = \dfrac{18}{6} = \boldsymbol{3}$

Median $= \dfrac{2 + 2}{2} = \boldsymbol{2}$

Mode $= \boldsymbol{2}$

Variance $=$

$\dfrac{1^2 + 2^2 + (-4)^2 + 1^2 + (-1)^2 + 1^2}{6}$

$= \dfrac{24}{6} = \boldsymbol{4}$

Standard deviation $= \sqrt{\dfrac{24}{6}} = \boldsymbol{2}$

12. $2(180 - A) = 5(90 - A) + 69$
(1)

$360 - 2A = 450 - 5A + 69$

$3A = 159$

$A = \boldsymbol{53°}$

13.
(72)

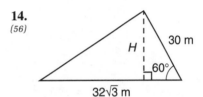

$A = 180° - 30° - 70°$

$\boldsymbol{A = 80°}$

$\dfrac{b}{\sin 30°} = \dfrac{10}{\sin 70°}$

$b = \dfrac{10 \sin 30°}{\sin 70°}$

$\boldsymbol{b = 5.32}$

$\dfrac{a}{\sin 80°} = \dfrac{10}{\sin 70°}$

$a = \dfrac{10 \sin 80°}{\sin 70°}$

$\boldsymbol{a = 10.48}$

14.
(56)

$H = 30 \sin 60° = 15\sqrt{3}\ \text{m}$

Area $= \dfrac{1}{2}BH = \dfrac{1}{2}\left(32\sqrt{3}\right)\left(15\sqrt{3}\right) = \boldsymbol{720\ \text{m}^2}$

15. $\begin{cases} (x - 3)^2 + y^2 \le 4^2 \\ y \le (x - 3)^2 \end{cases}$
(56)

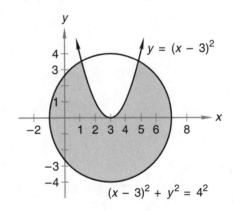

16. (a) $\ln e - \log 10 = 1 - 1 = \boldsymbol{0}$
(51, 59)

(b) $\log 10^4 + \log 10^{1/4} = 4 + \dfrac{1}{4} = \boldsymbol{\dfrac{17}{4}}$

(c) $\log_4 16 + 4^{\log_4 5} = 2 + 5 = \boldsymbol{7}$

17. $\frac{3}{2}\log_8 9 - \log_8 x = \log_8 9$
(59)

$$\log_8 9^{3/2} - \log_8 x = \log_8 9$$

$$\log_8 \frac{9^{3/2}}{x} = \log_8 9$$

$$\frac{27}{x} = 9$$

$$9x = 27$$

$$x = 3$$

18. $\ln x + \ln(x + 4) = \ln 5$
(51, 59)

$$\ln[x(x + 4)] = \ln 5$$

$$x(x + 4) = 5$$

$$x^2 + 4x - 5 = 0$$

$$(x + 5)(x - 1) = 0$$

$$x = 1, -5$$

$$x = 1$$

19. $y = \log_6 x$
(65)

$$6^y = x$$

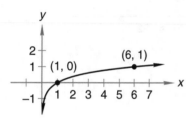

20. z score $= \frac{x - \mu}{\sigma} = \frac{2.8 - 2.5}{0.2} = 1.5$
(70)

$$.9332 = \mathbf{93.32\%}$$

Test 19, Form A

1.
(25)

$$R_G T_G + R_D T_D = \text{choc.}$$

$$\left(\frac{7}{3}\,\frac{\text{choc.}}{\text{min}}\right)T + \left(\frac{11}{4}\,\frac{\text{choc.}}{\text{min}}\right)(T - 2\text{ min}) = 45\text{ choc.}$$

$$\left(\frac{7}{3}\,\frac{\text{choc.}}{\text{min}}\right)T + \left(\frac{11}{4}\,\frac{\text{choc.}}{\text{min}}\right)T - \frac{11}{2}\text{ choc.} = 45\text{ choc.}$$

$$\left(\frac{61}{12}\,\frac{\text{choc.}}{\text{min}}\right)T = \frac{101}{2}\text{ choc.}$$

$$T = \frac{606}{61}\text{ min}$$

$$T = \mathbf{9.93\ min}$$

2. Students $= S$ seniors
(44)

Price $= 1000$ dollars

$$\text{Rate} = \frac{1000}{S}\,\frac{\text{dollars}}{\text{senior}}$$

$$\text{New Rate} = \frac{1000}{S - 20}\,\frac{\text{dollars}}{\text{senior}}$$

$$\text{Increase} = \frac{1000}{S - 20} - \frac{1000}{S}$$

$$= \frac{1000S - 1000(S - 20)}{S(S - 20)}$$

$$= \frac{1000S - 1000S + 20{,}000}{S^2 - 20S}$$

$$= \frac{\mathbf{20{,}000}}{S^2 - 20S}\,\frac{\textbf{dollars}}{\textbf{senior}}$$

3. $y = \dfrac{\begin{vmatrix} 7 & 5 \\ 3 & 6 \end{vmatrix}}{\begin{vmatrix} 7 & -2 \\ 3 & 4 \end{vmatrix}} = \dfrac{42 - 15}{28 + 6} = \dfrac{\mathbf{27}}{\mathbf{34}}$
(74)

4.
(73)

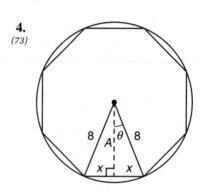

$$\theta = \frac{1}{2}\left(\frac{360°}{8}\right) = 22.5°$$

$$x = 8\sin 22.5° = 3.0615\text{ in.}$$

$$A = 8\cos 22.5° = 7.391\text{ in.}$$

$$\text{Area}_\Delta = \frac{3.0615 \times 7.391}{2} = 11.314\text{ in.}^2$$

$$\text{Area} = 16(11.314\text{ in.}^2) = \mathbf{181.02\ in.^2}$$

5. $9x^2 + 9y^2 - 18x + 36y - 36 = 0$
(63)

$$x^2 + y^2 - 2x + 4y = 4$$

$$(x^2 - 2x \quad) + (y^2 + 4y \quad) = 4$$

$$(x^2 - 2x + 1) + (y^2 + 4y + 4) = 9$$

$$(x - 1)^2 + (y + 2)^2 = 3^2$$

$$\textbf{Radius = 3; Center = (1, -2)}$$

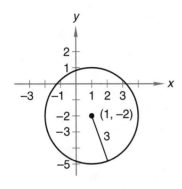

6. z score $= \dfrac{x - \mu}{\sigma} = \dfrac{75 - 50}{10} = 2.5$
(70)

$1 - 0.9938 = 0.0062 = \mathbf{0.62\%}$

7. $_nC_r = \dfrac{n!}{(n - r)!\,r!}$
(75)

$_{10}C_7 = \dfrac{10!}{(10 - 7)!\,7!} = \dfrac{10 \cdot 9 \cdot 8 \cdot 7!}{3 \cdot 2 \cdot 1 \cdot 7!} = \mathbf{120}$

8. $(3 \text{ cis } 110°)(4 \text{ cis } 100°) = (3)(4) \text{ cis } (110° + 100°)$
(64)

$= 12 \text{ cis } 210° = 12(\cos 210° + i \sin 210°)$

$= 12\left(-\dfrac{\sqrt{3}}{2} - \dfrac{1}{2}i\right) = \mathbf{-6\sqrt{3} - 6i}$

9. $\sec^2 x - 4 = 0$
(60)

$\sec^2 x = 4$

$\sec x = \pm 2$

$\cos x = \pm \dfrac{1}{2}$

$x = \dfrac{\pi}{3}, \dfrac{2\pi}{3}, \dfrac{4\pi}{3}, \dfrac{5\pi}{3}$

10. $c + 1.2c = 4.40$
(18)

$2.2c = 4.40$

$c = 2.00$

$c + 0.7c = 2.00 + 0.7(2.00) = \mathbf{\$3.40}$

11. Focus: $(h, k + p) = (4, 4)$
(68)

Vertex: $(h, k) = (4, -2)$

$k + p = 4$

$p = 4 - k = 4 - (-2) = 6$

$y - k = \dfrac{1}{4p}(x - h)^2$

$y - (-2) = \dfrac{1}{4(6)}(x - 4)^2$

$y = \dfrac{1}{24}(x - 4)^2 - 2$

Directrix: $y = k - p$

$y = -2 - 6$

$y = \mathbf{-8}$

Axis of symmetry: $x = h$

$x = \mathbf{4}$

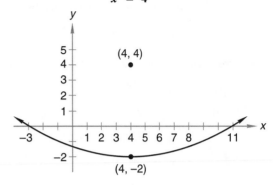

12. $\begin{cases} 3^2 \le x^2 + (y - 3)^2 \\ y > 3x + 3 \end{cases}$
(56)

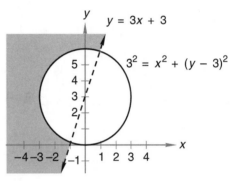

13. $\begin{vmatrix} 1 & d+3 \\ 1-d & 4 \end{vmatrix} = 4$
(69)

$4 - (1 - d)(d + 3) = 4$

$4 - (d + 3 - d^2 - 3d) = 4$

$d^2 + 2d + 1 = 4$

$d^2 + 2d - 3 = 0$

$(d + 3)(d - 1) = 0$

$d = \mathbf{-3, 1}$

14. $\dfrac{x^2}{4} + \dfrac{y^2}{16} = 1$
(71)

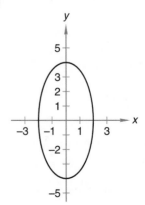

15. A_N = Anna's age now
(25)

B_N = Brandi's age now

$A_N + 3$ = Anna's age 3 years from now

$B_N - 9$ = Brandi's age 9 years ago

$B_N + 6$ = Brandi's age 6 years from now

$$\begin{cases} A_N = B_N - 7 \\ A_N + 3 = 2(B_N - 9) \end{cases}$$

$$A_N + 3 = 2(B_N - 9)$$
$$A_N = 2B_N - 21$$
$$A_N = B_N - 7$$
$$(2B_N - 21) = B_N - 7$$
$$B_N = 14$$

$$B_N + 6 = \textbf{20 yr}$$

16. $f\left(\dfrac{2\pi}{3}\right) + g\left(\dfrac{5\pi}{4}\right)f\left(\dfrac{3\pi}{2}\right)$
(39, 48)

$$= \sin^2\left(\dfrac{2\pi}{3}\right) + \cos^2\left(\dfrac{5\pi}{4}\right)\sin^2\left(\dfrac{3\pi}{2}\right)$$

$$= \sin^2(120°) + \cos^2(225°)\sin^2(270°)$$

$$= \left(\dfrac{\sqrt{3}}{2}\right)^2 + \left(-\dfrac{1}{\sqrt{2}}\right)^2(-1)^2 = \dfrac{3}{4} + \dfrac{1}{2} = \textbf{\dfrac{5}{4}}$$

17. $3\log_2 x - \dfrac{1}{2}\log_2 16 = 4$
(59)

$$\log_2 x^3 - \log_2 16^{(1/2)} = 4$$

$$\log_2 \dfrac{x^3}{\sqrt{16}} = 4$$

$$\dfrac{x^3}{4} = 2^4$$

$$x^3 = 64$$

$$x = \textbf{4}$$

18. $\csc x \tan x = \dfrac{1}{\sin x} \cdot \dfrac{\sin x}{\cos x} = \dfrac{1}{\cos x} = \textbf{sec } x$
(76)

19. Function $= \sin\theta$
(66)

Amplitude $= 3 - (-3) = 6$

Centerline $= -3$

Period $= 600°$

Coefficient $= \dfrac{360°}{600°} = \dfrac{3}{5}$

Phase angle $= 0°$

$$y = \textbf{-3} + \textbf{6 sin } \dfrac{\textbf{3}}{\textbf{5}}\boldsymbol{\theta}$$

20. $A = 180 - 125 - 25$
(72)

$$A = \textbf{30°}$$

$$\dfrac{b}{\sin 25°} = \dfrac{18}{\sin 125°}$$

$$b = \dfrac{18\sin 25°}{\sin 125°}$$

$$b = \textbf{9.29}$$

$$\dfrac{a}{\sin 30°} = \dfrac{18}{\sin 125°}$$

$$a = \dfrac{18\sin 30°}{\sin 125°}$$

$$a = \textbf{10.99}$$

Test 19, Form B

1. $\qquad R_J T_J + R_A T_A$ = holes
(25)

$$\left(\dfrac{5}{20}\dfrac{\text{hole}}{\text{min}}\right)T + \left(\dfrac{6}{30}\dfrac{\text{hole}}{\text{min}}\right)(T - 2\text{ min}) = 18\text{ holes}$$

$$\left(\dfrac{1}{4}\dfrac{\text{hole}}{\text{min}}\right)T + \left(\dfrac{1}{5}\dfrac{\text{hole}}{\text{min}}\right)T - \dfrac{2}{5}\text{ holes} = 18\text{ holes}$$

$$\left(\dfrac{9}{20}\dfrac{\text{hole}}{\text{min}}\right)T = \dfrac{92}{5}\text{ holes}$$

$$T = \dfrac{368}{9}\text{ min}$$

$$T = \textbf{40.89 min}$$

2. Students = J juniors
(44)

Price = 2000 dollars

Rate $= \dfrac{2000}{J}\dfrac{\text{dollars}}{\text{junior}}$

New Rate $= \dfrac{2000}{J - 30}\dfrac{\text{dollars}}{\text{junior}}$

Increase $= \dfrac{2000}{J - 30} - \dfrac{2000}{J}$

$$= \dfrac{2000J - 2000(J - 30)}{J(J - 30)}$$

$$= \dfrac{2000J - 2000J + 60,000}{J^2 - 30J}$$

$$= \dfrac{\textbf{60,000}}{J^2 - 30J}\dfrac{\textbf{dollars}}{\textbf{junior}}$$

3. $y = \dfrac{\begin{vmatrix} 2 & 11 \\ 3 & 9 \end{vmatrix}}{\begin{vmatrix} 2 & 4 \\ 3 & -2 \end{vmatrix}} = \dfrac{18 - 33}{-4 - 12} = \dfrac{-15}{-16} = \textbf{\dfrac{15}{16}}$
(74)

4.
(73)

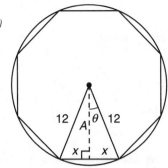

$$\theta = \frac{1}{2}\left(\frac{360°}{8}\right) = 22.5°$$

$x = 12 \sin 22.5° = 4.592 \text{ cm}$

$A = 12 \cos 22.5° = 11.087 \text{ cm}$

$$\text{Area}_\triangle = \frac{4.592 \times 11.087}{2} = 25.456 \text{ cm}^2$$

$\text{Area} = 16(25.456 \text{ cm}^2) = \textbf{407.30 cm}^2$

5.
(63)

$$3x^2 + 3y^2 - 18x + 24y = 0$$
$$x^2 + y^2 - 6x + 8y = 0$$
$$(x^2 - 6x \quad) + (y^2 + 8y \quad) = 0$$
$$(x^2 - 6x + 9) + (y^2 + 8y + 16) = 25$$
$$(x - 3)^2 + (y + 4)^2 = 5^2$$

Radius = 5; Center = (3, −4)

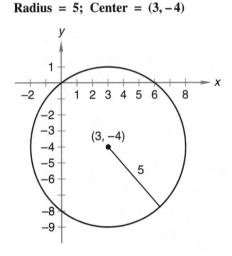

6. $z \text{ score} = \dfrac{x - \mu}{\sigma} = \dfrac{140 - 100}{20} = 2$
(70)

$1 - 0.9772 = 0.0228 = \textbf{2.28\%}$

7. $_nC_r = \dfrac{n!}{(n - r)!\,r!}$
(75)

$_{11}C_8 = \dfrac{11!}{(11 - 8)!\,8!} = \dfrac{11 \cdot 10 \cdot 9 \cdot 8!}{3 \cdot 2 \cdot 1 \cdot 8!} = \textbf{165}$

8. $(5 \text{ cis } 100°)(4 \text{ cis } 230°) = (5)(4) \text{ cis } (100° + 230°)$
(64)

$= 20 \text{ cis } 330° = 20(\cos 330° + i \sin 330°)$

$= 20\left(\dfrac{\sqrt{3}}{2} + i\left(\dfrac{-1}{2}\right)\right) = \textbf{10}\sqrt{\textbf{3}} - \textbf{10}\textbf{\textit{i}}$

9. $\csc^2 x - 4 = 0$
(60)

$$\csc^2 x = 4$$
$$\csc x = \pm 2$$
$$\sin x = \pm\frac{1}{2}$$
$$x = \frac{\pi}{6}, \frac{5\pi}{6}, \frac{7\pi}{6}, \frac{11\pi}{6}$$

10. $c + 1.3c = 57.50$
(18)

$$2.3c = 57.50$$
$$c = 25.00$$

$c + 0.8c = 25.00 + 0.8(25.00) = \textbf{\$45.00}$

11. Focus: $(h, k + p) = (3, 1)$
(68)

Vertex: $(h, k) = (3, -3)$

$$k + p = 1$$
$$p = 1 - k$$
$$p = 1 - (-3)$$
$$p = 4$$

$$y - k = \frac{1}{4p}(x - h)^2$$
$$y - (-3) = \frac{1}{4(4)}(x - 3)^2$$
$$y = \frac{1}{16}(x - 3)^2 - 3$$

Directrix: $y = k - p$
$$y = (-3) - 4$$
$$y = -7$$

Axis of symmetry: $x = h$
$$x = 3$$

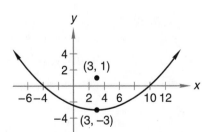

12.
(56)
$$\begin{cases} 2^2 \le x^2 + (y - 2)^2 \\ y < 2x - 1 \end{cases}$$

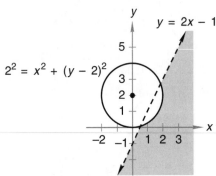

13.
(69)
$$\begin{vmatrix} a + 2 & 3 \\ 5 & a - 3 \end{vmatrix} = 9$$

$(a + 2)(a - 3) - 15 = 9$

$(a^2 - a - 6) - 15 = 9$

$a^2 - a - 21 = 9$

$a^2 - a - 30 = 0$

$(a + 5)(a - 6) = 0$

$a = -5, 6$

14.
(71)
$$\frac{x^2}{9} + \frac{y^2}{25} = 1$$

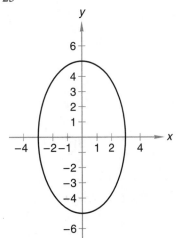

15. T_N = Thor's age now
(25)
L_N = Loki's age now

$L_N + 600$ = Loki's age 600 years from now

$T_N + 200$ = Thor's age 200 years from now

$T_N - 500$ = Thor's age 500 years ago

$$\begin{cases} T_N = L_N + 300 \\ L_N + 600 = 3(T_N - 500) \end{cases}$$

$L_N + 600 = 3(T_N - 1500)$

$L_N = 3T_N - 2100$

$T_N = L_N + 300$

$T_N = (3T_N - 2100) + 300$

$2T_N = 1800$

$T_N = 900$

$T_N + 200 = \textbf{1100 yr}$

16. $f\left(\dfrac{3\pi}{4}\right) + g\left(\dfrac{2\pi}{3}\right)f\left(\dfrac{3\pi}{2}\right)$
(39, 48)

$= \sin^2\left(\dfrac{3\pi}{4}\right) + \cos^2\left(\dfrac{2\pi}{3}\right)\sin^2\left(\dfrac{3\pi}{2}\right)$

$= \sin^2(135°) + \cos^2(120°)\sin^2(270°)$

$= \left(\dfrac{\sqrt{2}}{2}\right)^2 + \left(-\dfrac{1}{2}\right)^2(-1)^2 = \dfrac{2}{4} + \dfrac{1}{4} = \dfrac{3}{4}$

17. $3\log_2 x - \dfrac{1}{3}\log_2 8 = 5$
(59)

$\log_2 x^3 - \log_2 8^{(1/3)} = 5$

$\log_2 \dfrac{x^3}{2} = 5$

$\dfrac{x^3}{2} = 2^5$

$x^3 = 64$

$x = \textbf{4}$

18. $\sec x \cot x = \dfrac{1}{\cos x} \cdot \dfrac{\cos x}{\sin x} = \dfrac{1}{\sin x} = \textbf{csc } \textbf{\textit{x}}$
(76)

19. Function $= \cos \theta$
(66)
Amplitude $= 7 - (-1) = 8$

Centerline $= -1$

Period $= 540°$

Coefficient $= \dfrac{360°}{540°} = \dfrac{2}{3}$

Phase angle $= 135°$

$y = -1 + 8\cos\dfrac{2}{3}(\theta - 135°)$

20. $A = 180 - 120 - 33$
(72)
$A = \textbf{27}°$

$$\dfrac{b}{\sin 33°} = \dfrac{22}{\sin 120°}$$

$$b = \dfrac{22\sin 33°}{\sin 120°}$$

$b = \textbf{13.84}$

$$\frac{a}{\sin 27°} = \frac{22}{\sin 120°}$$

$$a = \frac{22 \sin 27°}{\sin 120°}$$

$$a = 11.53$$

Test 20, Form A

1. Exponents for x: 6 5 $\boxed{4}$ 3 2 1 0
(77) Exponents for y: 0 1 $\boxed{2}$ 3 4 5 6

Seventh row of Pascal's triangle:

1 6 $\boxed{15}$ 20 15 6 1

$$\mathbf{15x^4y^2}$$

2. Exponents for a: 4 3 2 1 0
(77) Exponents for b: 0 1 2 3 4

Fifth row of Pascal's triangle: 1 4 6 4 1

$$\mathbf{a^4 + 4a^3b + 6a^2b^2 + 4ab^3 + b^4}$$

3. $\qquad\qquad \log_2(x + 3) = \log_2(7 - x) + 2$
(59) $\log_2(x + 3) - \log_2(7 - x) = 2$

$$\log_2 \frac{x + 3}{7 - x} = 2$$

$$\frac{x + 3}{7 - x} = 2^2$$

$$x + 3 = 28 - 4x$$

$$5x = 25$$

$$\mathbf{x = 5}$$

4. $2x^2 + 18y^2 - 162 = 0$
(71)

$$2x^2 + 18y^2 = 162$$

$$\frac{x^2}{81} + \frac{y^2}{9} = 1$$

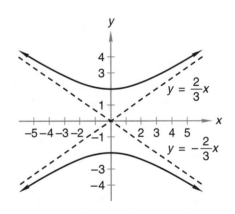

5. $\dfrac{\csc^2 x - \cot^2 x}{1 + \tan^2 x} = \dfrac{1}{\sec^2 x} = \mathbf{\cos^2 x}$
(76, 80)

6. $\qquad \begin{vmatrix} x + 2 & 2 \\ x + 1 & x + 8 \end{vmatrix} = 2$
(69)

$$(x + 2)(x + 8) - 2(x + 1) = 2$$

$$x^2 + 10x + 16 - 2x - 2 - 2 = 0$$

$$x^2 + 8x + 12 = 0$$

$$(x + 2)(x + 6) = 0$$

$$\mathbf{x = -2, -6}$$

7. $36y^2 - 16x^2 - 144 = 0$
(78)

$$36y^2 - 16x^2 = 144$$

$$\frac{y^2}{4} - \frac{x^2}{9} = 1$$

let $x = 0$, $y = \pm 2$

let $y = 0$, $x = \pm 3i$

Vertices $= \mathbf{(0, 2), (0, -2)}$

Asymptotes: $y = \dfrac{2}{3}x, \; y = -\dfrac{2}{3}x$

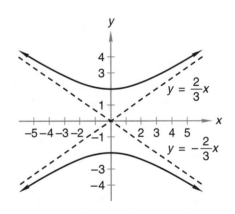

8. $r = \sqrt{1^2 + \left(-\sqrt{3}\right)^2} = 2$
(79)

$$\theta = \tan^{-1}\left(\frac{-\sqrt{3}}{1}\right) = 300°$$

$$\left(1 - \sqrt{3}i\right)^3 = (2 \text{ cis } 300°)^3$$

$$= 2^3 \text{ cis } [(3)(300°)] = 8 \text{ cis } 900° = 8 \text{ cis } 180°$$

$$= 8(\cos 180° + i \sin 180°) = 8(-1 + 0i) = \mathbf{-8}$$

9. $A = 180° - 100° - 35°$
(72)
$A = \mathbf{45°}$

$$\frac{c}{\sin 100°} = \frac{10}{\sin 35°}$$

$$c = \frac{10 \sin 100°}{\sin 35°}$$

$$c = \mathbf{17.17\ in.}$$

$$\frac{a}{\sin 45°} = \frac{10}{\sin 35°}$$

$$a = \frac{10 \sin 45°}{\sin 35°}$$

$$a = \mathbf{12.33\ in.}$$

10. Function $= \cos x$
(47, 66)
Amplitude $= 4 - (-6) = 10$

Centerline $= -6$

Period $= \dfrac{7\pi}{3} - \dfrac{\pi}{3} = 2\pi$

Coefficient $= \dfrac{2\pi}{2\pi} = 1$

Phase angle $= \dfrac{\pi}{3}$

$$y = \mathbf{-6 + 10 \cos \left(x - \frac{\pi}{3} \right)}$$

11. $[4 \text{ cis } (-45°)](-3 \text{ cis } 180°)$
(64)
$= (4)(-3) \text{ cis } (180° - 45°) = -12 \text{ cis } 135°$

$= -12(\cos 135° + i \sin 135°)$

$$= -12 \left(\frac{-\sqrt{2}}{2} + \frac{\sqrt{2}}{2} i \right) = \mathbf{6\sqrt{2} - 6\sqrt{2}\,i}$$

12.
(73)

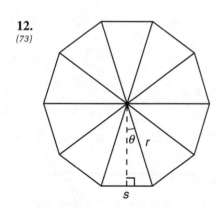

$$s = \frac{40}{10} = \mathbf{4\ cm}$$

$$\theta = \frac{1}{2} \left(\frac{360}{10} \right) = 18°$$

$$\sin \theta = \frac{\frac{1}{2}s}{r}$$

$$r = \frac{\frac{1}{2}s}{\sin \theta} = \frac{2}{\sin 18°} = \mathbf{6.47\ cm}$$

13. $\dfrac{\text{Side}_S}{\text{Side}_L} = \dfrac{4}{5}$
(5)

$$\frac{\text{Area}_S}{\text{Area}_L} = \left(\frac{\text{Side}_S}{\text{Side}_L} \right)^2 = \left(\frac{4}{5} \right)^2 = \mathbf{\frac{16}{25}}$$

14. $C = mN + b$
(62)

(a) $\begin{cases} 5600 = m10 + b \\ 3000 = m5 + b \end{cases}$
(b)

(a) $\quad\ \ 5600 = \ \ m10 + b$
(−b) $\ \ -3000 = -m5 \ - b$
$\qquad\overline{\ \ 2600 = \ \ m5}$
$\qquad\qquad m = 520$

(b) $3000 = 520(5) + b$
$\qquad b = 400$

$C = 520N + 400 = 520(4) + 400 = \mathbf{\$2480}$

15. $B = 6C$
(36)
Upstream:

$$(B - C)T_U = D_U$$
$$5CT_U = 100$$
$$CT_U = 20$$

Downstream:

$$(B + C)T_D = D_D$$
$$7C(T_U - 3) = 14$$
$$7CT_U - 21C = 14$$
$$CT_U - 3C = 2$$
$$(20) - 3C = 2$$
$$3C = 18$$
$$C = 6$$

$$B = 6C = \mathbf{36\ mph}$$

16.
(75)
$$_nC_r = \frac{n!}{(n-r)!r!}$$

$$_5C_2 = \frac{5!}{(5-2)!2!} = \frac{5 \cdot 4 \cdot 3!}{2 \cdot 1 \cdot 3!} = \mathbf{10}$$

17.
(79)
$$(125 \text{ cis } 60°)^{1/3} = \sqrt[3]{125} \text{ cis } \frac{60°}{3} = \mathbf{5 \text{ cis } 20°}$$

Angles differ by $\frac{360°}{3} = 120°$.

$5 \text{ cis } (20° + 120°) = \mathbf{5 \text{ cis } 140°}$

$5 \text{ cis } (20° + 240°) = \mathbf{5 \text{ cis } 260°}$

18. $1 = 1 \text{ cis } 0°$
(79)

$$\sqrt[3]{1}\left(\text{cis } \frac{0°}{3}\right) = 1 \text{ cis } 0° = 1(\cos 0° + i \sin 0°)$$

$$= 1(1 + 0i) = \mathbf{1}$$

$1 \text{ cis } (0° + 120°) = 1(\cos 120° + i \sin 120°)$

$$= 1\left(-\frac{1}{2} + \frac{\sqrt{3}}{2}i\right) = \mathbf{-\frac{1}{2} + \frac{\sqrt{3}}{2}i}$$

$1 \text{ cis } (0° + 240°) = 1(\cos 240° + i \sin 240°)$

$$= 1\left(-\frac{1}{2} - \frac{\sqrt{3}}{2}i\right) = \mathbf{-\frac{1}{2} - \frac{\sqrt{3}}{2}i}$$

19. $y = -\log_3 x$
(65)
$$y = \log_3 x^{-1}$$
$$x^{-1} = 3^y$$
$$x = \left(\frac{1}{3}\right)^y$$

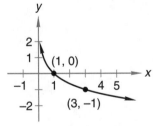

20. Focus: $(h, k+p) = (-2, 6)$
(68)
Vertex: $(h, k) = (-2, 0)$

$k + p = 6$
$\quad p = 6 - k = 6 - 0 = 6$

$$y - k = \frac{1}{4p}(x - h)^2$$

$$y - 0 = \frac{1}{4(6)}(x + 2)^2$$

$$y = \frac{1}{24}(x + 2)^2$$

Directrix: $y = k - p$
$\qquad\qquad y = 0 - 6$
$\qquad\qquad \mathbf{y = -6}$

Axis of symmetry: $x = h$
$\qquad\qquad\qquad\quad \mathbf{x = -2}$

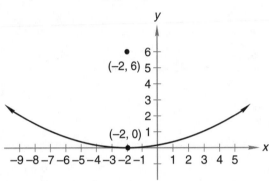

Test 20, Form B

1. Exponents for x: 5 4 3 $\boxed{2}$ 1 0
(77)
Exponents for y: 0 1 2 $\boxed{3}$ 4 5

Sixth row of Pascal's triangle:

1 5 10 $\boxed{10}$ 5 1

$\mathbf{10x^2y^3}$

2. Exponents for a: 5 4 3 2 1 0
(77)
Exponents for b: 0 1 2 3 4 5

Sixth row of Pascal's triangle: 1 5 10 10 5 1

$\mathbf{a^5 + 5a^4b + 10a^3b^2 + 10a^2b^3 + 5ab^4 + b^5}$

3.
(59)
$$\log_3(x + 1) = \log_3(1 - x) + 1$$

$$\log_3(x + 1) - \log_3(1 - x) = 1$$

$$\log_3 \frac{x + 1}{1 - x} = 1$$

$$\frac{x + 1}{1 - x} = 3^1$$

$$x + 1 = 3 - 3x$$

$$4x = 2$$

$$x = \frac{1}{2}$$

4. $20x^2 + 45y^2 - 180 = 0$
(71)
$$20x^2 + 45y^2 = 180$$
$$\frac{x^2}{9} + \frac{y^2}{4} = 1$$

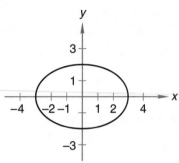

5. $\dfrac{\sec^2 x - \tan^2 x}{1 + \cot^2 x} = \dfrac{1}{\csc^2 x} = \sin^2 x$
(76, 80)

6. $\begin{vmatrix} x + 3 & x \\ x - 1 & 2x - 1 \end{vmatrix} = -8$
(69)
$$(x + 3)(2x - 1) - (x - 1)(x) = -8$$
$$2x^2 + 5x - 3 - x^2 + x + 8 = 0$$
$$x^2 + 6x + 5 = 0$$
$$(x + 5)(x + 1) = 0$$
$$x = -5, -1$$

7. $32x^2 - 50y^2 - 800 = 0$
(78)
$$32x^2 - 50y^2 = 800$$
$$\frac{x^2}{25} - \frac{y^2}{16} = 1$$

let $y = 0$, $x = \pm 5$

let $x = 0$, $y = \pm 4i$

Vertices = (5, 0), (–5, 0)

Asymptotes: $y = \dfrac{4}{5}x, \; y = -\dfrac{4}{5}x$

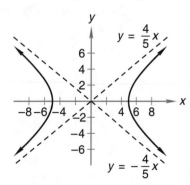

8. $r = \sqrt{1^2 + (-1)^2} = \sqrt{2}$
(79)
$$\theta = \tan^{-1}\left(\frac{-1}{1}\right) = -45°$$
$$(1 - i)^3 = \left(\sqrt{2} \; \text{cis} \, (-45°)\right)^3$$
$$= (\sqrt{2})^3 \; \text{cis} \, [(3)(-45°)] = 2\sqrt{2} \; \text{cis} \, (-135°)$$
$$= 2\sqrt{2}[\cos(-135°) + i \sin(-135°)]$$
$$= 2\sqrt{2}\left[-\frac{\sqrt{2}}{2} + i\left(-\frac{\sqrt{2}}{2}\right)\right] = -2 - 2i$$

9. $C = 180° - 85° - 30°$
(72)
$$C = 65°$$
$$\frac{b}{\sin 30°} = \frac{15}{\sin 85°}$$
$$b = \frac{15 \sin 30°}{\sin 85°}$$
$$b = 7.53 \text{ m}$$
$$\frac{c}{\sin 65°} = \frac{15}{\sin 85°}$$
$$c = \frac{15 \sin 65°}{\sin 85°}$$
$$c = 13.65 \text{ m}$$

10. Function $= \cos \theta$
(47, 66)
Amplitude $= 21 - 15 = 6$

Centerline $= 15$

Period $= \dfrac{5\pi}{4} - \left(-\dfrac{3\pi}{4}\right) = 2\pi$

Coefficient $= \dfrac{2\pi}{2\pi} = 1$

Phase angle $= \dfrac{\pi}{4}$

$$y = 15 + 6 \cos\left(x - \frac{\pi}{4}\right)$$

11. $(-5 \text{ cis } 210°)[6 \text{ cis } (-90°)]$
(64)
$$= (-5)(6) \text{ cis } (210° - 90°) = -30 \text{ cis } 120°$$
$$= -30(\cos 120° + i \sin 120°)$$
$$= -30\left(-\frac{1}{2} + \frac{\sqrt{3}}{2}i\right) = 15 - 15\sqrt{3}\,i$$

12.
(73)

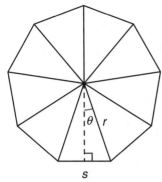

s

$$s = \frac{72}{9} = \textbf{8 in.}$$

$$\theta = \frac{1}{2}\left(\frac{360°}{9}\right) = 20°$$

$$\sin \theta = \frac{\frac{1}{2}s}{r}$$

$$r = \frac{\frac{1}{2}s}{\sin \theta} = \frac{4}{\sin 20°} = \textbf{11.70 in.}$$

13.
(5)
$$\frac{\text{Side}_S}{\text{Side}_L} = \frac{6}{7}$$

$$\frac{\text{Area}_S}{\text{Area}_L} = \left(\frac{\text{Side}_S}{\text{Side}_L}\right)^2 = \left(\frac{6}{7}\right)^2 = \frac{\textbf{36}}{\textbf{49}}$$

14. $C = mN + b$
(62)

(a) $\begin{cases} 6000 = m30 + b \\ \text{(b)} \quad 4400 = m20 + b \end{cases}$

(a) $\quad 6000 = m30 + b$
(−b) $\underline{-4400 = -m20 - b}$
$\quad\quad 1600 = m10$
$\quad\quad\quad m = 160$

(a) $6000 = 160(30) + b$
$\quad\quad b = 1200$

$C = 160N + 1200 = 160(8) + 1200 = \textbf{\$2480}$

15. $B = 7C$
(36)

Upstream:
$$(B - C)T_U = D_U$$
$$6CT_U = 96$$
$$CT_U = 16$$

Downstream:
$$(B + C)T_D = D_D$$
$$8C(T_U - 2) = 64$$
$$8CT_U - 16C = 64$$
$$CT_U - 2C = 8$$
$$(16) - 2C = 8$$
$$2C = 8$$
$$C = 4$$

$B = 7C = \textbf{28 mph}$

16. $_nC_r = \dfrac{n!}{(n - r)!r!}$
(75)

$$_{10}C_7 = \frac{10!}{(10 - 7)!7!} = \frac{10 \cdot 9 \cdot 8 \cdot 7!}{3 \cdot 2 \cdot 1 \cdot 7!} = \textbf{120}$$

17. $(216 \text{ cis } 30°)^{1/3} = \sqrt[3]{216} \text{ cis } \dfrac{30°}{3} = \textbf{6 cis 10°}$
(79)

Angles differ by $\dfrac{360°}{3} = 120°$.

$6 \text{ cis } (10° + 120°) = \textbf{6 cis 130°}$
$6 \text{ cis } (10° + 240°) = \textbf{6 cis 250°}$

18. $8i = 8 \text{ cis } 90°$
(79)

$$\sqrt[3]{8} \text{ cis } \frac{90°}{3} = 2 \text{ cis } 30° = 2(\cos 30° + i \sin 30°)$$

$$= 2\left(\frac{\sqrt{3}}{2} + \frac{1}{2}i\right) = \boldsymbol{\sqrt{3} + i}$$

$2 \text{ cis } (30° + 120°) = 2(\cos 150° + i \sin 150°)$

$$= 2\left(-\frac{\sqrt{3}}{2} + \frac{1}{2}i\right) = \boldsymbol{-\sqrt{3} + i}$$

$2 \text{ cis } (30° + 240°) = 2(\cos 270° + i \sin 270°)$
$= 2(0 + (-1)i) = \boldsymbol{-2i}$

19. $y = -\log_2 x$
(65)
$\quad y = \log_2 x^{-1}$
$x^{-1} = 2^y$
$$x = \left(\frac{1}{2}\right)^y$$

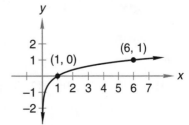

20. Focus: $(h, k + p) = (4, -1)$
(68)
Vertex: $(h, k) = (4, 0)$

$$k + p = -1$$
$$p = -1 - k$$
$$p = -1 - 0$$
$$p = -1$$

$$y - k = \frac{1}{4p}(x - h)^2$$

$$y - 0 = \frac{1}{4(-1)}(x - 4)^2$$

$$y = -\frac{1}{4}(x - 4)^2$$

Directrix: $y = k - p$
$$y = 0 - (-1)$$
$$y = 1$$

Axis of symmetry: $x = h$
$$x = 4$$

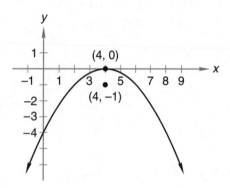

2. $y^2 - 16x^2 = 144$
(78)

$$\frac{y^2}{144} - \frac{x^2}{9} = 1$$

Let $x = 0$, $y = \pm 12$
Let $y = 0$, $x = \pm 3i$
Vertices: (0, 12), (0, –12)

Asymptotes: $y = \frac{12}{3}x$, $y = -\frac{12}{3}x$
$$y = 4x, \ y = -4x$$

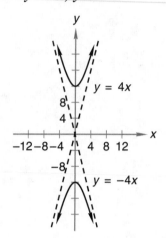

3. Rate $\times$ players $\times$ time = points
(44)
Rate(p players)(30 min) = 5 points

$$\text{Rate} = \frac{5}{30p} \frac{\text{points}}{\text{player-min}}$$

$$= \frac{1}{6p} \frac{\text{points}}{\text{player-min}}$$

Rate $\times$ players $\times$ time = points

$$\text{Time} = \frac{\text{points}}{\text{rate} \times \text{players}}$$

$$= \frac{t \text{ points}}{\frac{1}{6p} \frac{\text{points}}{\text{min-player}} (p + 2) \text{ players}}$$

$$= \frac{6pt}{p + 2} \text{ min}$$

4. $-8i = 8 \text{ cis } 270°$
(79)

$$8^{1/3} \text{ cis } \frac{270°}{3} = 2 \text{ cis } 90° = 2i$$

Angles differ by $\frac{360°}{3} = 120°$.

$$2 \text{ cis } (90° + 120°) = 2 \text{ cis } 210° = -\sqrt{3} - i$$
$$2 \text{ cis } (90° + 240°) = 2 \text{ cis } 330° = \sqrt{3} - i$$

Test 21, Form A

1. $C = mH + b$
(62)

(a) $\begin{cases} 1725 = m200 + b \\ 925 = m100 + b \end{cases}$
(b)

(a) $\quad 1725 = \quad m200 + b$
(–b) $\underline{-925 = -m100 - b}$
$\qquad 800 = m100$
$\qquad m = 8$

(b) $925 = 8(100) + b$
$\qquad b = 125$

$C = mH + 125 = 8(150) + 125 =$ **\$1325**

5. $16y^2 + 9x^2 = 144$
(71)

$$\frac{x^2}{16} + \frac{y^2}{9} = 1$$

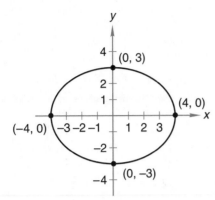

8.
(32)

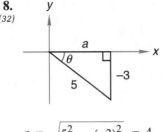

$$a = \sqrt{5^2 - (-3)^2} = 4$$

$$\cos\left[\text{Arcsin}\left(-\frac{3}{5}\right)\right] = \frac{4}{5}$$

$$\text{Area}_\Delta = \frac{5 \times 18.6603}{2} = 46.6508 \text{ m}^2$$

$$\text{Area} = 24(46.6508 \text{ m}^2) = \textbf{1119.62 m}^2$$

6. $\begin{cases} x^2 + y^2 - 2x + 4y - 11 \geq 0 \\ y \leq -(x + 2)^2 + 3 \end{cases}$
(56)

$$x^2 + y^2 - 2x + 4y - 11 \geq 0$$

$$(x^2 - 2x + 1) + (y^2 + 4y + 4) \geq 11 + 1 + 4$$

$$(x - 1)^2 + (y + 2)^2 \geq 4^2$$

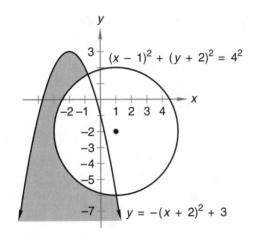

9. $3^{4x-2} = 5^{3x+1}$
(82)

$$\log 3^{4x-2} = \log 5^{3x+1}$$

$$(4x - 2)\log 3 = (3x + 1)\log 5$$

$$(4x - 2)(0.477) = (3x + 1)(0.699)$$

$$1.908x - 0.954 = 2.097x + 0.699$$

$$-0.189x = 1.653$$

$$x = \textbf{-8.75}$$

10. $\dfrac{\csc^3\theta - \csc\theta\cot^2\theta}{\csc\theta} - \sin^2\theta$
(76, 80)

$$= \frac{\csc\theta(\csc^2\theta - \cot^2\theta)}{\csc\theta} - \sin^2\theta$$

$$= 1 - \sin^2\theta = \textbf{cos}^2\,\theta$$

7.
(73)

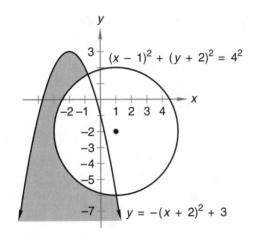

$$\frac{120 \text{ m}}{12} = 10 \text{ m}$$

$$x = \frac{10 \text{ m}}{2} = 5 \text{ m}$$

$$A = \frac{5}{\tan 15°} = 18.6603 \text{ m}$$

11. $(a + b)^5$
(77)

Exponents for a: 5 4 3 2 1 0

Exponents for b: 0 1 2 3 4 5

Sixth row of Pascal's triangle:

1 5 10 10 5 1

$$a^5 + 5a^4b + 10a^3b^2 + 10a^2b^3 + 5ab^4 + b^5$$

12. $\left(\dfrac{1}{2}\text{ cis }200°\right)^3 = \left(\dfrac{1}{2}\right)^3 \text{cis }(3 \cdot 200°)$
(79)

$$= \frac{1}{8}\text{ cis }600° = \frac{1}{8}\text{ cis }240°$$

$$= \frac{1}{8}\left(-\frac{1}{2} - \frac{\sqrt{3}}{2}i\right) = -\frac{1}{16} - \frac{\sqrt{3}}{16}i$$

13. (a) $\dfrac{6}{8} \cdot \dfrac{6}{8} = \dfrac{9}{16}$
(83)

(b) $\dfrac{6}{8} \cdot \dfrac{5}{7} = \dfrac{15}{28}$

14. P(four tails) $= \dfrac{1}{2} \cdot \dfrac{1}{2} \cdot \dfrac{1}{2} \cdot \dfrac{1}{2} = \dfrac{1}{16}$
(83)

15. z score $= \dfrac{x - \mu}{\sigma} = \dfrac{675 - 600}{150} = \dfrac{75}{150} = 0.5$
(70)

69.15% are less than 675, so

30.85% have at least 675 pages

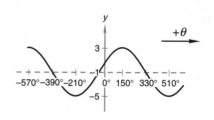

16.
(81)

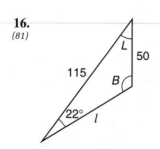

$\dfrac{115}{\sin B} = \dfrac{50}{\sin 22°}$

$\sin B = 0.8616$

$B = 120.50°$

$L = 180° - 120.50° - 22° = 37.50°$

$\dfrac{l}{\sin 37.50°} = \dfrac{50}{\sin 22°}$

$l = \textbf{81.25 m}$

17. $2 \sec^2 \dfrac{\theta}{2} + 3 \sec \dfrac{\theta}{2} - 2 = 0$
(50, 52)

$\left(2 \sec \dfrac{\theta}{2} - 1\right)\left(\sec \dfrac{\theta}{2} + 2\right) = 0$

$\sec \dfrac{\theta}{2} = \dfrac{1}{2}$	$\sec \dfrac{\theta}{2} = -2$
$\cos \dfrac{\theta}{2} = 2$	$\cos \dfrac{\theta}{2} = -\dfrac{1}{2}$
no answer	$\dfrac{\theta}{2} = 120°$
	$\theta = \textbf{240°}$

18. $y = -1 + 4 \sin \dfrac{1}{2}(\theta + 30°)$
(84)

Amplitude $= 4$

Centerline $= -1$

Period $= \dfrac{360°}{\dfrac{1}{2}} = 720°$

Phase angle $= -30°$

19. (a) $\log_3 x + \dfrac{1}{3} \log_3 8 = \dfrac{1}{2} \log_3 36$
(59)

$\log_3 8^{1/3} x = \log_3 36^{1/2}$

$2x = 6$

$x = \textbf{3}$

(b) $\log_2(2x + 4) - \dfrac{2}{3} \log_2 27 = 1$

$\log_2 \dfrac{(2x + 4)}{27^{2/3}} = 1$

$\dfrac{(2x + 4)}{9} = 2^1$

$2x + 4 = 18$

$2x = 14$

$x = \textbf{7}$

20. $a^2 = b^2 + c^2 - 2bc \cos A$
(81)

$a^2 = 11^2 + 15^2 - 2(11)(15) \cos 65°$

$a^2 = 121 + 225 - 139.5$

$a^2 = 206.5$

$a = \textbf{14.37 in.}$

$\dfrac{14.37}{\sin 65°} = \dfrac{15}{\sin B}$

$\sin B = 0.94604$

$B = \textbf{71.09°}$

$C = 180° - 65° - 71.09°$

$C = \textbf{43.91°}$

Test 21, Form B

1. $L = mC + b$
(62)

(a) $\begin{cases} 1280 = m250 + b \\ 530 = m100 + b \end{cases}$
(b)

(a) $1280 = m250 + b$
$(-b)$ $\underline{-530 = -m100 - b}$
$750 = m150$

$m = 5$

(b) $530 = 5(100) + b$

$b = 30$

$L = mC + b = 5(200) + 30 = \textbf{1030}$

2. $4y^2 - 16x^2 = 64$
(78)

$$\frac{y^2}{16} - \frac{x^2}{4} = 1$$

Let $x = 0$, $y = \pm 4$

Let $y = 0$, $x = \pm 2i$

Vertices: (0, 4), (0, -4)

Asymptotes: $y = \frac{4}{2}x$, $y = -\frac{4}{2}x$

$$y = 2x, \ y = -2x$$

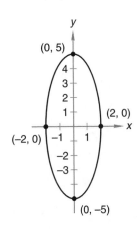

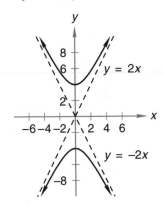

3. Rate $\times$ pods $\times$ time = seedlings or $RPT = S$
(44)

$R(p \text{ pods})(120 \text{ min}) = 7 \text{ seedlings}$

$$R = \frac{7}{120p} \frac{\text{seedlings}}{\text{pod-min}}$$

$RPT = S$

$$T = \frac{S}{RP}$$

$$T = \frac{z \text{ seedlings}}{\left(\dfrac{7}{120p} \dfrac{\text{seedlings}}{\text{pod-min}}\right)(p + 3) \text{ pods}}$$

$$T = \frac{120pz}{7(p + 3)} \text{ min}$$

4. $64i = 64 \text{ cis } 90°$
(79)

$$64^{1/3} \text{ cis } \frac{90°}{3} = 4 \text{ cis } 30° = \mathbf{2\sqrt{3} + 2i}$$

Angles differ by $\dfrac{360°}{3} = 120°$

$4 \text{ cis } (30° + 120°) = 4 \text{ cis } 150° = \mathbf{-2\sqrt{3} + 2i}$

$4 \text{ cis } (30° + 240°) = 4 \text{ cis } 270° = \mathbf{-4i}$

5. $4y^2 + 25x^2 = 100$
(71)

$$\frac{x^2}{4} + \frac{y^2}{25} = 1$$

6. $\begin{cases} y \geq (x - 1)^2 - 2 \\ x^2 + y^2 - 4x + 2y - 11 \leq 0 \end{cases}$
(56)

$$x^2 + y^2 - 4x + 2y - 11 \leq 0$$

$$(x^2 - 4x + 4) + (y^2 - 2y + 1) \leq 11 + 1 + 4$$

$$(x - 2)^2 + (y + 1)^2 \leq 4^2$$

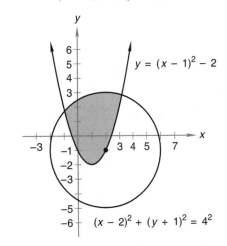

7.
(73)

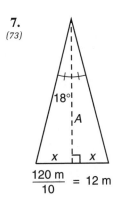

$$\frac{120 \text{ m}}{10} = 12 \text{ m}$$

$$x = \frac{12 \text{ m}}{2} = 6\text{m}$$

$$A = \frac{6}{\tan 18°} = 18.4661 \text{ m}$$

$$\text{Area}_\triangle = \frac{6 \times 18.4661}{2} = 55.3983 \text{ m}^2$$

$$\text{Area} = 20(55.3983 \text{ m}^2) = \mathbf{1107.97 \text{ m}^2}$$

Test Solutions

8.
(32)

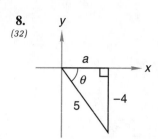

$$a = \sqrt{5^2 - (-4)^2} = 3$$

$$\cos\left[\text{Arcsin}\left(-\frac{4}{5}\right)\right] = \frac{3}{5}$$

9.
(82)

$$7^{2x+3} = 5^{3x-1}$$

$$\log 7^{2x+3} = \log 5^{3x-1}$$

$$(2x + 3)\log 7 = (3x - 1)\log 5$$

$$(2x + 3)(0.8451) = (3x - 1)(0.699)$$

$$1.690x + 2.535 = 2.097x + 0.699$$

$$0.407x = 3.234$$

$$x = \textbf{7.95}$$

10.
(76, 80)

$$\frac{\sec^2\theta\,\tan\theta - \tan^3\theta}{\tan\theta} - \cos^2\theta$$

$$= \frac{\tan\theta(\sec^2\theta - \tan^2\theta)}{\tan\theta} - \cos^2\theta$$

$$= 1 - \cos^2\theta = \textbf{sin}^2\,\boldsymbol{\theta}$$

11.
(77)

$(x + y)^4$

Exponents for x: 4 3 2 1 0

Exponents for y: 0 1 2 3 4

Fifth row of Pascal's triangle:

1 4 6 4 1

$$\boldsymbol{x^4 + 4x^3y + 6x^2y^2 + 4xy^3 + y^4}$$

12.
(79)

$$\left(\frac{1}{2}\text{ cis }150°\right)^4 = \left(\frac{1}{2}\right)^4\text{ cis }(4 \cdot 150°)$$

$$= \frac{1}{16}\text{ cis }600° = \frac{1}{16}\text{ cis }240°$$

$$= \frac{1}{16}\left(-\frac{1}{2} - \frac{\sqrt{3}}{2}i\right) = \boldsymbol{-\frac{1}{32} - \frac{\sqrt{3}}{32}i}$$

13.
(83)

(a) $\dfrac{3}{10} \cdot \dfrac{3}{10} = \dfrac{\textbf{9}}{\textbf{100}}$

(b) $\dfrac{3}{10} \cdot \dfrac{2}{9} = \dfrac{6}{90} = \dfrac{\textbf{1}}{\textbf{15}}$

14.
(83)

$P(\text{three heads}) = \dfrac{1}{2} \cdot \dfrac{1}{2} \cdot \dfrac{1}{2} = \dfrac{\textbf{1}}{\textbf{8}}$

15.
(70)

$z\text{ score} = \dfrac{x - \mu}{\sigma} = \dfrac{375 - 300}{50} = \dfrac{75}{50} = 1.5$

93.32% are less than 375, so

6.68% have at least 375 mushrooms

16.
(81)

$$\frac{126}{\sin B} = \frac{35}{\sin 15°}$$

$$\sin B = 0.9317$$

$$B = 111.30°$$

$$L = 180° - 111.30° - 15° = 53.70°$$

$$\frac{l}{\sin 53.70°} = \frac{35}{\sin 15°}$$

$$l = \textbf{109 m}$$

17.
(50, 52)

$$3\csc^2\frac{\theta}{2} - 4\csc\frac{\theta}{2} - 4 = 0$$

$$\left(3\csc\frac{\theta}{2} + 2\right)\left(\csc\frac{\theta}{2} - 2\right) = 0$$

$$\csc\frac{\theta}{2} = -\frac{2}{3} \qquad \csc\frac{\theta}{2} = 2$$

$$\sin\frac{\theta}{2} = -\frac{3}{2} \qquad \sin\frac{\theta}{2} = \frac{1}{2}$$

no answer $\qquad \dfrac{\theta}{2} = 30°, 150°$

$$\theta = \textbf{60°, 300°}$$

18.
(84)

$y = 2 - 3\sin\dfrac{1}{2}(\theta - 60°)$

Amplitude = 3

Centerline = 2

$\text{Period} = \dfrac{360°}{\dfrac{1}{2}} = 720°$

Phase angle = 60°

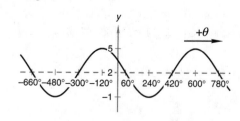

19. (a) $\log_2 x + \dfrac{1}{3}\log_2 8 = \dfrac{1}{2}\log_2 49$
(59)

$$\log_2 8^{1/3} x = \log_2 49^{1/2}$$

$$2x = 7$$

$$x = \dfrac{7}{2}$$

(b) $\log_3(2x - 4) - \dfrac{2}{3}\log_3 8 = 1$

$$\log_3 \dfrac{(2x - 4)}{8^{2/3}} = 1$$

$$\dfrac{2x - 4}{4} = 3^1$$

$$2x - 4 = 12$$

$$2x = 16$$

$$x = \mathbf{8}$$

20. $a^2 = b^2 + c^2 - 2bc \cos A$
(81)

$$a^2 = 13^2 + 10^2 - 2(13)(10)\cos 55°$$

$$a^2 = 169 + 100 - 149.13$$

$$a^2 = 119.87$$

$$a = \mathbf{10.95\ in.}$$

$$\dfrac{10.95}{\sin 55°} = \dfrac{13}{\sin B}$$

$$\sin B = 0.9726$$

$$B = \mathbf{76.57°}$$

$$C = 180° - 76.57° - 55°$$

$$C = \mathbf{48.43°}$$

Test 22, Form A

1. (a) $\dfrac{4}{12} \cdot \dfrac{4}{12} = \dfrac{1}{9}$
(83)

(b) $\dfrac{4}{12} \cdot \dfrac{3}{11} = \dfrac{1}{11}$

2. $P(<7) = \dfrac{15}{36} = \dfrac{5}{12}$
(83)

3. $R_B = 1,\ R_L = \dfrac{1}{12},\ T_L = T_B$
(85)

$$R_L T_L = S \qquad R_B T_B = S + 60$$

$$S = \dfrac{T}{12} \qquad S = T - 60$$

$$\dfrac{T}{12} = T - 60$$

$$\dfrac{11}{12}T = 60$$

$$T = 65\dfrac{5}{11}\ \text{min}$$

4.
(84)

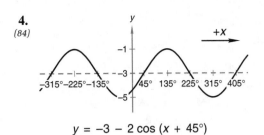

$$y = -3 - 2\cos(x + 45°)$$

5. $\qquad 3\sin^2 4\theta = \cos 4\theta - 1$
(50, 85)

$$3(1 - \cos^2 4\theta) = \cos 4\theta - 1$$

$$3\cos^2 4\theta + \cos 4\theta - 4 = 0$$

$$(3\cos 4\theta + 4)(\cos 4\theta - 1) = 0$$

$$\cos 4\theta = -\dfrac{4}{3} \qquad \cos 4\theta = 1$$

no answer $\qquad 4\theta = 0°, 360°, 720°, 1080°$

$$\theta = \mathbf{0°, 90°, 180°, 270°}$$

6. $\qquad b^2 = a^2 + c^2 - 2ac \cos B$
(81)

$$\cos B = \dfrac{a^2 + c^2 - b^2}{2ac}$$

$$\cos B = \left(\dfrac{10^2 + 4^2 - 12^2}{2(10)(4)}\right) = -0.35$$

$$B = \mathbf{110.49°}$$

7. $\qquad x^2 - 4y^2 = 100$
(78)

$$\dfrac{x^2}{100} - \dfrac{y^2}{25} = 1$$

Let $y = 0$, $x = \pm 10$

Let $x = 0$, $y = \pm 5i$

Vertices: $(\pm 10, 0)$

Asymptotes: $y = \pm \dfrac{1}{2}x$

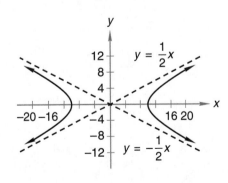

8. $y = \dfrac{\begin{vmatrix} 2 & -1 \\ -3 & -4 \end{vmatrix}}{\begin{vmatrix} 2 & -7 \\ -3 & 5 \end{vmatrix}} = \dfrac{-8 - 3}{10 - 21} = 1$
(74)

9.
(82)

$$2^{7x-1} = 7^{2x+1}$$

$$\log 2^{7x-1} = \log 7^{2x+1}$$

$$(7x - 1)(0.3010) = (2x + 1)(0.8451)$$

$$2.107x - 0.3010 = 1.6902x + 0.8451$$

$$0.4168x = 1.1461$$

$$x = \mathbf{2.75}$$

10. $2x + y = 3$
(58)

$$y = -2x + 3$$

The line perpendicular to the given line has a slope of $\dfrac{1}{2}$, so

$$y = \frac{1}{2}x + b$$

$$(1) = \frac{1}{2}(2) + b$$

$$b = 0$$

$$y = \frac{1}{2}x$$

$$(-2x + 3) = \frac{1}{2}x$$

$$\frac{5}{2}x = 3$$

$$x = \frac{6}{5}$$

$$y = \frac{1}{2}x = \frac{1}{2} \cdot \frac{6}{5} = \frac{3}{5}$$

$$(2, 1), \left(\frac{6}{5}, \frac{3}{5}\right)$$

$$D = \sqrt{\left(2 - \frac{6}{5}\right)^2 + \left(1 - \frac{3}{5}\right)^2}$$

$$= \sqrt{\left(\frac{4}{5}\right)^2 + \left(\frac{2}{5}\right)^2} = \frac{2\sqrt{5}}{5}$$

11. $\cos\left(\theta - \dfrac{\pi}{2}\right) = \cos\theta\cos\dfrac{\pi}{2} + \sin\theta\sin\dfrac{\pi}{2}$
(87)

$$= \mathbf{\sin\theta}$$

12. $(81 \text{ cis } 180°)^{1/4} = 81^{1/4}\left(\text{cis }\dfrac{180°}{4}\right)$
(79)

$$= 3 \text{ cis } 45°, 3 \text{ cis } 135°, 3 \text{ cis } 225°, 3 \text{ cis } 315°$$

$$= \mathbf{\frac{3\sqrt{2}}{2} + \frac{3\sqrt{2}}{2}i, -\frac{3\sqrt{2}}{2} + \frac{3\sqrt{2}}{2}i,}$$

$$\mathbf{-\frac{3\sqrt{2}}{2} - \frac{3\sqrt{2}}{2}i, \frac{3\sqrt{2}}{2} - \frac{3\sqrt{2}}{2}i}$$

13. $\tan(A - B) = \dfrac{\sin(A - B)}{\cos(A - B)}$
(87)

$$= \frac{\sin A\cos B - \cos A\sin B}{\cos A\cos B + \sin A\sin B}$$

$$= \frac{\dfrac{\sin A\cos B}{\cos A\cos B} - \dfrac{\cos A\sin B}{\cos A\cos B}}{\dfrac{\cos A\cos B}{\cos A\cos B} + \dfrac{\sin A\sin B}{\cos A\cos B}}$$

$$\tan(A - B) = \mathbf{\frac{\tan A - \tan B}{1 + \tan A\tan B}}$$

14. $\dfrac{2}{3}\log_3 8 - \log_3(3x + 2) + \log_3(x + 2)$
(59)

$$= \log_3 4$$

$$\log_3 \frac{8^{2/3}(x + 2)}{3x + 2} = \log_3 4$$

$$\frac{4(x + 2)}{3x + 2} = 4$$

$$4x + 8 = 12x + 8$$

$$8x = 0$$

$$x = \mathbf{0}$$

15. $\dfrac{\csc\theta}{\sec\theta - \tan\theta} - \dfrac{\csc\theta}{\sec\theta + \tan\theta}$
(80, 87)

$$= \frac{\csc\theta\left[(\sec\theta + \tan\theta) - (\sec\theta - \tan\theta)\right]}{\sec^2\theta - \tan^2\theta}$$

$$= \frac{2\csc\theta\tan\theta}{1} = 2\frac{1}{\sin\theta} \cdot \frac{\sin\theta}{\cos\theta} = \mathbf{2\sec\theta}$$

16.
(81)

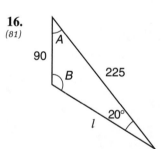

$$\frac{225}{\sin B} = \frac{90}{\sin 20°}$$

$$B = 121.23°$$

$$A = 180° - 121.23° - 20° = 38.77°$$

$$\frac{l}{\sin 38.77°} = \frac{90}{\sin 20°}$$

$$l = \mathbf{164.78 \text{ ft}}$$

17. $25x^2 + 4y^2 = 100$
(71)

$$\frac{x^2}{4} + \frac{y^2}{25} = 1$$

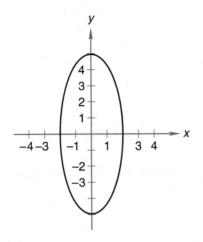

Test 22, Form B

1. (a) $\dfrac{3}{15} \cdot \dfrac{3}{15} = \dfrac{1}{25}$
(83)

(b) $\dfrac{3}{15} \cdot \dfrac{2}{14} = \dfrac{1}{35}$

2. $P(< 8) = \dfrac{21}{36} = \dfrac{7}{12}$
(83)

3. $R_B = 1$, $R_L = \dfrac{1}{12}$, $T_L = T_B$
(85)

$$R_L T_L = S \qquad\qquad R_B T_B = S + 30$$

$$S = \dfrac{T}{12} \qquad\qquad S = T - 30$$

$$\dfrac{T}{12} = T - 30$$

$$\dfrac{11}{12}T = 30$$

$$T = 32\dfrac{8}{11} \text{ min}$$

18. $A_t = A_0 e^{kt}$
(88)

$$320 = 480 e^{k100}$$

$$e^{k100} = \dfrac{2}{3}$$

$$k100 = -0.4055$$

$$k = -0.004055$$

$$A_t = \mathbf{480}e^{-0.004055t}$$

$$240 = 480 e^{-0.004055t}$$

$$-0.004055t = \ln\dfrac{1}{2}$$

$$t = \mathbf{170.94 \ hr}$$

4.
(84)

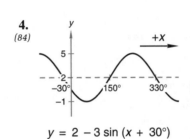

$$y = 2 - 3 \sin (x + 30°)$$

5. $\qquad 2\cos^2 2\theta = 3 \sin 2\theta$
(50, 85)

$$2\left(1 - \sin^2 2\theta\right) = 3 \sin 2\theta$$

$$2 \sin^2 2\theta + 3 \sin 2\theta - 2 = 0$$

$$(2 \sin 2\theta - 1)(\sin 2\theta + 2) = 0$$

$$\sin 2\theta = \dfrac{1}{2} \qquad\qquad \sin 2\theta = -2$$

$$2\theta = 30°, 150°, 390°, 510° \qquad \text{no answer}$$

$$\theta = \mathbf{15°, 75°, 195°, 255°}$$

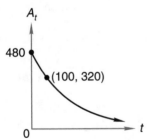

19. $12 + (25)(-4) = \mathbf{-88}$
(86)

20. (a) $\begin{cases} a_1 + 20d = 28 \\ a_1 + 49d = -59 \end{cases}$
(86)

(b) $\qquad a_1 + 49d = -59$

(-a) $\underline{-a_1 - 20d = -28}$

$$29d = -87$$

$$d = -3$$

(a) $a_1 + 20(-3) = 28$

$$a_1 = 88$$

88, 85, 82

6. $\qquad b^2 = a^2 + c^2 - 2ac \cos B$
(81)

$$\cos B = \dfrac{a^2 + c^2 - b^2}{2ac}$$

$$\cos B = \left(\dfrac{9^2 + 3^2 - 11^2}{2(9)(3)}\right) = -0.574$$

$$B = \mathbf{125.03°}$$

7. $x^2 - 16y^2 = 64$
(78)

$$\frac{x^2}{64} - \frac{y^2}{4} = 1$$

Let $y = 0$, $x = \pm 8$

Let $x = 0$, $y = \pm 2i$

Vertices: $(\pm 8, 0)$

Asymptotes: $y = \pm\dfrac{1}{4}x$

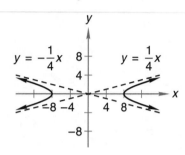

8. $y = \dfrac{\begin{vmatrix} 3 & 1 \\ -2 & 5 \end{vmatrix}}{\begin{vmatrix} 3 & -4 \\ -2 & 5 \end{vmatrix}} = \dfrac{15 - (-2)}{15 - 8} = \dfrac{17}{7}$
(74)

9.
(82)

$$3^{11x-4} = 11^{3x+4}$$

$$\log 3^{11x-4} = \log 11^{3x+4}$$

$$(11x - 4)(0.4771) = (3x + 4)(1.041)$$

$$5.248x - 1.908 = 3.124x + 4.166$$

$$2.124x = 6.074$$

$$x = 2.87$$

10. $y - 3x = 15$
(58)

$$y = 3x + 15$$

The line perpendicular to the given line has a slope of $-\dfrac{1}{3}$, so

$$y = -\frac{1}{3}x + b$$

$$(-1) = -\frac{1}{3}(3) + b$$

$$b = 0$$

$$y = -\frac{1}{3}x$$

$$(3x + 15) = -\frac{1}{3}x$$

$$\frac{10}{3}x = -15$$

$$x = -\frac{9}{2}$$

$$y = -\frac{1}{3}x = -\frac{1}{3}\left(-\frac{9}{2}\right) = \frac{3}{2}$$

$$(3, -1), \left(-\frac{9}{2}, \frac{3}{2}\right)$$

$$D = \sqrt{\left(3 - \left(-\frac{9}{2}\right)\right)^2 + \left(-1 - \frac{3}{2}\right)^2}$$

$$= \sqrt{\left(\frac{15}{2}\right)^2 + \left(-\frac{5}{2}\right)^2} = \frac{5\sqrt{10}}{2}$$

11. $\sin\left(\theta - \dfrac{\pi}{2}\right) = \sin\theta\cos\dfrac{\pi}{2} - \cos\theta\sin\dfrac{\pi}{2}$
(87)

$$= -\cos\theta$$

12. $(64\text{ cis }180°)^{1/3} = 64^{1/3}\left(\text{cis }\dfrac{180°}{3}\right)$
(79)

$$= 4\text{ cis }60°,\ 4\text{ cis }180°,\ 4\text{ cis }300°$$

$$= 2 + 2\sqrt{3}i,\ -4,\ 2 - 2\sqrt{3}i$$

13. $\tan(A + B) = \dfrac{\sin(A + B)}{\cos(A + B)}$
(87)

$$= \frac{\sin A\cos B + \cos A\sin B}{\cos A\cos B - \sin A\sin B}$$

$$= \frac{\dfrac{\sin A\cos B}{\cos A\cos B} + \dfrac{\cos A\sin B}{\cos A\cos B}}{\dfrac{\cos A\cos B}{\cos A\cos B} - \dfrac{\sin A\sin B}{\cos A\cos B}}$$

$$\tan(A + B) = \frac{\tan A + \tan B}{1 - \tan A\tan B}$$

14. $\dfrac{2}{3}\log_3 8 - \log_3(x - 1) + \log_3(3x + 5)$
(59)

$$= \log_3 28$$

$$\log_3\frac{8^{2/3}(3x + 5)}{x - 1} = \log_3 28$$

$$\frac{4(3x + 5)}{x - 1} = 28$$

$$12x + 20 = 28x - 28$$

$$16x = 48$$

$$x = 3$$

15. $\dfrac{\sec\theta}{\csc\theta - \cot\theta} - \dfrac{\sec\theta}{\csc\theta + \cot\theta}$
(80, 87)

$$= \frac{\sec\theta[(\csc\theta + \cot\theta) - (\csc\theta - \cot\theta)]}{\csc^2\theta - \cot^2\theta}$$

$$= \frac{2\sec\theta\cot\theta}{1} = 2\frac{1}{\cos\theta}\cdot\frac{\cos\theta}{\sin\theta} = 2\csc\theta$$

16.
(81)

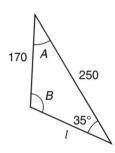

$$\frac{250}{\sin B} = \frac{170}{\sin 35°}$$
$$B = 122.49°$$

$$A = 180° - 122.49° - 35° = 22.51°$$

$$\frac{l}{\sin 22.51°} = \frac{170}{\sin 35°}$$
$$l = \textbf{113.47 ft}$$

17. $16y^2 + 9x^2 = 144$
(71)

$$\frac{x^2}{16} + \frac{y^2}{9} = 1$$

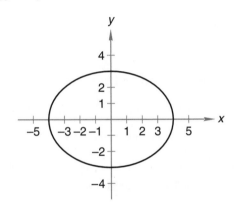

18. $A_t = A_0 e^{kt}$
(88)

$$200 = 800e^{k60}$$

$$e^{k60} = \frac{1}{4}$$

$$k60 = -1.3863$$

$$k = -0.0231$$

$$A_t = \textbf{800}e^{-\textbf{0.0231}t}$$

$$400 = 800e^{-0.0231t}$$

$$-0.0231t = \ln\frac{1}{2}$$

$$t = \textbf{30 s}$$

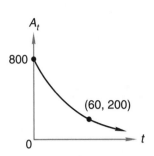

19. $9 + (20)(-3) = \textbf{-51}$
(86)

20. (a) $\begin{cases} a_1 + 28d = 92 \\ a_1 + 47d = 168 \end{cases}$
(86) (b)

(b) $\quad a_1 + 47d = 168$

(−a) $\dfrac{-a_1 - 28d = -92}{19d = 76}$

$$d = 4$$

(a) $a_1 + 28(4) = 92$

$$a_1 = -20$$

$$\textbf{-20, -16, -12}$$

Test 23, Form A

1. $16x^2 - 25y^2 = 400$
(78)

$$\frac{x^2}{25} - \frac{y^2}{16} = 1$$

Vertices: $(\pm 5, 0)$

Asymptotes: $y = \pm\dfrac{4}{5}x$

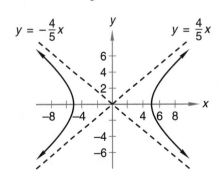

Test Solutions

2.
(89)

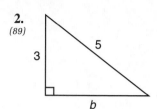

$b^2 + 3^2 = 5^2$

$b = \sqrt{16} = 4$

$$\frac{x^2}{16} + \frac{y^2}{25} = 1$$

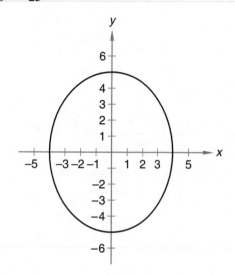

3. $A_t = A_0 e^{kt}$
(88)

$700 = 1000 e^{k30}$

$30k = \ln \dfrac{7}{10}$

$k = -0.01189$

$300 = 1000 e^{-0.01189t}$

$t = \mathbf{101.26\ min}$

4. $N,\ N + 2,\ N + 4$
(7)

$N(N + 4) = 15(N + 2) - 54$

$N^2 + 4N = 15N - 24$

$N^2 - 11N + 24 = 0$

$(N - 8)(N - 3) = 0$

$N = 8$

8, 10, 12

5. (a) $a_4 = 4(-5)^3 = \mathbf{-500}$
(91)

(b) $3r^3 = -24$

$r = -2$

$3,\ 3r,\ 3r^2,\ -24$

−6, 12

6. Amplitude $= 1$
(84)

Centerline $= 2$

Period $= \dfrac{2\pi}{2} = \pi$

Phase angle $= \dfrac{\pi}{4}$

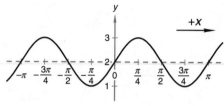

$$y = 2 + \cos 2\left(x - \frac{\pi}{4}\right)$$

7. $16^{3x-2} = 64^{4-x}$
(82)

$2^{4(3x-2)} = 2^{6(4-x)}$

$4(3x - 2) = 6(4 - x)$

$12x - 8 = 24 - 6x$

$18x = 32$

$x = \dfrac{16}{9}$

8. $(-16)^{1/4} = (16\ \mathrm{cis}\ 180°)^{1/4} = 16^{1/4}\ \mathrm{cis}\ \dfrac{180°}{4}$
(79)

$= 2\ \mathrm{cis}\ 45°,\ 2\ \mathrm{cis}\ 135°,\ 2\ \mathrm{cis}\ 225°,\ 2\ \mathrm{cis}\ 315°$

$= \sqrt{2} + \sqrt{2}i,\ -\sqrt{2} + \sqrt{2}i,\ -\sqrt{2} - \sqrt{2}i,\ \sqrt{2} - \sqrt{2}i$

9. $\sin(A + A) = \sin A \cos A + \cos A \sin A$
(87, 90)

$\mathbf{\sin 2A = 2\sin A \cos A}$

10. $-52 + 18(6) = \mathbf{56}$
(86)

11. (a) $\begin{cases} a_1 + 8d = -51 \\ a_1 + 3d = -1 \end{cases}$
(86)   (b)

(a) $\quad a_1 + 8d = -51$

(−b) $\underline{-a_1 - 3d = \quad 1}$

$\qquad\qquad 5d = -50$

$\qquad\qquad d = -10$

(b) $a_1 + 3(-10) = -1$

$\qquad\qquad a_1 = 29$

29, 19, 9, −1

12. (a) $\dfrac{3}{12} \cdot \dfrac{4}{12} = \dfrac{1}{12}$
(83)

(b) $\dfrac{3}{12} \cdot \dfrac{4}{11} = \dfrac{1}{11}$

13. $R_L = \dfrac{1}{12}$, $R_B = 1$
(85)

$R_L T = R_B T - 45$

$\dfrac{1}{12}T = (1)T - 45$

$\dfrac{11}{12}T = 45$

$T = \mathbf{49\dfrac{1}{11} \ min}$

14. $P(Q \cup R) = P(Q) + P(R) - P(Q \cap R)$
(92)

$= \dfrac{4}{52} + \dfrac{26}{52} - \dfrac{2}{52} = \dfrac{28}{52} = \mathbf{\dfrac{7}{13}}$

15. $3^{\log_3 9 - 2\log_3 6 + 4\log_3 2 - 2\log_3 \sqrt{3}}$
(59)

$= 3^{\log_3 9} \cdot 3^{\log_3 6^{-2}} \cdot 3^{\log_3 2^4} \cdot 3^{\log_3 (\sqrt{3})^{-2}}$

$= (9)\left(\dfrac{1}{6^2}\right)(2^4)\left(\dfrac{1}{(\sqrt{3})^2}\right) = \dfrac{9 \cdot 16}{36 \cdot 3} = \mathbf{\dfrac{4}{3}}$

16. (a) $\qquad\qquad 2\tan^2 2\theta = 3\sec 2\theta$
(85)

$2(\sec^2 2\theta - 1) = 3\sec 2\theta$

$2\sec^2 2\theta - 3\sec 2\theta - 2 = 0$

$(2\sec 2\theta + 1)(\sec 2\theta - 2) = 0$

$\sec 2\theta = -\dfrac{1}{2} \qquad \sec 2\theta = 2$

no answer $\qquad 2\theta = 60°, 300°, 420°, 660°$

$\theta = \mathbf{30°, 150°, 210°, 330°}$

(b) $\cot^2 \theta = 3$

$\cot \theta = \pm\sqrt{3}$

$\theta = \mathbf{30°, 150°, 210°, 330°}$

17. $2\log(x + 2) - \log(x + 6) = \log 2 + \log(x - 1)$
(59)

$\log \dfrac{(x + 2)^2}{x + 6} = \log 2(x - 1)$

$x^2 + 4x + 4 = 2(x^2 + 5x - 6)$

$x^2 + 4x + 4 = 2x^2 + 10x - 12$

$x^2 + 6x - 16 = 0$

$(x + 8)(x - 2) = 0$

$x = \mathbf{2}$

18. (a) $\text{antilog}_2(-1) = 2^{-1} = \mathbf{\dfrac{1}{2}}$
(67)

(b) $\text{antilog}_{1/2}(-1) = \left(\dfrac{1}{2}\right)^{-1} = \dfrac{1}{\frac{1}{2}} = \mathbf{2}$

19. (a) $\dfrac{\sec^2 x}{\sec^2 x - 1} - 1 = \dfrac{\tan^2 x + 1}{\tan^2 x} - \dfrac{\tan^2 x}{\tan^2 x}$
(80)

$= \dfrac{\tan^2 x + 1 - \tan^2 x}{\tan^2 x} = \dfrac{1}{\tan^2 x} = \mathbf{\cot^2 x}$

(b) $\dfrac{\cos^2 \theta - \sin^2 \theta}{\cos^4 \theta - \sin^4 \theta}$

$= \dfrac{\cos^2 \theta - \sin^2 \theta}{(\cos^2 \theta - \sin^2 \theta)(\cos^2 \theta + \sin^2 \theta)}$

$= \dfrac{1}{\cos^2 \theta + \sin^2 \theta} = \dfrac{1}{1} = \mathbf{1}$

20. $a^2 = b^2 + c^2 - 2bc \cos A$
(81)

$\cos A = \left(\dfrac{b^2 + c^2 - a^2}{2bc}\right)$

$\cos A = \left(\dfrac{11^2 + 8^2 - 10^2}{2(11)(8)}\right)$

$\cos A = 0.483$

$A = \mathbf{61.12°}$

$\dfrac{10}{\sin 61.12°} = \dfrac{11}{\sin B}$

$\sin B = 0.9632$

$B = \mathbf{74.41°}$

Test 23, Form B

1. $9x^2 - 4y^2 = 900$
(78)

$\dfrac{x^2}{100} - \dfrac{y^2}{225} = 1$

Vertices: $(\pm 10, 0)$

Asymptotes: $y = \pm\dfrac{3}{2}x$

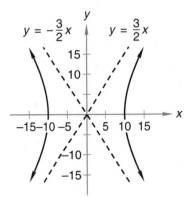

Test Solutions

2.
(89)

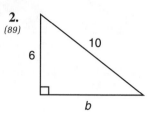

$$b^2 + 6^2 = 10^2$$
$$b = \sqrt{64} = 8$$

$$\frac{x^2}{64} + \frac{y^2}{100} = 1$$

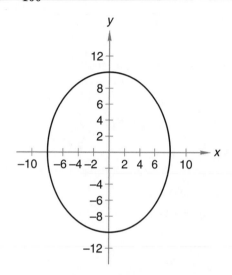

3. $A_t = A_0 e^{kt}$
(88)

$$25 = 30e^{k52}$$

$$52k = \ln \frac{5}{6}$$

$$k = -0.003506$$

$$20 = 30e^{-0.003506t}$$

$$t = \textbf{115.65 min}$$

4. $N, N + 2, N + 4$
(7)

$$N(N + 2) = 13(N + 4) - 26$$
$$N^2 + 2N = 13N + 26$$
$$N^2 - 11N - 26 = 0$$
$$(N + 2)(N - 13) = 0$$
$$N = 13$$

13, 15, 17

5. (a) $a_3 = 3(-3)^2 = \textbf{27}$
(91)

(b) $2r^3 = -16$
$$r = -2$$
$$2, 2r, 2r^2, -16$$
$$\textbf{-4, 8}$$

6. Amplitude $= 1$
(84) Centerline $= 3$

Period $= \dfrac{2\pi}{4} = \dfrac{\pi}{2}$

Phase angle $= -\dfrac{\pi}{4}$

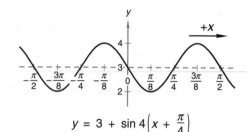

$$y = 3 + \sin 4\left(x + \frac{\pi}{4}\right)$$

7. $81^{x-3} = 9^{3-x}$
(82)

$$3^{4(x-3)} = 3^{2(3-x)}$$
$$4(x - 3) = 2(3 - x)$$
$$4x - 12 = 6 - 2x$$
$$6x = 18$$
$$x = \textbf{3}$$

8. $(16)^{1/4} = (16 \text{ cis } 0°)^{1/4} = 16^{1/4} \text{ cis } \dfrac{0°}{4}$
(79)

$$= 2 \text{ cis } 0°, 2 \text{ cis } 90°, 2 \text{ cis } 180°, 2 \text{ cis } 270°$$
$$= \textbf{2, 2i, -2, -2i}$$

9. $\cos (A + A) = \cos A \cos A - \sin A \sin A$
(87, 90)

$$\cos 2A = \cos^2 A - \sin^2 A$$
$$\cos 2A = (1 - \sin^2 A) - \sin^2 A$$
$$\textbf{cos } 2A = 1 - 2 \sin^2 A$$

10. $12 + 16(3) = \textbf{60}$
(86)

11. (a) $\begin{cases} a_1 + 4d = 8 \\ a_1 + 6d = 12 \end{cases}$
(86)

(b) $a_1 + 6d = 12$

(–a) $\underline{-a_1 - 4d = -8}$
$$2d = 4$$
$$d = 2$$

(b) $a_1 + 6(2) = 12$
$$a_1 = 0$$

0, 2, 4

12. (a) $\dfrac{4}{12} \cdot \dfrac{3}{12} = \dfrac{1}{12}$
(83)

(b) $\dfrac{4}{12} \cdot \dfrac{3}{11} = \dfrac{1}{11}$

13. $R_L = \dfrac{1}{12}$, $R_B = 1$
(85)

$$R_L T = R_B T - 15$$

$$\frac{1}{12}T = (1)T - 15$$

$$\frac{11}{12}T = 15$$

$$T = 16\frac{4}{11} \text{ min}$$

14. $P(K \cup B) = P(K) + P(B) - P(K \cap B)$
(92)

$$= \frac{4}{52} + \frac{26}{52} - \frac{2}{52} = \frac{28}{52} = \frac{7}{13}$$

15. $2^{\log_2 8 - 2\log_2 2 + 3\log_2 1 - 2\log_2 \sqrt{3}}$
(59)

$$= 2^{\log_2 8} \cdot 2^{\log_2 2^{-2}} \cdot 2^{\log_2 1^3} \cdot 2^{\log_2 (\sqrt{3})^{-2}}$$

$$= (8)\left(\frac{1}{2^2}\right)(1^3)\left(\frac{1}{(\sqrt{3})^2}\right) = \frac{8 \cdot 1}{4 \cdot 3} = \frac{2}{3}$$

16. (a)
(85)

$$2\cot^2 2\theta = 3\csc 2\theta$$

$$2(\csc^2 2\theta - 1) = 3\csc 2\theta$$

$$2\csc^2 2\theta - 3\csc 2\theta - 2 = 0$$

$$(2\csc 2\theta + 1)(\csc 2\theta - 2) = 0$$

$$\cos 2\theta = -\frac{1}{2}$$

no answer

$$\csc 2\theta = 2$$

$$2\theta = 30°, 150°, 390°, 510°$$

$$\theta = \mathbf{15°, 75°, 195°, 255°}$$

(b) $\tan^2 \theta = 3$

$$\tan \theta = \pm\sqrt{3}$$

$$\theta = \mathbf{60°, 120°, 240°, 300°}$$

17. $2\ln(x+5) - \ln(x+2) = \ln 2 + \ln(x+9)$
(59)

$$\ln \frac{(x+5)^2}{x+2} = \ln 2(x+9)$$

$$x^2 + 10x + 25 = 2(x^2 + 11x + 18)$$

$$x^2 + 10x + 25 = 2x^2 + 22x + 36$$

$$x^2 + 12x + 11 = 0$$

$$(x+11)(x+1) = 0$$

$$x = -1$$

18. (a) $\operatorname{antilog}_3(-1) = 3^{-1} = \dfrac{1}{3}$
(67)

(b) $\operatorname{antilog}_{1/3}(-1) = \left(\dfrac{1}{3}\right)^{-1} = \dfrac{1}{\frac{1}{3}} = \mathbf{3}$

19. (a) $\dfrac{\csc^2 x}{\csc^2 x - 1} - 1 = \dfrac{1 + \cot^2 x}{\cot^2 x} - \dfrac{\cot^2 x}{\cot^2 x}$
(80)

$$= \frac{1 + \cot^2 x - \cot^2 x}{\cot^2 x} = \frac{1}{\cot^2 x} = \mathbf{\tan^2 x}$$

(b) $\dfrac{\sec^2 \theta + \tan^2 \theta}{\sec^4 \theta - \tan^4 \theta}$

$$= \frac{\sec^2 \theta + \tan^2 \theta}{(\sec^2 \theta - \tan^2 \theta)(\sec^2 \theta + \tan^2 \theta)}$$

$$= \frac{1}{\sec^2 \theta - \tan^2 \theta} = \frac{1}{1} = \mathbf{1}$$

20. $a^2 = b^2 + c^2 - 2bc \cos A$
(81)

$$\cos A = \left(\frac{b^2 + c^2 - a^2}{2bc}\right)$$

$$\cos A = \left(\frac{16^2 + 10^2 - 12^2}{2(16)(10)}\right)$$

$$\cos A = 0.6625$$

$$A = \mathbf{48.51°}$$

$$\frac{12}{\sin 48.51°} = \frac{16}{\sin B}$$

$$\sin B = 0.9988$$

$$B = \mathbf{87.15°}$$

Test 24, Form A

1. $\tan 2A = \dfrac{\sin 2A}{\cos 2A} = \dfrac{2\sin A \cos A}{\cos^2 A - \sin^2 A}$
(90)

$$= \frac{\dfrac{2\sin A \cos A}{\cos A \cos A}}{\dfrac{\cos^2 A}{\cos^2 A} - \dfrac{\sin^2 A}{\cos^2 A}} = \frac{\mathbf{2\tan A}}{\mathbf{1 - \tan^2 A}}$$

2. $x^2 + 7x + 19 = 0$
(46)

$$x = \frac{-7 \pm \sqrt{7^2 - (4)(1)(19)}}{2(1)}$$

$$= \frac{-7 \pm \sqrt{-27}}{2} = \frac{-7}{2} \pm \frac{3\sqrt{3}}{2}i$$

$$\left(x + \frac{7}{2} - \frac{3\sqrt{3}}{2}i\right)\left(x + \frac{7}{2} + \frac{3\sqrt{3}}{2}i\right)$$

3. Rate × women × time = jobs or $RWT = J$
(44)

$R(w \text{ women})(10 \text{ days}) = j \text{ jobs}$

$$\text{Rate} = \frac{j}{10w} \frac{\text{jobs}}{\text{women-days}}$$

$RWT = J$

$$T = \frac{J}{RW}$$

$$T = \frac{j + 28 \text{ jobs}}{\dfrac{j}{10w} \dfrac{\text{jobs}}{\text{women-days}} (w + n) \text{ women}}$$

$$T = \frac{10w(j + 28)}{j(w + n)} \textbf{ days}$$

4. $\dfrac{x^2}{36} + \dfrac{y^2}{9} = 1$
(89)

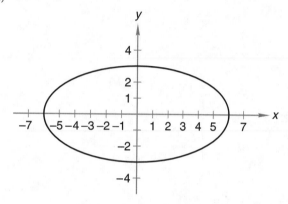

5. (a) $\begin{cases} a_1 + 8d = 20 \\ (b)\ a_1 + 13d = -10 \end{cases}$
(86)

(a) $\quad a_1 + 8d = 20$

(−b) $\dfrac{-a_1 - 13d = 10}{}$

$\quad\quad\quad -5d = 30$

$\quad\quad\quad\quad d = -6$

(a) $a_1 + 8(-6) = 20$

$\quad\quad\quad a_1 = 68$

68, 62, 56

6. $5 + 2i$
(95)

$$r \text{ cis } \theta = \sqrt{5^2 + 2^2} \text{ cis}\left(\tan^{-1}\left(\frac{2}{5}\right)\right)$$

$$= 5.39 \text{ cis } 21.80°$$

$$(5 + 2i)^{1/4} = (5.39)^{1/4} \text{ cis}\left(\frac{21.80°}{4}\right)$$

$$= \textbf{1.52 cis 5.45°, 1.52 cis 95.45°,}$$
$$\textbf{1.52 cis 185.45°, 1.52 cis 275.45°}$$

7. (a) $y = 7 + 2 \csc x$
(94)

(b) $y = \cot \theta$

8.
(94)

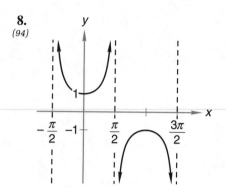

$y = \sec x$

9.
(94)

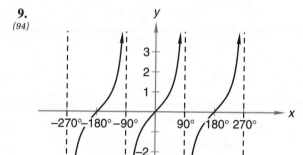

$y = \tan x$

10.
(96)

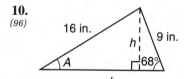

$$\frac{9}{\sin A} = \frac{16}{\sin 68°}$$

$$\sin A = \frac{9 \sin 68°}{16}$$

$$A = \textbf{31.44°}$$

$h = 16 \sin 31.44° = 8.345$

$b = 16 \cos 31.44° + 9 \cos 68° = 17.022$

$$\text{Area} = \frac{1}{2}bh = \frac{1}{2}(17.022)(8.345)$$

$$\textbf{Area} = \textbf{71.02 in.}^2$$

11.
(81)

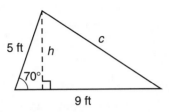

$$c = \sqrt{5^2 + 9^2 - 2(5)(9)\cos 70°}$$

c = 8.67 ft

$$h = 5\sin 70°$$

$$\text{Area} = \frac{1}{2}bh = \frac{1}{2}(9)(5\sin 70°)$$

Area = 21.14 ft²

12. $P(R \cup W) = P(R) + P(W) - P(R \cap W)$
(92)

$$= \frac{3}{11} + \frac{6}{11} - \frac{2}{11} = \frac{7}{11}$$

13.
(85)

$$\tan^2 \theta - \sec \theta = -1$$

$$\left(\sec^2 \theta - 1\right) - \sec \theta = -1$$

$$\sec^2 \theta - \sec \theta = 0$$

$$\sec \theta(\sec \theta - 1) = 0$$

$$\sec \theta = 0 \qquad \sec \theta - 1 = 0$$

no answer $\qquad \sec \theta = 1$

$$\theta = 0°$$

14.
(73)

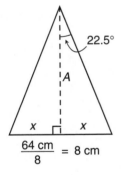

$$\frac{64 \text{ cm}}{8} = 8 \text{ cm}$$

$$x = \frac{8 \text{ cm}}{2} = 4 \text{ cm}$$

$$A = \frac{4}{\tan 22.5°} = 9.657 \text{ cm}$$

$$\text{Area}_\triangle = \frac{9.657 \times 4}{2} = 19.314 \text{ cm}^2$$

$$\text{Area} = (16)(19.314) = \textbf{309.02 cm}^2$$

15. The line perpendicular to the given line has a slope
(58) of $\frac{1}{2}$, so

$$y = \frac{1}{2}x + b$$

$$(0) = \frac{1}{2}(0) + b$$

$$b = 0$$

$$y = \frac{1}{2}x$$

$$(-2x + 2) = \frac{1}{2}x$$

$$\frac{5}{2}x = 2$$

$$x = \frac{4}{5}$$

$$y = \frac{1}{2}x = \frac{1}{2}\left(\frac{4}{5}\right) = \frac{2}{5}$$

$$(0, 0), \left(\frac{4}{5}, \frac{2}{5}\right)$$

$$D = \sqrt{\left(\frac{4}{5}\right)^2 + \left(\frac{2}{5}\right)^2} = \sqrt{\frac{20}{25}} = \frac{2\sqrt{5}}{5}$$

16. $A_t = A_0 e^{kt}$
(88)

$$2 = e^{k20}$$

$$20k = \ln 2$$

$$k = 0.034657$$

$$e^{(0.034657)(180)} = \textbf{511.97}$$

17. Center line $= -4$
(66)

Amplitude $= 2$

$$\text{Period} = \frac{360°}{\frac{2}{3}} = 540°$$

Phase angle $= 30°$

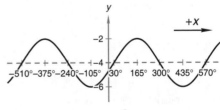

$$y = -4 + 2\sin \frac{2}{3}(x - 30°)$$

18.
(82)

$$10^{3x+1} = 14^{2x+1}$$

$$\log 10^{3x+1} = \log 14^{2x+1}$$

$$3x + 1 = (2x + 1)\log 14$$

$$x(3 - 2\log 14) = \log 14 - 1$$

$$x = \frac{\log 14 - 1}{3 - 2\log 14} = 0.21$$

$$RWT = J$$

$$T = \frac{J}{RW}$$

$$T = \frac{2j \text{ jobs}}{\dfrac{j}{15w}\dfrac{\text{jobs}}{\text{women-hr}}(w - 5)\text{ women}}$$

$$T = \frac{30w}{w - 5}\text{ hr}$$

19. $\log_5(3x + 3) - \log_5(x - 3) = \dfrac{2}{3}\log_5 27$
(59)

$$\log_5\frac{3x + 3}{x - 3} = \log_5 27^{2/3}$$

$$(3x + 3) = (9)(x - 3)$$

$$3x + 3 = 9x - 27$$

$$6x = 30$$

$$x = 5$$

4. $\dfrac{x^2}{49} + \dfrac{y^2}{9} = 1$
(89)

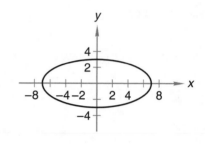

20. $\dfrac{\cos\theta}{1 + \sin\theta} \cdot \dfrac{\cos\theta}{\cos\theta} = \dfrac{\cos^2\theta}{(1 + \sin\theta)\cos\theta}$
(93)

$$= \frac{1 - \sin^2\theta}{(1 + \sin\theta)\cos\theta} = \frac{(1 + \sin\theta)(1 - \sin\theta)}{(1 + \sin\theta)\cos\theta}$$

$$= \frac{1 - \sin\theta}{\cos\theta}$$

5. (a) $\begin{cases} a_1 + 10d = 42 \\ a_1 + 15d = 57 \end{cases}$
(86) (b)

$$\text{(b)} \quad a_1 + 15d = 57$$

$$\text{(-a)} \quad \underline{-a_1 - 10d = -42}$$

$$5d = 15$$

$$d = 3$$

Test 24, Form B

1. $\tan 2A = \dfrac{\sin 2A}{\cos 2A} = \dfrac{2\sin A\cos A}{\cos^2 A - \sin^2 A}$
(90)

$$= \frac{\dfrac{2\sin A\cos A}{\cos A\cos A}}{\dfrac{\cos^2 A}{\cos^2 A} - \dfrac{\sin^2 A}{\cos^2 A}} = \frac{2\tan A}{1 - \tan^2 A}$$

(b) $a_1 + 15(3) = 57$

$$a_1 = 12$$

12, 15, 18, 21

6. $2 + 3i$
(95)

$$r\operatorname{cis}\theta = \sqrt{2^2 + 3^2}\ \operatorname{cis}\left(\tan^{-1}\left(\frac{3}{2}\right)\right)$$

$$= 3.61\operatorname{cis}56.31°$$

$$(2 + 3i)^{1/3} = (3.61)^{1/3}\operatorname{cis}\left(\frac{56.31°}{3}\right)$$

$$= \textbf{1.53 cis 18.77°, 1.53 cis 138.77°,}$$
$$\textbf{1.53 cis 258.77°}$$

2. $x^2 - 4x + 5 = 0$
(46)

$$x = \frac{-(-4) \pm \sqrt{(-4)^2 - 4(1)(5)}}{2(1)}$$

$$= \frac{4 \pm \sqrt{-4}}{2} = 2 \pm i$$

$$(x - 2 - i)(x - 2 + i)$$

3. Rate × women × time = jobs or $RWT = J$
(44)

$$R(w\text{ women})(15\text{ hr}) = j\text{ jobs}$$

$$\text{Rate} = \frac{j}{15w}\frac{\text{jobs}}{\text{women-hr}}$$

7. (a) $y = 3 + 7\csc x$
(94)
(b) $y = \cot\theta$

8.
(94)

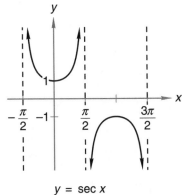

$y = \sec x$

9.
(94)

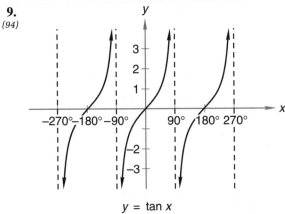

$y = \tan x$

10.
(96)

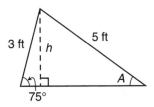

$$\frac{3}{\sin A} = \frac{5}{\sin 75°}$$

$$\sin A = \frac{3 \sin 75°}{5}$$

$$A = \mathbf{35.42°}$$

$h = 5 \sin 35.42° = 2.90$

$b = 5 \cos 35.42° + 3 \cos 75° = 4.85$

$$\text{Area} = \frac{1}{2}bh = \frac{1}{2}(4.85)(2.90)$$

$$\textbf{Area} = \mathbf{7.03 \ ft^2}$$

11.
(81)

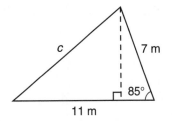

Note: Figure not drawn to scale

$$c = \sqrt{7^2 + 11^2 - 2(7)(11) \cos 85°}$$

$$c = \mathbf{12.51 \ m}$$

$$h = 7 \sin 85°$$

$$\text{Area} = \frac{1}{2}bh = \frac{1}{2}(11)(7 \sin 85°)$$

$$\textbf{Area} = \mathbf{38.35 \ m^2}$$

12. $P(H \cup W) = P(H) + P(W) - P(H \cap W)$
(92)
$$= \frac{4}{10} + \frac{3}{10} - \frac{1}{10} = \frac{6}{10} = \frac{3}{5}$$

13.
(85)
$$\sec^2 \theta + \tan \theta = 1$$
$$\left(\sec^2 \theta - 1\right) + \tan \theta = 0$$
$$\left(\tan^2 \theta\right) + \tan \theta = 0$$
$$\tan \theta(\tan \theta + 1) = 0$$

$\tan \theta = 0 \qquad\qquad \tan \theta + 1 = 0$
$\quad \theta = \mathbf{0°, 180°} \qquad\qquad \tan \theta = -1$
$$\theta = \mathbf{135°, 315°}$$

14.
(73)

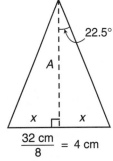

$$\frac{32 \ cm}{8} = 4 \ cm$$

$$x = \frac{4 \ cm}{2} = 2 \ cm$$

$$A = \frac{2}{\tan 22.5°} = 4.828 \ cm$$

$$\text{Area}_\Delta = \frac{2 \times 4.828}{2} = 4.828 \ cm^2$$

$$\text{Area} = (16)\left(4.828 \ cm^2\right) = \mathbf{77.25 \ cm^2}$$

Test Solutions

15. The line perpendicular to the given line has a slope
(58)
of $-\dfrac{2}{3}$, so

$$y = -\frac{2}{3}x + b$$

$$(1) = -\frac{2}{3}(0) + b$$

$$b = 1$$

$$y = -\frac{2}{3}x + 1$$

$$\left(\frac{3}{2}x - 3\right) = -\frac{2}{3}x + 1$$

$$\frac{13}{6}x = 4$$

$$x = \frac{24}{13}$$

$$y = \frac{3}{2}\left(\frac{24}{13}\right) - 3 = -\frac{3}{13}$$

$$(0, 1), \left(\frac{24}{13}, -\frac{3}{13}\right)$$

$$D = \sqrt{\left(\frac{24}{13}\right)^2 + \left(-\frac{3}{13} - 1\right)^2} = \sqrt{\frac{832}{169}} = \frac{8\sqrt{13}}{13}$$

16. $\quad A_t = A_0 e^{kt}$
(88)
$$2 = e^{k10}$$

$$10k = \ln 2$$

$$k = 0.06931$$

$$e^{(0.06931)(15)} = \textbf{2.83}$$

17. Center line = -5
(66)
Amplitude = 8

Period = $\dfrac{360°}{\dfrac{3}{2}} = 240°$

Phase angle = $-60°$

$$y = -5 + 8 \sin \frac{3}{2}(\theta + 60°)$$

18. $\quad 10^{2x+3} = 7^{x-1}$
(82)
$$\log 10^{2x+3} = \log 7^{x-1}$$

$$2x + 3 = (x - 1)\log 7$$

$$x(2 - \log 7) = -\log 7 - 3$$

$$x = \frac{-\log 7 - 3}{2 - \log 7} = \textbf{-3.33}$$

19. $\quad \log_5\left(x - \dfrac{1}{2}\right) = \log_5(x + 6) - \dfrac{1}{2}\log_5 4$
(59)

$$\log_5\left(x - \frac{1}{2}\right) = \log_5 \frac{x + 6}{4^{1/2}}$$

$$2\left(x - \frac{1}{2}\right) = x + 6$$

$$2x - 1 = x + 6$$

$$x = \textbf{7}$$

20. $\quad \dfrac{\cos \theta}{1 - \sin \theta} \cdot \dfrac{\cos \theta}{\cos \theta} = \dfrac{\cos^2 \theta}{(1 - \sin \theta)\cos \theta}$
(93)

$$= \frac{1 - \sin^2 \theta}{(1 - \sin \theta)\cos \theta} = \frac{(1 - \sin \theta)(1 + \sin \theta)}{(1 - \sin \theta)\cos \theta}$$

$$= \frac{1 + \sin\theta}{\cos\theta}$$

Test 25, Form A

1. Distance = m mi, rate = $r \dfrac{\text{mi}}{\text{hr}}$
(28)

Time = $\dfrac{\text{distance}}{\text{rate}} = \dfrac{m}{r}$ hr

New distance = $(m + 7)$ mi

New rate = $\dfrac{\text{new distance}}{\text{new time}} = \dfrac{(m + 7) \text{ mi}}{\dfrac{m}{r} \text{ hr}}$

$$= \frac{r(m + 7)}{m} \frac{\textbf{mi}}{\textbf{hr}}$$

2. Purchases = t things, price = d dollars
(44)

Rate = $\dfrac{d}{t} \dfrac{\text{dollars}}{\text{thing}}$

New rate = $\left(\dfrac{d}{t} + k\right) \dfrac{\text{dollars}}{\text{thing}} = \left(\dfrac{d + kt}{t}\right) \dfrac{\text{dollars}}{\text{thing}}$

New rate $\times N$ = price

$$\left(\frac{d + kt}{t}\right) \frac{\text{dollars}}{\text{things}} \times N = 50 \text{ dollars}$$

$$N = \frac{50 \text{ dollars}}{\dfrac{(d + kt)}{t} \dfrac{\text{dollars}}{\text{thing}}}$$

$$= \frac{50t}{d + kt} \textbf{ things}$$

3. (a) $y = \log_5 13$
(98)

$$5^y = 13$$

$$y \log 5 = \log 13$$

$$y = \frac{\log 13}{\log 5} = \mathbf{1.59}$$

(b) $y = \log_7 63$

$$7^y = 63$$

$$y \log 7 = \log 63$$

$$y = \frac{\log 63}{\log 7} = \mathbf{2.13}$$

4. $\left(\dfrac{1}{x + 2}\right) 7^{\log_7\left(x^2 + 5x + 6\right) - \log_7 (x+3)}$
(98)

$$= \frac{1}{x + 2}\, 7^{\log_7 \frac{x^2 + 5x + 6}{x+3}}$$

$$= \frac{1}{x + 2} \cdot \frac{(x + 3)(x + 2)}{(x + 3)}$$

$$= \frac{x + 2}{x + 2} = \mathbf{1}$$

5. Radius = 11 in.
(73) Side of square = 2(11) = 22 in.

Perimeter = 4(22) = **88 in.**

6. Arithmetic mean = $\dfrac{x + y}{2} = \dfrac{11 + 23}{2} = \mathbf{17}$
(99)

Geometric mean = $\pm\sqrt{xy} = \pm\sqrt{11 \cdot 23} = \pm\sqrt{\mathbf{253}}$

7. $a_n = a_1 r^{(n-1)}$
(99)

$$a_5 = 162\left(\frac{2}{3}\right)^4 = \mathbf{32\ ft}$$

8. $\left(R_M + R_B\right)T = \text{jobs}$
(25)

$$\left(\frac{2}{m} + \frac{2}{b}\right)\frac{\text{jobs}}{\text{hr}}\, T = 1 \text{ job}$$

$$\left(\frac{2b + 2m}{mb}\ \frac{\text{jobs}}{\text{hr}}\right)T = 1 \text{ job}$$

$$T = \frac{1 \text{ job}}{\dfrac{2b + 2m}{mb}\ \dfrac{\text{jobs}}{\text{hr}}}$$

$$T = \frac{mb}{2m + 2b}\ \mathbf{hr}$$

9. $-7 + 5i$
(95)

$$r \operatorname{cis} \theta = \sqrt{(-7)^2 + 5^2}\ \operatorname{cis}\left[\tan^{-1}\left(\frac{5}{-7}\right)\right]$$

$$= 8.60 \operatorname{cis} 144.46°$$

$$(-7 + 5i)^{1/3} = (8.60)^{1/3} \operatorname{cis}\left(\frac{144.46°}{3}\right)$$

$$= \mathbf{2.05\ cis\ 48.15°,\ 2.05\ cis\ 168.15°,}$$
$$\mathbf{2.05\ cis\ 288.15°}$$

10. $y = 1 + \csc \theta$
(84, 94) Amplitude = 1

Centerline = 1

Coefficient = $\dfrac{360}{360} = 1$

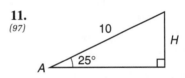

11.
(97)

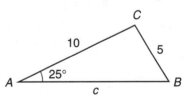

$H = 10 \sin 25° = 4.23$

$a = 5,\ b = 10$

$H < a < b$ so there are two possible triangles:

$$\frac{5}{\sin 25°} = \frac{10}{\sin B}$$

$$\sin B = \frac{10 \sin 25°}{5} = 0.845265$$

$$B = \mathbf{57.70°}$$

$$C = 180° - 25° - 57.70°$$

$$C = \mathbf{97.30°}$$

$$\frac{c}{\sin 97.30°} = \frac{5}{\sin 25°}$$

$$c = \frac{5 \sin 97.30°}{\sin 25°}$$

$$c = \mathbf{11.74}$$

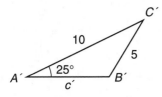

$B' = 180° - 57.70°$

$\boldsymbol{B' = 122.30°}$

$C' = 180° - 25° - 122.30°$

$\boldsymbol{C' = 32.70°}$

$$\frac{c'}{\sin 32.70°} = \frac{5}{\sin 25°}$$

$$c' = \frac{5 \sin 32.70°}{\sin 25°}$$

$$\boldsymbol{c' = 6.39}$$

12.
(88)
$$\begin{cases} A_0 = 600,000 \\ A_0 e^{k30} = 15,000 \end{cases}$$

$$600,000 e^{k30} = 15,000$$

$$e^{k30} = \frac{1}{40}$$

$$30k = \ln \frac{1}{40}$$

$$k = -0.12296$$

$$600,000 e^{-0.12296t} = 5$$

$$-0.12296t = \ln \frac{5}{600,000}$$

$$t = \boldsymbol{95.11 \ yr}$$

13. $a_1, a_1 r, a_1 r^2, a_1 r^3$
(91)
$$a_1 r^3 = 2(3)^3 = \boldsymbol{54}$$

14.
(99)
$$\begin{cases} \pm\sqrt{xy} = 8 \\ x - y = 30 \end{cases}$$

$$x - y = 30$$

$$x = 30 + y$$

$$\pm\sqrt{xy} = 8$$

$$\pm\sqrt{(30 + y)y} = 8$$

$$y^2 + 30y = 64$$

$$y^2 + 30y - 64 = 0$$

$$(y + 32)(y - 2) = 0$$

$$y = -32, 2$$

If $y = 2$, $x = 30 + 2 = 32$

so, $\pm\sqrt{(2)(32)} = \pm\sqrt{64} = 8$ correct

If $y = -32$, $x = 30 - 32 = -2$

so, $\pm\sqrt{(-2)(-32)} = \pm\sqrt{64} = 8$ correct

$\boldsymbol{x = -2, \ y = -32 \ and \ x = 32, \ y = 2}$

15.
(85)
$$2 \sin^2 x = 13 \cos x - 5$$

$$2(1 - \cos^2 x) - 13 \cos x + 5 = 0$$

$$2 \cos^2 x + 13 \cos x - 7 = 0$$

$$(2 \cos x - 1)(\cos x + 7) = 0$$

$$\cos x = \frac{1}{2} \qquad \cos x = -7$$

$$\qquad\qquad\qquad \text{no answer}$$

$$x = \frac{\pi}{3}, \frac{5\pi}{3}$$

16.
(92)
$$\ _nP_r = \frac{n!}{(n - r)!}$$

$$\ _{10}P_6 = \frac{10!}{(10 - 6)!}$$

$$\boldsymbol{\ _{10}P_6 = 151,200}$$

$$\ _nC_r = \frac{n!}{(n - r)! \, r!}$$

$$\ _{10}C_6 = \frac{10!}{(10 - 6)! \, 6!}$$

$$\boldsymbol{\ _{10}C_6 = 210}$$

17.
(89)

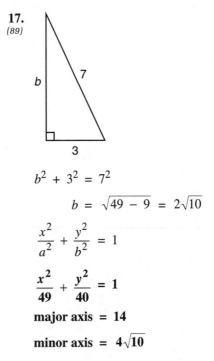

$$b^2 + 3^2 = 7^2$$

$$b = \sqrt{49 - 9} = 2\sqrt{10}$$

$$\frac{x^2}{a^2} + \frac{y^2}{b^2} = 1$$

$$\boldsymbol{\frac{x^2}{49} + \frac{y^2}{40} = 1}$$

major axis = 14

minor axis = $4\sqrt{10}$

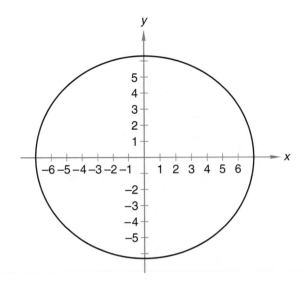

New rate $= \dfrac{\text{new distance}}{\text{new time}} = \dfrac{(k+12)\text{ km}}{\dfrac{k}{r}\text{ hr}}$

$= \dfrac{r(k+12)}{k}\ \dfrac{\text{km}}{\text{hr}}$

2. Purchases $= r$ books, price $= d$ dollars
(44)

Rate $= \dfrac{d}{r}\ \dfrac{\text{dollars}}{\text{book}}$

New rate $= \left(\dfrac{d}{r} - c\right)\dfrac{\text{dollars}}{\text{book}}$

$= \left(\dfrac{d-cr}{r}\right)\dfrac{\text{dollars}}{\text{book}}$

New rate $\times N =$ price

$\left(\dfrac{d-cr}{r}\right)\dfrac{\text{dollars}}{\text{book}} \times N = 20$ dollars

$N = \dfrac{20\text{ dollars}}{\dfrac{d-cr}{r}\ \dfrac{\text{dollars}}{\text{book}}}$

$= \dfrac{20r}{d-cr}\ \textbf{books}$

18. $\log_2\left(\log_2 x\right) = 3$
(98)

$\log_2 x = 2^3$

$x = 2^8$

$x = \textbf{256}$

19. $\dfrac{2\sin^2 x + \cos 2x}{\sec x}$
(93)

$= \dfrac{2\left(1-\cos^2 x\right)+\left(2\cos^2 x - 1\right)}{\sec x}$

$= \dfrac{2 - 2\cos^2 x + 2\cos^2 x - 1}{\sec x}$

$= \dfrac{1}{\sec x} = \textbf{cos } \textbf{x}$

20. $f(x) = \sqrt{9 - x^2}$
(21)

$y^2 = 9 - x^2$

$y^2 + x^2 = 3^2$

semicircle

radius $= 3$

center $= (0, 0)$

E.

Test 25, Form B

1. Distance $= k$ km, rate $= r\ \dfrac{\text{km}}{\text{hr}}$
(28)

Time $= \dfrac{\text{distance}}{\text{rate}} = \dfrac{k}{r}$ hr

New distance $= (k + 12)$ km

3. (a) $\quad y = \log_9 85$
(98)

$9^y = 85$

$y \log 9 = \log 85$

$y = \dfrac{\log 85}{\log 9} = \textbf{2.02}$

(b) $\quad y = \log_3 28$

$3^y = 28$

$y \log 3 = \log 28$

$y = \dfrac{\log 28}{\log 3} = \textbf{3.03}$

4. $\left(\dfrac{1}{x+6}\right)4^{\log_4\left(x^2+3x-18\right)-\log_4(x-3)}$
(98)

$= \dfrac{1}{x+6}\,4^{\log_4\frac{x^2+3x-18}{x-3}}$

$= \dfrac{1}{x+6}\cdot\dfrac{(x+6)(x-3)}{(x-3)}$

$= \dfrac{x+6}{x+6} = \textbf{1}$

5. Radius = 12 ft
(73) Side of square = 2(12) = 24 ft

Perimeter = 4(24) = **96 ft**

6. Arithmetic mean = $\dfrac{x + y}{2} = \dfrac{23 + 41}{2} = \mathbf{32}$
(99)

Geometric mean = $\pm\sqrt{xy} = \pm\sqrt{23 \cdot 41} = \pm\sqrt{\mathbf{943}}$

7. $a_n = a_1 r^{(n-1)}$
(99)

$a_5 = 243\left(\dfrac{1}{3}\right)^4 = \mathbf{3\ ft}$

8. $\qquad (R_J + R_K)T = \text{sections}$
(25)

$\left(\dfrac{2}{r} + \dfrac{1}{p}\right) \dfrac{\text{sections}}{\text{hr}}\, T = 6\ \text{sections}$

$\left(\dfrac{2p + r}{rp}\dfrac{\text{sections}}{\text{hr}}\right) T = 6\ \text{sections}$

$\qquad\qquad T = \dfrac{6\ \text{sections}}{\dfrac{2p + r}{rp}\ \dfrac{\text{sections}}{\text{hr}}}$

$\qquad\qquad T = \dfrac{6rp}{2p + r}\ \mathbf{hr}$

9. $-6 + 3i$
(95)

$r\ \text{cis}\ \theta = \sqrt{(-6)^2 + 3^2}\ \text{cis}\left[\tan^{-1}\left(\dfrac{3}{-6}\right)\right]$

$\qquad = 6.71\ \text{cis}\ 153.43°$

$(-6 + 3i)^{1/3} = (6.71)^{1/3}\ \text{cis}\ \dfrac{153.43°}{3}$

$\qquad = \mathbf{1.89\ cis\ 51.14°,\ 1.89\ cis\ 171.14°,}$

$\qquad \mathbf{1.89\ cis\ 291.14°}$

10. $y = -2 + \csc\theta$
(84, 94)

Amplitude = 1

Centerline = −2

Coefficient = $\dfrac{360}{360} = 1$

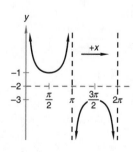

11.
(97)

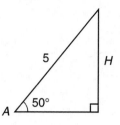

$H = 5\sin 50° = 3.83$

$a = 4,\ b = 5$

$H < a < b$ so there are two triangles possible:

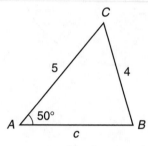

$\dfrac{4}{\sin 50°} = \dfrac{5}{\sin B}$

$\sin B = \dfrac{5\sin 50°}{4}$

$B = \mathbf{73.25°}$

$C = 180° - 50° - 73.25°$

$C = \mathbf{56.75°}$

$\dfrac{c}{\sin 56.75°} = \dfrac{4}{\sin 50°}$

$c = \dfrac{4\sin 56.75°}{\sin 50°}$

$c = \mathbf{4.37}$

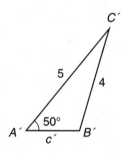

$B' = 180° - 73.25°$

$B' = \mathbf{106.75°}$

$C' = 180° - 50° - 106.75°$

$C' = \mathbf{23.25°}$

$\dfrac{c'}{\sin 23.25°} = \dfrac{4}{\sin 50°}$

$c' = \dfrac{4\sin 23.25°}{\sin 50°}$

$c' = \mathbf{2.06}$

12.
(88)
$$\begin{cases} A_0 = 800{,}000 \\ A_0 e^{k25} = 20{,}000 \end{cases}$$

$$800{,}000\, e^{k25} = 20{,}000$$

$$e^{k25} = \frac{1}{40}$$

$$25k = \ln \frac{1}{40}$$

$$k = -0.147555$$

$$800{,}000\, e^{-0.147555t} = 1$$

$$-0.147555t = \ln \frac{1}{800{,}000}$$

$$t = \textbf{92.12 yr}$$

13. $a_1, a_1 r, a_1 r^2, a_1 r^3, a_1 r^4$
(91)

$$a_1 r^3 = 4(-2)^4 = \textbf{64}$$

14.
(99)
$$\begin{cases} \pm\sqrt{xy} = 6 \\ x - y = 5 \end{cases}$$

$$x - y = 5$$

$$x = 5 + y$$

$$\pm\sqrt{xy} = 6$$

$$\pm\sqrt{(5 + y)y} = 6$$

$$y^2 + 5y = 36$$

$$y^2 + 5y - 36 = 0$$

$$(y + 9)(y - 4) = 0$$

$$y = -9, 4$$

If $y = 4$, $x = 5 + 4 = 9$

so, $\pm\sqrt{(9)(4)} = \pm\sqrt{36} = 6$ correct

If $y = -9$, $x = 5 - 9 = -4$

so, $\pm\sqrt{(-4)(-9)} = \pm\sqrt{36} = 6$ correct

$x = \textbf{9}, y = \textbf{4}$ and $x = \textbf{-4}, y = \textbf{-9}$

15.
(85)
$$2\cos^2 x = 13\sin x - 5$$

$$2(1 - \sin^2 x) - 13\sin x + 5 = 0$$

$$2\sin^2 x + 13\sin x - 7 = 0$$

$$(2\sin x - 1)(\sin x + 7) = 0$$

$$\sin x = \frac{1}{2} \qquad \sin x = -7$$
$$\qquad\qquad\qquad\text{no answer}$$

$$x = \frac{\pi}{6}, \frac{5\pi}{6}$$

16.
(92)
$$_nP_r = \frac{n!}{(n - r)!}$$

$$_{13}P_5 = \frac{13!}{(13 - 5)!}$$

$$_{13}P_5 = \textbf{154,440}$$

$$_nC_r = \frac{n!}{(n - r)!\, r!}$$

$$_{13}C_5 = \frac{13!}{(13 - 5)!\, 5!}$$

$$_{13}C_5 = \textbf{1287}$$

17.
(89)

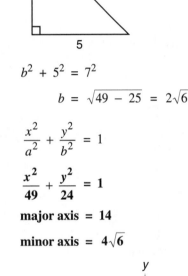

$$b^2 + 5^2 = 7^2$$

$$b = \sqrt{49 - 25} = 2\sqrt{6}$$

$$\frac{x^2}{a^2} + \frac{y^2}{b^2} = 1$$

$$\frac{x^2}{\textbf{49}} + \frac{y^2}{\textbf{24}} = \textbf{1}$$

major axis = 14

minor axis = $4\sqrt{6}$

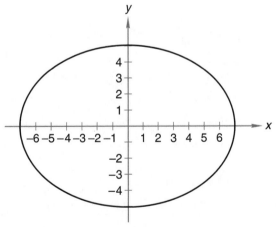

18. $\log_3 (\log_3 x) = 2$
(98)

$$\log_3 x = 3^2$$

$$x = 3^9$$

$$x = \textbf{19,683}$$

19.
(93)
$$\frac{2\sin^2 x + \cos 2x}{\csc x}$$

$$= \frac{2(1 - \cos^2 x) + (2\cos^2 x - 1)}{\csc x}$$

$$= \frac{2 - 2\cos^2 x + 2\cos^2 x - 1}{\csc x}$$

$$= \frac{1}{\csc x} = \sin x$$

20. $f(x) = 3 - 3^{-x} = 3 - \left(\frac{1}{3}\right)^x$
(21)

Exponential

x	-1	0
y	0	2

D.

Test 26, Form A

1. $a_n = a_1 r^{(n-1)}$
(99)

$$a_4 = 250\left(\frac{3}{5}\right)^3 = \textbf{54 ft}$$

2.
(101)
$$\begin{vmatrix} 3 & 1 & 1 \\ 6 & 1 & 9 \\ 5 & 0 & 2 \end{vmatrix} = (6 + 45 + 0) - (5 + 0 + 12)$$

$$= 51 - 17 = \textbf{34}$$

3. $_{10}P_6 = \dfrac{10!}{4!} = \textbf{151,200}$
(92)

$$_{10}C_6 = \frac{10!}{6!4!} = \textbf{210}$$

4. $2\log(x^2 - 1) - 2\log y - 3\log(x + 1)$
(103)
$$+ \log(y + xy)$$

$$= \log(x^2 - 1)^2 - \log y^2 - \log(x + 1)^3$$
$$+ \log(y + xy)$$

$$= \log\frac{(x^2 - 1)^2(y + xy)}{y^2(x + 1)^3}$$

$$= \log\frac{(x + 1)(x - 1)(x + 1)(x - 1)y(x + 1)}{y^2(x + 1)(x + 1)(x + 1)}$$

$$= \log\frac{(x - 1)^2}{y}$$

5. $x =$
(101)
$$\frac{\begin{vmatrix} 2 & -4 & 1 \\ -10 & 2 & -3 \\ -1 & 2 & 0 \end{vmatrix}}{\begin{vmatrix} 2 & -4 & 1 \\ 0 & 2 & -3 \\ -3 & 2 & 0 \end{vmatrix}}$$

$$= \frac{(0 - 12 - 20) - (-2 - 12 + 0)}{(0 - 36 + 0) - (-6 - 12 + 0)}$$

$$= \frac{-32 + 14}{-36 + 18} = \frac{-18}{-18} = \textbf{1}$$

6. (a) $\log_6 15 = y$
(98)
$$6^y = 15$$
$$\log 6^y = \log 15$$
$$y \log 6 = \log 15$$
$$y = \frac{\log 15}{\log 6} = \textbf{1.51}$$

(b) $\log_{15} 6 = y$
$$15^y = 6$$
$$\log 15^y = \log 6$$
$$y \log 15 = \log 6$$
$$y = \frac{\log 6}{\log 15} = \textbf{0.66}$$

7. $\sin(A + B) = \sin A \cos B + \cos A \sin B$
(100)
$$\sin 345° = \sin(120° + 225°)$$
$$= \sin 120° \cos 225° + \cos 120° \sin 225°$$
$$= \left(\frac{\sqrt{3}}{2}\right)\left(-\frac{\sqrt{2}}{2}\right) + \left(-\frac{1}{2}\right)\left(-\frac{\sqrt{2}}{2}\right)$$
$$= -\frac{\sqrt{6}}{4} + \frac{\sqrt{2}}{4} = \frac{\sqrt{2} - \sqrt{6}}{4}$$

8.
(98)
$$\log_4 x = \sqrt{\log_4 x}$$
$$(\log_4 x)^2 = \log_4 x$$
$$(\log_4 x)^2 - \log_4 x = 0$$
$$(\log_4 x)(\log_4 x - 1) = 0$$

$$\log_4 x = 0 \qquad \log_4 x - 1 = 0$$
$$x = 4^0 \qquad\qquad \log_4 x = 1$$
$$x = 1 \qquad\qquad\qquad x = 4^1$$
$$x = \textbf{4}$$

9. $-27 = 27 \text{ cis } 180°$
(79)

$27^{1/3} \text{ cis } \dfrac{180°}{3} = 3 \text{ cis } 60° = \dfrac{3}{2} + \dfrac{3\sqrt{3}}{2}i$

$3 \text{ cis } (60° + 120°) = 3 \text{ cis } 180° = \mathbf{-3}$

$3 \text{ cis } (60° + 240°) = 3 \text{ cis } 300° = \dfrac{3}{2} - \dfrac{3\sqrt{3}}{2}i$

10. (a) $\text{pH} = -\log \text{H}^+ = -\log\left(7.9 \times 10^{-9}\right) = \mathbf{8.10}$
(103)

(b) $\text{H}^+ = 10^{-\text{pH}} = 10^{-3.2} = \mathbf{6.31 \times 10^{-4}}$

11. $y = -2 + 3 \cos \dfrac{1}{2}(\theta - 100°)$
(84)

Amplitude $= 3$

Centerline $= -2$

Period $= \dfrac{360°}{\dfrac{1}{2}} = 720°$

Phase angle $= 100°$

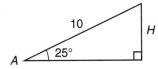

12. $F = 3x,\ S = -2y^2$
(102)

Exponents of F	5	4	3	2	1	0
Exponents of S	0	1	2	3	4	5
Coefficients	1	5	10	10	5	1

$10F^2S^3 = 10(3x)^2(-2y^2)^3 = \mathbf{-720x^2y^6}$

13. $\cos(x + y) = \cos x \cos y - \sin x \sin y$
(100)

$\underline{\cos(x - y) = \cos x \cos y + \sin x \sin y}$

$\cos(x + y) + \cos(x - y) = 2 \cos x \cos y$

$\mathbf{\cos x \cos y = \dfrac{1}{2}\left[\cos(x + y) + \cos(x - y)\right]}$

14.
(97)

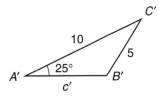

$H = 10 \sin 25° = 4.23$

$a = 5,\ b = 10$

$H < a < b$, so there are two possible triangles.

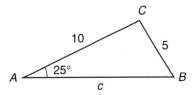

$\dfrac{5}{\sin 25°} = \dfrac{10}{\sin B}$

$\sin B = \dfrac{10 \sin 25°}{5}$

$B = \mathbf{57.70°}$

$C = 180° - 25° - 57.70°$

$C = \mathbf{97.30°}$

$\dfrac{c}{\sin 97.30°} = \dfrac{5}{\sin 25°}$

$c = \dfrac{5 \sin 97.30°}{\sin 25°}$

$c = \mathbf{11.74}$

$B' = 180° - 57.70°$

$B' = \mathbf{122.30°}$

$C' = 180° - 25° - 122.30°$

$C' = \mathbf{32.70°}$

$\dfrac{c'}{\sin 32.70°} = \dfrac{5}{\sin 25°}$

$c' = \dfrac{5 \sin 32.70°}{\sin 25°}$

$c' = \mathbf{6.39}$

15. $\sin 2x = \sin x$
(90)

$2 \sin x \cos x = \sin x$

$2 \sin x \cos x - \sin x = 0$

$\sin x(2 \cos x - 1) = 0$

$\sin x = 0 \qquad 2 \cos x - 1 = 0$

$x = \mathbf{0, \pi} \qquad 2 \cos x = 1$

$\cos x = \dfrac{1}{2}$

$x = \mathbf{\dfrac{\pi}{3}, \dfrac{5\pi}{3}}$

16.
(93)
$$\frac{1 - 3 \sin x - 4 \sin^2 x}{\cos^2 x}$$

$$= \frac{(1 - 4 \sin x)(1 + \sin x)}{1 - \sin^2 x}$$

$$= \frac{(1 - 4 \sin x)(1 + \sin x)}{(1 - \sin x)(1 + \sin x)}$$

$$= \frac{1 - 4 \sin x}{1 - \sin x}$$

17.
(103)
$$\log \left(\frac{xy^2}{z^4} \right) = \log (xy^2) - \log z^4$$

$$= \log x + \log y^2 - \log z^4$$

$$= \log x + 2 \log y - 4 \log z$$

18. (a)
(104)
$$S_n = \frac{a_1(1 - r^n)}{1 - r}$$

$$S_{10} = \frac{-6(1 - (-2)^{10})}{1 - (-2)} = \frac{-6(1 - 1024)}{3}$$

$$= 2046$$

(b) $a_n = a_1 + d(n - 1)$

$$a_{10} = -6 + (-2)(10 - 1) = -24$$

$$S_n = \frac{n}{2}(a_1 + a_n)$$

$$S_{10} = \frac{10}{2}[-6 + (-24)] = 5(-30) = -150$$

19.
(88)
$$A_t = 48e^{kt}$$

$$42 = 48e^{50k}$$

$$0.875 = e^{50k}$$

$$-0.13353 = 50k$$

$$k = -0.0026706$$

$$A_t = 48e^{-0.0026706t}$$

$$25 = 48e^{-0.0026706t}$$

$$0.52083 = e^{-0.0026706t}$$

$$-0.65233 = -0.0026706t$$

$$t = 244.26 \text{ min}$$

20. (a) $y = \tan \theta$
(94)

(b) Function $= \sec x$

Amplitude $= 8 - 2 = 6$

Centerline $= 2$

Coefficient $= \dfrac{360°}{360°} = 1$

$y = 2 + 6 \sec x$

Test 26, Form B

1.
(99)
$$a_n = a_1 r^{(n - 1)}$$

$$a_3 = 50\left(\frac{2}{5}\right)^2 = \textbf{8 ft}$$

2.
(101)
$$\begin{vmatrix} 2 & 0 & 1 \\ 3 & 1 & 2 \\ 1 & 2 & 3 \end{vmatrix} = (6 + 0 + 6) - (1 + 8 + 0)$$

$$= 12 - 9 = \textbf{3}$$

3.
(92)
$$_9P_3 = \frac{9!}{6!} = \textbf{504}$$

$$_9C_3 = \frac{9!}{3!6!} = \textbf{84}$$

4.
(103)
$$\log (y^2 - 1) - 3 \log x - 2 \log (y + 1)$$
$$+ \log (x + xy)$$

$$= \log (y^2 - 1) - \log x^3 - \log (y + 1)^2$$
$$+ \log (x + xy)$$

$$= \log \frac{(y^2 - 1)(x + xy)}{x^3(y + 1)^2}$$

$$= \log \frac{(y + 1)(y - 1)x(1 + y)}{x^3(y + 1)(y + 1)}$$

$$= \log \frac{(y - 1)}{x^2}$$

5.
(101)
$$x = \frac{\begin{vmatrix} 0 & 2 & 1 \\ 5 & -1 & -1 \\ 12 & -2 & -3 \end{vmatrix}}{\begin{vmatrix} 1 & 2 & 1 \\ 3 & -1 & -1 \\ 5 & -2 & -3 \end{vmatrix}}$$

$$= \frac{(0 - 24 - 10) - (-12 + 0 - 30)}{(3 - 10 - 6) - (-5 + 2 - 18)}$$

$$= \frac{-34 + 42}{-13 + 21} = \frac{8}{8} = \textbf{1}$$

6. (a) $\log_7 12 = y$
(98)

$$7^y = 12$$

$$\log 7^y = \log 12$$

$$y \log 7 = \log 12$$

$$y = \frac{\log 12}{\log 7} = \textbf{1.28}$$

(b) $\log_{12} 7 = y$

$$12^y = 7$$

$$\log 12^y = \log 7$$

$$y \log 12 = \log 7$$

$$y = \frac{\log 7}{\log 12} = \mathbf{0.78}$$

7. $\sin (A + B) = \sin A \cos B + \cos A \sin B$
(100)

$\sin 285° = \sin (150° + 135°)$

$\quad = \sin 150° \cos 135° + \cos 150° \sin 135°$

$$= \left(\frac{1}{2}\right)\left(-\frac{\sqrt{2}}{2}\right) + \left(-\frac{\sqrt{3}}{2}\right)\left(\frac{\sqrt{2}}{2}\right)$$

$$= -\frac{\sqrt{2}}{4} - \frac{\sqrt{6}}{4} = \frac{-\sqrt{2} - \sqrt{6}}{4}$$

8. $\qquad \log_9 y = \sqrt{\log_9 y}$
(98)

$$(\log_9 y)^2 = \log_9 y$$

$$(\log_9 y)^2 - \log_9 y = 0$$

$$\log_9 y(\log_9 y - 1) = 0$$

$$\log_9 y = 0 \qquad \log_9 y - 1 = 0$$

$$y = 9^0 \qquad \log_9 y = 1$$

$$y = \mathbf{1} \qquad \quad y = 9^1$$

$$y = \mathbf{9}$$

9. $-81 = 81 \text{ cis } 180°$
(79)

$$81^{1/4} \text{ cis } \frac{180°}{4} = 3 \text{ cis } 45° = \frac{3\sqrt{2}}{2} + \frac{3\sqrt{2}}{2}i$$

$$3 \text{ cis } (45° + 90°) = 3 \text{ cis } 135°$$

$$= -\frac{3\sqrt{2}}{2} + \frac{3\sqrt{2}}{2}i$$

$$3 \text{ cis } (45° + 180°) = 3 \text{ cis } 225°$$

$$= -\frac{3\sqrt{2}}{2} - \frac{3\sqrt{2}}{2}i$$

$$3 \text{ cis } (45° + 270°) = 3 \text{ cis } 315°$$

$$= \frac{3\sqrt{2}}{2} - \frac{3\sqrt{2}}{2}i$$

10. (a) $\text{pH} = -\log \text{H}^+ = -\log\left(4.3 \times 10^{-10}\right) = \mathbf{9.37}$
(103)

(b) $\text{H}^+ = 10^{-\text{pH}} = 10^{-2.3} = \mathbf{5.01 \times 10^{-3}}$

11. $y = 2 + 2 \cos \frac{1}{3}(\theta - 60°)$
(84)

Amplitude $= 2$

Centerline $= 2$

$$\text{Period} = \frac{360°}{\frac{1}{3}} = 1080°$$

Phase angle $= 60°$

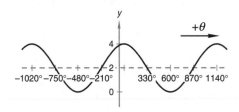

12. $F = 2x, \; S = -3y^2$
(102)

Exponents of F	5	4	3	2	1	0
Exponents of S	0	1	2	3	4	5
Coefficients	1	5	10	10	5	1

$$10F^3S^2 = 10(2x)^3(-3y^2)^2 = \mathbf{720x^3y^4}$$

13. $-\cos (x + y) = -\cos x \cos y + \sin x \sin y$
(100)

$$\underline{\cos (x - y) = \cos x \cos y + \sin x \sin y}$$

$$\cos (x - y) - \cos (x + y) = 2 \sin x \sin y$$

$$\sin x \sin y = \frac{1}{2}[\cos (x - y) - \cos (x + y)]$$

14.
(97)

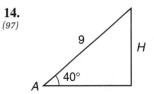

$H = 9 \sin 40° = 5.79$

$a = 7, \; b = 9$

$H < a < b$, so there are two possible triangles.

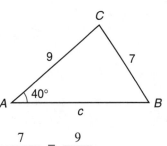

$$\frac{7}{\sin 40°} = \frac{9}{\sin B}$$

$$\sin B = \frac{9 \sin 40°}{7}$$

$$B = \mathbf{55.73°}$$

$$C = 180° - 40° - 55.73°$$

$$C = \mathbf{84.27°}$$

$$\frac{c}{\sin 84.27°} = \frac{7}{\sin 40°}$$

$$c = \frac{7 \sin 84.27°}{\sin 40°}$$

$$c = \mathbf{10.84}$$

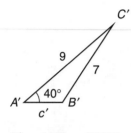

$$B' = 180° - 55.73°$$

$$B' = \mathbf{124.27°}$$

$$C' = 180° - 40° - 124.27°$$

$$C' = \mathbf{15.73°}$$

$$\frac{c'}{\sin 15.73°} = \frac{7}{\sin 40°}$$

$$c' = \frac{7 \sin 15.73°}{\sin 40°}$$

$$c' = \mathbf{2.95}$$

15.
(90)

$$\sin 2x = \cos x$$

$$2 \sin x \cos x = \cos x$$

$$2 \sin x \cos x - \cos x = 0$$

$$\cos x(2 \sin x - 1) = 0$$

$$\cos x = 0 \qquad\qquad 2 \sin x - 1 = 0$$

$$x = \frac{\pi}{2}, \frac{3\pi}{2} \qquad 2 \sin x = 1$$

$$\sin x = \frac{1}{2}$$

$$x = \frac{\pi}{6}, \frac{5\pi}{6}$$

16.
(93)

$$\frac{1 - 3 \cos x - 4 \cos^2 x}{\sin^2 x}$$

$$= \frac{(1 - 4 \cos x)(1 + \cos x)}{1 - \cos^2 x}$$

$$= \frac{(1 - 4 \cos x)(1 + \cos x)}{(1 - \cos x)(1 + \cos x)} = \mathbf{\frac{1 - 4 \cos x}{1 - \cos x}}$$

17. $\log\left(\dfrac{x^3 y}{z^2}\right) = \log(x^3 y) - \log z^2$
(103)

$$= \log x^3 + \log y - \log z^2$$

$$= \mathbf{3 \log x + \log y - 2 \log z}$$

18. (a) $S_n = \dfrac{a_1(1 - r^n)}{1 - r}$
(104)

$$S_7 = \frac{5(1 - 3^7)}{1 - 3} = \frac{5(-2186)}{-2} = \mathbf{5465}$$

(b) $a_n = a_1 + d(n - 1)$

$$a_7 = 5 + 3(7 - 1) = 23$$

$$S_n = \frac{n}{2}(a_1 + a_n)$$

$$S_7 = \frac{7}{2}(5 + 23) = \mathbf{98}$$

19.
(88)

$$A_t = 62e^{kt}$$

$$48 = 62e^{40k}$$

$$0.774203 = e^{40k}$$

$$-0.25592 = 40k$$

$$k = -0.006398$$

$$A_t = 62e^{-0.006398t}$$

$$30 = 62e^{-0.006398t}$$

$$0.48387 = e^{-0.006398t}$$

$$-0.72594 = -0.006398t$$

$$t = \mathbf{113.46 \ min}$$

20. (a) $y = \cot \theta$
(94)

(b) Function $= \sec x$

Amplitude $= -2 - (-3) = 1$

Centerline $= -3$

Coefficient $= \dfrac{360°}{360°} = 1$

$$y = \mathbf{-3 + \sec x}$$

Test 27, Form A

1.
(44)

$$(R_B + R_M)T = \text{problems}$$

$$\left(\frac{p}{2} + \frac{x}{h}\right)\frac{\text{problems}}{\text{hr}}T = 400 \text{ problems}$$

$$\left(\frac{ph + 2x}{2h}\right)\frac{\text{problems}}{\text{hr}}T = 400 \text{ problems}$$

$$T = \frac{800h}{ph + 2x} \text{ hours}$$

2.
(105)
$$\begin{vmatrix} -3 & 2 & 4 \\ 0 & 1 & -2 \\ -1 & 7 & 0 \end{vmatrix}$$

$$= -3\begin{vmatrix} 1 & -2 \\ 7 & 0 \end{vmatrix} - 2\begin{vmatrix} 0 & -2 \\ -1 & 0 \end{vmatrix} + 4\begin{vmatrix} 0 & 1 \\ -1 & 7 \end{vmatrix}$$

$$= -3(14) - 2(-2) + 4(1) = \mathbf{-34}$$

3.
(96, 72)

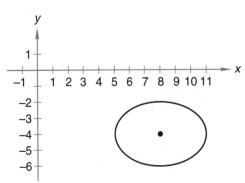

$h = 6 \sin 65° = 5.438$

$a = 6 \cos 65° = 2.536$

$b^2 + h^2 = 10^2$

$\quad b = \sqrt{10^2 - (5.438)^2} = 8.392$

$A = \dfrac{1}{2}(a + b)h$

$\quad = \dfrac{1}{2}(2.536 + 8.392)(5.438) = \mathbf{29.71\ m^2}$

4. $-3 + 4i$
(95)

$r \operatorname{cis} \theta = \sqrt{(-3)^2 + (4)^2}\ \operatorname{cis}\left[\tan^{-1}\left(\dfrac{4}{-3}\right)\right]$

$\quad = 5 \operatorname{cis} 126.87°$

$(-3 + 4i)^{1/4} = 5^{1/4} \operatorname{cis}\left(\dfrac{126.87°}{4}\right)$

$\quad\quad = \mathbf{1.50\ cis\ 31.72°,\ 1.50\ cis\ 121.72°,}$
$\quad\quad\ \ \mathbf{1.50\ cis\ 211.72°,\ 1.50\ cis\ 301.72°}$

5. $\quad y = \log_7 4$
(98)

$\quad 7^y = 4$

$\quad \ln 7^y = \ln 4$

$\quad y \ln 7 = \ln 4$

$\quad\quad y = \dfrac{\ln 4}{\ln 7}$

6. (a) $\text{pH} = -\log \text{H}^+ = -\log\left(4.1 \times 10^{-5}\right) = \mathbf{4.39}$
(103)

$\quad$ (b) $\text{H}^+ = 10^{-\text{pH}} = 10^{-3.7}$

$\quad\quad\quad = \mathbf{2.0 \times 10^{-4}\ moles\ per\ liter}$

7.
(102)

Exponents of $3x^2$		6	5	4	3	2	1	0	
Exponents of $(-2y)$		0	1	2	3	4	5	6	
Coefficients		1	6	15	20	15	6	1	

$$20\left(3x^2\right)^3(-2y)^3 = \mathbf{-4320x^6y^3}$$

8. $\dfrac{\sqrt[4]{2300}\ \sqrt[3]{4800}}{\sqrt{5400}} = \mathbf{1.59}$
(103)

9. (a) $\quad\quad \cos^2 x - \sin^2 x = -1$
(85, 52)

$\quad\quad\ \left(1 - \sin^2 x\right) - \sin^2 x = -1$

$\quad\quad\quad\quad 1 - 2\sin^2 x + 1 = 0$

$\quad\quad\quad\quad\quad 2\left(1 - \sin^2 x\right) = 0$

$\quad\quad\quad\quad\quad\quad \sin^2 x = 1$

$\quad\quad\quad\quad\quad\quad \sin x = \pm 1$

$\quad\quad\quad\quad\quad\quad x = \dfrac{\pi}{2}, \dfrac{3\pi}{2}$

$\quad$ (b) $1 + \sqrt{3}\tan 2x = 0$

$\quad\quad\quad\quad \tan 2x = -\dfrac{1}{\sqrt{3}}$

$\quad\quad\quad\quad 2x = \dfrac{5\pi}{6}, \dfrac{11\pi}{6}, \dfrac{17\pi}{6}, \dfrac{23\pi}{6}$

$\quad\quad\quad\quad x = \dfrac{5\pi}{12}, \dfrac{11\pi}{12}, \dfrac{17\pi}{12}, \dfrac{23\pi}{12}$

10. $\quad\quad 4x^2 + 9y^2 - 64x + 72y + 364 = 0$
(106)

$4\left(x^2 - 16x \quad\right) + 9\left(y^2 + 8y \quad\right) = -364$

$4\left(x^2 - 16x + 64\right) + 9\left(y^2 + 8y + 16\right) = 36$

$\quad\quad\quad 4(x - 8)^2 + 9(y + 4)^2 = 36$

$\quad\quad\quad \dfrac{(x - 8)^2}{9} + \dfrac{(y + 4)^2}{4} = 1$

center $= (8, -4)$

major axis $= 6$

minor axis $= 4$

11.
(106)

$$16x^2 - y^2 + 32x + 2y - 1 = 0$$

$$16(x^2 + 2x \quad) - (y^2 - 2y \quad) = 1$$

$$16(x^2 + 2x + 1) - (y^2 - 2y + 1) = 1$$

$$16(x + 1)^2 - (y - 1)^2 = 16$$

$$\frac{(x + 1)^2}{1} - \frac{(y - 1)^2}{16} = 1$$

center = (–1, 1)

If: $y = 1$

$$(x + 1)^2 = 1$$

$$x + 1 = \pm 1$$

$$x = -1 \pm 1 = 0, -2$$

vertices = (0, 1); (–2, 1)

asymptotes:

$y = 4x + b$	$y = -4x + b$
$1 = 4(-1) + b$	$1 = -4(-1) + b$
$b = 5$	$b = -3$
$y = 4x + 5$	$y = -4x - 3$

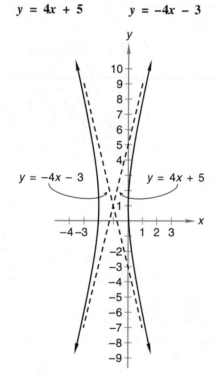

12. Rate $= \dfrac{d}{t} \dfrac{\text{dollars}}{\text{ticket}}$
(44)

New Rate $= \dfrac{d}{t} - x = \dfrac{d - xt}{t} \dfrac{\text{dollars}}{\text{ticket}}$

Rate $\times N = $ dollars

$$\frac{d - xt}{t} \frac{\text{dollars}}{\text{ticket}} \times N = 500 \text{ dollars}$$

$$N = \frac{500t}{d - xt} \text{ tickets}$$

13. $A = \begin{bmatrix} 2 & 6 \\ 4 & 3 \end{bmatrix}$, $\quad B = \begin{bmatrix} 1 & 0 \\ -3 & -4 \end{bmatrix}$
(108)

$$A + B = \begin{bmatrix} 2 + 1 & 6 + 0 \\ 4 - 3 & 3 - 4 \end{bmatrix}$$

$$A + B = \begin{bmatrix} 3 & 6 \\ 1 & -1 \end{bmatrix}$$

$$A - B = \begin{bmatrix} 2 - 1 & 6 - 0 \\ 4 + 3 & 3 + 4 \end{bmatrix}$$

$$A - B = \begin{bmatrix} 1 & 6 \\ 7 & 7 \end{bmatrix}$$

$$2A = \begin{bmatrix} 2 \cdot 2 & 2 \cdot 6 \\ 2 \cdot 4 & 2 \cdot 3 \end{bmatrix}$$

$$2A = \begin{bmatrix} 4 & 12 \\ 8 & 6 \end{bmatrix}$$

14. $\log_5 \left(\dfrac{25 \sqrt[3]{x^4 y^5}}{z^{-2}} \right)$
(103)

$$= \log_5 25 + \log_5 x^{4/3} y^{5/3} - \log_5 z^{-2}$$

$$= \log_5 5^2 + \log_5 x^{4/3} + \log_5 y^{5/3} - \log_5 z^{-2}$$

$$= 2 + \frac{4}{3} \log_5 x + \frac{5}{3} \log_5 y + 2 \log_5 z$$

15. $6 - \dfrac{6}{2} + \dfrac{6}{4} - \dfrac{6}{8} + \ldots$
(107)

$$a_1 = 6, \quad r = -\frac{1}{2}$$

$$S = \frac{a_1}{1 - r} = \frac{6}{1 - \left(-\dfrac{1}{2}\right)} = 4$$

16. (a)
(94)

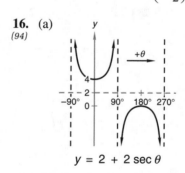

$$y = 2 + 2 \sec \theta$$

(b)

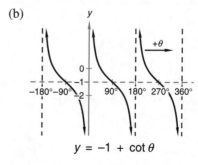

$$y = -1 + \cot \theta$$

17. log $(x + 3) - \log (2x - 3) = 2 \log \sqrt{2}$
(59)
$$\log \frac{x + 3}{2x - 3} = \log \left(\sqrt{2}\right)^2$$
$$\frac{x + 3}{2x - 3} = 2$$
$$x + 3 = 4x - 6$$
$$3x = 9$$
$$x = \mathbf{3}$$

18. $\dfrac{1 + \cos 2x}{\csc x \sin 2x} = \dfrac{1 + \left(2 \cos^2 x - 1\right)}{\dfrac{1}{\sin x} \cdot 2 \sin x \cos x}$
(93, 90)

$$= \frac{2 \cos^2 x}{2 \cos x} = \mathbf{\cos x}$$

19. Function $= \sin x$
(57, 66)
Centerline $= 2$

Amplitude $= 3$

Period $= \dfrac{2\pi}{\dfrac{1}{2}} = 4\pi$

Phase angle $= \pi$

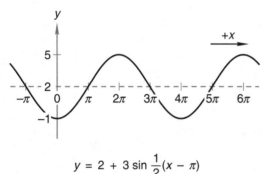

$$y = 2 + 3 \sin \frac{1}{2}(x - \pi)$$

20. (a) $y = \tan \theta$
(94)
(b) $y = 9 + 3 \csc x$

Test 27, Form B

1.
(44)
$$\left(R_J + R_D\right)T = \text{wrestlers}$$
$$\left(\frac{4}{9} + \frac{3}{m}\right)\frac{\text{wrestlers}}{\text{min}} \, T = 15 \text{ wrestlers}$$
$$\left(\frac{4m + 27}{9m}\right)\frac{\text{wrestlers}}{\text{min}} \, T = 15 \text{ wrestlers}$$
$$T = \frac{135m}{4m + 27} \text{ min}$$

2. $\begin{vmatrix} 4 & 2 & -3 \\ -2 & 1 & 0 \\ -1 & 7 & 0 \end{vmatrix}$
(105)

$$= 4 \begin{vmatrix} 1 & 0 \\ 7 & 0 \end{vmatrix} - 2 \begin{vmatrix} -2 & 0 \\ -1 & 0 \end{vmatrix} + 3 \begin{vmatrix} -2 & 1 \\ -1 & 7 \end{vmatrix}$$
$$= 4(0) - 2(0) + 3(-13) = \mathbf{-39}$$

3.
(96, 72)

$h = 7 \sin 55° = 5.734$

$a = 7 \cos 55° = 4.015$

$b^2 + h^2 = 11^2$

$$b = \sqrt{11^2 - (5.734)^2} = 9.387$$

$A = \dfrac{1}{2}(a + b)h$

$$= \frac{1}{2}(4.015 + 9.387)(5.734) = \mathbf{38.42 \text{ m}^2}$$

4. $-4 + 3i$
(95)
$$r \operatorname{cis} \theta = \sqrt{(-4)^2 + 3^2} \operatorname{cis} \left[\tan^{-1}\left(\frac{3}{-4}\right)\right]$$
$$= 5 \operatorname{cis} 143.13°$$

$$(-4 + 3i)^{1/4} = 5^{1/4} \operatorname{cis} \left(\frac{143.13°}{4}\right)$$
$$= \mathbf{1.50 \operatorname{cis} 35.78°, \ 1.50 \operatorname{cis} 125.78°,}$$
$$\mathbf{1.50 \operatorname{cis} 215.78°, \ 1.50 \operatorname{cis} 305.78°}$$

5. $\quad y = \log_9 5$
(98)
$$9^y = 5$$
$$\ln 9^y = \ln 5$$
$$y \ln 9 = \ln 5$$
$$y = \frac{\ln 5}{\ln 9}$$

6. (a) pH $= -\log \text{H}^+ = -\log \left(2.6 \times 10^{-2}\right) = \mathbf{1.59}$
(103)
(b) $\text{H}^+ = 10^{-\text{pH}} = 10^{-11.6}$

$$= \mathbf{2.51 \times 10^{-12} \text{ moles per liter}}$$

Test Solutions

7.
(102)

Exponents of $2x$	4	3	**2**	1	0
Exponents of $(-4y^2)$	0	1	**2**	3	4
Coefficients	1	4	**6**	4	1

$$6(2x)^2(-4y^2)^2 = \mathbf{384x^2y^4}$$

8.
(103)
$$\frac{\sqrt[3]{1600}\ \sqrt[7]{20{,}000}}{\sqrt{2300}} = \mathbf{1.00}$$

9. (a)
(85, 52)
$$2\cos^2 x + \cos x - 1 = 0$$
$$(2\cos x - 1)(\cos x + 1) = 0$$

$$2\cos x - 1 = 0 \qquad \cos x + 1 = 0$$
$$2\cos x = 1 \qquad \cos x = -1$$
$$\cos x = \frac{1}{2} \qquad x = \pi$$
$$x = \frac{\pi}{3}, \frac{5\pi}{3}$$

(b) $1 - \sqrt{3}\tan 2x = 0$
$$\tan 2x = \frac{1}{\sqrt{3}}$$
$$2x = \frac{\pi}{6}, \frac{7\pi}{6}, \frac{13\pi}{6}, \frac{19\pi}{6}$$
$$x = \frac{\pi}{12}, \frac{7\pi}{12}, \frac{13\pi}{12}, \frac{19\pi}{12}$$

10.
(106)
$$9x^2 + 4y^2 - 72x + 64y + 364 = 0$$
$$9(x^2 - 8x \quad) + 4(y^2 + 16y \quad) = -364$$
$$9(x^2 - 8x + 16) + 4(y^2 + 16y + 64) = 36$$
$$9(x - 4)^2 + 4(y + 8)^2 = 36$$
$$\frac{(x - 4)^2}{4} + \frac{(y + 8)^2}{9} = 1$$

center = $(4, -8)$

major axis = **6**

minor axis = **4**

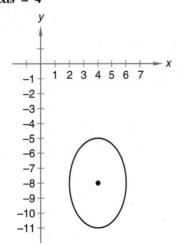

11.
(106)
$$16y^2 - x^2 + 32y + 2x - 1 = 0$$
$$16(y^2 + 2y \quad) - (x^2 - 2x \quad) = 1$$
$$16(y^2 + 2y + 1) - (x^2 - 2x + 1) = 16$$
$$16(y + 1)^2 - (x - 1)^2 = 16$$
$$\frac{(y + 1)^2}{1} - \frac{(x - 1)^2}{16} = 1$$

center = $(1, -1)$

If: $\quad x = 1$
$$(y + 1)^2 = 1$$
$$y + 1 = \pm 1$$
$$y = -1 \pm 1 = 0, -2$$

vertices = $(1, 0); (1, -2)$

asymptotes:

$$y = \frac{1}{4}x + b \qquad\qquad y = -\frac{1}{4}x + b$$
$$-1 = \frac{1}{4}(1) + b \qquad -1 = -\frac{1}{4}(1) + b$$
$$b = -\frac{5}{4} \qquad\qquad b = -\frac{3}{4}$$
$$y = \frac{1}{4}x - \frac{5}{4} \qquad y = -\frac{1}{4}x - \frac{3}{4}$$

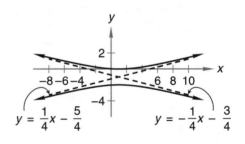

$$y = \frac{1}{4}x - \frac{5}{4} \qquad\qquad y = -\frac{1}{4}x - \frac{3}{4}$$

12.
(44)
$$\text{Rate} = \frac{c}{p}\ \frac{\text{cents}}{\text{pack}}$$

$$\text{New Rate} = \frac{c}{p} - d\ \frac{\text{cents}}{\text{pack}} = \frac{c - dp}{p}\ \frac{\text{cents}}{\text{pack}}$$

$$\text{Rate} \times N = \text{cents}$$
$$\frac{c - dp}{p}\ \frac{\text{cents}}{\text{pack}} \times N = 1000 \text{ cents}$$
$$N = \frac{1000p}{c - dp}\ \textbf{packs}$$

13. $A = \begin{bmatrix} 2 & 2 \\ 2 & 0 \end{bmatrix}, \qquad B = \begin{bmatrix} 2 & 5 \\ 2 & 2 \end{bmatrix}$
(108)

$A + B = \begin{bmatrix} 2+2 & 2+5 \\ 2+2 & 0+2 \end{bmatrix}$

$A + B = \begin{bmatrix} 4 & 7 \\ 4 & 2 \end{bmatrix}$

$A - B = \begin{bmatrix} 2-2 & 2-5 \\ 2-2 & 0-2 \end{bmatrix}$

$A - B = \begin{bmatrix} 0 & -3 \\ 0 & -2 \end{bmatrix}$

$2B = \begin{bmatrix} 2\cdot2 & 2\cdot5 \\ 2\cdot2 & 2\cdot2 \end{bmatrix}$

$2B = \begin{bmatrix} 4 & 10 \\ 4 & 4 \end{bmatrix}$

14. $\log_6\left(\dfrac{36\sqrt[4]{x^2 y^9}}{z}\right)$
(103)

$= \log_6 36 + \log_6 x^{2/4}y^{9/4} - \log_6 z$

$= \log_6 6^2 + \log_6 x^{1/2} + \log_6 y^{9/4} - \log_6 z$

$= 2 + \dfrac{1}{2}\log_6 x + \dfrac{9}{4}\log_6 y - \log_6 z$

15. $2 + \dfrac{1}{2} + \dfrac{1}{8} + \dfrac{1}{32} + \ldots$
(107)

$a_1 = 2, \ r = \dfrac{1}{4}$

$S = \dfrac{a_1}{1-r} = \dfrac{2}{1-\frac{1}{4}} = \dfrac{8}{3}$

16. (a)
(94)

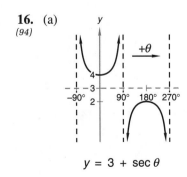

$y = 3 + \sec\theta$

(b)

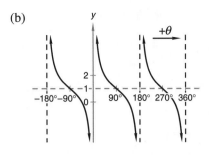

$y = \cot\theta + 1$

17. $\log(x+3) - \log x = 6\log\sqrt[3]{3}$
(59)

$\log\dfrac{x+3}{x} = \log\left(\sqrt[3]{3}\right)^6$

$\dfrac{x+3}{x} = 3^2$

$x + 3 = 9x$

$8x = 3$

$x = \dfrac{3}{8}$

18. $\dfrac{1-\cos 2x}{\sec x \sin 2x} = \dfrac{1-(1-2\sin^2 x)}{\frac{1}{\cos x}\cdot 2\sin x\cos x}$
(93, 90)

$= \dfrac{2\sin^2 x}{2\sin x} = \sin x$

19. Function $= \sin x$
(57, 66)

Centerline $= 1$

Amplitude $= 2$

Period $= \dfrac{2\pi}{\frac{1}{2}} = 4\pi$

Phase angle $= -\pi$

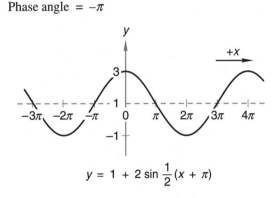

$y = 1 + 2\sin\dfrac{1}{2}(x+\pi)$

20. (a) $y = -2\tan\theta$
(94)

(b) $y = 3 + 2\csc x$

Test 28, Form A

1. $P(\text{both blue}) = \dfrac{4}{9} \cdot \dfrac{3}{8} = \dfrac{12}{72} = \dfrac{1}{6}$
(83)

2. $y = \begin{vmatrix} 3 & 0 & 0 \\ 1 & 5 & -3 \\ 1 & -2 & 1 \\ 3 & 2 & 0 \\ 1 & 0 & -3 \\ 1 & 1 & 1 \end{vmatrix}$
(101)

$= \dfrac{(15 + 0 + 0) - (0 + 18 + 0)}{(0 - 6 + 0) - (0 - 9 + 2)}$

$= \dfrac{15 - 18}{-6 + 7} = -3$

3. $0.0\overline{439} = \dfrac{439}{10,000} + \left(\dfrac{1}{1000}\right)\left(\dfrac{439}{10,000}\right)$
(109)

$+ \left(\dfrac{1}{1000}\right)^2\left(\dfrac{439}{10,000}\right) + \dots$

$a_1 = \dfrac{439}{10,000}, \ r = \dfrac{1}{1000}$

$S = \dfrac{a_1}{1 - r} = \dfrac{\frac{439}{10,000}}{1 - \frac{1}{1000}} = \dfrac{\frac{439}{10,000}}{\frac{999}{1000}} = \dfrac{439}{9990}$

4. $a_1 = 132, \ r = \dfrac{1}{4}$
(107)

$S = 132 + \left(\dfrac{1}{4}\right)132 + \left(\dfrac{1}{4}\right)^2 132 + \dots$

$S = \dfrac{a_1}{1 - r} = \dfrac{132}{1 - \frac{1}{4}} = \dfrac{132}{\frac{3}{4}} = 176$

$\text{Total} = 176 + (176 - 132) = 220 \text{ ft}$

5. $a_1 = -4, \ r = -3$
(91, 104)

(a) $a_n = a_1 r^{n-1}$

$a_{10} = (-4)(-3)^9 = 78,732$

(b) $S_n = \dfrac{a_1(1 - r^n)}{1 - r}$

$S_{10} = \dfrac{(-4)\left[1 - (-3)^{10}\right]}{1 - (-3)} = 59,048$

6. (a) $H^+ = 10^{-pH} = 10^{-11.8}$
(103)

$= 1.58 \times 10^{-12} \text{ mole per liter}$

(b) $pH = -\log H^+ = -\log\left(3.25 \times 10^{-8}\right) = 7.49$

7. $x^2 + 9y^2 + 10x + 18y - 2 = 0$
(106)

$\left(x^2 + 10x \quad\right) + 9\left(y^2 + 2y \quad\right) = 2$

$\left(x^2 + 10x + 25\right) + 9\left(y^2 + 2y + 1\right) = 36$

$(x + 5)^2 + 9(y + 1)^2 = 36$

$\dfrac{(x + 5)^2}{36} + \dfrac{(y + 1)^2}{4} = 1$

center $= (-5, -1)$

major axis $= 12$

minor axis $= 4$

Major axis is horizontal.

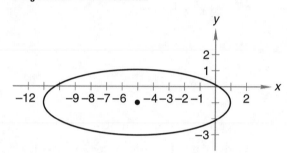

8. $4x^2 - y^2 - 24x + 2y - 1 = 0$
(106)

$4\left(x^2 - 6x \quad\right) - \left(y^2 - 2y \quad\right) = 1$

$4\left(x^2 - 6x + 9\right) - \left(y^2 - 2y + 1\right) = 36$

$4(x - 3)^2 - (y - 1)^2 = 36$

$\dfrac{(x - 3)^2}{9} - \dfrac{(y - 1)^2}{36} = 1$

center $= (3, 1)$

If $y = 1$, then

$\dfrac{(x - 3)^2}{9} = 1$

$x = 3 \pm 3 = 6, 0$

vertices $= (6, 1), (0, 1)$

asymptotes:

$y = 2x + b$	$y = -2x + b$
$1 = 2(3) + b$	$1 = -2(3) + b$
$b = -5$	$b = 7$
$y = 2x - 5$	$y = -2x + 7$

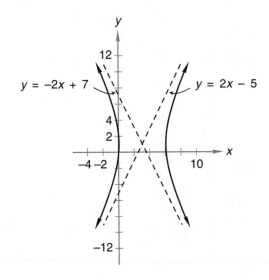

$y = -2x + 7$ $y = 2x - 5$

12.
(44)
$$\text{Rate} = \frac{d}{n} \frac{\text{dollars}}{\text{ticket}}$$

$$\text{New rate} = \left(\frac{d}{n} - 10\right) \frac{\text{dollars}}{\text{ticket}}$$

$$= \frac{d - 10n}{n} \frac{\text{dollars}}{\text{ticket}}$$

$$\text{New rate} \times N = \text{dollars}$$

$$\frac{d - 10n}{n} \frac{\text{dollars}}{\text{ticket}} \times N = 250 \text{ dollars}$$

$$N = \frac{250n}{d - 10n} \text{ tickets}$$

9.
(59)
$$9^{\log_3 12 + 2 \log_3 2 - \log_3 6}$$

$$= 9^{\log_3 12 + \log_3 4 + \log_3 \frac{1}{6}}$$

$$= 3^{2\left(\log_3 12 + \log_3 4 + \log_3 \frac{1}{6}\right)}$$

$$= 3^{\log_3 12^2 + \log_3 4^2 + \log_3 \left(\frac{1}{6}\right)^2}$$

$$= 3^{\log_3 \frac{(144)(16)}{36}} = \frac{(144)(16)}{36} = \mathbf{64}$$

13.
(98)
$$\log \sqrt[4]{x^3} + \log \sqrt[4]{x^5} = \frac{2}{3} \log 27$$

$$\log x^{3/4} x^{5/4} = \log 27^{2/3}$$

$$\log x^{8/4} = \log 9$$

$$x^2 = 9$$

$$x = \pm 3$$

$$x = \mathbf{3}$$

10.
(111)
$$\log_3(x - 2) < 3$$

$$(x - 2) < 3^3$$

$$x < 29$$

$$(x - 2) > 0$$

$$x > 2$$

$$\mathbf{2 < x < 29}$$

14.
(103)
$$\frac{\left(\sqrt[3]{406 \times 10^3}\right)^2}{\sqrt{807 \times 10^{17}}} = \mathbf{6.10 \times 10^{-7}}$$

15.
(48, 52)
$$\tan^2 2\theta = 1$$

$$\tan 2\theta = \pm 1$$

$$2\theta = 45°, 135°, 225°, 315°, 405°, 495°, 585°,$$
$$675°$$

$$\theta = \mathbf{22.50°, 67.50°, 112.50°, 157.50°, 202.50°,}$$
$$\mathbf{247.50°, 292.50°, 337.50°}$$

11.
(88)
$$\begin{cases} 120 = A_0 e^{k5} \\ 400 = A_0 e^{k15} \end{cases}$$

$$\frac{400}{120} = \frac{A_0 e^{k15}}{A_0 e^{k5}}$$

$$\frac{10}{3} = e^{k10}$$

$$10k = \ln \frac{10}{3}$$

$$k = 0.1204$$

$$120 = A_0 e^{(0.1204)5}$$

$$A_0 = 120 e^{-0.602}$$

$$A_0 = 65.73$$

$$A_{25} = 65.73 e^{(0.1204)25} = \mathbf{1333 \text{ aliens}}$$

16.
(90)
$$\frac{2 \cot x}{\cot^2 x + 1} = \frac{2 \cot x}{\csc^2 x} = \frac{\frac{2 \cos x}{\sin x}}{\frac{1}{\sin^2 x}}$$

$$= 2 \sin x \cos x = \mathbf{\sin 2x}$$

17.
(40)
$$-\log_3 (m + 1) + 2 \log_3 m + \log_3 \left(m^2 - 1\right)$$

$$- \log_3 \left(m^2 + m\right)$$

$$= \log_3 \frac{m^2\left(m^2 - 1\right)}{(m + 1)\left(m^2 + m\right)}$$

$$= \log_3 \frac{m^2(m + 1)(m - 1)}{(m + 1)m(m + 1)} = \mathbf{\log_3 \frac{m(m - 1)}{m + 1}}$$

18. $F = 2x$, $S = -3y^2$, $n = 11$, and $k = 5$
(112)

$$\frac{n!}{(n - k + 1)! \, (k - 1)!} F^{n-k+1} S^{k-1}$$

$$= \frac{11!}{(11 - 5 + 1)! \, (5 - 1)!} F^{11-5+1} S^{5-1}$$

$$= \frac{11!}{7! 4!} F^7 S^4 = 330(2x)^7 \left(-3y^2\right)^4$$

$$= \mathbf{3,421,440} x^7 y^8$$

19. $(1)^{1/3} = (\text{cis } 0°)^{1/3} = \text{cis } 0°, \text{cis } 120°, \text{cis } 240°$
(79)

$$= \mathbf{1}, -\frac{1}{2} + \frac{\sqrt{3}}{2} i, \; -\frac{1}{2} - \frac{\sqrt{3}}{2} i$$

20.
(110)

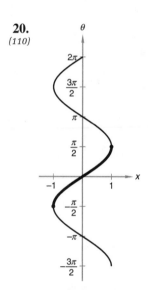

$\theta = \arcsin x$

Domain $= \left\{ x \in \mathbb{R} \mid -1 \le x \le 1 \right\}$

Range $= \left\{ \theta \in \mathbb{R} \mid -\dfrac{\pi}{2} \le \theta \le \dfrac{\pi}{2} \right\}$

$\text{Arcsin} \left(-\dfrac{\sqrt{2}}{2} \right) = -\dfrac{\pi}{4}$

$\text{Arcsin} \left(\dfrac{\sqrt{2}}{2} \right) = \dfrac{\pi}{4}$

$\text{Arcsin} (-1) = -\dfrac{\pi}{2}$

Test 28, Form B

1. $P(\text{both green}) = \dfrac{6}{11} \cdot \dfrac{5}{10} = \dfrac{30}{110} = \dfrac{\mathbf{3}}{\mathbf{11}}$
(83)

2. $y = \dfrac{\begin{vmatrix} 3 & 0 & 1 \\ 0 & -3 & -3 \\ 1 & 1 & 1 \end{vmatrix}}{\begin{vmatrix} 3 & 4 & 1 \\ 0 & 1 & -3 \\ 1 & 1 & 1 \end{vmatrix}}$
(101)

$$= \frac{(-9 + 0 + 0) - (-3 - 9 + 0)}{(3 - 12 + 0) - (1 - 9 + 0)}$$

$$= \frac{-9 + 12}{-9 + 8} = \mathbf{-3}$$

3. $0.0\overline{311} = \dfrac{311}{10,000} + \left(\dfrac{1}{1000}\right)\left(\dfrac{311}{10,000}\right)$
(109)

$$+ \left(\dfrac{1}{1000}\right)^2 \left(\dfrac{311}{10,000}\right) + \dots$$

$$a_1 = \frac{311}{10,000}, \; r = \frac{1}{1000}$$

$$S = \frac{a_1}{1 - r} = \frac{\dfrac{311}{10,000}}{1 - \dfrac{1}{1000}} = \frac{\dfrac{311}{10,000}}{\dfrac{999}{1000}} = \frac{\mathbf{311}}{\mathbf{9990}}$$

4. $a_1 = 132$, $r = \dfrac{1}{3}$
(107)

$$S = 132 + \left(\frac{1}{3}\right)132 + \left(\frac{1}{3}\right)^2 132 + \dots$$

$$S = \frac{a_1}{1 - r} = \frac{132}{1 - \dfrac{1}{3}} = \frac{132}{\dfrac{2}{3}} = 198$$

Total $= 198 + (198 - 132) = \mathbf{264 \text{ ft}}$

5. $a_1 = 5$, $r = -2$
(91, 104)

(a) $a_n = a_1 r^{n-1}$

$a_9 = (5)(-2)^8 = \mathbf{1280}$

(b) $S_n = \dfrac{a_1(1 - r^n)}{1 - r}$

$$S_{10} = \frac{(5)\left[1 - (-2)^9\right]}{1 - (-2)} = \mathbf{855}$$

6. (a) $H^+ = 10^{-pH} = 10^{-4.3}$
(103)
$= 5.01 \times 10^{-5}$ mole per liter

(b) $pH = -\log H^+ = -\log\left(7.94 \times 10^{-12}\right) = 11.10$

7. $x^2 + 4y^2 + 6x - 16y + 9 = 0$
(106)
$\left(x^2 + 6x \quad\right) + 4\left(y^2 - 4y \quad\right) = -9$

$\left(x^2 + 6x + 9\right) + 4\left(y^2 - 4y + 4\right) = 16$

$(x + 3)^2 + 4(y - 2)^2 = 16$

$$\frac{(x + 3)^2}{16} + \frac{(y - 2)^2}{4} = 1$$

center $= (-3, 2)$
major axis $= 8$
minor axis $= 4$
Major axis is horizontal.

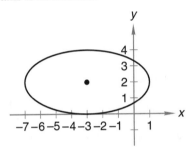

8. $x^2 - 9y^2 - 4x + 72y - 149 = 0$
(106)
$\left(x^2 - 4x \quad\right) - 9\left(y^2 - 8y \quad\right) = 149$

$\left(x^2 - 4x + 4\right) - 9\left(y^2 - 8y + 16\right) = 9$

$(x - 2)^2 - 9(y - 4)^2 = 9$

$$\frac{(x - 2)^2}{9} - \frac{(y - 4)^2}{1} = 1$$

center $= (2, 4)$
If $y = 4$, then

$$\frac{(x - 2)^2}{9} = 1$$

$x = 2 \pm 3 = 5, -1$

vertices $= (5, 4), (-1, 4)$
asymptotes:

$y = \frac{1}{3}x + b \qquad y = -\frac{1}{3}x + b$

$4 = \frac{1}{3}(2) + b \qquad 4 = -\frac{1}{3}(2) + b$

$b = \frac{10}{3} \qquad\qquad b = \frac{14}{3}$

$y = \frac{1}{3}x + \frac{10}{3} \qquad y = -\frac{1}{3}x + \frac{14}{3}$

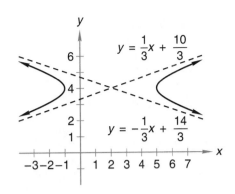

$y = \frac{1}{3}x + \frac{10}{3}$

$y = -\frac{1}{3}x + \frac{14}{3}$

9. $4^{\log_2 3 + 2\log_2 2 - \log_2 5}$
(59)
$= 4^{\log_2 3 + \log_2 4 - \log_2 5}$

$= 2^{2\left(\log_2 3 + \log_2 4 - \log_2 5\right)}$

$= 2^{\log_2 3^2 + \log_2 4^2 - \log_2 5^2}$

$= 2^{\log_2 \frac{(9)(16)}{25}} = \frac{(9)(16)}{25} = \frac{144}{25}$

10. $\log_2(x - 3) < 4$
(111)
$(x - 3) < 2^4$

$x < 19$

$(x - 3) > 0$

$x > 3$

$3 < x < 19$

11. $\begin{cases} 70 = A_0 e^{k5} \\ 225 = A_0 e^{k30} \end{cases}$
(88)

$\frac{225}{70} = \frac{A_0 e^{k30}}{A_0 e^{k5}}$

$\frac{45}{14} = e^{k25}$

$25k = \ln\frac{45}{14}$

$k = 0.04670$

$70 = A_0 e^{(0.04760)5}$

$A_0 = 70e^{-0.23352}$

$A_0 = 55.42$

$A_{50} = 55.42e^{(0.04670)50} = \textbf{572 sightings}$

12. Rate = $\dfrac{y}{x}\dfrac{\text{dollars}}{\text{copy}}$
(44)

New rate = $\left(\dfrac{y}{x} + 5\right)\dfrac{\text{dollars}}{\text{copy}} = \dfrac{y + 5x}{x}\dfrac{\text{dollars}}{\text{copy}}$

New rate $\times\ N$ = dollars

$\dfrac{y + 5x}{x}\dfrac{\text{dollars}}{\text{copy}} \times N = 50$ dollars

$N = \dfrac{50x}{y + 5x}$ copies

13. $\log \sqrt[3]{x^7} + \log \sqrt[3]{x^2} = \dfrac{3}{4}\log 16$
(98)

$\log x^{7/3}x^{2/3} = \log 16^{3/4}$

$\log x^{9/3} = \log 8$

$x^3 = 2^3$

$x = 2$

14. $\dfrac{\left(\sqrt[3]{619 \times 10^5}\right)^2}{\sqrt{502 \times 10^{19}}} = 2.21 \times 10^{-6}$
(103)

15. $\sin^2 2\theta = 1$
(48, 52)

$\sin 2\theta = \pm 1$

$2\theta = 90°, 270°, 450°, 630°$

$\theta = 45°, 135°, 225°, 315°$

16. $\dfrac{2\tan x}{\tan^2 x + 1} = \dfrac{2\tan x}{\sec^2 x} = \dfrac{\frac{2\sin x}{\cos x}}{\frac{1}{\cos^2 x}}$
(90)

$= 2\sin x \cos x = \sin 2x$

17. $-\log_4 (n + 2) + 3\log_4 n + \log_4 (n^2 - 4)$
(40)

$- \log_3 (n^2 + n)$

$= \log_4 \dfrac{(n^3)(n^2 - 4)}{(n + 2)(n^2 + n)}$

$= \log_4 \dfrac{(n^3)(n - 2)(n + 2)}{(n + 2)n(n + 1)} = \log_4 \dfrac{n^2(n - 2)}{n + 1}$

18. $F = 2x^2$, $S = -5y$, $n = 10$, and $k = 5$
(112)

$\dfrac{n!}{(n - k + 1)!\,(k - 1)!}\,F^{n-k+1}S^{k-1}$

$= \dfrac{10!}{(10 - 5 + 1)!\,(5 - 1)!}\,F^{10-5+1}S^{5-1}$

$= \dfrac{10!}{6!\,4!}\,F^6 S^4 = 210(2x^2)^6(-5y)^4$

$= 8,400,000\,x^{12}y^4$

19. $(i)^{1/3} = (\text{cis } 90°)^{1/3} = \text{cis } 30°,\ \text{cis } 150°,\ \text{cis } 270°$
(79)

$= \dfrac{\sqrt{3}}{2} + \dfrac{1}{2}i,\ -\dfrac{\sqrt{3}}{2} + \dfrac{1}{2}i,\ -i$

20.
(110)

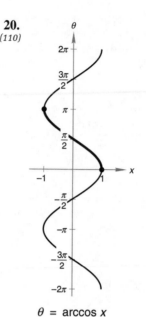

$\theta = \arccos x$

Domain $= \left\{x \in \mathbb{R}\ |\ -1 \le x \le 1\right\}$

Range $= \left\{x \in \mathbb{R}\ |\ 0 \le \theta \le \pi\right\}$

$\text{Arccos}\left(-\dfrac{\sqrt{2}}{2}\right) = \dfrac{3\pi}{4}$

$\text{Arccos}\left(\dfrac{\sqrt{2}}{2}\right) = \dfrac{\pi}{4}$

$\text{Arccos}\,(-1) = \pi$

Test 29, Form A

1. $P(3 \cup H) = P(3) + P(H) - P(3 \cap H)$
(92)

$= \dfrac{4}{52} + \dfrac{13}{52} - \dfrac{1}{52} = \dfrac{16}{52} = \dfrac{4}{13}$

2. $x = \dfrac{\begin{vmatrix} 0 & -2 & 0 \\ 5 & 0 & 3 \\ -7 & 2 & -5 \end{vmatrix}}{\begin{vmatrix} 3 & -2 & 0 \\ 1 & 0 & 3 \\ -1 & 2 & -5 \end{vmatrix}}$
(101)

$= \dfrac{(0 + 42 + 0) - (0 + 0 + 50)}{(0 + 6 + 0) - (0 + 18 + 10)}$

$= \dfrac{42 - 50}{6 - 28} = \dfrac{-8}{-22} = \dfrac{4}{11}$

3.
(108)
$$\begin{bmatrix} 2 & 0 \\ 2 & -3 \\ 4 & 1 \end{bmatrix} \cdot \begin{bmatrix} 1 & 3 \\ 2 & -5 \end{bmatrix}$$

$$= \begin{bmatrix} 2 \cdot 1 + 0 \cdot 2 & 2 \cdot 3 + 0 \cdot (-5) \\ 2 \cdot 1 + (-3) \cdot 2 & 2 \cdot 3 + (-3)(-5) \\ 4 \cdot 1 + 1 \cdot 2 & 4 \cdot 3 + 1(-5) \end{bmatrix}$$

$$= \begin{bmatrix} \mathbf{2} & \mathbf{6} \\ \mathbf{-4} & \mathbf{21} \\ \mathbf{6} & \mathbf{7} \end{bmatrix}$$

4.
(110)

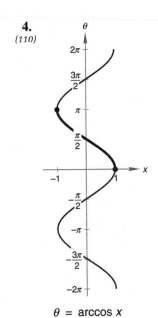

$\theta = \arccos x$

Domain $= \left\{ x \in \mathbb{R} \mid -1 \le x \le 1 \right\}$

Range $= \left\{ \theta \in \mathbb{R} \mid 0 \le \theta \le \pi \right\}$

$\textbf{Arccos} \left(\dfrac{\sqrt{3}}{2} \right) = \dfrac{\pi}{6}$

$\textbf{Arccos} \left(-\dfrac{\sqrt{3}}{2} \right) = \dfrac{5\pi}{6}$

$\textbf{Arccos} \, (0) = \dfrac{\pi}{2}$

5. $\log_4 (x - 2) > 2$
(111)
$$x - 2 > 4^2$$
$$x > 18$$

$$x - 2 > 0$$
$$x > 2$$

$$\boldsymbol{x > 18}$$

6. $F = 2x^3$, $S = (-y)$, $n = 12$, and $k = 8$
(112)

$$\frac{n!}{(n - k + 1)!\,(k - 1)!} F^{n-k+1} S^{k-1}$$

$$= \frac{12!}{(12 - 8 + 1)!\,(8 - 1)!} F^{(12-8+1)} S^{(8-1)}$$

$$= \frac{12!}{5!7!} F^5 S^7 = 792\left(2x^3\right)^5 (-y)^7 = \mathbf{-25{,}344x^{15}y^7}$$

7.
(113)
$$\begin{array}{r|rrrr} 2 & 1 & -5 & 1 & 12 \\ & & 2 & -6 & -10 \\ \hline & 1 & -3 & -5 & 2 \end{array}$$

$$\frac{x^3 - 5x^2 + x + 12}{x - 2} = x^2 - 3x - 5 + \frac{2}{x - 2}$$

8. $y = \cot (x - \pi)$
(94)

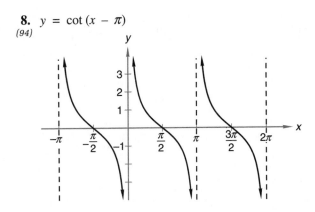

9.
(93)
$$\frac{\sin^2 x}{1 - \cos x} = \frac{1 - \cos^2 x}{1 - \cos x} \cdot \frac{\dfrac{1}{\cos^2 x}}{\dfrac{1}{\cos^2 x}}$$

$$= \frac{\sec^2 x - 1}{\sec^2 x - \sec x} = \frac{(\sec x - 1)(\sec x + 1)}{\sec x(\sec x - 1)}$$

$$= \frac{\mathbf{1 + \sec x}}{\mathbf{\sec x}}$$

10. $f(x) = (x - 1)(x - 2)^2$
(114)
The graph crosses the x axis at $x = 1$.
The graph is tangent to the x axis at $x = 2$.
y-intercept $= (0, -4)$

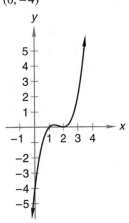

11. $\underline{2|}$ 1 −2 0 5 −10
(113)
          2   0 0 10
          ─────────────────
          1   0 0 5   0

The remainder is zero, so **2** is a zero of the polynomial.

12. $(x + 3)6^{\log_6(x^2 - 5x + 6) - \log_6(x^2 - 9)}$
(40, 59)

$= (x + 3)6^{\log_6 \frac{x^2 - 5x + 6}{x^2 - 9}}$

$= \dfrac{(x + 3)(x^2 - 5x + 6)}{x^2 - 9}$

$= \dfrac{(x + 3)(x - 3)(x - 2)}{(x - 3)(x + 3)} = x - 2$

13. $\sin x + \sin y = 2 \sin \dfrac{x + y}{2} \cos \dfrac{x - y}{2}$
(100)

$\sin 105° + \sin 15°$

$= 2 \sin \dfrac{105° + 15°}{2} \cos \dfrac{105° - 15°}{2}$

$= 2 \sin 60° \cos 45° = 2\left(\dfrac{\sqrt{3}}{2}\right)\left(\dfrac{\sqrt{2}}{2}\right) = \dfrac{\sqrt{6}}{2}$

14. $4.\overline{13}$
(109)
$a_1 = 0.13,\ r = 0.01$

$4.\overline{13} = 4 + \dfrac{a_1}{1 - r} = 4 + \dfrac{0.13}{1 - 0.01}$

$= 4 + \dfrac{0.13}{.99} = 4 + \dfrac{13}{99} = \dfrac{409}{99}$

15. $\cos 2x - \sin x = 0$
(90, 84)

$\left(1 - 2 \sin^2 x\right) - \sin x = 0$

$2 \sin^2 x + \sin x - 1 = 0$

$(2 \sin x - 1)(\sin x + 1) = 0$

$2 \sin x - 1 = 0 \qquad \sin x + 1 = 0$

$\sin x = \dfrac{1}{2} \qquad\qquad \sin x = -1$

$\qquad\qquad\qquad\qquad x = \dfrac{3\pi}{2}$

$x = \dfrac{\pi}{6}, \dfrac{5\pi}{6}$

16. $\log(x - y) + 2 \log z - \log(x^2 z - y^2 z)$
(40)

$= \log \dfrac{(x - y)z^2}{x^2 z - y^2 z} = \log \dfrac{z^2(x - y)}{z(x^2 - y^2)}$

$= \log \dfrac{z(x - y)}{(x - y)(x + y)} = \log \dfrac{z}{x + y}$

17. $P(x) = 2x^3 - 5x^2 + 2x + 5$
(115)

$\underline{-2|}$ 2 −5   2   5
           −4 18 −40
         ──────────────────
          2 −9 20 −35

$P(-2) = -35$

18. $\qquad 9x^2 + 4y^2 + 54x - 8y + 49 = 0$
(106)
$9(x^2 + 6x + 9) + 4(y^2 - 2y + 1) = 36$

$9(x + 3)^2 + 4(y - 1)^2 = 36$

$\dfrac{(x + 3)^2}{4} + \dfrac{(y - 1)^2}{9} = 1$

Center: $(-3, 1)$

Length of major axis $= 6$

Length of minor axis $= 4$

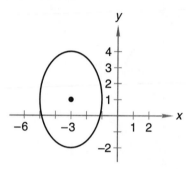

19. $y = x^3 - 2x + 1$
(116)
$\quad$ Radius $= \left(|-2| + 1\right) = 3$, y-intercept $= (0, 1)$

x	y
−2	−3
−1	2
0	1
1	0
2	5

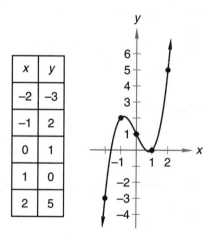

20. C.
(114)

Test 29, Form B

1. $P(4 \cup S) = P(4) + P(S) - P(4 \cap S)$
(92)
$$= \frac{4}{52} + \frac{13}{52} - \frac{1}{52} = \frac{16}{52} = \frac{4}{13}$$

2. $x = \dfrac{\begin{vmatrix} 3 & 2 & 0 \\ -1 & 0 & 6 \\ -2 & 2 & 4 \end{vmatrix}}{\begin{vmatrix} 3 & 2 & 0 \\ -2 & 0 & 6 \\ 1 & 2 & 4 \end{vmatrix}}$
(101)

$$= \frac{(0 - 24 + 0) - (0 + 36 - 8)}{(0 + 12 + 0) - (0 + 36 - 16)}$$

$$= \frac{-24 - 28}{12 - 20} = \frac{-52}{-8} = \frac{13}{2}$$

3. $\begin{bmatrix} 4 & 1 \\ 2 & -5 \\ 4 & 3 \end{bmatrix} \cdot \begin{bmatrix} -2 & -3 \\ 2 & 3 \end{bmatrix}$
(108)

$$= \begin{bmatrix} 4 \cdot (-2) + 1 \cdot 2 & 4 \cdot (-3) + 1 \cdot 3 \\ 2 \cdot (-2) + (-5) \cdot 2 & 2 \cdot (-3) + (-5) \cdot 3 \\ 4 \cdot (-2) + 3 \cdot 2 & 4 \cdot (-3) + 3 \cdot 3 \end{bmatrix}$$

$$= \begin{bmatrix} -6 & -9 \\ -14 & -21 \\ -2 & -3 \end{bmatrix}$$

4.
(110)

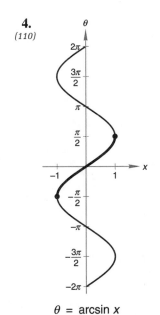

$\theta = \arcsin x$

Domain $= \left\{ x \in \mathbb{R} \mid -1 \le x \le 1 \right\}$

Range $= \left\{ \theta \in \mathbb{R} \mid -\dfrac{\pi}{2} \le \theta \le \dfrac{\pi}{2} \right\}$

$\text{Arcsin}\left(\dfrac{\sqrt{3}}{2}\right) = \dfrac{\pi}{3}$

$\text{Arcsin}\left(-\dfrac{\sqrt{3}}{2}\right) = -\dfrac{\pi}{3}$

$\text{Arcsin}\,(0) = 0$

5. $\log_3(x - 1) > 2$
(111)
$$x - 1 > 3^2$$
$$x > 10$$
$$x - 1 > 0$$
$$x > 1$$
$$x > 10$$

6. $F = 2a^3$, $S = (-b^2)$, $n = 8$, and $k = 3$
(112)

$$\frac{n!}{(n - k + 1)!\,(k - 1)!}\, F^{n-k+1} S^{k-1}$$

$$= \frac{8!}{(8 - 3 + 1)!\,(3 - 1)!}\, F^{(8-3+1)} S^{(3-1)}$$

$$= \frac{8!}{6!2!}\, F^6 S^2 = 28\left(2a^3\right)^6\left(-b^2\right)^2$$

$$= 1792\,a^{18}\,b^4$$

7. $3\mid\ \begin{array}{rrrrrr} 1 & 0 & -7 & -5 & 1 & -12 \\ & 3 & 9 & 6 & 3 & 12 \\ \hline 1 & 3 & 2 & 1 & 4 & 0 \end{array}$
(113)

$$\frac{x^5 - 7x^3 - 5x^2 + x - 12}{x - 3}$$

$$= x^4 + 3x^3 + 2x^2 + x + 4$$

8. $y = \tan(x - \pi)$
(94)

9.
(93)
$$\frac{\cos^2 x}{1 - \sin x} = \frac{1 - \sin^2 x}{1 - \sin x} \cdot \frac{\frac{1}{\sin^2 x}}{\frac{1}{\sin^2 x}}$$

$$= \frac{\csc^2 x - 1}{\csc^2 x - \csc x} = \frac{(\csc x - 1)(\csc x + 1)}{\csc x(\csc x - 1)}$$

$$= \frac{1 + \csc x}{\csc x}$$

10. $f(x) = (x + 2)(x - 1)^2$
(114)

The graph crosses the x axis at $x = -2$.

The graph is tangent to the x axis at $x = 1$.

y-intercept $= (0, 2)$

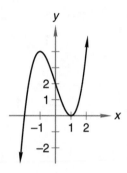

11.
(113)

$$3 \big| \begin{array}{ccccc} 2 & -3 & -5 & 6 & -51 \\ & 6 & 9 & 12 & 54 \\ \hline 2 & 3 & 4 & 18 & 3 \end{array}$$

There is a remainder, so 3 is not a zero of the polynomial.

12. $(x - 4)7^{\log_7(x^2 - 3x - 28) - \log_7(x^2 - 16)}$
(40, 59)

$$= (x - 4)7^{\log_7 \frac{x^2 - 3x - 28}{x^2 - 16}}$$

$$= \frac{(x - 4)(x^2 - 3x - 28)}{x^2 - 16}$$

$$= \frac{(x - 4)(x - 7)(x + 4)}{(x - 4)(x + 4)} = x - 7$$

13. $\cos x + \cos y = 2 \cos \frac{x + y}{2} \cos \frac{x - y}{2}$
(100)

$$\cos 105° + \cos 15°$$

$$= 2 \cos \frac{105° + 15°}{2} \cos \frac{105° - 15°}{2}$$

$$= 2 \cos 60° \cos 45° = 2\left(\frac{1}{2}\right)\left(\frac{\sqrt{2}}{2}\right) = \frac{\sqrt{2}}{2}$$

14. $4.\overline{21}$
(109)

$a_1 = 0.21, \ r = 0.01$

$$4.\overline{21} = 4 + \frac{a_1}{1 - r} = 4 + \frac{0.21}{1 - 0.01}$$

$$= 4 + \frac{0.21}{0.99} = 4 + \frac{21}{99} = \frac{417}{99}$$

15.
(90, 84)

$$\cos 2x - \cos x = 0$$

$$\left(2 \cos^2 x - 1\right) - \cos x = 0$$

$$2 \cos^2 x - \cos x - 1 = 0$$

$$(2 \cos x + 1)(\cos x - 1) = 0$$

$$2 \cos x + 1 = 0 \qquad\qquad \cos x - 1 = 0$$

$$\cos x = -\frac{1}{2} \qquad\qquad \cos x = 1$$

$$\qquad\qquad\qquad\qquad x = 0$$

$$x = \frac{2\pi}{3}, \frac{4\pi}{3}$$

16. $\ln (x + y) + 2 \ln z - \ln \left(y^2 z - x^2 z\right)$
(98)

$$= \ln \frac{(x + y)z^2}{y^2 z - x^2 z} = \ln \frac{z^2(x + y)}{z(y - x)(y + x)}$$

$$= \ln \frac{z(x + y)}{(y - x)(y + x)} = \ln \frac{z}{y - x}$$

17. $P(x) = 3x^3 + 4x^2 + 5x + 6$
(115)

$$-3 \big| \begin{array}{cccc} 3 & 4 & 5 & 6 \\ & -9 & 15 & -60 \\ \hline 3 & -5 & 20 & -54 \end{array}$$

$$P(-3) = -54$$

18.
(106)

$$9x^2 + 4y^2 - 54x - 16y + 61 = 0$$

$$9\left(x^2 - 6x + 9\right) + 4\left(y^2 - 4y + 4\right) = 36$$

$$9(x - 3)^2 + 4(y - 2)^2 = 36$$

$$\frac{(x - 3)^2}{4} + \frac{(y - 2)^2}{9} = 1$$

Center: (3, 2)

Length of major axis = 6

Length of minor axis = 4

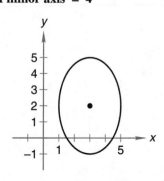

19. $y = 2x^3 - 3x + 2$
(116)
Radius $= \left(|-3| + 1\right) = 4$, y-intercept $= (0, 2)$

x	y
−1	3
0	2
1	1

20. D.
(114)

Test 30, Form A

1. $153 = 17 \cdot 3 \cdot 3$
(117)
$42 = 7 \cdot 3 \cdot 2$

No. Both numbers have 3 as a common factor.

2. $\quad 2|\ \ 1 \ -2 \ -9 \ \ 18$
(118)
$\qquad \qquad 2 \ \ \ 0 \ -18$
$\qquad \overline{1 \ \ \ 0 \ -9 \ \ \ \ 0}$

$(x - 2)(x^2 - 9) = 0$

$x^2 = 9$

Other roots are **3, −3**

3. Integral factors: $\dfrac{\{1, -1, 3, -3\}}{\{1, -1, 2, -2, 4, -4\}}$
(117)
Possible rational roots:

$\pm 1, \pm \dfrac{1}{2}, \pm \dfrac{1}{4}, \pm 3, \pm \dfrac{3}{2}, \pm \dfrac{3}{4}$

4. $y = x^3 - 4x^2 + x + 1$
(116)
Radius $= |-4| + 1 = \mathbf{5}$

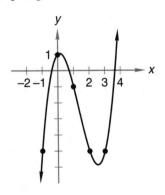

x	y
−1	−5
0	1
1	−1
2	−5
3	−5

5. $\quad -2|\ \ 4 \ \ \ 2 \ \ \ 3 \ \ \ \ 1$
(115)
$\qquad \qquad \quad -8 \ \ 12 \ -30$
$\qquad \overline{\quad 4 \ -6 \ \ 15 \ -29}$

$P(-2) = \mathbf{-29}$

6. $A_t = A_0 e^{kt}$
(88)
$10 = 20e^{14k}$

$0.5 = e^{14k}$

$k = -0.04951$

$5 = 20e^{-0.04951t}$

$t = \mathbf{28 \ days}$

7. $A \cdot B = \begin{bmatrix} 2 & 3 \\ 1 & 0 \\ 2 & 1 \end{bmatrix} \begin{bmatrix} -3 & 2 & 1 \\ 3 & 0 & 7 \end{bmatrix}$
(108)

$= \begin{bmatrix} 2(-3) + 3(3) & 2(2) + 3(0) & 2(1) + 3(7) \\ 1(-3) + 0(3) & 1(2) + 0(0) & 1(1) + 0(7) \\ 2(-3) + 1(3) & 2(2) + 1(0) & 2(1) + 1(7) \end{bmatrix}$

$= \begin{bmatrix} \mathbf{3} & \mathbf{4} & \mathbf{23} \\ \mathbf{-3} & \mathbf{2} & \mathbf{1} \\ \mathbf{-3} & \mathbf{4} & \mathbf{9} \end{bmatrix}$

8. $A = \begin{bmatrix} 1 & 3 \\ 2 & 4 \end{bmatrix}$
(120)

$A^{-1} = \dfrac{1}{(4)(1) - (2)(3)} \begin{bmatrix} 4 & -3 \\ -2 & 1 \end{bmatrix}$

$= -\dfrac{1}{2} \begin{bmatrix} 4 & -3 \\ -2 & 1 \end{bmatrix} = \begin{bmatrix} \mathbf{-2} & \dfrac{\mathbf{3}}{\mathbf{2}} \\ \mathbf{1} & -\dfrac{\mathbf{1}}{\mathbf{2}} \end{bmatrix}$

9. $\log_3 \left(\dfrac{(x + 1)^3 \sqrt{y}}{\sqrt{y + 3}\ (x + 1)^2} \right)$
(103)

$= \log_3 \left(\dfrac{(x + 1)\sqrt{y}}{\sqrt{y + 3}} \right)$

$= \log_3 (x + 1) + \log_3 y^{1/2} - \log_3 (y + 3)^{1/2}$

$= \mathbf{\log_3 (x + 1) + \dfrac{1}{2} \log_3 y - \dfrac{1}{2} \log_3 (y + 3)}$

10. $f(x) = \text{Arctan } x$
(110)

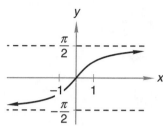

Domain $= \{x \in \mathbb{R} \mid -\infty < x < \infty\}$

Range $= \left\{f(x) \in \mathbb{R} \mid -\dfrac{\pi}{2} < f(x) < \dfrac{\pi}{2}\right\}$

Arctan 1 $= \dfrac{\pi}{4}$

Arctan (–1) $= -\dfrac{\pi}{4}$

Arctan $\sqrt{3}$ $= \dfrac{\pi}{3}$

11. $f(x) = x(x - 2)(x + 2)$
(114)

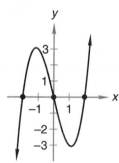

12. $4x^2 - y^2 + 8x - 4y - 4 = 0$
(106)
$$4(x^2 + 2x + 1) - (y^2 + 4y + 4) = 4$$

$$\dfrac{(x + 1)^2}{1} - \dfrac{(y + 2)^2}{4} = 1$$

center: $(-1, -2)$

vertices: $(0, -2), (-2, -2)$

asymptotes: $y = 2x, \; y = -2x - 4$

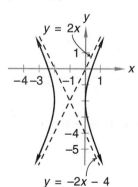

13. $\dfrac{n!}{(n - k + 1)!\,(k - 1)!}\,F^{n-k+1}S^{k-1}$
(112)

$$= \dfrac{9!}{(9 - 6 + 1)!\,(6 - 1)!}\,(3x^2)^4\left(-\dfrac{1}{x}\right)^5$$

$$= \dfrac{9!}{4!5!}\,3^4 x^8\left(-\dfrac{1}{x}\right)^5 = -10{,}206x^3$$

14. $4^{2x+3} = 8^{4x-1}$
(82)
$$\left(2^2\right)^{2x+3} = \left(2^3\right)^{4x-1}$$

$$2^{4x+6} = 2^{12x-3}$$

$$4x + 6 = 12x - 3$$

$$8x = 9$$

$$x = \dfrac{9}{8}$$

15. $\sin 2x + 2\sin^2 x + \cos 2x$
(90)
$$= (2\sin x \cos x) + 2\sin^2 x + \left(\cos^2 x - \sin^2 x\right)$$

$$= \cos^2 x + \sin^2 x + 2\sin x \cos x$$

$$= \mathbf{1 + 2\sin x \cos x}$$

16. $2\cot^2 x + 3\csc x = 0$
(85)
$$2\left(\csc^2 x - 1\right) + 3\csc x = 0$$

$$2\csc^2 x + 3\csc x - 2 = 0$$

$$(2\csc x - 1)(\csc x + 2) = 0$$

$2\csc x - 1 = 0$	$\csc x + 2 = 0$
$2\csc x = 1$	$\csc x = -2$
$\csc x = \dfrac{1}{2}$	$x = \dfrac{7\pi}{6}, \dfrac{11\pi}{6}$
no answer	

17. $y = x^3 + 2x^2 - x - 2$
(119)

upper bound

$$\begin{array}{r|rrrr} 1 & 1 & 2 & -1 & -2 \\ & & 1 & 3 & 2 \\ \hline & 1 & 3 & 2 & 0 \end{array}$$

All signs are positive,
so **upper bound = 1.**

lower bound

$$\begin{array}{r|rrrr} -3 & 1 & 2 & -1 & -2 \\ & & -3 & 3 & -6 \\ \hline & 1 & -1 & 2 & -8 \end{array}$$

Signs alternate, so
lower bound = –3.

18. $(-i)^{1/3} = (\text{cis } 270°)^{1/3} = \text{cis}\left(\dfrac{270°}{3}\right)$
(95)

$$= \text{cis } 90°, \text{cis } (90° + 120°), \text{cis } (90° + 240°)$$

$$= \text{cis } 90°, \text{cis } 210°, \text{cis } 330°$$

$$= \boldsymbol{i}, \; -\dfrac{\sqrt{3}}{2} - \dfrac{1}{2}\boldsymbol{i}, \; \dfrac{\sqrt{3}}{2} - \dfrac{1}{2}\boldsymbol{i}$$

19. (a) $p(x) = x^4 - x^3 - 3x^2 - x + 2$
(119)
   2 sign changes

   There are either 2 or 0 positive real roots.

   (b) $p(-x) = x^4 + x^3 - 3x^2 + x + 2$

   2 sign changes

   There are either 2 or 0 negative real roots.

20. $\begin{cases} R_T T_T = 200 \\ R_H T_H = 560 \end{cases}$
(25)

$$R_T T_T = 200$$

$$\left(R_H - 10\right)\left(\frac{1}{2} T_H\right) = 200$$

$$\frac{1}{2} R_H T_H - 5T_H = 200$$

$$\frac{1}{2}(560) - 5T_H = 200$$

$$-5T_H = -80$$

$$T_H = 16 \text{ hr}$$

$$R_H T_H = 560$$

$$R_H(16) = 560$$

$$R_H = \textbf{35 mph}$$

Test 30, Form B

1. $51 = 17 \cdot 3$
(117)
$340 = 17 \cdot 5 \cdot 2 \cdot 2$

   No. Both numbers have 17 as a common factor.

2. $\begin{array}{r} 3 \,\vert\; 1 \;\; -3 \;\; -4 \;\;\; 12 \\ 3 \;\;\;\; 0 \;\; -12 \\ \hline 1 \;\;\;\; 0 \;\; -4 \;\;\;\; 0 \end{array}$
(118)

$$(x - 3)(x^2 - 4) = 0$$

$$x^2 = 4$$

   Other roots are **2, -2**

3. Integral factors: $\dfrac{\{1, -1, 2, -2\}}{\{1, -1, 2, -2, 3, -3, 6, -6\}}$
(117)

   Possible rational roots:

$$\pm 1, \pm\frac{1}{2}, \pm\frac{1}{3}, \pm\frac{1}{6}, \pm 2, \pm\frac{2}{3}$$

4. $y = x^3 - 4x^2 + 6x + 1$
(116)
   Radius $= |6| + 1 = 7$

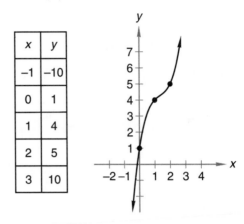

x	y
-1	-10
0	1
1	4
2	5
3	10

5. $\begin{array}{r} -3 \,\vert\; 4 \;\; -2 \;\;\;\; 2 \;\;\;\; -1 \\ -12 \;\; 42 \;\; -132 \\ \hline 4 \;\; -14 \;\; 44 \;\; -133 \end{array}$
(115)

$$P(-3) = \textbf{-133}$$

6. $A_t = A_0 e^{kt}$
(88)
$$15 = 30 e^{20k}$$

$$0.5 = e^{20k}$$

$$k = -0.03466$$

$$7 = 30 e^{-0.03466t}$$

$$t = \textbf{42 days}$$

7. $A \cdot B = \begin{bmatrix} 4 & 2 \\ 4 & 1 \\ 4 & 0 \end{bmatrix}\begin{bmatrix} 6 & 9 & 1 \\ 1 & 2 & 7 \end{bmatrix}$
(108)

$$= \begin{bmatrix} 4(6) + 2(1) & 4(9) + 2(2) & 4(1) + 2(7) \\ 4(6) + 1(1) & 4(9) + 1(2) & 4(1) + 1(7) \\ 4(6) + 0(1) & 4(9) + 0(2) & 4(1) + 0(7) \end{bmatrix}$$

$$= \begin{bmatrix} \textbf{26} & \textbf{40} & \textbf{18} \\ \textbf{25} & \textbf{38} & \textbf{11} \\ \textbf{24} & \textbf{36} & \textbf{4} \end{bmatrix}$$

8. $A = \begin{bmatrix} 4 & 3 \\ 2 & 1 \end{bmatrix}$
(120)

$$A^{-1} = \frac{1}{(1)(4) - (2)(3)}\begin{bmatrix} 1 & -3 \\ -2 & 4 \end{bmatrix}$$

$$= -\frac{1}{2}\begin{bmatrix} 1 & -3 \\ -2 & 4 \end{bmatrix} = \begin{bmatrix} -\dfrac{1}{2} & \dfrac{3}{2} \\ 1 & -2 \end{bmatrix}$$

9.
(103)
$$\log_4 \left(\frac{\sqrt[3]{y}\,(x-1)^2}{\sqrt{z+1}\,(x-1)^3} \right)$$

$$= \log_4 \left(\frac{\sqrt[3]{y}}{\sqrt{z+1}\,(x-1)} \right)$$

$$= \log_4 y^{1/3} - \log_4 (z+1)^{1/2} - \log_4 (x-1)$$

$$= \frac{1}{3} \log_4 y - \frac{1}{2} \log_4 (z+1) - \log_4 (x-1)$$

10. $f(x) = \text{Arctan } x$
(110)

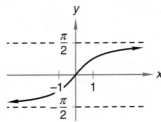

Domain $= \left\{ x \in \mathbb{R} \mid -\infty < x < \infty \right\}$

Range $= \left\{ f(x) \in \mathbb{R} \mid -\dfrac{\pi}{2} < f(x) < \dfrac{\pi}{2} \right\}$

$\text{Arctan } (1) = \dfrac{\pi}{4}$

$\text{Arctan } (-\sqrt{3}) = -\dfrac{\pi}{3}$

$\text{Arctan } \left(\dfrac{1}{\sqrt{3}} \right) = \dfrac{\pi}{6}$

11. $f(x) = x(x-1)(x+3)$
(114)

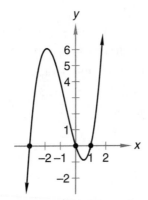

12.
(106)
$$4y^2 - x^2 + 8y - 4x - 4 = 0$$
$$4(y^2 + 2y + 1) - (x^2 + 4x + 4) = 4$$
$$\frac{(y+1)^2}{1} - \frac{(x+2)^2}{4} = 1$$

center: $(-2, -1)$

vertices: $(-2, 0), (-2, -2)$

asymptotes: $y = \dfrac{1}{2}x, \; y = -\dfrac{1}{2}x - 2$

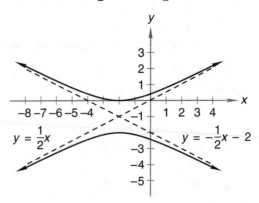

13.
(112)
$$\frac{n!}{(n-k+1)!\,(k-1)!} F^{n-k+1} S^{k-1}$$

$$= \frac{9!}{(9-6+1)!\,(6-1)!} (2x^2)^4 \left(-\frac{1}{x} \right)^5$$

$$= \frac{9!}{4!5!}\, 2^4 x^8 \left(-\frac{1}{x} \right)^5 = -2016x^3$$

14.
(82)
$$4^{4x-1} = 8^{2x+3}$$
$$(2^2)^{4x-1} = (2^3)^{2x+3}$$
$$2^{8x-2} = 2^{6x+9}$$
$$8x - 2 = 6x + 9$$
$$2x = 11$$
$$x = \frac{11}{2}$$

15.
(90)
$$(\cos x + \sin x)^2 - 1$$
$$= \cos^2 x + 2\cos x \sin x + \sin^2 x - 1$$
$$= \cos^2 x + 2\cos x \sin x - \cos^2 x$$
$$= 2\cos x \sin x = \sin 2x$$

16.
(85)
$$2\cot^2 x - 3\csc x = 0$$
$$2(\csc^2 x - 1) - 3\csc x = 0$$
$$2\csc^2 x - 3\csc x - 2 = 0$$
$$(2\csc x + 1)(\csc x - 2) = 0$$

$$2\csc x + 1 = 0 \qquad \csc x - 2 = 0$$
$$2\csc x = -1 \qquad\quad \csc x = 2$$
$$\csc x = -\frac{1}{2} \qquad\quad x = \frac{\pi}{6}, \frac{5\pi}{6}$$

no answer

17. $y = 3x^3 + x^2 - x + 1$
(119)

upper bound	lower bound

upper bound:
```
1| 3  1  -1  1
      3   4  3
   ─────────────
   3  4   3  4
```

All signs are positive,
so **upper bound = 1.**

lower bound:
```
-1| 3  1  -1  1
      -3   2  -1
   ─────────────
   3  -2   1  0
```

Signs alternate, so
lower bound = -1.

18. $i^{1/3} = (\text{cis } 90°)^{1/3} = \text{cis}\left(\dfrac{90°}{3}\right)$
(95)

$= \text{cis } 30°, \text{cis } (30° + 120°), \text{cis } (30° + 240°)$

$= \text{cis } 30°, \text{cis } 150°, \text{cis } 270°$

$= \dfrac{\sqrt{3}}{2} + \dfrac{1}{2}i, \ -\dfrac{\sqrt{3}}{2} + \dfrac{1}{2}i, \ -i$

19. (a) $p(x) = x^4 + x^3 - 3x^2 - x - 2$
(119)

1 sign change

There is 1 positive real root.

(b) $p(-x) = x^4 - x^3 - 3x^2 + x - 2$

3 sign changes

There are either 3 or 1 negative real roots.

20. $\begin{cases} R_{JA}T_{JA} = 5 \\ R_E T_E = 12 \end{cases}$
(25)

$R_E T_E = 12$

$(R_{JA} + 1)(2T_{JA}) = 12$

$2R_{JA}T_{JA} + 2T_{JA} = 12$

$R_{JA}T_{JA} + T_{JA} = 6$

$(5) + T_{JA} = 6$

$T_{JA} = 1 \text{ hr}$

$R_{JA}T_{JA} = 5$

$R_{JA}(1) = 5$

$R_{JA} = 5 \ \dfrac{\textbf{pitches}}{\textbf{hr}}$

Test 31, Form A

1. Rate $= \dfrac{k}{h} \dfrac{\text{mi}}{\text{hr}}$
(28)

New time $= (h + 1)$ hr

New distance $= (k + 3)$ mi

New rate $= \dfrac{k + 3}{h + 1} \dfrac{\textbf{mi}}{\textbf{hr}}$

2. $\begin{cases} y = 1 & \text{if } -\infty < x \le 0 \\ y = x & \text{if } 0 < x \le 2 \\ y = 2 - x & \text{if } 0 < x \le \infty \end{cases}$
(121)

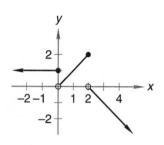

3. $xy = 8$
(123)

$y = \dfrac{8}{x}, \ x \ne 0$

$x = \dfrac{8}{y}, \ y \ne 0$

asymptotes: $y = 0, \ x = 0$

x	1	2	4	8	-1	-2	-4	-8
y	8	4	2	1	-8	-4	-2	-1

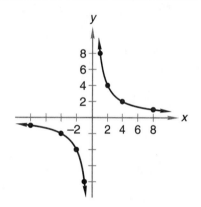

4. $f(x) = [x] + 1$
(121)

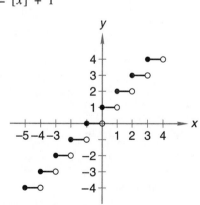

Test Solutions

5. Possible rational roots: ±1, ±2, ±4
(118)

$\begin{array}{r|rrrr} 1 & 1 & -4 & 6 & -4 \\ & & 1 & -3 & 3 \\ \hline & 1 & -3 & 3 & -1 \end{array}$
$\qquad$
$\begin{array}{r|rrrr} -1 & 1 & -4 & 6 & -4 \\ & & -1 & 5 & -11 \\ \hline & 1 & -5 & 11 & -15 \end{array}$

$\begin{array}{r|rrrr} 2 & 1 & -4 & 6 & -4 \\ & & 2 & -4 & 4 \\ \hline & 1 & -2 & 2 & 0 \end{array}$

$x^3 - 4x^2 + 6x - 4 = (x - 2)(x^2 - 2x + 2)$

Use the quadratic formula to find the roots of

$x^2 - 2x + 2 = 0$

$$x = \frac{2 \pm \sqrt{4 - 4(1)(2)}}{2(1)}$$

$$= \frac{2 \pm \sqrt{-4}}{2} = 1 \pm i$$

The roots are: **2, 1 + i**, and **1 – i**

6.
(73)

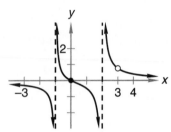

$s = \dfrac{24}{6} = 4$

$\theta = \dfrac{1}{2}\left(\dfrac{360°}{6}\right) = 30°$

$\sin \theta = \dfrac{\frac{1}{2}s}{r}$

$r = \dfrac{s}{2 \sin \theta} = \dfrac{4}{2 \sin 30°} = \textbf{4 in.}$

7. (a) $p(x) = 4x^3 + 2x^2 + 7x + 9$
(119)
   No sign changes.
   There are no positive real roots.

   (b) $p(-x) = -4x^3 + 2x^2 - 7x + 9$
   3 sign changes.
   There are either 3 or 1 negative real roots.

8. For $-\infty < x \le -1$
(121)
$\qquad y = mx + b, \; m = 1, \; b = 1$
$\qquad y = x + 1$

For $-1 < x \le 1$
$\qquad y = -2$

For $1 < x < \infty$
$\qquad y = mx + b, \; m = 1, \; b = -1$
$\qquad y = x - 1$

$$\begin{cases} y = x + 1 & \text{if } -\infty < x \le -1 \\ y = -2 & \text{if } -1 < x \le 1 \\ y = x - 1 & \text{if } 1 < x < \infty \end{cases}$$

9. $y = \dfrac{x^2 - 3x}{(x + 1)(x - 2)(x - 3)}$
(122)

$\qquad = \dfrac{x(x - 3)}{(x + 1)(x - 2)(x - 3)}$

$\qquad = \dfrac{x}{(x + 1)(x - 2)} \quad (x \ne 3)$

10. $P(\text{both purple}) = \dfrac{4}{10} \cdot \dfrac{3}{9} = \dfrac{2}{15}$
(83)

11. (a) $C = 180° - 40° - 70° = \textbf{70°}$
(96, 72)

   (b) $\dfrac{a}{\sin 70°} = \dfrac{12}{\sin 40°}$

   $\qquad a = \dfrac{12 \sin 70°}{\sin 40°}$

   $\qquad a = \textbf{17.54 in.}$

   (c) Area $= \dfrac{1}{2}a(12 \sin C)$

   $\qquad = \dfrac{1}{2}\left(\dfrac{12 \sin 70°}{\sin 40°}\right)(12 \sin 70°)$

   $\qquad = \textbf{98.91 in.}^2$

12. (a) $x^2 - 4x + y^2 = 0$ is a **circle.**
(123)
   (b) $9x^2 + 4y^2 = 36$ is an **ellipse.**
   (c) $x^2 - 4y^2 = 4$ is a **hyperbola.**
   (d) $x^2 + 4x - 4y - 2 = 0$ is a **parabola.**
   (e) $x^2 + y^2 - 3x + 4y - 9 = 0$ is a **circle.**

13. $9x^2 + 4y^2 = 36$
(71)

$$\frac{x^2}{4} + \frac{y^2}{9} = 1$$

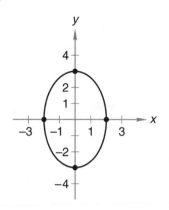

14. $\Delta x = \frac{3}{4}(x_2 - x_1) = \frac{3}{4}(6 - 2) = 3$
(124)

$$\Delta y = \frac{3}{4}(y_2 - y_1) = \frac{3}{4}(6 - 4) = \frac{3}{2}$$

$$(x_1 + \Delta x, \ y_1 + \Delta y) = \left(2 + 3, \ 4 + \frac{3}{2}\right)$$

$$= \left(5, \ \frac{11}{2}\right)$$

15. $y = 2x^4 - 8x^2 = 2(x^4 - 4x^2)$
(116)

Region of interest: $|-4| + 1 = 5$

x	−2	−1	0	1	2
y	0	−6	0	−6	0

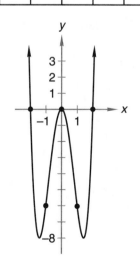

16. $\log_{1/3}(x - 2) > 2$
(111)

$$(x - 2) < \left(\frac{1}{3}\right)^2$$

$$x - 2 < \frac{1}{9}$$

$$x < 2\frac{1}{9}$$

$$x - 2 > 0$$

$$x > 2$$

$$\mathbf{2 < x < 2\frac{1}{9}}$$

17. $\sin 2x - \cos x = 0$
(76, 90)

$$2 \sin x \cos x - \cos x = 0$$

$$\cos x (2 \sin x - 1) = 0$$

$\cos x = 0 \qquad\qquad 2 \sin x - 1 = 0$

$x = \dfrac{\pi}{2}, \dfrac{3\pi}{2} \qquad\qquad \sin x = \dfrac{1}{2}$

$$x = \frac{\pi}{6}, \frac{5\pi}{6}$$

18. $\cos 3x = \cos(2x + x)$
(100)

$= \cos 2x \cos x - \sin 2x \sin x$

$= (\cos^2 x - \sin^2 x) \cos x - (2 \sin x \cos x) \sin x$

$= \cos^3 x - \sin^2 x \cos x - 2 \sin^2 x \cos x$

$= \cos^3 x - (1 - \cos^2 x) \cos x - 2(1 - \cos^2 x) \cos x$

$= \cos^3 x - \cos x + \cos^3 x - 2 \cos x + 2 \cos^3 x$

$= \mathbf{4 \cos^3 x - 3 \cos x}$

19. If i is a root, then $-i$ is a root.
(118)

$$\frac{x^4 - 3x^2 - 4}{(x - i)(x + i)} = \frac{x^4 - 3x^2 - 4}{x^2 + 1}$$

$$= \frac{(x^2 - 4)(x^2 + 1)}{x^2 + 1} = x^2 - 4$$

$$x^2 - 4 = 0$$

$$x^2 = 4$$

$$x = \pm 2$$

The other roots are: $\mathbf{-i, \ 2, \ and \ -2}$

20. C.
(114)

Test 31, Form B

1. Rate = $\dfrac{t}{h}$ $\dfrac{\text{thermometers}}{\text{hr}}$
(28)

New time = $(h - 3)$ hrs

New number of thermometers = $t + 2$

New rate = $\dfrac{t + 2}{h - 3}$ $\dfrac{\textbf{thermometers}}{\textbf{hr}}$

2. $\begin{cases} y = 3 & \text{if } -\infty < x \le 1 \\ y = x & \text{if } 1 < x \le 3 \\ y = -x + 1 & \text{if } 3 < x \le \infty \end{cases}$
(121)

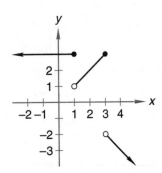

3. $xy = 9$
(123)

$y = \dfrac{9}{x}, \ x \ne 0$

$x = \dfrac{9}{y}, \ y \ne 0$

asymptotes: $y = 0, \ x = 0$

x	9	3	1	−1	−3	−9
y	1	3	9	−9	−3	−1

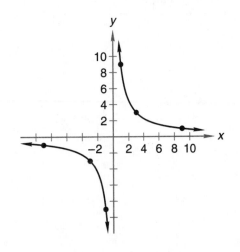

4. $f(x) = [x] - 1$
(121)

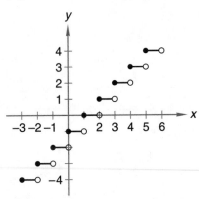

5. Possible rational roots: $\pm 1, \pm 3, \pm 5, \pm 15$
(118)

$\begin{array}{r|rrrr} 1 & 1 & -2 & 2 & -15 \\ & & 1 & -1 & 1 \\ \hline & 1 & -1 & 1 & 14 \end{array}$ $\begin{array}{r|rrrr} -1 & 1 & -2 & 2 & -15 \\ & & -1 & 3 & -5 \\ \hline & 1 & -3 & 5 & -20 \end{array}$

$\begin{array}{r|rrrr} 3 & 1 & -2 & 2 & -15 \\ & & 3 & 3 & 15 \\ \hline & 1 & 1 & 5 & 0 \end{array}$

$x^3 - 2x^2 + 2x - 15 = (x - 3)(x^2 + x + 5)$

Use the quadratic formula to find the roots of

$x^2 + x + 5 = 0$

$x = \dfrac{-1 \pm \sqrt{1 - 4(1)(5)}}{2(1)}$

$= \dfrac{-1 \pm \sqrt{-19}}{2} = -\dfrac{1}{2} \pm \dfrac{\sqrt{19}}{2}i$

The roots are: $\mathbf{3}$, $-\dfrac{1}{2} + \dfrac{\sqrt{19}}{2}i$, **and** $-\dfrac{1}{2} - \dfrac{\sqrt{19}}{2}i$

6.
(73)

$s = \dfrac{30}{6} = 5$

$\theta = \dfrac{1}{2}\left(\dfrac{360°}{6}\right) = 30°$

$\sin \theta = \dfrac{\dfrac{1}{2}s}{r}$

$r = \dfrac{s}{2 \sin \theta} = \dfrac{5}{2 \sin 30°} = \textbf{5 in.}$

7. (a) $p(x) = 6x^3 - 2x^2 - 3x + 7$
(119)
    2 sign changes.

    There are either 2 or 0 positive real roots.

(b) $p(-x) = -6x^3 - 2x^2 + 3x + 7$

    1 sign change.

    There is 1 negative real root.

8. For $-\infty < x \le -1$
(121)
    $y = -1$

For $-1 < x \le 1$

    $y = mx + b$, $m = -1$, $b = 0$

    $y = -x$

For $1 < x < \infty$

    $y = 1$

$$\begin{cases} y = -1 \text{ if } -\infty < x \le -1 \\ y = -x \text{ if } -1 < x \le 1 \\ y = 1 \quad \text{ if } 1 < x < \infty \end{cases}$$

9. $y = \dfrac{x^2 + 4x}{(x + 2)(x - 1)(x + 4)}$
(122)

$\quad = \dfrac{x(x + 4)}{(x + 2)(x - 1)(x + 4)}$

$\quad = \dfrac{x}{(x + 2)(x - 1)} \quad (x \ne -4)$

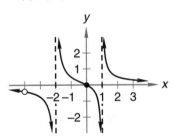

10. $P(\text{both are green}) = \dfrac{7}{12} \cdot \dfrac{6}{11} = \dfrac{7}{22}$
(83)

11. (a) $C = 180° - 120° - 25° = \mathbf{35°}$
(96, 72)

(b) $\dfrac{a}{\sin 120°} = \dfrac{6}{\sin 25°}$

$\quad a = \dfrac{6 \sin 120°}{\sin 25°}$

$\quad a = \mathbf{12.30 \text{ ft}}$

(c) Area $= \dfrac{1}{2}a(6 \sin C)$

$\quad = \dfrac{1}{2}\left(\dfrac{6 \sin 120°}{\sin 25°}\right)(6 \sin 35°)$

$\quad = \mathbf{21.16 \text{ ft}^2}$

12. (a) $x^2 - 4y^2 = 4$ is a **hyperbola.**
(123)
(b) $2x^2 - 4x + y^2 = 0$ is an **ellipse.**

(c) $x^2 + y^2 - 6x + 4y + 9 = 0$ is a **circle.**

(d) $xy = 8$ is a **hyperbola.**

(e) $x^2 + 4x - 4y - 2 = 0$ is a **parabola.**

13. $x^2 + y^2 - 6x + 4y + 9 = 0$
(71)
$\quad (x^2 - 6x + 9) + (y^2 + 4y + 4) = 4$

$\quad\quad (x - 3)^2 + (y + 2)^2 = 2^2$

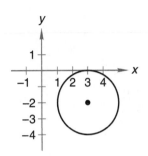

14. $\Delta x = \dfrac{2}{3}(x_2 - x_1) = \dfrac{2}{3}(7 - 1) = 4$
(124)

$\quad \Delta y = \dfrac{2}{3}(y_2 - y_1) = \dfrac{2}{3}(6 - 3) = 2$

$\quad (x_1 + \Delta x, y_1 + \Delta y) = (1 + 4, 3 + 2) = \mathbf{(5, 5)}$

15. $y = 3x^3 - 9x = 3(x^3 - 3x)$
(116)
    Region of interest: $|-3| + 1 = 4$

x	-2	-1	0	1	2
y	-6	6	0	-6	6

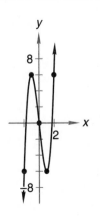

16. $\log_{1/2}(x - 3) > 3$
(111)

$$(x - 3) < \left(\frac{1}{2}\right)^3$$

$$x - 3 < \frac{1}{8}$$

$$x < 3\frac{1}{8}$$

$$x - 3 > 0$$

$$x > 3$$

$$\mathbf{3 < x < 3\frac{1}{8}}$$

17. $\sin 2x - \sin x = 0$
(90)

$$2 \sin x \cos x - \sin x = 0$$

$$\sin x (2 \cos x - 1) = 0$$

$$\sin x = 0 \qquad\qquad 2 \cos x - 1 = 0$$

$$\mathbf{x = 0, \pi}$$

$$\cos x = \frac{1}{2}$$

$$x = \frac{\pi}{3}, \frac{5\pi}{3}$$

18. $\sin 3x = \sin(2x + x)$
(76, 90)

$$= \sin 2x \cos x + \cos 2x \sin x$$

$$= (2 \sin x \cos x)\cos x + \left(1 - 2 \sin^2 x\right) \sin x$$

$$= 2 \sin x \cos^2 x + \sin x - 2 \sin^3 x$$

$$= 2 \sin x \left(1 - \sin^2 x\right) + \sin x - 2 \sin^3 x$$

$$= 2 \sin x - 2 \sin^3 x + \sin x - 2 \sin^3 x$$

$$= \mathbf{3 \sin x - 4 \sin^3 x}$$

19. If $2i$ is a root, then $-2i$ is a root.
(118)

$$\frac{x^4 + 3x^2 - 4}{(x - 2i)(x + 2i)} = \frac{x^4 + 3x^2 - 4}{x^2 + 4}$$

$$= \frac{\left(x^2 + 4\right)\left(x^2 - 1\right)}{x^2 + 4} = x^2 - 1$$

$$x^2 - 1 = 0$$

$$x^2 = 1$$

$$x = \pm 1$$

The other roots are: $\mathbf{-2i, 1,}$ and $\mathbf{-1}$

20. **D.**
(114)

Advanced Math
Test Masters

Test Forms

Instructions

Tests are an important component of the Saxon program. We believe that concepts and skills should be continually tested. However, tests should only be administered after the concepts and skills have been thoroughly practiced. Therefore, we recommend that tests be administered according to the testing schedule printed on the back side of this page.

Note: Optional student answer forms are located at the back of this booklet. These forms should provide sufficient writing space so that students can show all of their work along with their answers.

Advanced Math

Testing Schedule

Test to be administered:	Covers material up through:	Give after teaching:
Test 1	Lesson 4	Lesson 8
Test 2	Lesson 8	Lesson 12
Test 3	Lesson 12	Lesson 16
Test 4	Lesson 16	Lesson 20
Test 5	Lesson 20	Lesson 24
Test 6	Lesson 24	Lesson 28
Test 7	Lesson 28	Lesson 32
Test 8	Lesson 32	Lesson 36
Test 9	Lesson 36	Lesson 40
Test 10	Lesson 40	Lesson 44
Test 11	Lesson 44	Lesson 48
Test 12	Lesson 48	Lesson 52
Test 13	Lesson 52	Lesson 56
Test 14	Lesson 56	Lesson 60
Test 15	Lesson 60	Lesson 64
Test 16	Lesson 64	Lesson 68
Test 17	Lesson 68	Lesson 72
Test 18	Lesson 72	Lesson 76
Test 19	Lesson 76	Lesson 80
Test 20	Lesson 80	Lesson 84
Test 21	Lesson 84	Lesson 88
Test 22	Lesson 88	Lesson 92
Test 23	Lesson 92	Lesson 96
Test 24	Lesson 96	Lesson 100
Test 25	Lesson 100	Lesson 104
Test 26	Lesson 104	Lesson 108
Test 27	Lesson 108	Lesson 112
Test 28	Lesson 112	Lesson 116
Test 29	Lesson 116	Lesson 120
Test 30	Lesson 120	Lesson 124
Test 31	Lesson 124	Lesson 125

1. Twice the complement of angle A is $40°$ less than the supplement of angle A. Find the measure of angle A.

2. The ratio of velites to principes was 7 to 3. If there were 1200 principes, how many velites were there?

3. In a taste test, 56% of the people polled preferred brand D. If a total of 728 people polled preferred brand D, how many people were polled?

4. Construct an angle which is congruent to $\angle ABC$, then bisect it.

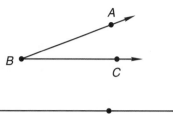

5. Construct a perpendicular to $\overline{DE}$ at F.

6. Construct a triangle whose sides have lengths a, b, and c.

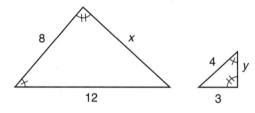

7. Solve: $\begin{cases} 3x + 5y = -22 \\ x - 2y = 0 \end{cases}$

8. Solve: $2(x - x^0 + 1) = -4(2x - 5)$

9. Add: $\dfrac{4}{x} - \dfrac{2}{x - 1} + \dfrac{1}{x(x - 1)}$

10. Simplify: $\dfrac{4^{-1}x^{-2}y^3}{2^2(xy)^{-4}}$

11. The lengths of the sides of a triangle are 7 cm, 5 cm, and 5 cm. Is the triangle a right triangle, an acute triangle, or an obtuse triangle?

12. Find x and y.

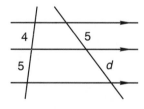

13. Find a, b, and c.

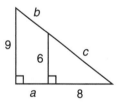

14. Find d.

15. Find x and y.

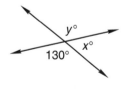

16. An equilateral triangle has a perimeter of 30 cm and an area of $25\sqrt{3}$ cm^2. Find the altitude of the triangle.

17. A sphere has a radius of 3 inches. Find the volume and surface area of the sphere.

18. In the circle, O is the center. The radius of the circle is $\sqrt{7}$ meters. Find the area of the shaded sectors.

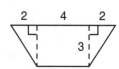

19. Find the volume of the cone whose base is shown and whose altitude is 6 cm. Dimensions are in centimeters.

20. Evaluate: $x^2 - 3y^2 + 2(x - y)(x^2 + 2xy + y^2)^0$ if $x = 2$ and $y = 1$

1. Three times the complement of angle A is $50°$ more than the supplement of angle A. Find the measure of angle A.

2. The ratio of corporations to endangered species was 8 to 5. If there were 1500 endangered species, how many corporations were there?

3. In a preference test, 38% of the people polled liked the art of Vincent van Gogh. If 874 of the people polled liked Vincent van Gogh's art, how many people were polled?

4. Construct an angle which is congruent to $\angle ABC$, then bisect it.

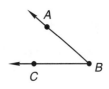

5. Construct a perpendicular to $\overline{DE}$ at F.

6. Construct a triangle with side lengths a, b, and c.

7. Solve: $\begin{cases} 2x + 5y = 24 \\ 2x - y = 0 \end{cases}$

8. Solve: $4(x + x^0 + 2) = 3(3x - 1)$

9. Add: $\dfrac{3}{x + 1} - \dfrac{2}{x} + \dfrac{1}{x(x + 1)}$

10. Simplify: $\dfrac{3^{-1}x^{-3}y^2}{2^3(xy)^{-1}}$

11. The lengths of the sides of a triangle are 7 cm, 6 cm, and 6 cm. Is this triangle a right triangle, an acute triangle, or an obtuse triangle?

12. Find x and y.

13. Find e, f, and g.

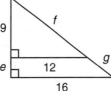

14. Find x.

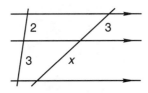

15. Find x and y.

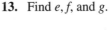

16. An equilateral triangle has a perimeter of 6 km and an area of $\sqrt{3}$ km^2. Find the altitude of the triangle.

17. A sphere has a radius of 2 miles. Find the volume and surface area of the sphere.

18. In the circle shown, O is the center. The radius of the circle is $\sqrt{5}$ cm. Find the area of the shaded sectors.

19. Find the volume of the cone whose base is shown and whose altitude is 9 m. Dimensions are in meters.

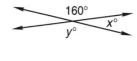

20. Evaluate: $x^3 - 2y^2 + 2(y - x)(6x^5 + 3xy^4 + x^2)^0$ if $x = 3$ and $y = 4$

Advanced Mathematics by Saxon

1. The ratio of horseshoes to shamrocks was 11 to 2, and five times the number of shamrocks was 3 less than the number of horseshoes. How many were shamrocks?

2. Debbie had a total of twenty-five nickels and dimes. If the value of the coins was $1.75, how many of each coin did she have?

3. Find three consecutive odd integers such that twice the sum of the first and second is one less than three times the third.

4. Is the following argument valid or invalid?

    All parrots are named Polly.
    She is named Polly.
    ─────────────────────────
    Therefore, she is a parrot.

5. Write the contrapositive of the following statement:
   If an animal is furry, then it is a cat.

Solve:

6. $\dfrac{1}{2} + \dfrac{2}{x+1} = \dfrac{3}{4}$

7. $\sqrt{3x-2} - \sqrt{4} = 5$

8. $\begin{cases} x + y + z = 2 \\ 3x + 2y + z = 7 \\ 4x - y - 2z = 9 \end{cases}$

Simplify:

9. $\left(\sqrt{5} - \sqrt{2}\right)\left(\sqrt{5} + \sqrt{2}\right)$

10. $\dfrac{\sqrt{x^4 y^2}\, xy^{-2}}{\sqrt[3]{x^3 y^6 (xy)^2}}$

11. $5i^2 - 7i^4 + 3i^3 - 1$

12. $(i - 2)(i - 3)$

13. Use construction to divide $\overline{YZ}$ into 3 congruent segments.

14. Find the length of diagonal $\overline{AC}$ in the rectangular solid shown. Dimensions are in feet.

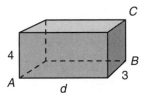

15. The circle is tangent to three sides of the rectangle. Find the area of the shaded region of this figure. Dimensions are in centimeters.

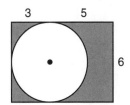

16. Find x.

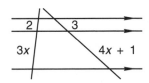

17. In $\triangle XYZ$, $\overline{YW}$ is the angle bisector of $\angle XYZ$. Find c.

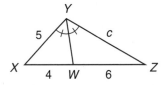

18. Two 7-sided polygons are similar. A side of the larger polygon is 6 times as long as the corresponding side of the smaller polygon. What is the ratio of the area of the larger polygon to the area of the smaller polygon?

19. Given: $\triangle DLW$ is a right triangle
    $\overline{KC} \perp \overline{LW}$

    Outline a proof that shows:

    $\dfrac{DW}{LW} = \dfrac{CW}{KW}$

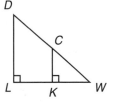

20. Find the surface area of the right circular cone whose slant height is 8 in. and whose base has a radius of 4 in.

Advanced Mathematics by Saxon

1. The ratio of diamonds to stars was 3 to 11, and three times the number of diamonds was 2 less than the number of stars. How many were diamonds?

2. Jen had a total of twenty-one nickels and dimes. If the value of the coins was $1.55, how many of each coin did she have?

3. Find three consecutive even integers such that twice the sum of the first and second is eight more than three times the third.

4. Is the following argument valid or invalid?

   > All poets are waiting for Godot.
   > Gogo is waiting for Godot.
   > ───────────────────────────
   > Therefore, Gogo is a poet.

5. Write the contrapositive of the following statement:

   > If a cat is purring, then it is happy.

Solve:

6. $\dfrac{1}{3} + \dfrac{4}{x + 2} = \dfrac{5}{6}$

7. $\sqrt{6x - 2} - \sqrt{9} = 5$

8. $\begin{cases} x + y + z = 2 \\ 2x + 3y + z = 6 \\ 2x + 4y - z = 7 \end{cases}$

Simplify:

9. $(\sqrt{7} - \sqrt{3})(\sqrt{7} + \sqrt{3})$

10. $\dfrac{\sqrt[3]{x^6 y^3} x^{-1} y^2}{\sqrt{x^4 y^2 (xy)^3}}$

11. $7i^3 - 6i^2 + 4i^3 + 1$

12. $(4 - i)(2 - i)$

13. Use construction to divide $\overline{MJ}$ into 3 congruent segments.

14. Find the length of diagonal $\overline{AC}$ in the rectangular solid shown. Dimensions are in centimeters.

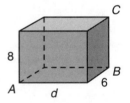

15. The circle is tangent to two sides of the rectangle. Find the area of the shaded region of this figure. Dimensions are in centimeters.

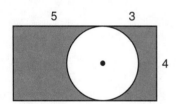

16. Find x.

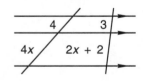

17. In $\triangle ABC$, $\overline{BN}$ is the angle bisector of $\angle ABC$. Find z.

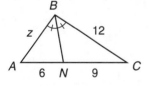

18. Two 6-sided polygons are similar. A side of the larger polygon is 7 times as long as the corresponding side of the smaller polygon. What is the ratio of the area of the larger polygon to the area of the smaller polygon?

19. Given: $\triangle DMV$ is a right triangle
    $\overline{BN} \perp \overline{MV}$

    Outline a proof that shows:

    $\dfrac{DV}{MV} = \dfrac{BV}{NV}$

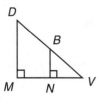

20. Find the surface area of the right circular cone whose slant height is 9 in. and whose base has a radius of 3 in.

Advanced Mathematics by Saxon

1. The ratio of Reisingers to Ochsenbeins was 5 to 2. If their combined total at the wedding was 350, how many were not Reisingers?

2. Find the sum of the measures of the interior angles and the sum of the measures of the exterior angles of a regular decagon (10-sided figure).

3. A total of 52 dogs and cats were on the ranch. If three times the number of dogs exceeded the number of cats by four, how many of each were on the ranch?

4. The triangle and the circle are tangent at three points as shown. Find x and y.

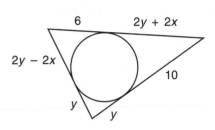

5. Find x, y, and z.

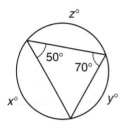

6. Begin with $ax^2 + bx + c = 0$ and derive the quadratic formula.

7. Use the quadratic formula to solve: $2x^2 = 4x - 5$

8. Solve by completing the square: $5 + 2x^2 = -6x$

9. Solve: $\sqrt{3m + 7} + \sqrt{3m} = 7$

10. Simplify: $\sqrt{2}\sqrt{-8} - \sqrt{2}\sqrt{-2}\sqrt{-2} + 2\sqrt{-2}\sqrt{-2}\sqrt{-2}$

11. Is the following argument valid or invalid?

> All math teachers are nice.
> Jim is a math teacher.
> ———————————————
> Therefore, Jim is nice.

12. Find a, b, and c.

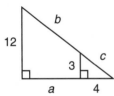

Simplify:

13. $\dfrac{a^{-2} + m^{-3}}{a^{-3}m^2}$

14. $\dfrac{\sqrt{a^2 b^4}\left(a^3 b^{-2}\right)^3}{\sqrt[3]{a^6 b^{-9}}\left(\sqrt{a}\right)^{-1}}$

15. $\dfrac{3 - 2i + 3i^3}{1 - i}$

16. A sphere has a radius of 12 inches. Find the volume and surface area of the sphere.

17. Given: R is the midpoint of $\overline{MS}$
$\overline{TR} \perp \overline{MS}$

Outline a proof that shows: $\overline{TM} \cong \overline{TS}$

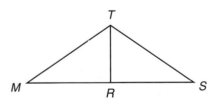

18. State the congruency postulate that can be used to prove: $\triangle BCA \cong \triangle DAC$.

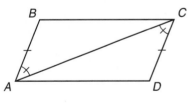

19. Construct a perpendicular from $\overline{AB}$ that passes through P.

20. Construct a line parallel to $\overleftrightarrow{CD}$ that passes through X.

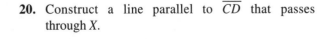

       Advanced Mathematics **by Saxon**

1. The ratio of priests to acolytes was 2 to 3. If their combined total was 85, how many were not acolytes?

2. Find the sum of the measures of the interior angles and the sum of the measures of the exterior angles of a regular nonagon (9-sided figure).

3. A total of 128 blue cars and red cars were in the parking lot. If the number of blue cars exceeded three times the number of red cars by four, how many of each car were in the parking lot?

4. The triangle and the circle are tangent at three points as shown. Find x and y.

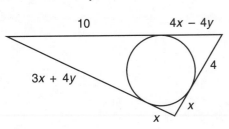

5. Find x, y, and z.

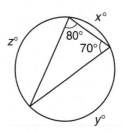

6. Begin with $ax^2 + bx + c = 0$ and derive the quadratic formula.

7. Use the quadratic formula to solve: $3x^2 = 2x - 4$

8. Solve by completing the square: $-7 + 2x^2 = 4x$

9. Solve: $\sqrt{5y - 9} + \sqrt{5y} = 9$

10. Simplify: $\sqrt{3}\sqrt{-3} + \sqrt{-9}\sqrt{9}\sqrt{3} - 3i\sqrt{-3}\sqrt{-3}$

11. Is the following argument valid or invalid?

> All English teachers like Shakespeare.
> Mrs. Backer is an English teacher.
> _____
> Therefore, Mrs. Backer likes Shakespeare.

12. Find a, b, and c.

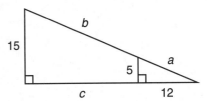

Simplify:

13. $\dfrac{x^{-1} + y^{-3}}{x^2 y^{-4}}$

14. $\dfrac{\sqrt{a^4 b^2}\left(a^3 b^{-2}\right)^2}{\sqrt[3]{a^3 b^{-6}}\left(\sqrt{b}\right)^{-1}}$

15. $\dfrac{i^3 + 3 - (-3i)}{2 - i}$

16. A sphere has a radius of 9 centimeters. Find the volume and surface area of the sphere.

17. Given: B is the midpoint of $\overline{AC}$
    $\overline{TB} \perp \overline{AC}$

    Outline a proof that shows: $\overline{TA} \cong \overline{TC}$

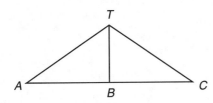

18. State the congruency postulate that can be used to prove: $\triangle ACB \cong \triangle CAD$

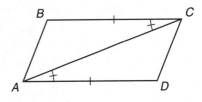

19. Construct a perpendicular from $\overline{XY}$ that passes through Q.

20. Construct a line parallel to $\overline{MN}$ that passes through P.

Advanced Mathematics by Saxon

1. In a mixture of gold and silver, 420 ounces of gold were required to make 900 ounces of the mixture. How much silver was required to make 2100 ounces of the mixture?

2. An airplane is flying at an altitude of 4000 ft above the ground. The pilot sights an object on the ground at an angle of depression of 30°. What is the slant range from the airplane to the object?

3. Find the equation of the line that passes through $(-2, 5)$ and is perpendicular to the line $2x = 5 - 3y$.

4. Convert $-4.5\hat{i} + 3.7\hat{j}$ to polar coordinates. (Write four forms for the point.)

5. Convert $-5\underline{/-342°}$ to rectangular coordinates.

6. Simplify: $\left(3x^{5/2} - 7y^{7/2}\right)\left(3x^{5/2} + 7y^{7/2}\right)$

7. Solve: $\begin{cases} \dfrac{1}{2}x - \dfrac{1}{4}y = \dfrac{1}{2} \\ 0.2y - 0.2z = 1 \\ -\dfrac{1}{8}x + \dfrac{1}{4}z = -\dfrac{1}{4} \end{cases}$

8. Solve for c: $y = v\left(\dfrac{ax}{b} + \dfrac{m}{c}\right)$

Simplify:

9. $\dfrac{1 + 5\sqrt{3}}{3\sqrt{3} - 5}$

10. $\dfrac{a^{-7}b^5 + b^3a^{-3}}{a^{-2}b^4}$

11. Given: $\overline{ZW}$ is the angle bisector of $\angle XZY$
     $\overline{XZ} \cong \overline{YZ}$

     Write a two-column proof to prove:
     $\overline{XW} \cong \overline{YW}$

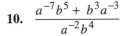

12. In $\triangle ABC$, $\overline{AD}$ is the angle bisector of $\angle BAC$. Find x.

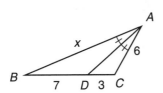

13. Find a, b, and h.

14. Simplify: $\sqrt{5}\sqrt{2}\sqrt{-5}\sqrt{-2} - \sqrt{5}\sqrt{2}i\sqrt{5}\sqrt{2}i^3 - \sqrt{-25}$

Find x.

15.

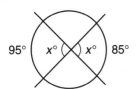

16.

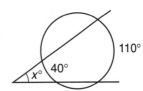

17.

18.

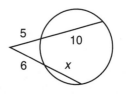

19. Write the contrapositive of the major premise of this syllogism to help determine whether the following argument is valid or invalid:

> All non-algebra students are not with it.
> Eric is with it.
> ————————————————
> Therefore, Eric is an algebra student.

20. Kelly's test scores are 88, 100, 95, and 84. What does she need on the last test in order to average 90 on her tests?

Advanced Mathematics **by Saxon**

1. In a mixture of copper and zinc, 700 tons of copper were required to make 1010 tons of the mixture. How much zinc was required to make 1818 tons of the mixture?

2. An airplane is flying at an altitude of 60 ft above the ground. The pilot sights an object on the ground at an angle of depression of 30°. What is the slant range from the airplane to the object?

3. Find the equation of the line that passes through $(-4, 6)$ and is perpendicular to the line $2x = \frac{1}{2}y - 3$.

4. Convert $-2.5\hat{i} + 3.1\hat{j}$ to polar coordinates. (Write four forms for the point.)

5. Convert $-4\underline{/-330°}$ to rectangular coordinates.   **6.** Simplify: $\left(2x^{3/2} - 3y^{5/2}\right)\left(2x^{3/2} + 3y^{5/2}\right)$

7. Solve: $\begin{cases} \dfrac{1}{4}y - \dfrac{2}{5}z = \dfrac{1}{10} \\ 0.5x + 0.5z = 2.5 \\ \dfrac{3}{4}x + \dfrac{5}{2}y = 8 \end{cases}$ **8.** Solve for d: $y = r\left(\dfrac{bx}{c} + \dfrac{a}{d}\right)$

Simplify:

9. $\dfrac{1 + 3\sqrt{2}}{4\sqrt{2} - 3}$ **10.** $\dfrac{h^5 r^{-7} + r^{-2}h^3}{h^6 r^{-4}}$

11. Given: $\overline{DA}$ is the angle bisector of $\angle BDC$
$\overline{BD} \cong \overline{CD}$

Write a two-column proof to prove:
$\overline{BA} \cong \overline{CA}$

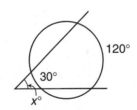

12. In $\triangle XYZ$, $\overline{XW}$ is the angle bisector of $\angle YXZ$. Find k.   **13.** Find q, r, and t.

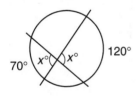   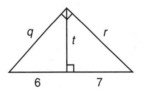

14. Simplify: $\sqrt{6}\sqrt{3}\sqrt{-6}\sqrt{-3} - \sqrt{6}\sqrt{3}i\sqrt{6}\sqrt{3}i^3 - \sqrt{-36}$

Find x.

15.   **16.**

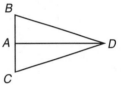

17.   **18.**

      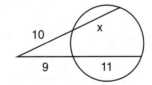

19. Write the contrapositive of the major premise of this syllogism to help determine whether the following argument is valid or invalid.

All non-egalitarians are not emancipated.
Sven is emancipated.
_____
Therefore, Sven is an egalitarian.

20. Smith's test scores are 87, 99, 93, and 81. What does he need on the last test in order to average 90 on his tests?

      Advanced Mathematics **by Saxon**

1. Draw the necessary reference triangles and evaluate. Do not use a calculator.

   (a) $\dfrac{\sqrt{3}}{2}\sin 30°$

   (b) $4\cos 45°$

   (c) $\dfrac{\sqrt{3}}{3}\tan 60°$

2. How many liters of a 74% glycol solution must be added to 67 liters of a 31% glycol solution to get a 59% glycol solution?

3. Given: $\overline{AC} \parallel \overline{DF}$
   $\overline{BC} \parallel \overline{EF}$

   Write a two-column proof to prove:
   $\triangle ABC \sim \triangle DEF$

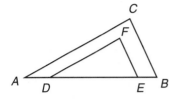

4. Solve: $\begin{cases} x^2 + y^2 = 16 \\ y - x = 2 \end{cases}$

5. Divide $x^3 + 5x - 6$ by $x - 3$.

6. Factor: $27x^3y^9 - 8z^{12}$

7. Factor: $8x^{4n+1} - 12x^{7n+3}$

8. Simplify: $\dfrac{2i^3 - 4i^4 + i^2}{3 + 3i + \sqrt{-16}}$

9. Reds varied directly as blues squared and inversely as greens. When there were 160 reds, there were 4 blues and 2 greens. How many reds were there when there were 7 blues and 10 greens?

Simplify:

10. $\dfrac{a}{a + \dfrac{a}{c + \dfrac{a}{b}}}$

11. $\dfrac{\dfrac{3x}{y^2} + \dfrac{2z}{xy}}{\dfrac{x}{y} - \dfrac{z}{x}}$

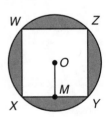

12. $\left(3x^4y\right)^{-2}\left(\dfrac{3x^2y}{xy}\right)^2$

13. The sum of the digits of a two-digit counting number is 6. When the digits are reversed, the number is 18 greater than the original number. What was the original number?

14. A kite is flying at the end of a straight string that has a length of 300 feet. The string makes an angle of 70° with the ground. How high above the ground is the kite?

15. In the figure shown, square $WXYZ$ is inscribed in circle O. Also, $\overline{OM} \perp \overline{XY}$ and $OM = 7$. Find the area of the shaded region.

16. Given: $\overline{LM} \cong \overline{ON}$
    $\overline{LM} \parallel \overline{ON}$

    Write a two-column proof to prove:
    $\triangle LPM \cong \triangle OPN$

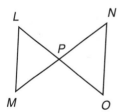

17. Simplify by factoring the numerator: $\dfrac{x^{4a} - y^{4a}}{x^{2a} + y^{2a}}$

18. Find the equation of a line which passes through $(4, -1)$ and is parallel to the line $x + 4y = 3$.

Find x.

19.

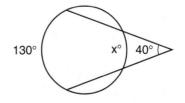

20.

1. Draw the necessary reference triangles and evaluate. Do not use a calculator.

   (a) $\dfrac{1}{2}\cos 60°$

   (b) $\sqrt{3}\tan 30°$

   (c) $6\sin 45°$

2. How many liters of a 76% glycol solution must be added to 69 liters of a 33% glycol solution to get a 61% glycol solution?

3. Given: $\overline{LM} \parallel \overline{OP}$
   $\overline{MN} \parallel \overline{PQ}$

   Write a two-column proof to prove:
   $\triangle LMN \sim \triangle OPQ$

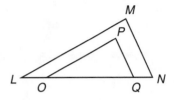

4. Solve: $\begin{cases} y - x = 3 \\ x^2 + y^2 = 17 \end{cases}$

5. Divide $x^3 + 4x^2 + 10$ by $x + 3$.

6. Factor: $64y^{12} - 8x^9 z^3$

7. Factor: $3x^{8n+2} - 9x^{5n+3}$

8. Simplify: $\dfrac{3i^2 - 4i^3 - 2i^4}{2 + \sqrt{-9} + 4i}$

9. Yins varied directly as yangs and inversely as jades squared. When there were 15 yins, there were 90 yangs and 6 jades. How many yins were there when there were 64 yangs and 4 jades?

Simplify:

10. $\dfrac{n}{n + \dfrac{n}{x + \dfrac{n}{y}}}$

11. $\dfrac{\dfrac{3x}{yz} + \dfrac{2z}{x}}{\dfrac{y}{x} - \dfrac{x}{z}}$

12. $\left(2xy^3\right)^{-3}\left(\dfrac{2xy^2}{xy}\right)^2$

13. The sum of the digits of a two-digit counting number is 9. When the digits are reversed, the number is 45 greater than the original number. What was the original number?

14. A parasailer is flying at the end of a straight cord that has a length of 150 feet. The cord makes an angle of 50° with the ground. How high above the ground is the parasailer?

15. In the figure shown, square $ABCD$ is inscribed in circle O. Also, $\overline{OM} \perp \overline{BC}$ and $OM = 5$. Find the area of the shaded region.

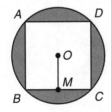

16. Given: $\overline{QR} \cong \overline{UV}$
    $\overline{QR} \parallel \overline{UV}$

    Write a two-column proof to prove:
    $\triangle QRT \cong \triangle UVT$

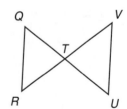

17. Simplify by factoring the numerator: $\dfrac{x^{4m} - y^{4n}}{x^{2m} + y^{2n}}$

18. Find the equation of a line which passes through $(2, -2)$ and is parallel to the line $x + 3y = 4$.

Find x.

19.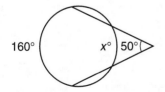

20.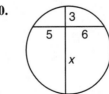

Advanced Mathematics **by Saxon**

1. The sum of the digits of a two-digit counting number is 11. When the digits are reversed, the new number is 27 more than the original number. What was the original number?

2. Which of the following sets of ordered pairs are functions?
   (a) $\{(2, -1), (5, 2), (3, -2), (2, 1), (6, 1)\}$ (b) $\{(7, 2), (9, 3), (13, -1), (-7, 2)\}$
   (c) $\{(-1, 2), (8, 3), (5, 2), (3, 2)\}$ (d) $\{(9, 4), (1,6), (2, 4), (1, -3)\}$

3. Graph the following sets on the real number line.
   (a) $\{x \in \mathbb{R} \mid |x - 2| < 1\}$ (b) $\{x \in \mathbb{R} \mid |x - 2| > 1\}$

4. Convert $3\hat{i} + 16\hat{j}$ to polar coordinates. (Write four forms for this point.)

5. Let $f(x) = x^2 - x + 3$. Evaluate: (a) $f(-2)$ (b) $f(10)$

6. Factor: (a) $64a^3b^9 - 125p^6$ (b) $x^{4m} - y^{4n}$

7. A solid is made up of a hemisphere, a right circular cylinder, and a right circular cone, as shown. Find the volume of the solid.

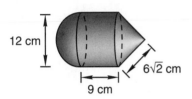

12 cm $6\sqrt{2}$ cm   9 cm

8. Find the domain of the function defined by each equation:
   (a) $f(x) = \sqrt{x + 2}$ (b) $g(x) = \dfrac{1}{x^2 - 4}$

9. Convert $5\angle{-138°}$ to rectangular coordinates.   10. Factor: $4x^{5n+2} - 8x^{8n+1}$

Sketch the graph of each function:

11. $y = 5^x$ 12. $y = \left(\dfrac{1}{5}\right)^x$

13. Determine whether each graph represents the graph of a function. If so, determine whether the graph is a one-to-one function or not.

(a) 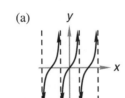   (b) 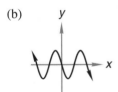   (c) 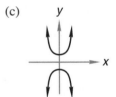   (d)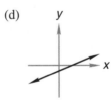

14. Cuzelle has a total of 40 coins worth $5.60. All coins are either nickels, dimes or quarters. If the number of quarters is the same as the number of nickels, how many of each coin does he have?

15. Given: $\overline{WF} \cong \overline{ZF}$
    $\overline{XF} \cong \overline{YF}$

    Write a two-column proof to prove:
    $\triangle XFW \cong \triangle YFZ$

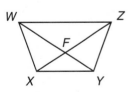

16. Solve: $\begin{cases} x^2 + y^2 = 9 \\ x^2 - y^2 = 5 \end{cases}$ 17. Simplify: $(x + y)(xy^{-1} - x^{-1}y)^{-1}$

18. Draw reference triangles to evaluate $\dfrac{1}{2} \tan 60° - \dfrac{1}{\sqrt{2}} \sin 45° + \sqrt{3} \cos 30°$. Do not use a calculator.

19. A sphere has a volume of 972π cubic inches. Find the surface area of the sphere.

20. How much water should be added to 77 gallons of a 37% salt solution to get a 30% salt solution?

     Advanced Mathematics by Saxon

1. The sum of the digits of a two-digit counting number is 11. When the digits are reversed, the new number is 9 more than the original number. What was the original number?

2. Which of the following sets of ordered pairs are functions?
   (a) $\{(8, 2), (12, 4), (3, 2), (5, 4)\}$
   (b) $\{(3, -1), (6, 2), (3, -2), (5, 1)\}$
   (c) $\{(1, 2), (2, 2), (3, 2), (3, 1)\}$
   (d) $\{(5, 6), (6, 7), (7, 6), (6, 5)\}$

3. Graph the following sets on the real number line.
   (a) $\{x \in \mathbb{R} \mid |x + 1| < 2\}$
   (b) $\{x \in \mathbb{R} \mid |x + 1| > 2\}$

4. Convert $4\hat{i} + 7\hat{j}$ to polar coordinates. (Write four forms for this point.)

5. Let $f(x) = x^2 - 2x + 3$. Evaluate: (a) $f(2)$ (b) $f(-3)$

6. Factor: (a) $27x^3y^6 - 8d^9$ (b) $x^{4a} - y^{4b}$

7. A solid is made up of a hemisphere, a right circular cylinder, and a right circular cone, as shown. Find the volume of the solid.

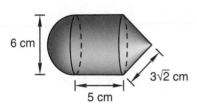

6 cm

$3\sqrt{2}$ cm

5 cm

8. Find the domain of the function defined by each equation:
   (a) $f(x) = \sqrt{x + 3}$
   (b) $g(x) = \dfrac{1}{x^2 - 16}$

9. Convert $3\underline{/-125°}$ to rectangular coordinates.
10. Factor: $3x^{6n+2} - 6x^{7n+1}$

Sketch the graph of each function:

11. $y = 3^x$
12. $y = \left(\dfrac{1}{3}\right)^x$

13. Determine whether each graph represents the graph of a function. If so, determine whether the graph is a one-to-one function or not.

(a)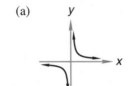
(b)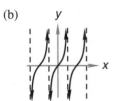
(c)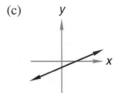
(d)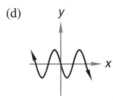

14. Grout has a total of 43 coins worth $3.95. All coins are either nickels, dimes, or quarters. If the number of nickels is 6 more than the number of dimes, how many of each coin does he have?

15. Given: $\overline{AE} \cong \overline{DE}$
    $\overline{BE} \cong \overline{CE}$

    Write a two-column proof to prove:
    $\triangle AEB \cong \triangle DEC$

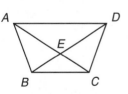

16. Solve: $\begin{cases} x^2 + y^2 = 4 \\ x^2 - y^2 = 2 \end{cases}$
17. Simplify: $(x - y)(xy^{-1} + x^{-1}y)^{-1}$

18. Draw reference triangles to evaluate $\sqrt{3} \tan 60° + \sqrt{2} \cos 45° - 2\sqrt{3} \tan 30°$. Do not use a calculator.

19. A sphere has a volume of 2304π cubic miles. Find the surface area of the sphere.

20. How much water should be added to 414 ounces of a 21% alcohol solution to get an 18% alcohol solution?

Advanced Mathematics by Saxon

1. Draw the necessary reference triangles and evaluate $2 \sin 30° + 3 \cos 60° - 2 \tan 45°$. Do not use a calculator.

2. Find the domain of the function $f(x) = \dfrac{\sqrt{x - 20}}{x^2 - 3x - 4}$.

3. If $f(x) = 4 \cos x$, find $f(300°)$. Do not use a calculator.

4. Evaluate $\dfrac{9!}{3!6!}$. Do not use a calculator.   5. If $f(x) = x^2 - x$, find $f(x + h)$.

6. Ten years ago, Anne was half as old as Sylvia was then. Five years from now, Anne will be as old as Sylvia was five years ago. How old is Sylvia now?

7. Solve for x:

    (a) $\log_x 3 = \dfrac{1}{2}$ (b) $\log_2 \dfrac{1}{16} = x$ (c) $\log_4 x = 2$

8. Solve for t: $3s = \dfrac{2}{3p}\left(\dfrac{6z}{t} - \dfrac{5q}{r}\right)$ 9. Simplify: $\dfrac{\sqrt{-3}\sqrt{-3} - \sqrt{-25} + \sqrt{4}\sqrt{-4}\sqrt{4}}{2 + 3i^3}$

10. Sketch the graph of the function: $y = \dfrac{1}{x + 4}$

11. Chris can mow the lawn in 20 minutes. His mother can mow the lawn in 30 minutes. Chris works for 10 minutes before his mother begins to help. How long do they work together to complete the job?

12. Given: A is the midpoint of $\overline{DC}$

    $\angle D \cong \angle C$

    Write a two-column proof to prove:

    $\overline{ED} \cong \overline{BC}$

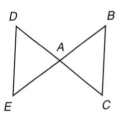

13. While building the addition to Ponderosa High School, the electricians found that it took 5 men to wire 4 rooms in 6 hours. The foreman added 9 more men to the job. How many hours would it take them to do 28 rooms?

14. Dolphins varied directly as tuna and inversely as sharks squared. When there were 50 dolphins, there were 125 tuna and 5 sharks. How many dolphins were there when there were 16 tuna and only 2 sharks?

Factor:

15. $9x^{2n+3} + 18x^{5n+1}$ 16. $125a^9b^3 - 8c^3d^6$

17. Determine whether each graph represents the graph of a function. If so, determine whether the graph is a one-to-one function or not.

    (a) 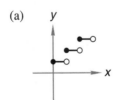   (b) 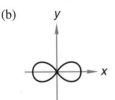   (c) 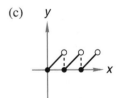   (d)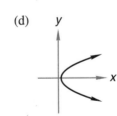

18. Simplify: $\dfrac{x^{a+3}\left(\sqrt{y^4}\right)^{2a}}{y^{2a-2}}$

19. Let $f(x) = 2x$ and $g(x) = 1 - x^2$. Evaluate:

    (a) $(fg)(4)$ (b) $(f/g)(4)$ (c) $(f \circ g)(4)$

20. The space shuttle traveled at v meters per second for l meters and was 5 seconds late for its reentry window. How fast should the shuttle have traveled to make it to the window on time?

Advanced Mathematics by Saxon

Test 7, Form B **SHOW YOUR WORK** Name: _____

1. Draw the necessary reference triangles and evaluate $3 \cos 60° - \dfrac{1}{2} \tan 45° + 2 \sin 30°$. Do not use a calculator.

2. Find the domain of the function $f(x) = \dfrac{\sqrt{x + 5}}{x^2 + x - 6}$.

3. If $f(x) = 4 \sin x$, find $f(330°)$. Do not use a calculator.

4. Evaluate $\dfrac{8!}{4!4!}$. Do not use a calculator.   5. If $f(x) = x^2 + x$, find $f(x + h)$.

6. Fifteen years ago, Phil was twice as old as Darell was then. Three years from now, Darell will be as old as Phil was four years ago. How old is Phil now?

7. Solve for x:

   (a) $\log_x 2 = \dfrac{1}{2}$ (b) $\log_3 \dfrac{1}{3} = x$ (c) $\log_2 x = -3$

8. Solve for l: $3s = \dfrac{3}{2t}\left(\dfrac{8d}{l} - \dfrac{3m}{d}\right)$ 9. Simplify: $\dfrac{\sqrt{-16} + \sqrt{9}\sqrt{-9}\sqrt{-9} - \sqrt{-5}\sqrt{5}}{2 - 3i^3}$

10. Sketch the graph of the function: $y = \dfrac{1}{x - 2}$

11. Machiavelli can mow the lawn in 30 minutes. Karl can mow the lawn in 20 minutes. Machiavelli works for 10 minutes before Karl begins to help. How long do they work together to complete the job?

12. Given: N is the midpoint of $\overline{MO}$
       $\angle M \cong \angle O$

    Write a two-column proof to prove:
       $\overline{LM} \cong \overline{PO}$

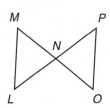

13. While occupying new territory in northern Gaul, the Roman militia found that it took 12 men to scout 3 acres in 4 hours. The governor added 12 more men to do the job. How many hours would it take them to scout 18 acres?

14. Dancers varied directly as band members squared and inversely as conductors. When there were 250 dancers, there were 10 band members and 2 conductors. How many dancers were there when there were 3 band members and 15 conductors?

Factor:

15. $13x^{5n+2} - 26x^{3n+1}$ 16. $64x^3y^6 - 27z^9w^3$

17. Determine whether each graph represents the graph of a function. If so, determine whether the graph is a one-to-one function or not.

(a) 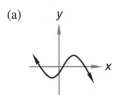   (b) 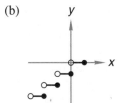   (c) 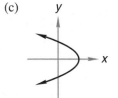   (d)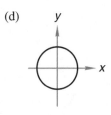

18. Simplify: $\dfrac{y^{b+2}\left(\sqrt{x^6}\right)^{2b}}{x^{3b-1}}$

19. Let $f(x) = 2 - x$ and $g(x) = 3x^2$. Evaluate:

   (a) $(fg)(3)$ (b) $(f/g)(3)$ (c) $(f \circ g)(3)$

20. The airplane travelled at m kilometers per minute for d kilometers and was 7 minutes late to its destination. How fast should the airplane have traveled to make it to its destination on time?

Advanced Mathematics **by Saxon**

Test 8, Form A   **SHOW YOUR WORK**   Name: _____

1. The boat traveled k miles per hour for t hours and was 40 miles short of the goal when the gun went off. If the skipper tried again, how long would it take to reach the goal if she increased the rate of travel by 10 mph?

2. Evaluate $\dfrac{9!}{5!4!}$. Do not use a calculator.

3. If $f(x) = \dfrac{\sqrt{x-10}}{x^2 - 4x - 5}$, find the domain of f.

4. Evaluate $\sin 30° - \cos 300° + \cos 180° + \sin 90°$. Do not use a calculator.

5. Find the resultant of $7\underline{/20°} + 5\underline{/36°}$. Write the answer in polar coordinates.

6. Find four consecutive positive integers such that the product of the first two is 6 greater than the product of 3 and the fourth.

7. Sketch the graph of each function: (a) $y = -x^2$ (b) $y = \dfrac{1}{-x^2}$

8. Evaluate. Do not use a calculator.

   (a) $\text{Arcsin } \dfrac{1}{2}$

   (b) $\text{Arcsin}\left(-\dfrac{1}{2}\right)$

9. The graph of the function $f(x) = \sqrt{x}$ is shown on the left below. The graph on the right is the same graph reflected in the x axis. Write the equation of the graph on the right.

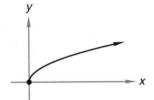
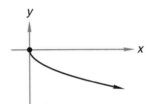

10. Factor: $49a^{4n+3} - 7a^{6n+5}$

11. Simplify: $\dfrac{1}{b + \dfrac{2x}{1 + \dfrac{3}{c}}}$

12. Solve for x:

   (a) $\log_x 49 = 2$

   (b) $\log_5 \dfrac{1}{125} = x$

   (c) $\log_{1/4} x = 3$

13. Jim is five years older than Dot. Twenty years ago, Dot was half as old as Jim is now. How old is Jim now?

14. Given: $\overline{AC} \cong \overline{BC}$
    $\overline{CD} \perp \overline{AB}$

    Write a two-column proof to prove:
    $\triangle CDA \cong \triangle CDB$

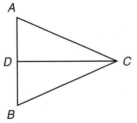

15. Simplify: $\dfrac{z^{3+b}\left(\sqrt{z^3}\right)^{b+2}}{z^{2b-1}}$

16. Find the inverse function of $y = 7x + 3$.

17. Solve: $\begin{cases} y^2 - x^2 = 4 \\ y + 3x = 2 \end{cases}$

18. Simplify: $\dfrac{\sqrt{3}\sqrt{-3}\sqrt{2}\sqrt{-2} - \sqrt{-16} + \sqrt{-5}\sqrt{5}}{1 + \sqrt{-16}i^3}$

19. If $f(x) = 2x^2 - x + 3$, find $f(x + h) - f(x)$.

20. How much of a 70% alcohol solution and how much of a 30% alcohol solution should be mixed to make 5 liters of a 50% alcohol solution?

Advanced Mathematics **by Saxon**

SHOW YOUR WORK   Name: _____

1. The ship sailed at k miles per hour for a hours and was 20 miles short of the village when the horn was sounded. If the Vikings tried again, how long would it take to reach the village if they increased the rate of travel by 35 mph?

2. Evaluate $\dfrac{8!}{6!\,2!}$. Do not use a calculator.   3. If $f(x) = \dfrac{\sqrt{x-5}}{x^2 - 6x - 7}$, find the domain of f.

4. Evaluate $\cos 60° - \sin 270° + \sin 330° + \cos 90°$. Do not use a calculator.

5. Find the resultant of $9\underline{/15°} + 6\underline{/55°}$. Write the answer in polar coordinates.

6. Find three consecutive negative integers such that the product of the first two is 26 greater than the square of the third.

7. Sketch the graph of each function: (a) $y = |x|$ (b) $y = \dfrac{1}{|x|}$

8. Evaluate. Do not use a calculator.

    (a) $\text{Arcsin } \dfrac{\sqrt{3}}{2}$ (b) $\text{Arcsin}\left(-\dfrac{\sqrt{3}}{2}\right)$

9. The graph of the function $f(x) = \sqrt{x}$ is shown on the left below. The graph on the right is the same graph reflected in the y axis. Write the equation of the graph on the right.

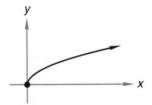   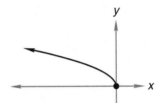

10. Factor: $6a^{3n+1} - 42a^{5n+4}$ 11. Simplify: $\dfrac{1}{a + \dfrac{3b}{2 + \dfrac{4}{x}}}$

12. Solve for x:

    (a) $\log_x 27 = 3$ (b) $\log_6 \dfrac{1}{36} = x$ (c) $\log_{1/7} x = -2$

13. Greg is eight years younger than Marsha. Six years ago, Greg was half as old as Marsha is now. How old is Marsha now?

14. Given: $\overline{XY} \cong \overline{ZY}$
           $\overline{MY} \perp \overline{XZ}$

    Write a two-column proof to prove:
       $\triangle YMX \cong \triangle YMZ$

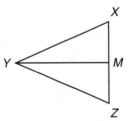

15. Simplify: $\dfrac{y^{2-b}\left(y^3\right)^{b+1}}{\sqrt[3]{y^{4b}}}$ 16. Find the inverse function of $y = 5x - 2$.

17. Solve: $\begin{cases} y^2 - x^2 = 9 \\ y + 3 = 2x \end{cases}$ 18. Simplify: $\dfrac{\sqrt{4}\sqrt{-4}\sqrt{-4} + \sqrt{-25} + \sqrt{-3}\sqrt{3}}{1 + \sqrt{-4}i^3}$

19. If $f(x) = x^2 - 6x + 1$, find $f(x + h) - f(x)$.

20. How much of a 10% alcohol solution and how much of a 40% alcohol solution should be mixed to make 1 liter of a 25% alcohol solution?

***Advanced Mathematics* by Saxon**

1. John found that his plane could fly at 6 times the speed of the wind. He flew 700 miles upwind in 3 hours more than it took to fly 560 miles downwind. What was the speed of the plane in still air?

2. Find the number that is $\frac{2}{5}$ of the way from $-3\frac{2}{5}$ to $5\frac{3}{5}$.

3. Find the equilibrant of $2\underline{/123°}$ and $4\underline{/252°}$. Write the answer in polar coordinates.

4. If a rectangle's length is increased by 30% and its width is decreased by 30%, what is the percent change in area?

5. Evaluate $\dfrac{10!}{3!7!}$. Do not use a calculator.

6. Evaluate: $\displaystyle\sum_{j=1}^{3} \dfrac{2^j}{2+j}$

7. If $f(x) = \dfrac{1}{x}$, find $f(x+h) - f(x)$.

8. Factor: $8x^6y^9 - 64a^3b^{12}$

9. If $f(\theta) = \cos\theta$ and $g(\theta) = \tan\theta$, find $f(540°) + g(225°)$. Do not use a calculator.

10. Evaluate: (a) $\sin(\text{Arctan } 1)$ (b) $\tan\left(\text{Arccos } \dfrac{1}{2}\right)$. Do not use a calculator.

11. The data points in the table below came from an experiment that involved salt (S) and carbon (C). Note that in the graph to the right the horizontal and vertical scales are different. The position of the line that best fits the data points is estimated. Write the equation that expresses salt as a function of carbon ($S = mC + b$).

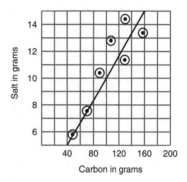

Carbon in grams	48	70	90	108	130	132	158
Salt in grams	5.8	7.5	10.4	12.8	11.3	14.4	13.4

12. The class ran m feet at z feet per minute and arrived at lunch 3 minutes late. How fast should they have run to have arrived on time?

13. Five students could do 100 math problems in 2 hours. How long would it take 10 students to do 1000 math problems?

14. Erica could do 10 math problems in 20 minutes. Penny could do 15 math problems in 25 minutes. If they worked together, how many minutes would it take Erica and Penny to do 30 math problems?

15. If $f(x) = \dfrac{\sqrt{x-3}}{x^2 - 5x + 6}$, find the domain of f.

16. Find the inverse function of $y = \dfrac{7}{8}x - \dfrac{1}{4}$.

17. Given: $\angle ABC \cong \angle DCB$
$\qquad\angle BCA \cong \angle CBD$

Write a two-column proof to prove:
$\overline{AC} \cong \overline{DB}$

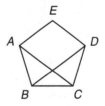

18. Solve for x: (a) $\log_x \dfrac{27}{64} = 3$ (b) $\log_3 \dfrac{1}{27} = x$ (c) $\log_{1/3} x = -4$

19. The graph of $f(x) = \sqrt{x}$ is shown on the left. On the right, the graph is reflected in the y axis. Write the equation of the graph on the right.

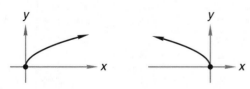

20. In the figure shown, $\overline{EF}$ is the median of trapezoid $ABCD$. Find x.

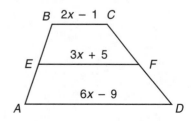

1. Thumbalina found that her goose could fly at 3 times the speed of the wind. She traveled 138 miles upwind in one hour less than it took her to fly 368 miles downwind. How fast could the goose fly in still air?

2. Find the number that is $\frac{2}{3}$ of the way from $-5\frac{1}{3}$ to $9\frac{2}{3}$.

3. Find the equilibrant of $2\underline{/165°}$ and $3\underline{/214°}$. Write the answer in polar coordinates.

4. If a rectangle's length is increased by 50% and its width is decreased by 70%, what is the percent change in area?

5. Evaluate $\dfrac{9!}{3!6!}$. Do not use a calculator.

6. Evaluate: $\displaystyle\sum_{q=1}^{3} \dfrac{3^q}{3+q}$

7. If $f(x) = \dfrac{1}{x}$, find $f(x+h) - f(x)$.

8. Factor: $27x^3y^9 - 8q^6z^{12}$

9. If $h(\theta) = \tan\theta$ and $k(\theta) = \cos\theta$, find $h(315°) + k(420°)$. Do not use a calculator.

10. Evaluate: (a) $\cos\left(\text{Arctan }\sqrt{3}\right)$ (b) $\sin\left(\text{Arccos }\dfrac{\sqrt{3}}{2}\right)$. Do not use a calculator.

11. The data points in the table below came from an experiment that involved Badgers (B) and Termites (T). Note that in the graph the horizontal and vertical scales are different. The position of the line that best fits the data points is estimated. Write the equation that expresses termites as a function of badgers ($T = mB + c$).

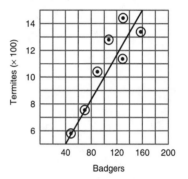

Badgers	48	70	90	108	130	132	158
Termites	580	750	1040	1280	1130	1440	1340

12. The herd stampeded d feet at r feet per minute and arrived at the OK corral 7 minutes late. How fast should the herd have stampeded to have arrived on time?

13. Six soccer players could eat 60 hot dogs in 15 minutes. How long would it take 12 soccer players to eat 96 hot dogs?

14. Barney could label 5 rocks in 10 minutes. Fife could label 3 rocks in 8 minutes. If they work together, how many minutes would it take Barney and Fife to label 49 rocks?

15. If $f(x) = \dfrac{\sqrt{x+2}}{x^2 - 5x - 14}$, find the domain of f.

16. Find the inverse function of $y = \dfrac{10}{11}x + \dfrac{1}{22}$.

17. Given: $\angle XYZ \cong \angle VZY$
$\angle XZY \cong \angle VYZ$

Write a two-column proof to prove:
$\overline{XZ} \cong \overline{VY}$

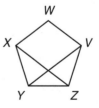

18. Solve for x: (a) $\log_x \dfrac{8}{125} = 3$ (b) $\log_6 \dfrac{1}{36} = x$ (c) $\log_{1/4} x = -2$

19. The graph of $f(x) = -\sqrt{x}$ is shown on the left. On the right, the graph is reflected in the y axis. Write the equation of the graph on the right.

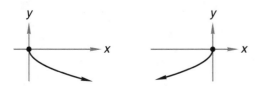

20. In the figure shown, $\overline{EF}$ is the median of trapezoid $ABCD$. Find x.

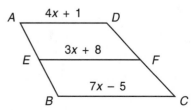

Advanced Mathematics by Saxon

1. The great runner could travel 10 miles at 5 mph and then run 6 miles at 2 mph. What should be her speed for the next 8 miles so that her overall average speed would be 4 mph?

2. The data points in the table below relate the number of textbooks sold (S) to the price per textbook (P). Note that in the graph the horizontal and vertical scales are different. The position of the line that best fits this data has been estimated. Write the equation that expresses the number of textbooks sold as a function of the price per textbook ($S = mP + b$).

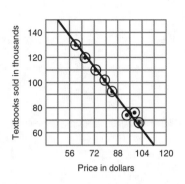

Price per book (in dollars)	60	66	73	79	84	94	99	102
Number sold (in thousands)	130	120	110	102	93	74	76	68

3. Find the equation of the line that is equidistant from the points $(5, 2)$ and $(0, -4)$. Write the equation in slope-intercept form.

4. A multiple choice quiz has 5 questions, and there are 4 possible choices to each question. How many different sets of answers are possible?

5. Write the quadratic equation with a lead coefficient of 1 whose roots are 3 and 2.

6. If $f(x) = 2x^2 - 3$, find $\dfrac{f(x + h) - f(x)}{h}$.

7. Evaluate: $\displaystyle\sum_{k=2}^{5} \left(\dfrac{k^2}{3} - k \right)$

8. Mark watched an ant crawl through an arc of 40° along the rim of his melon, which was cut in half. If the radius of the melon was 7 inches, how far did the ant crawl?

9. Find the coordinates of the point half way between $(-2, 6)$ and $(6, -4)$.

Solve for x:

10. $\log_{96} 3 + \log_{96} 5 = \log_{96} (5 + x)$

11. $\log_{20} (2x + 6) - \log_{20} 2 = \log_{20} 8$

12. $4 \log_b x = \log_b 16$

13. $\log_3 \dfrac{1}{81} = x$

Evaluate. Do not use a calculator.

14. $\sin \dfrac{\pi}{2} - \cos \dfrac{3\pi}{4} - \tan \dfrac{\pi}{6}$

15. $\sin \left(\text{Arctan} \dfrac{3}{4} \right)$

16. Use the point-slope form to find a general form of the equation of the line whose slope is -3 and that passes through the point $(-1, 7)$. Then transform the equation to the double-intercept form.

17. The airplane flew m miles at r mph and arrived 2 hours late. How fast should the airplane have flown to have arrived on time?

18. Tim can build 3 shelves in one day and Al can build 4 shelves in 2 days. If Al starts work one day before Tim, how long will they work together to build 22 shelves?

19. The graph of the function $f(x) = \frac{1}{x}$ is centered at the origin as shown on the left below. The graph on the right is the same graph translated so that it is centered at $(0, 1)$. Write the equation of the graph on the right.

20. Given: $\overline{AB}$ bisects $\angle CAD$
$\overline{AB}$ bisects $\angle CBD$

Write a two-column proof to prove:
$\triangle ACB \cong \triangle ADB$

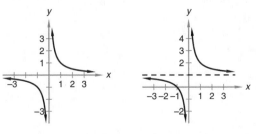

       Advanced Mathematics by Saxon

1. Ian could run 8 miles at 4 mph and then run 4 miles at 2 mph. What should his speed be for the next 6 miles so that his overall average speed would be 3 mph?

2. The data points in the table below relate the number of books sold (S) to the price per book (P). Note that in the graph the horizontal and vertical scales are different. The position of the line that best fits this data has been estimated. Write the equation that expresses the number of books sold as a function of the price per book ($S = mP + b$).

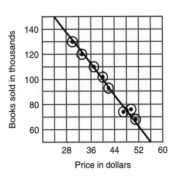

Price per book (in dollars)	30	33	37	40	42	47	50	51
Number sold (in thousands)	130	120	110	102	93	74	76	68

3. Find the equation of the line that is equidistant from the points $(4, 3)$ and $(0, -2)$. Write the equation in slope-intercept form.

4. A multiple choice quiz has 7 questions, and there are 3 possible choices for each question. How many different sets of answers are possible?

5. Write the quadratic equation with a lead coefficient of 1 whose roots are –3 and 5.

6. If $f(x) = 3x^2 - 4$, find $\dfrac{f(x + h) - f(x)}{h}$

7. Evaluate: $\displaystyle\sum_{k=3}^{6} \left(\dfrac{k^2}{2} - 2k \right)$

8. Blind Io watched a scarab beetle crawl through an arc of $60°$ on a disc with a radius of 100 mm. How far did the beetle crawl?

9. Find the coordinate of the point halfway between $(-8, 7)$ and $(14, -15)$.

Solve for x:

10. $\log_{87} 4 + \log_{87} 3 = \log_{87} (4 + x)$

11. $\log_{20} (3x + 9) - \log_{20} 2 = \log_{20} 12$

12. $5 \log_b x = \log_b 32$

13. $\log_4 \dfrac{1}{64} = x$

Evaluate. Do not use a calculator.

14. $\cos \pi - \sin \dfrac{3\pi}{2} - \tan \dfrac{11\pi}{6}$

15. $\sin \left(\text{Arctan} \dfrac{12}{5} \right)$

16. Use the point-slope form to find a general form of the equation of the line whose slope is –2 and that passes through the point $(2, -1)$. Then transform the equation to the double-intercept form.

17. The flock migrated k kilometers at s kilometers per day and arrived two days late. How fast should the flock have flown to have arrived at the breeding grounds on time?

18. C.J. can haul 6 loads in 3 days, and Faye can haul 5 loads in 2 days. If C.J. starts work one day before Faye, how long will they work together to haul 20 loads?

19. The graph of the function $f(x) = -\dfrac{1}{x}$ is centered at the origin as shown on the left below. The graph on the right is the same graph translated so that it is centered at $(-2, 2)$. Write the equation of the graph on the right.

20. Given: $\overline{YW}$ bisects $\angle XYZ$
$\overline{YW}$ bisects $\angle XWZ$

Write a two column proof to prove:
$\triangle YXW \cong \triangle YZW$

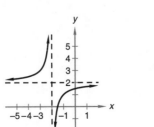

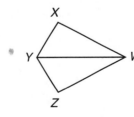

     Advanced Mathematics **by Saxon**

1. At the smoked turkey sale, Safemart sold t turkeys for d dollars. Good Cafe was able to buy them for $2 less per turkey. How many turkeys could Good Cafe purchase for $1000?

2. A spider crawls through an arc of 50°. How far does the spider crawl if the diameter of the circle is 100 inches?

3. Sketch the graph of the function: $y = \left(\dfrac{1}{2}\right)^{-2x}$

4. By how much does $_6P_4$ exceed $_6P_2$?

5. Solve for x:

   (a) $3 \log_2 x = 2 \log_2 8$

   (b) $\log_9 \dfrac{1}{81} = x$

   (c) $\log_x 81 = 4$

6. Evaluate. Do not use a calculator.

   (a) Arctan 1

   (b) Arccos (-1)

   (c) $\sin\left(\text{Arccos}\left(-\dfrac{3}{5}\right)\right)$

7. Simplify: $\log_2 2^3 + \log_3 3^2 - \log_5 5^2$

8. Solve for x: $\log_7 (x + 8) - \log_7 (x - 1) = \log_7 10$

9. Sketch the graph of each function: (a) $f(x) = |x + 3| - 2$ (b) $g(x) = \dfrac{1}{|x + 3| - 2}$

10. Find the equation of the line that is equidistant from points $(3, -2)$ and $(-3, 4)$. Write the equation in slope-intercept form.

11. If $f(x) = \dfrac{\sqrt{-x}}{x^3 + 2x^2 - 3x}$, find the domain of f.

12. Evaluate: $\displaystyle\sum_{j=2}^{4} (3j - j^2)$

13. Determine if $f(x) = \dfrac{1}{x - 2}$ and $g(x) = \dfrac{2x + 1}{x}$ are inverse functions by computing their compositions.

14. Find the standard form of the equation of a circle whose center is at $(2, 5)$ and whose radius is 4.

15. Given: $\overline{AC} \cong \overline{DC}$
    $\overline{BC} \cong \overline{EC}$

    Write a two-column proof to prove:
    $$\angle A \cong \angle D$$

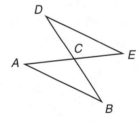

16. Evaluate: $\cos \dfrac{13\pi}{6} - \tan \dfrac{8\pi}{3}$

17. The second period College Algebra class of 33 students could do n problems in x hours. If 3 students were absent, how long would it take to do 100 problems?

18. Find the coordinates of the point halfway between $(2, 4)$ and $(12, -2)$.

19. Evaluate: $\sec 600° + \cot 315°$. Do not use a calculator.

20. Write the equation of this sinusoid.

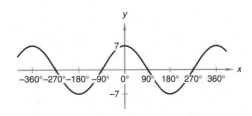

1. At the guitar amp sale, Mahoney's sold t amps for m dollars. Eddie was able to buy them for $15 less per amp. How many amps could Eddie purchase for $3000?

2. The goat runs through an arc of 70° around the hitching post. How far did the goat run if he was 150 inches from the post?

3. Sketch the graph of the function: $y = \left(\dfrac{1}{3}\right)^{-2x}$

4. By how much does $_5P_4$ exceed $_5P_2$?

5. Solve for x:

   (a) $4 \log_3 x = 2 \log_3 9$

   (b) $\log_4 \dfrac{1}{64} = x$

   (c) $\log_x 32 = 5$

6. Evaluate. Do not use a calculator.

   (a) Arcsin 1

   (b) Arctan (-1)

   (c) $\cos\left(\text{Arcsin}\left(-\dfrac{4}{5}\right)\right)$

7. Simplify: $\log_3 3^4 + \log_5 5^3 - \log_2 2^4$

8. Solve for x: $\log_9 (x + 2) - \log_9 (x - 3) = \log_9 6$

9. Sketch the graph of each function: (a) $f(x) = |x - 2| - 3$ (b) $g(x) = \dfrac{1}{|x - 2| - 3}$

10. Find the equation of the line that is equidistant from points $(-3, 3)$ and $(5, -1)$. Write the equation in slope-intercept form.

11. If $f(x) = \dfrac{\sqrt{2 - x}}{x^3 + 3x^2 - 4x}$, find the domain of f.

12. Evaluate: $\displaystyle\sum_{i=1}^{3} \left(4i - 2i^2\right)$

13. Determine if $f(x) = \dfrac{1}{2x + 1}$ and $g(x) = \dfrac{1 - x}{2x}$ are inverse functions by computing their compositions.

14. Find the standard form of the equation of a circle whose center is at $(-3, 2)$ and whose radius is 5.

15. Given: $\overline{LN} \cong \overline{PN}$

    $\overline{MN} \cong \overline{ON}$

    Write a two-column proof to prove:

    $\angle L \cong \angle P$

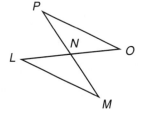

16. Evaluate: $\sin \dfrac{13\pi}{6} + \tan \dfrac{8\pi}{3}$

17. The sixth hour ceramics class of 22 students could make b vases in 9 hours. If 2 students were absent, how long would it take to make 30 vases?

18. Find the coordinates of the point halfway between $(4, 12)$ and $(2, 2)$.

19. Evaluate: $\sec 240° + \cot 495°$. Do not use a calculator.

20. Write the equation of this sinusoid.

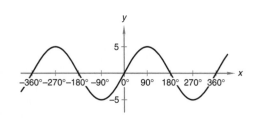

Advanced Mathematics by Saxon

1. Use the midpoint formula method to find the equation of the perpendicular bisector of the line segment whose endpoints are (−2, 3) and (−6, 1). Write the equation in double-intercept form.

2. Seven math books and three literature books are on a shelf. How many ways can they be arranged if the math books are kept together and the literature books are kept together?

3. The teacher can write 18 words on the board in 3 minutes. The student can write 24 words in 6 minutes. The student began to write for 2 minutes before the teacher begins to help. How long would it take them together to finish writing a total of 88 words?

4. One thousand liters of a solution was available, but the solution was 60% alcohol. Barney needed a solution which was 45% alcohol. How many liters of alcohol had to be extracted so that the solution would be 45% alcohol?

5. Determine whether the graph of each equation is symmetric about the x axis, the y axis, or the origin:

(a)

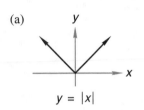

$y = |x|$

(b)

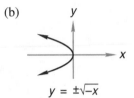

$y = \pm\sqrt{-x}$

6. Evaluate. Do not use a calculator.

(a) $\text{Arctan } \sqrt{3}$

(b) $\sin\left(\text{Arctan}\left(-\dfrac{3}{4}\right)\right)$

Solve for x:

7. $\dfrac{1}{2} \log_{15} 9 + \log_{15} (x + 1) = \log_{15} 12$

8. $3 \log_7 1 = 2 \log_7 (x - 7)$

Evaluate. Do not use a calculator.

9. $\sec 780° + \cos (-540°) + \sin 630°$

10. $\csc^2 \dfrac{3\pi}{4} - \tan^3 \dfrac{5\pi}{4} + \sin^3 \dfrac{\pi}{2}$

11. Let $f(x) = 4x^2$ and $g(x) = x - \dfrac{3}{x}$. Evaluate: (a) $(f - g)(3)$ (b) $(f/g)(3)$ (c) $(f \circ g)(3)$

12. Find the standard form of the equation of a circle whose center is at (−2, 3) and whose radius is 5.

13. Sketch the graph of the function $f(x) = \left(\dfrac{1}{2}\right)^{-x-2}$.

14. Sketch the graph of each function: (a) $g(x) = |x - 4| - 2$ (b) $h(x) = \dfrac{1}{|x - 4| - 2}$

15. How many three digit counting numbers less than 500 have digits that are all even?

16. In the Ptomaine Cafeteria, the cook made c cookies which fed s students for 10 days. How many days would it take m more students to eat the same amount of cookies?

Write the equations of the following sinusoids:

17.

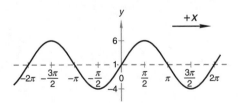

18.

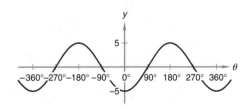

19. Factor $x^2 - 4x + 6$ over the set of complex numbers.

20. Write the quadratic equation with a lead coefficient of 1 whose roots are $1 + 2i$ and $1 - 2i$.

     Advanced Mathematics **by Saxon**

1. Use the midpoint formula method to find the equation of the perpendicular bisector of the line segment whose endpoints are $(2, -3)$ and $(6, -1)$. Write the equation in double-intercept form.

2. Four phonics books and five philosophy books are on a shelf. How many ways can they be arranged if the phonics books are kept together and the philosophy books are kept together?

3. The grizzled old mountain man can chop 2 cords of wood in 1 day. The young lad can chop 2 cords in 3 days. The young lad chops alone for 2 days, and then the old man joins in. How long must they work together before a total of 12 cords have been chopped?

4. Five hundred liters of a solution was available, but the solution was 75% alcohol. Alberto needed a solution which was 30% alcohol. How many liters of alcohol had to be extracted so that the solution would be 30% alcohol?

5. Determine whether the graph of each equation is symmetric about the x axis, the y axis, or the origin:

(a)

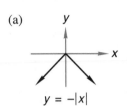

$y = -|x|$

(b)

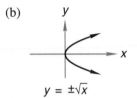

$y = \pm\sqrt{x}$

6. Evaluate. Do not use a calculator.

   (a) $\text{Arctan } \dfrac{1}{\sqrt{3}}$

   (b) $\sin\left(\text{Arctan}\left(-\dfrac{5}{12}\right)\right)$

Solve for x:

7. $\dfrac{1}{2}\log 16 + \log(x + 2) = 5\log 2$

8. $\log_8(x - 8) = \dfrac{2}{3}\log_8 27$

Evaluate. Do not use a calculator.

9. $\csc^2(-750°) + \tan 495° + \cos 630°$

10. $\csc^2 \dfrac{7\pi}{6} - \cot^3 \dfrac{3\pi}{4} + \sin^3\left(-\dfrac{\pi}{2}\right)$

11. Let $f(x) = 3x^2$ and $g(x) = x - \dfrac{2}{x}$. Evaluate: (a) $(f - g)(2)$ (b) $(f/g)(2)$ (c) $(f \circ g)(2)$

12. Find the standard form of the equation of a circle whose center is at $(4, -4)$ and whose radius is 6.

13. Sketch the graph of the function $f(x) = \left(\dfrac{1}{3}\right)^{-x-1}$

14. Sketch the graph of each function: (a) $g(x) = |x + 2| - 3$ (b) $h(x) = \dfrac{1}{|x + 2| - 3}$

15. How many three digit counting numbers less than 700 have digits that are all even?

16. At the factory, w workers made p products in 8 days. How many days would it take x more workers to make the same number of products?

Write the equations of the following sinusoids:

17.

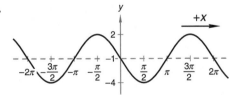

18.

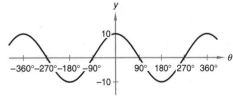

19. Factor $x^2 + 5x + 8$ over the set of complex numbers.

20. Write the quadratic equation with a lead coefficient of 1 whose roots are $2 - 3i$ and $2 + 3i$.

Advanced Mathematics by Saxon

1. Use the midpoint formula method to find the equation of the perpendicular bisector of the line segment whose endpoints are (4, –3) and (–2, –5). Write the equation in general form.

2. The nurse was aghast. She knew that g gallons of milk would feed s infants for 12 days, but she had $s + 15$ infants to feed. How many days would m gallons of milk last?

3. Find the equation of the line that is equidistant from the points (–2, –5) and (3, 4) using the locus definition method. Write the equation in slope-intercept form.

4. Chere can do 2 jobs in 3 days, and Stacey can do 5 jobs in 6 days. Chere works for 3 days, and then Stacey begins to help. How many days will it take them working together to do 74 jobs?

5. Write the quadratic equation with a lead coefficient of 1 whose roots are $1 + 4i$ and $1 - 4i$.

6. The school bus went d miles in h hours but arrived 3 hours late. How fast should the bus have traveled to have arrived on time?

7. Given the function $f(x) = |x|$, write the equation of the function g whose graph is the graph of f translated 3 units to the left and 4 units down. Sketch the graph of the new function g.

8. Solve the following equations if $0° \leq \theta < 360°$:

   (a) $\cos \theta = -\dfrac{\sqrt{3}}{2}$

   (b) $\sin \dfrac{\theta}{2} - \dfrac{1}{2} = 0$

9. Find the equation of the following sinusoid:

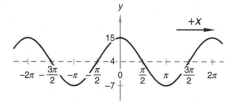

10. The following data comes from an experiment performed to determine if there is a relationship between the percentage of blood hemoglobin (H) in dogs and the number of red blood cells (C) they possess. Use a graphing calculator to find the equation of the line which best fits the data and gives the number of red blood cells (in millions per mm^3) as a function of the percentage of blood hemoglobin ($C = mH + b$). Also find the correlation coefficient for this scientific data and discuss whether or not the line is a good model for the data.

Blood hemoglobin %	93	99	96	80	98
Red blood cells	8.4	8.5	8.1	6.2	7.9

11. Evaluate: $\sec^2\left(-\dfrac{13\pi}{6}\right) - \csc^2 \dfrac{5\pi}{4}$

12. Write 4500 as a power whose base is e.

13. Sketch the graph of the function $f(x) = \left(\dfrac{1}{3}\right)^{x-2}$.

14. The graph of the function $f(x) = \sqrt{x}$ is shown on the left. The graph on the right is the same graph reflected in the y axis and translated 2 units to the right. Write the equation of the graph on the right.

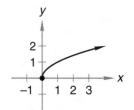

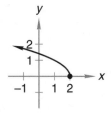

15. Given: $\overline{AD} \parallel \overline{BC}$
    $\overline{DC} \parallel \overline{AB}$

    Write a two-column proof to prove: $\overline{AD} \cong \overline{BC}$

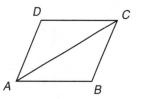

16. Evaluate: Arctan (sin 90°)

17. Find: log 5.6

18. Find: ln 5.6

19. How many positive integers are there less than 900 such that all digits are odd?

20. How many ways can the letters A, B, C, D, E, and F be arranged in a row 4 at a time if neither A nor C can be second and E must be third? Repetition is permitted.

Advanced Mathematics **by Saxon**

1. Use the midpoint formula method to find the equation of the perpendicular bisector of the line segment whose endpoints are $(3, -2)$ and $(5, 4)$. Write the equation in general form.

2. The accountant was disappointed. He knew that d dollars would finance j bands for 7 days at the festival, but he had to pay $j + 3$ bands. How many days would n dollars last?

3. Find the equation of the line that is equidistant from the points $(5, -3)$ and $(3, 2)$ using the locus definition method. Write the equation in slope-intercept form.

4. Hadrian could do 5 jobs in 8 days, and Lief could do 1 job in 2 days. Lief works for 4 days, and then Hadrian begins to help. How many days will it take them working together to do 74 jobs?

5. Write the quadratic equation with a lead coefficient of 1 whose roots are $1 + 2i$ and $1 - 2i$.

6. The bullet train went x kilometers in t hours but arrived 1 hour late. How fast should the train have traveled to have arrived on time?

7. Given the function $f(x) = |x|$, write the equation of the function g whose graph is the graph of f translated 2 units to the right and 3 units down. Sketch the graph of the new function g.

8. Solve the following equations if $0° \le \theta < 360°$:

    (a) $\sin \theta = -\dfrac{\sqrt{3}}{2}$

    (b) $\tan \dfrac{\theta}{2} - \sqrt{3} = 0$

9. Find the equation of the following sinusoid:

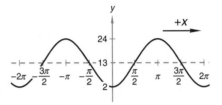

10. The following data comes from an experiment performed to determine if there is a relationship between the percentage of alkaloids (A) in human blood and the number of carcinogens (C) in human blood. Use a graphing calculator to find the equation of the line which best fits the data and gives the number of carcinogens (in parts per million) as a function of the percentage of alkaloids ($C = mA + b$). Also find the correlation coefficient for this scientific data and discuss whether or not the line is a good model for the data.

Alkaloid %	11.5	8.2	8.9	10.1	6.9
Carcinogens	33	24	30	29	16

11. Evaluate: $\tan^2\left(\dfrac{4\pi}{3}\right) - \sec^2\left(-\dfrac{11\pi}{6}\right)$

12. Write 4900 as a power whose base is e.

13. Sketch the graph of the function $f(x) = \left(\dfrac{1}{2}\right)^{x-2}$.

14. The graph of the function $f(x) = \sqrt{-x}$ is shown on the left. The graph on the right is the same graph reflected in the x axis and translated 3 units to the left. Write the equation of the graph on the right.

15. Given: $\overline{HI} \parallel \overline{KJ}$
    $\overline{HK} \parallel \overline{IJ}$

    Write a two-column proof to prove: $\overline{IJ} \cong \overline{HK}$

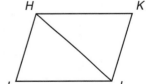

16. Evaluate: Arccos (tan 45°)

17. Find: log 6.3

18. Find: ln 6.3

19. How many positive integers are there less than 800 such that all digits are even?

20. How many ways can the letters $Z, Y, X, W, V,$ and U be arranged in a row 5 at a time if U cannot be first, X cannot be second, and Z must be third? Repetition is permitted.

      Advanced Mathematics by Saxon

1. Smith was traveling x miles to Boston at m miles per hour and arrived 2 hours late for the party. How fast should he have traveled to have arrived on time?

2. Snow White and the Seven Dwarves sat around a circular table. How many seating arrangements were possible?

3. On the outbound leg of a 450 mile trip, the plane flew at a slow speed. On the trip back (also 450 miles), the pilot tripled the speed of the plane. How fast did the plane travel on the trip back if the total traveling time was 8 hours?

4. How many distinguishable permutations can be formed from the letters in the word success?

5. Complete the square to graph $y = x^2 - 2x + 4$.

Solve for x.

6. $2 \ln 2 + 2 \ln 3 = 2 \ln (x + 4)$

7. $\log_9 12x - 3 \log_9 2 = 1$

8. The wheels on the toy car have a diameter of 2 inches and are revolving at 60 radians per second. What is the linear velocity of the toy car in feet per minute?

9. (a) Write 6300 as 10 raised to a power.   (b) Write 6300 as e raised to a power.

10. Let $f(x) = \sqrt{x}$ and $g(x) = \sqrt{x - 6}$. Which of the following statements is true?

    A. The graph of g is the graph of f translated six units to the right.

    B. The graph of g is the graph of f translated six units to the left.

    C. The graph of g is the graph of f translated six units up.

    D. The graph of g is the graph of f translated six units down.

11. Simpich had e elves who worked h hours to get d number of dolls made. Then n elves went on vacation. How many hours would it take the remaining elves to make s dolls?

12. Andrea went to the greeting card store because they were selling c cards for t cents. When she arrived the store announced a blue light special of 20 cents less on each card. How many cards could Andrea now buy for five dollars?

13. Write the equation of the following sinusoid: 14. Find the area of this triangle.

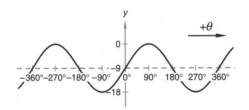

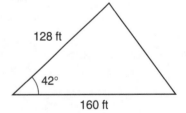

15. Find the area of the segment bounded by an arc of measure 80° and the chord joining the endpoints of the arc in a circle of radius 10 feet.

16. The latitude of the U.S. Air Force Academy is 39° north of the equator. If the diameter of the earth is 7920 miles, how far is the U.S. Air Force Academy from the equator?

17. Factor $x^2 - 5x + 8$ over the set of complex numbers.

Solve the following equations given that $0° \le \theta < 360°$:

18. $3 \tan 3\theta - \sqrt{3} = 0$

19. $3 \csc \dfrac{\theta}{2} - 2\sqrt{3} = 0$

20. Find the equation of the line equidistant from the points $(2, 4)$ and $(-4, -4)$. Write the equation in double intercept form.

Advanced Mathematics by Saxon

1. Amy was driving m miles to Atlanta at v miles per hour and arrived 3 hours late for the rave. How fast should she have driven to have arrived on time?

2. Buddha and ten of his students sat around a circular table. How many seating arrangements were possible?

3. Ben flew a distance of 480 miles at a moderate speed. On the trip back (also 480 miles), Ben doubled the speed of the plane. How fast did Ben fly on the trip back if the total traveling time was 6 hours?

4. How many distinguishable permutations can be formed from the letters in the word sassy?

5. Complete the square to graph $y = x^2 - 4x + 2$.

Solve for x:

6. $2 \ln 3 + 2 \ln 2 = 2 \ln (x + 2)$

7. $\log_6 9x - 2 \log_6 3 = 1$

8. The wheels of the party van have a diameter of 2 feet and are revolving at 2000 radians per minute. What is the linear velocity of the party van in inches per second?

9. (a) Write 6900 as 10 raised to a power.   (b) Write 6900 as e raised to a power.

10. Let $f(x) = \sqrt{x}$ and $g(x) = \sqrt{x} + 4$. Which of the following statements is true?

   A. The graph of g is the graph of f translated four units to the right.

   B. The graph of g is the graph of f translated four units to the left.

   C. The graph of g is the graph of f translated four units up.

   D. The graph of g is the graph of f translated four units down.

11. Travis had d kindred who worked t hours to get m number of drums made. Then k kindred left. How many hours would it take the remaining kindred to make r drums?

12. Seth went to the music store because they were selling p tapes for c cents. When he arrived the store announced a special of 10 cents less on each tape. How many tapes could Seth now buy for six dollars?

13. Write the equation of the following sinusoid: 14. Find the area of this triangle.

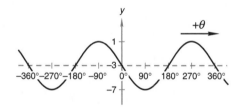

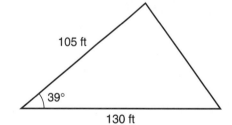

15. Find the area of the segment bounded by an arc of measure 70° and the chord joining the endpoints of the arc in a circle of radius 12 feet.

16. The latitude of the U.S. Military Academy is 44° north of the equator. If the diameter of the earth is 7920 miles, how far is the U.S. Military Academy from the equator?

17. Factor $x^2 + 2x + 9$ over the set of complex numbers.

Solve the following equations given that $0° \leq \theta < 360°$:

18. $3 \sec 2\theta - 2\sqrt{3} = 0$

19. $2 \sin \dfrac{\theta}{3} - \sqrt{2} = 0$

20. Find the equation of the line equidistant from the points $(7, 1)$ and $(-1, -5)$. Write the equation in double intercept form.

Advanced Mathematics **by Saxon**

1. The wheel was rolling along at 400 radians per minute. What was its linear velocity in miles per hour if the radius was 20 meters?

2. There are three identical red flags, two identical blue flags, and five identical green flags. How many different patterns are possible if the flags are displayed vertically on a flagpole?

3. Write the equation of the following sinusoid in terms of the cosine function:

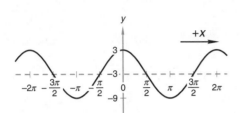

4. Find the area of this trapezoid.

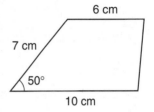

5. The central angle of a sector of a circle is 1.2 radians. Find the area of the sector if the radius is 4 m.

6. (a) Write 41,000 as 10 raised to a power.   (b) Write 41,000 as e raised to a power.

7. Sketch the graphs of the equations $y = x^2 - 4x + 2$ and $y = -x + 4$. Shade the region(s) that satisfies the system of inequalities:

$$\begin{cases} y \geq x^2 - 4x + 2 \\ y \leq -x + 4 \end{cases}$$

8. Find the standard form of the equation of a circle whose radius is 7 and whose center is $(4, -5)$.

Solve the following equations given that $0° \leq \theta < 360°$:

9. $\cos^2 \theta - 1 = 0$

10. $2 \sin \theta \cos \theta = \cos \theta$

Solve for x:

11. $\log_{20} (x + 2) + \log_{20} (x + 3) = 1$

12. $\dfrac{4}{5} \log_8 32 - \log_8 (x + 2) = \log_8 2$

13. Simplify: $4^{\log_4 \sqrt{2} + \log_4 \sqrt{6}}$

14. Evaluate: $\sin^2 \dfrac{7\pi}{6} + \cos^2 \dfrac{11\pi}{6} - \tan^3 \dfrac{3\pi}{4}$

15. Find the distance between the point $(3, 1)$ and the line $y = x - 4$.

16. Factor $x^2 - 3x + 3$ over the set of complex numbers.

17. Uncle Donald could do 2 jobs in 3 days and Cousin Kelly could do 4 jobs in 7 days. Cousin Kelly worked alone for 3 days before Uncle Donald joined in. How long would they have to work together to complete a total of 8 jobs?

18. The helicopter could fly at 4 times the speed of the wind. Thus, it could travel 600 miles downwind in 1 hour more than it took to travel 300 miles upwind. What was the speed of the helicopter in still air?

Find the domain and range of each function whose graph is shown.

19.

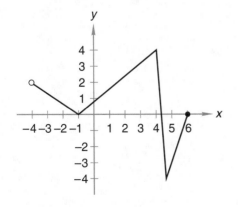

20.

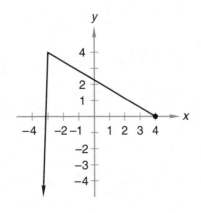

1. The wheel was rolling along at 20 radians per second. What was its linear velocity in miles per hour if the radius was 2 meters?

2. There are four identical blue shirts, two identical green shirts, and three identical yellow shirts. How many different patterns are possible if the shirts are hung in a row on a clothesline?

3. Write the equation of the following sinusoid in terms of the cosine function:

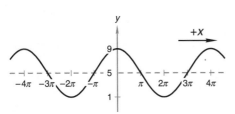

4. Find the area of this trapezoid.

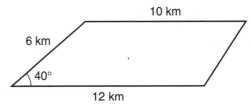

5. The central angle of a sector of a circle is 3.4 radians. Find the area of the sector if the radius is 3 cm.

6. (a) Write 3,800 as 10 raised to a power.   (b) Write 3,800 as e raised to a power.

7. Sketch the graphs of the equations $y = x^2 - 2x - 2$ and $y = \frac{1}{2}x - 1$. Shade the region(s) that satisfies the system of inequalities:

$$\begin{cases} y \geq x^2 - 2x - 2 \\ y \leq \frac{1}{2}x - 1 \end{cases}$$

8. Find the standard form of the equation of a circle whose radius is 4 and whose center is $(2, -3)$.

Solve the following equations given that $0° \leq \theta < 360°$:

9. $\sin^2 \theta - 1 = 0$

10. $2 \sin \theta \cos \theta = \sin \theta$

Solve for x:

11. $\log_{14}(2x + 3) + \log_{14}(x + 3) = 1$

12. $\frac{4}{3} \log_3 8 - \log_3(x + 3) = \log_3 2$

13. Simplify: $9^{\log_9 \sqrt{3} + \log_9 \sqrt{6}}$

14. Evaluate: $\sin^2 \frac{4\pi}{3} - \cos^3 \frac{3\pi}{2} + \tan^2 \frac{5\pi}{4}$

15. Find the distance between the point $(-3, 1)$ and the line $y = -x + 4$.

16. Factor $x^2 - x + 6$ over the set of complex numbers.

17. Dr. Rubin could examine 7 patients in 2 days and Dr. Chu could examine 3 patients in 1 day. Dr. Rubin worked alone for 3 days before Dr. Chu joined in. How long would they have to work together to examine a total of 50 patients?

18. The genetically altered platypus could swim at 5 times the speed of the river. Thus, it could travel 180 miles downstream in 1 hour less than it took to travel 160 miles upstream. What was the speed of the platypus in still water?

Find the domain and range of each function whose graph is shown.

19.

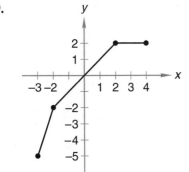

20.

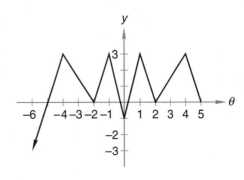

Advanced Mathematics **by Saxon**

1. Find the area of the segment bounded by an arc of measure $135°$ and the chord which joins the endpoints of the arc in a circle of radius 2 cm.

2. The wheel had an angular velocity of 500 radians per minute. How fast was the wheel rolling along in kilometers per hour if the radius of the wheel was 170 centimeters?

3. The total cost of production varied linearly with the number produced. When 20 were produced, the cost was $450. When 30 were produced, the cost was $650. Write an equation that gives the cost as a function of the number produced, and find out what it would cost if 100 were produced.

4. The mean of a distribution that is approximately normal is 83 and the standard deviation is 3. Use the standard deviation to tell how the data is distributed with respect to the mean.

5. Solve for x: $\begin{cases} cx + by = d \\ px + qy = f \end{cases}$

6. Multiply $(\sqrt{3} \text{ cis } 15°)(2 \text{ cis } 45°)$ and express the answer in rectangular coordinates. Give an exact answer.

7. Thom traveled t miles in s hours and then traveled m miles in z hours. If he maintained his overall average rate, how long would it take him to travel 150 miles?

8. The equation $x^2 + y^2 - 2x + 8y + 8 = 0$ is the equation of a circle. Complete the square to change this equation to standard form. Find the radius and the coordinates of the center of the circle and then graph the circle.

9. Solve the equation given that $0° \le \theta < 360°$: $\sin \theta \cos 2\theta - \cos 2\theta = 0$

10. Make a stem-and-leaf plot given the following data: 42, 57, 64, 33, 46, 59, 44, 71, 49, 55, 54, 32.

11. The measurements are 407, 591, 604, 488, 544, 474, 691, and 645. Use a graphing calculator to find the mean and the standard deviation and to find min x, Q_1, med, Q_3, and max x. Use this data to draw a box-and-whisker plot.

12. Evaluate: $\sin\left(\text{Arctan } \dfrac{1}{4}\right)$

13. Evaluate: $\tan^2(-405°) - \sec^2(-405°) + \cos 900°$

14. Find the area of this trapezoid in square centimeters.

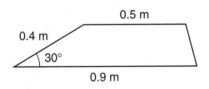

15. Write the equation of the sinusoid in terms of the sine function:

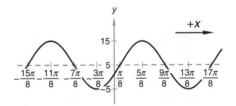

Solve for x:

16. $\log_7 (x + 3) - \log_7 x = \log_7 4$

17. $\log x + \log (x - 3) = 1$

18. Sketch the graphs of the equations $y = -(x - 1)^2 + 5$ and $y = x + 2$. Shade the region(s) that satisfies the system of inequalities:

$$\begin{cases} y \le -(x - 1)^2 + 5 \\ y \le x + 2 \end{cases}$$

19. Find the range, mean, median, mode, variance, and standard deviation for the following data: 12, 7, 8, 9, 11, 8, 15.

20. If $f(x) = x(x + 2)$, find $\dfrac{f(x + h) - f(x - h)}{2h}$.

Advanced Mathematics by Saxon

1. Find the area of the segment bounded by an arc of measure 150° and the chord which joins the endpoints of the arc in a circle of radius 3 km.

2. The hoop had an angular velocity of 300 radians per minute. How fast was the hoop rolling along in kilometers per hour if the diameter of the hoop was 50 centimeters?

3. The total cost of production varied linearly with the number produced. When 10 were produced, the cost was $172. When 25 were produced, the cost was $412. Write an equation that gives the cost as a function of the number produced, and find out what it would cost if 20 were produced.

4. The mean of a distribution that is approximately normal is 92 and the standard deviation is 2. Use the standard deviation to tell how the data is distributed with respect to the mean.

5. Solve for x: $\begin{cases} cx + dy = f \\ wx + zy = t \end{cases}$

6. Multiply $(2 \text{ cis } 75°)[\sqrt{3} \text{ cis } (-15°)]$ and express the answer in rectangular coordinates. Give an exact answer.

7. Travis ran t miles in h hours and then ran r miles in m hours. If he maintained his overall average rate, how long would it take him to run 26 miles?

8. The equation $x^2 + y^2 + 2x - 4y - 4 = 0$ is the equation of a circle. Complete the square to change this equation to standard form. Find the radius and the coordinates of the center of the circle and then graph the circle.

9. Solve the equation given that $0° \le \theta < 360°$: $\tan \theta \sin 2\theta + \sin 2\theta = 0$

10. Make a stem-and-leaf plot given the following data: 43, 56, 63, 34, 48, 57, 47, 68, 49, 56, 53, 32.

11. The measurements are 408, 590, 606, 486, 546, 473, 693, and 644. Use a graphing calculator to find the mean and the standard deviation and to find min x, Q_1, med, Q_3, and max x. Use this data to draw a box-and-whisker plot.

12. Evaluate: $\sin\left(\text{Arctan } \dfrac{2}{5}\right)$

13. Evaluate: $\tan^2 225° - \sec^2 225° + \cos(-540°)$

14. Find the area of this trapezoid in square centimeters.

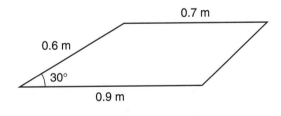

15. Write the equation of the sinusoid in terms of the sine function:

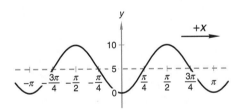

Solve for x:

16. $\log_5(x + 2) - \log_5 x = \log_5 3$

17. $\log x + \log(x + 3) = 1$

18. Sketch the graphs of the equations $y = (x - 1)^2 - 5$ and $y = -x - 2$. Shade the region(s) that satisfies the system of inequalities:

$$\begin{cases} y \ge (x - 1)^2 - 5 \\ y \le -x - 2 \end{cases}$$

19. Find the range, mean, median, mode, variance, and standard deviation for the following data: 13, 8, 7, 11, 8, 10, 6.

20. If $f(x) = x(x + 1)$, find $\dfrac{f(x + h) - f(x - h)}{2h}$.

Advanced Mathematics **by Saxon**

1. The price of the hamburger meat varied linearly with the weight of the package. If a package of hamburger meat weighed 6 lb, the price was $7.80; but if a package only weighed 2 lb, the price was only $2.60. How much would a 10 lb package of hamburger meat cost?

2. Sam traveled m miles in h hours and then traveled n miles in $(2h - 1)$ hours. At his average rate, how long would it take him to travel 50 miles?

3. Find: (a) $\text{antilog}_6 3$ (b) $\text{antilog}_3 2$

4. Solve for y: $\begin{cases} ax + by = c \\ dx + fy = g \end{cases}$

5. Use the result of problem 4 to solve for y: $\begin{cases} 2x + y = 7 \\ 5x + 8y = 1 \end{cases}$

6. Sketch the graph of $y = \log_3 x$.

7. (a) Convert $3 - 4i$ to polar coordinates.   (b) Convert $7 \text{ cis } 240°$ to rectangular coordinates. Give an exact answer.

8. The wheels of Erica's car had a diameter of 30 inches. If she was traveling at 26 miles per hour, what was the angular velocity of the wheels in radians per minute?

9. Find the range, mean, median, mode, variance, and standard deviation for the following data: 5, 4, 12, 3, 5, 7.

10. Write the equation of part (a) as a sine function and part (b) as a cosine function:

(a)

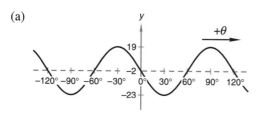

(b)

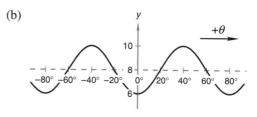

11. Simplify: $9 \ln e^2 + 4^{\log_4 6 - \log_4 2} - 7^{\log_7 21 + \log_7 1}$

12. Multiply $[5 \text{ cis } (-70°)](3 \text{ cis } 280°)$ and express the answer in rectangular coordinates. Give an exact answer.

13. Graph the solution to the system of inequalities: $\begin{cases} y \geq (x + 3)^2 - 2 \\ y \leq x + 3 \end{cases}$

14. The equation $x^2 + y^2 - 6x - 8y + 21 = 0$ is the equation of a circle. Complete the square to change this equation to standard form. Find the radius and the coordinates of the center of the circle and then graph the circle.

15. The measurements are 255, 380, 410, 296, 314, 389, 312, 294, 368, 254, 398, and 353. Use a graphing calculator to find the mean and the standard deviation and to find min x, Q_1, med, Q_3, and max x. Use this data to draw a box-and-whisker plot.

16. The test scores were normally distributed with a mean of 43 and a standard deviation of 3.
    (a) Approximately what percentage of the scores lies between 40 and 46?
    (b) Approximately what percentage of the scores lies between 43 and 46?

17. Solve for x: $\ln (x + 3) = \ln 4 + \ln (x - 3)$

18. A parabola has $y = -2$ for its directrix and its focus is at $(0, 2)$. Find the coordinates of the vertex and write the equation for the parabola.

19. Solve the equations below given that $0 \leq x < 2\pi$:

    (a) $\cos 2x + \dfrac{1}{2} = 0$

    (b) $(\sqrt{3} \tan x + 1)(2 \sin x - \sqrt{3}) = 0$

20. Find the area of this triangle.

50 in.   150°

20 in.

Advanced Mathematics **by Saxon**

1. The price of the hamburger meat varied linearly with the weight of the package. If a package of hamburger meat weighed 5 lb, the price was $8.45; but if a package only weighed 2 lb, the price was only $3.38. How much would a 10 lb package of hamburger meat cost?

2. Aaron traveled j inches in t seconds and then traveled k inches in $(4t - 2)$ seconds. At his average rate, how long would it take him to travel 10 inches?

3. Find: (a) $\text{antilog}_5 2$ (b) $\text{antilog}_9 3$

4. Solve for y: $\begin{cases} dx + cy = f \\ gx + hy = j \end{cases}$

5. Use the result of problem 4 to solve for y: $\begin{cases} 9x + y = 6 \\ x + y = 10 \end{cases}$

6. Sketch the graph of $y = \log_2 x$.

7. (a) Convert $4 - 3i$ to polar coordinates.   (b) Convert $9 \text{ cis } 300°$ to rectangular coordinates. Give an exact answer.

8. The wheels of Kim's car had a diameter of 36 inches. If she was traveling at 40 miles per hour, what was the angular velocity of the wheels in radians per minute?

9. Find the range, mean, median, mode, variance, and standard deviation for the following data: 5, 10, 14, 9, 10, 6.

10. Write the equation of part (a) as a sine function and part (b) as a cosine function:

(a)

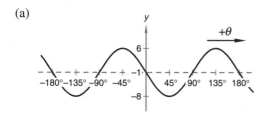

(b)

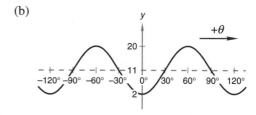

11. Simplify: $7^{\log_7 4 - 2 \log_7 2} + 3^{\log_3 5 + \log_3 2} - 2 \ln e^3$

12. Multiply $[4 \text{ cis } (-20°)](5 \text{ cis } 170°)$ and express the answer in rectangular coordinates. Give an exact answer.

13. Graph the solution to the system of inequalities: $\begin{cases} y \leq (x - 1)^2 + 3 \\ y \leq x + 4 \end{cases}$

14. The equation $x^2 + y^2 - 8x + 6y + 16 = 0$ is the equation of a circle. Complete the square to change this equation to standard form. Find the radius and the coordinates of the center of the circle and then graph the circle.

15. The measurements are 305, 247, 416, 538, 454, 322, 444, 306, 200, 520, 239, and 296. Use a graphing calculator to find the mean and the standard deviation and to find min x, Q_1, med, Q_3, and max x. Use this data to draw a box-and-whisker plot.

16. The test scores were normally distributed with a mean of 68 and a standard deviation of 4.
    (a) Approximately what percentage of the scores lies between 64 and 72?
    (b) Approximately what percentage of the scores lies between 68 and 72?

17. Solve for x: $\ln (x + 5) = \ln 3 + \ln (x - 5)$

18. A parabola has $y = -5$ for its directrix and its focus is at $(0, 5)$. Find the coordinates of the vertex and write the equation for the parabola.

19. Solve the equations below given that $0 \leq x < 2\pi$:

    (a) $\sin 2x + \dfrac{\sqrt{3}}{2} = 0$

    (b) $(2 \sin x - 1)(2 \cos x - \sqrt{2}) = 0$

20. Find the area of this triangle.

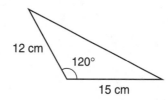

Advanced Mathematics by Saxon

1. The reflecting surface of a parabolic antenna has the shape formed when the parabola $y = \frac{1}{36}x^2$ is rotated about its axis of symmetry. If the measurements are in feet, how far from the vertex should the receiver be placed if it is to be at the focus?

2. A parabola has its vertex at $(-2, 1)$ and its focus at $(-2, -1)$. Write the equations of the parabola, the directrix, and the axis of symmetry. Graph the parabola.

3. Find: (a) $\text{antilog}_7 2$ (b) $\text{antilog}_8 (-2)$

4. Solve for x: $\begin{vmatrix} x + 2 & -2 \\ 1 & x \end{vmatrix} = 5$

5. If m varies directly as y, inversely as p^2, and inversely as the square root of n, what happens to m when y is multiplied by 2, p is tripled, and n is quadrupled?

6. Multiply $(6 \text{ cis } 72°)(-3 \text{ cis } 48°)$ and express the answer in rectangular coordinates. Give an exact answer.

7. How many distinguishable ways can 5 identical blue marbles and 2 identical yellow marbles be arranged in a line?

8. Melissa can do 2 jobs in 3 hours; when Krista helps, together they manage to do 8 jobs in 3 hours. How long would it take Krista to do one job?

9. Graph the ellipse: $\dfrac{x^2}{9} + \dfrac{y^2}{4} = 1$

10. Solve $\cos \theta + 2 \cos^2 \theta = 1$ given that $0° \le \theta < 360°$.

11. Find the range, mean, median, mode, variance, and standard deviation for the following data: 5, 1, 7, 2, 5, 4.

12. Two times the supplement of an angle exceeds 5 times the complement of the same angle by $126°$. What is the angle?

13. Solve this triangle for the unknown parts.

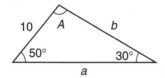

14. Find the area of this triangle.

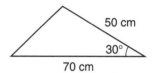

15. Graph the solution to the system of inequalities: $\begin{cases} (x - 4)^2 + y^2 \ge 4 \\ y \ge (x - 4)^2 \end{cases}$

16. Simplify:

    (a) $\log 10 - \ln e$

    (b) $\log 10^3 + \log 10^{1/3}$

    (c) $\log_3 9 + 3^{\log_3 7}$

17. Solve for x: $\dfrac{2}{3} \log_4 8 - 3 \log_4 x = \log_4 4$

18. Solve for x: $\ln x + \ln (x + 2) = \ln 3$

19. Sketch the graph of $y = \log_4 x$.

20. The weight of German shepherd puppies born in Parker Vet Hospital in the past 9 years is approximately normally distributed around a mean of 3.2 pounds with a standard deviation of 0.5 pounds. What percentage of the puppies weighed less than 2.7 pounds?

Advanced Mathematics by Saxon

1. The reflecting surface of a parabolic antenna has the shape formed when the parabola $y = \frac{1}{16}x^2$ is rotated about its axis of symmetry. If the measurements are in feet, how far from the vertex should the receiver be placed if it is to be at the focus?

2. A parabola has its vertex at $(2, -1)$ and its focus at $(2, 1)$. Write the equations of the parabola, the directrix, and the axis of symmetry. Graph the parabola.

3. Find: (a) $\text{antilog}_3 3$ (b) $\text{antilog}_5 (-2)$

4. Solve for x: $\begin{vmatrix} x + 1 & -3 \\ 4 & x \end{vmatrix} = 18$

5. If t varies inversely as y^2, directly as m, and inversely as the square root of n, what happens to t when y is multiplied by 5, m is multiplied by 3, and n is multiplied by 9?

6. Multiply $(2 \text{ cis } 84°)(-3 \text{ cis } 66°)$ and express the answer in rectangular coordinates. Give an exact answer.

7. How many distinguishable ways can 4 identical green marbles and 3 identical red marbles be arranged in a line?

8. Jeremy can do 3 jobs in 5 hours; when Brian helps, together they manage to do 65 jobs in 25 hours. How long would it take Brian to do one job?

9. Graph the ellipse: $\dfrac{x^2}{16} + \dfrac{y^2}{1} = 1$

10. Solve $\sin \theta + 2 \sin^2 \theta = 1$ given that $0° \le \theta < 360°$.

11. Find the range, mean, median, mode, variance, and standard deviation for the following data: 2, 1, 7, 2, 4, 2.

12. Two times the supplement of an angle exceeds 5 times the complement of the same angle by 69°. What is the angle?

13. Solve this triangle for the unknown parts.

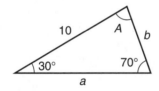

14. Find the area of this triangle.

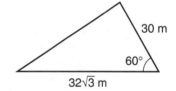

15. Graph the solution to the system of inequalities: $\begin{cases} (x - 3)^2 + y^2 \ge 4^2 \\ y \le (x - 3)^2 \end{cases}$

16. Simplify:

    (a) $\ln e - \log 10$

    (b) $\log 10^4 + \log 10^{1/4}$

    (c) $\log_4 16 + 4^{\log_4 5}$

17. Solve for x: $\dfrac{3}{2} \log_8 9 - \log_8 x = \log_8 9$

18. Solve for x: $\ln x + \ln (x + 4) = \ln 5$

19. Sketch the graph of $y = \log_6 x$.

20. The magnitude of earthquakes in the Martian Archipelago over the last 12 years have been approximately normally distributed around a mean of 2.5 on the Richter scale with a standard deviation of 0.2 R. What percentage of the quakes registered under 2.8 on the Richter Scale?

Advanced Mathematics by Saxon

1. Alan could eat 7 chocolates in 3 minutes and Anil could eat 11 chocolates in 4 minutes. How many minutes would it take them to consume 45 chocolates if Alan started eating 2 minutes before Anil joined in?

2. The senior class decided to have a picnic. A total of S seniors pledged to contribute equally for the $1000 fund. If 20 refused to honor their commitment, how much more would each of the rest of the seniors have to pay?

3. Use Cramer's Rule to solve for y: $\begin{cases} 7x - 2y = 5 \\ 3x + 4y = 6 \end{cases}$

4. An 8-sided regular polygon (regular octagon) is inscribed in a circle whose radius is 8 inches. Find the area of the polygon.

5. Find the radius and coordinates of the center of the circle whose equation is $9x^2 + 9y^2 - 18x + 36y - 36 = 0$. Graph the circle.

6. The scores on a standardized test are normally distributed with a mean of 50 and a standard deviation of 10. What is the percentage of scores that are greater than 75? Use the Standard Normal Table.

7. How many ways can a committee of 7 people be selected from a group of 10 people?

8. Multiply $(3 \operatorname{cis} 110°)(4 \operatorname{cis} 100°)$ and express the answer in rectangular coordinates. Give an exact answer.

9. Solve $\sec^2 x - 4 = 0$ given that $0 \le x < 2\pi$.

10. The flowers were marked up 120% of the cost to get a selling price of $4.40. They did not sell well, so the florist reduced the mark up to 70% of the cost. What was the new selling price?

11. A parabola has its vertex at $(4, -2)$ and its focus at $(4, 4)$. Write the equations of the parabola, the directrix, and the axis of symmetry. Graph the parabola.

12. Graph the solution to the system of inequalities: $\begin{cases} 9 \le x^2 + (y - 3)^2 \\ y > 3x + 3 \end{cases}$

13. Solve for d: $\begin{vmatrix} 1 & d + 3 \\ 1 - d & 4 \end{vmatrix} = 4$

14. Graph the ellipse: $\dfrac{x^2}{4} + \dfrac{y^2}{16} = 1$

15. Anna is seven years younger than Brandi. Three years from now Anna will be twice as old as Brandi was nine years ago. How old will Brandi be six years from now?

16. If $f(x) = \sin^2 x$ and $g(x) = \cos^2 x$, find $f\left(\dfrac{2\pi}{3}\right) + g\left(\dfrac{5\pi}{4}\right)f\left(\dfrac{3\pi}{2}\right)$.

17. Solve for x: $3 \log_2 x - \dfrac{1}{2} \log_2 16 = 4$

18. Show: $\csc x \tan x = \sec x$

19. Write the equation of the sinusoid as a sine function.

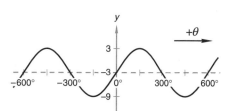

20. Solve this triangle for the unknown parts.

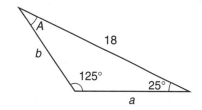

Advanced Mathematics by Saxon

1. John could play 5 holes of golf in 20 minutes and Allan could play 6 holes in 30 minutes. How many minutes would it take them to play 18 holes if John started playing 2 minutes before Allan joined in?

2. The junior class decided to plan the Prom. A total of J juniors pledged to contribute equally for the $2000 fund. If 30 refused to honor their commitment, how much more would each of the rest of the juniors have to pay?

3. Use Cramer's rule to solve for y: $\begin{cases} 2x + 4y = 11 \\ 3x - 2y = 9 \end{cases}$

4. An 8 sided regular polygon (regular octagon) is inscribed in a circle whose radius is 12 cm. Find the area of the polygon.

5. Find the radius and coordinates of the center of the circle whose equation is $3x^2 + 3y^2 - 18x + 24y = 0$. Graph the circle.

6. The scores on a standardized test are normally distributed with a mean of 100 and a standard deviation of 20. What is the percentage of scores that are greater than 140? Use the Standard Normal Table.

7. How many ways can a posse of 8 be selected from a group of 11 cowboys?

8. Multiply $(5 \text{ cis } 100°)(4 \text{ cis } 230°)$ and express the answer in rectangular coordinates. Give an exact answer.

9. Solve $\csc^2 x - 4 = 0$ given that $0 \le x < 2\pi$.

10. The tennis shoes were marked up 130% of the cost to get a selling price of $57.50. They did not sell well, so the cobbler reduced the mark up to 80% of the cost. What was the new selling price?

11. A parabola has its vertex at $(3, -3)$ and its focus at $(3, 1)$. Write the equations of the parabola, the directrix, and the axis of symmetry. Graph the parabola.

12. Graph the solution to the system of inequalities: $\begin{cases} 4 \le x^2 + (y - 2)^2 \\ y > 2x - 1 \end{cases}$

13. Solve for a: $\begin{vmatrix} a + 2 & 3 \\ 5 & a - 3 \end{vmatrix} = 9$

14. Graph the ellipse: $\dfrac{x^2}{16} + \dfrac{y^2}{4} = 1$

15. Thor is three hundred years older than Loki. Six hundred years from now Loki will be 3 times as old as Thor was 500 years ago. How old will Thor be two hundred years from now?

16. If $f(x) = \sin^2 x$ and $g(x) = \cos^2 x$, find $f\left(\dfrac{3\pi}{4}\right) + g\left(\dfrac{2\pi}{3}\right) f\left(\dfrac{3\pi}{2}\right)$.

17. Solve for x: $3\log_2 x - \dfrac{1}{3}\log_2 8 = 5$

18. Show: $\sec x \cot x = \csc x$

19. Write the equation of the sinusoid as a cosine function.

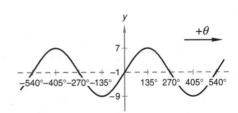

20. Solve this triangle for the unknown parts.

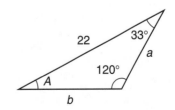

1. Write the third term of $(x + y)^6$.

2. Write all five terms of $(a + b)^4$.

3. Solve for x: $\log_2 (x + 3) = \log_2 (7 - x) + 2$

4. Write the equation in standard form and graph the ellipse: $2x^2 + 18y^2 - 162 = 0$

5. Show: $\dfrac{\csc^2 x - \cot^2 x}{1 + \tan^2 x} = \cos^2 x$

6. Solve for x: $\begin{vmatrix} x + 2 & 2 \\ x + 1 & x + 8 \end{vmatrix} = 2$

7. Given the hyperbola $36y^2 - 16x^2 - 144 = 0$, write the equation in standard form and find the coordinates of the vertices and the equations of the asymptotes. Graph the hyperbola.

8. Use De Moivre's theorem to find $(1 - \sqrt{3}i)^3$. Write the answer in rectangular coordinates. Give an exact answer.

9. Solve this triangle for the unknown parts.

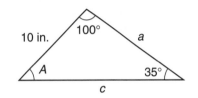

10. Write the equation of this sinusoid as a cosine function.

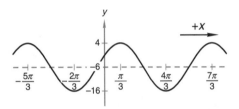

11. Multiply $\left[4 \text{ cis } (-45°)\right](-3 \text{ cis } 180°)$ and express the answer in rectangular coordinates. Give an exact answer.

12. The perimeter of a regular 10-sided polygon (regular decagon) is 40 cm. What is the length of one of the sides of the polygon? What is the radius of the circle that can be circumscribed about the polygon?

13. Two 6-sided polygons (hexagons) are similar. The ratio of a side of the larger hexagon to a corresponding side of the smaller hexagon is 5 to 4. What is the ratio of the area of the smaller polygon to the area of the larger polygon?

14. The labor expense varied linearly with the number of men who worked. If 10 men worked, the cost was $5600. If only 5 men worked, the cost was $3000. What would be the cost if only 4 men worked?

15. The boat could sail at 6 times the speed of the current in the river. Thus, the boat could go 100 miles upstream in 3 hours more than it took to go 14 miles downstream. What was the speed of the boat in still water?

16. How many different 2-player bridge teams could be formed from 5 players?

17. Find the three cube roots of 125 cis 60° and express them in polar coordinates.

18. Find the three cube roots of 1 and express them in rectangular coordinates. Give exact answers.

19. Sketch the graph of the function $y = -\log_3 x$.

20. A parabola has its vertex at $(-2, 0)$ and its focus at $(-2, 6)$. Write the equations of the parabola, the directrix, and the axis of symmetry. Graph the parabola.

Advanced Mathematics **by Saxon**

1. Write the fourth term of $(x + y)^5$.

2. Write all six terms of $(a + b)^5$.

3. Solve for x: $\log_3 (x + 1) = \log_3 (1 - x) + 1$

4. Write the equation in standard form and graph the ellipse: $20x^2 + 45y^2 - 180 = 0$

5. Show: $\dfrac{\sec^2 x - \tan^2 x}{1 + \cot^2 x} = \sin^2 x$

6. Solve for x: $\begin{vmatrix} x + 3 & x \\ x - 1 & 2x - 1 \end{vmatrix} = -8$

7. Given the hyperbola $32x^2 - 50y^2 - 800 = 0$, write the equation in standard form and find the coordiantes of the vertices and the equations of the asymptotes. Graph the hyperbola.

8. Use DeMoivre's theorem to find $(1 - i)^3$. Write the answer in rectangular coordinates. Give an exact answer.

9. Solve this triangle for the unknown parts.

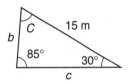

10. Write the equation of this sinusoid as a cosine function.

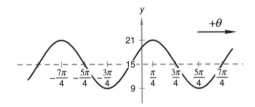

11. Multiply $(-5 \text{ cis } 210°)[6 \text{ cis } (-90°)]$ and express the answer in rectangular coordinates. Give an exact answer.

12. The perimeter of a regular 9-sided polygon (regular nonagon) is 72 inches. What is the length of one of the sides of the polygon? What is the radius of the circle that can be circumscribed about the polygon?

13. Two 3-sided polygons (triangles) are similar. The ratio of a side of the larger triangle to a corresponding side of the smaller triangle is 7 to 6. What is the ratio of the area of the smaller triangle to the area of the larger triangle?

14. The production expense varied linearly with the number of people who worked. If 30 people worked, the cost was $6000. If only 20 people worked, the cost was $4400. What would be the cost if only 8 people worked?

15. The boat could sail at 7 times the speed of the current in the river. Thus, the boat could go 96 miles upstream in 2 hours more than it took to go 64 miles downstream. What was the speed of the boat in still water?

16. How many different ways can a 7 player basketball team be selected if there are 10 players trying out for the team?

17. Find the three cube roots of $216 \text{ cis } 30°$ and express them in polar coordinates.

18. Find the three cube roots of $8i$ and express them in rectangular coordinates. Give exact answers.

19. Sketch the graph of the function $y = -\log_2 x$.

20. A parabola has its vertex at $(4, 0)$ and its focus at $(4, -1)$. Write the equations of the parabola, the directrix, and the axis of symmetry. Graph the parabola.

Advanced Mathematics **by Saxon**

1. The cost varied linearly with the number of hours the staff worked. When the staff worked 200 hours the cost was $1725, and when the staff worked 100 hours the cost was $925. What would it cost if the staff worked 150 hours?

2. Given the hyperbola $y^2 - 16x^2 = 144$, write the equation in standard form and find the coordinates of the vertices and the equations of the asymptotes. Graph the hyperbola.

3. If p players could score 5 points in 30 minutes, how many minutes would it take 2 more players to score t points?

4. Write three cube roots of $-8i$ in rectangular coordinates. Give exact answers.

5. Write the equation in standard form and graph the ellipse: $16y^2 + 9x^2 = 144$.

6. Graph the solution to the system of inequalities:
$$\begin{cases} x^2 + y^2 - 2x + 4y - 11 \geq 0 \\ y \leq -(x + 2)^2 + 3 \end{cases}$$

7. The perimeter of a 12-sided regular polygon is 120 meters. Find the area of the polygon in square meters.

8. Evaluate: $\cos\left[\text{Arcsin}\left(-\dfrac{3}{5}\right)\right]$

9. Solve: $3^{4x-2} = 5^{3x+1}$

10. Show: $\dfrac{\csc^3 \theta - \csc \theta \cot^2 \theta}{\csc \theta} - \sin^2 \theta = \cos^2 \theta$

11. Write all six terms of $(a + b)^5$.

12. Use De Moivre's theorem to find $\left(\dfrac{1}{2} \text{ cis } 200°\right)^3$. Write the answer in rectangular coordinates. Give an exact answer.

13. The urn contained 8 marbles. Six were white and two were blue. Two marbles were randomly drawn. What is the probability that both were white (a) with replacement and (b) without replacement?

14. A fair coin is tossed 4 times. What is the probability that it will come up tails every time?

15. A graduate student in education looks at several high school math textbooks and records the number of pages each contains. She then decides that the data is normally distributed with a mean of 600 pages and a standard deviation of 150 pages. If the student is correct, what percentage of high school math textbooks would have at least 675 pages?

16. Two wires are attached to a vertical pole from a point on the ground. The angle between the wires is 22°. The longer wire is 115 meters long and is attached to the top of the pole. The shorter wire is attached to a point 50 meters below the top of the pole. Find the length of the shorter wire.

17. Solve $2 \sec^2 \dfrac{\theta}{2} + 3 \sec \dfrac{\theta}{2} - 2 = 0$ given that $0° \leq \theta < 360°$.

18. Sketch the graph of $y = -1 + 4 \sin \dfrac{1}{2}(\theta + 30°)$.

19. Solve for x:

(a) $\log_3 x + \dfrac{1}{3} \log_3 8 = \dfrac{1}{2} \log_3 36$

(b) $\log_2 (2x + 4) - \dfrac{2}{3} \log_2 27 = 1$

20. Solve this triangle for the unknown parts.

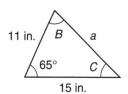

Advanced Mathematics by Saxon

1. The number of locusts varied linearly with the number of crops. When 250 crops grew up, 1280 locusts appeared, and when 100 crops grew up, 530 locusts appeared. How many locusts will appear if 200 crops grow?

2. Given the hyperbola $4y^2 - 16x^2 = 64$, write the equation in standard form and find the coordinates of the vertices and the equations of the asymptotes. Graph the hyperbola.

3. If p pods could create 7 seedlings in 120 minutes, how many minutes would it take 3 more pods to make z seedlings?

4. Write three cube roots of $64i$ in rectangular coordinates. Give exact answers.

5. Write the equation in standard form and graph the ellipse: $4y^2 + 25x^2 = 100$.

6. Graph the solution to the system of inequalities:

$$\begin{cases} y \geq (x - 1)^2 - 2 \\ x^2 + y^2 - 4x + 2y - 11 \leq 0 \end{cases}$$

7. The perimeter of a 10-sided regular polygon is 120 meters. Find the area of the polygon in square meters.

8. Evaluate: $\cos\left[\text{Arcsin}\left(-\dfrac{4}{5}\right)\right]$

9. Solve: $7^{2x+3} = 5^{3x-1}$

10. Show: $\dfrac{\sec^2\theta\tan\theta - \tan^3\theta}{\tan\theta} - \cos^2\theta = \sin^2\theta$

11. Write all five terms of $(x + y)^4$.

12. Use De Moivre's theorem to find $\left(\dfrac{1}{2}\,\text{cis}\,150°\right)^4$. Write the answer in rectangular coordinates. Give an exact answer.

13. The urn contained 10 marbles. Seven were red and three were black. Two marbles were randomly drawn. What is the probability that both were black (a) with replacement and (b) without replacement?

14. A fair coin is tossed 3 times. What is the probability that it will come up heads every time?

15. The Hopi Shaman observes several patches of mushrooms and records the number of mushrooms in each patch. The Shaman then decides that the population counts are normally distributed with a mean of 300 mushrooms and a standard deviation of 50 mushrooms. If the Shaman is correct, what percentage of mushroom patches would have at least 375 mushrooms?

16. Two wires are attached to a vertical pole from a point on the ground. The angle between the wires is 15°. The longer wire is 126 meters long and is attached to the top of the pole. The shorter wire is attached to a point 35 meters below the top of the pole. Find the length of the shorter wire.

17. Solve $3\csc^2\dfrac{\theta}{2} - 4\csc\dfrac{\theta}{2} - 4 = 0$ given that $0° \leq \theta < 360°$.

18. Sketch the graph of $y = 2 - 3\sin\dfrac{1}{2}(\theta - 60°)$.

19. Solve for x:

(a) $\log_2 x + \dfrac{1}{3}\log_2 8 = \dfrac{1}{2}\log_2 49$

(b) $\log_3 (2x - 4) - \dfrac{2}{3}\log_3 8 = 1$

20. Solve this triangle for the unknown parts.

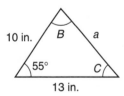

Advanced Mathematics **by Saxon**

1. The urn contains 3 white marbles, 4 green marbles, and 5 red marbles. Two marbles are randomly drawn. What is the probability that both are green (a) with replacement and (b) without replacement?

2. A pair of dice is rolled. What is the probability that the number rolled will be less than 7?

3. How soon after noon will the hands of the clock be together again?

4. Sketch the graph of $y = -3 - 2\cos(x + 45°)$.

5. Solve $3\sin^2 4\theta = \cos 4\theta - 1$ given that $0° \le \theta < 360°$.

6. Find the measure of the largest angle.

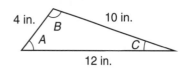

7. Given the hyperbola $x^2 - 4y^2 = 100$, write the equation in standard form and find the coordinates of the vertices and the equations of the asymptotes. Graph the hyperbola.

8. Use Cramer's Rule to solve for y: $\begin{cases} 2x - 7y = -1 \\ -3x + 5y = -4 \end{cases}$

9. Solve for x: $2^{7x-1} = 7^{2x+1}$

10. Find the distance from the point $(2, 1)$ to the line $2x + y = 3$.

11. Simplify $\cos\left(\theta - \dfrac{\pi}{2}\right)$ by using the sum and difference identity. Use exact values.

12. Write the four fourth roots of $81 \text{ cis } 180°$ in rectangular coordinates. Give exact answers.

13. Develop the identity for $\tan(A - B)$ by using the identities for $\sin(A - B)$ and $\cos(A - B)$.

14. Solve for x: $\dfrac{2}{3}\log_3 8 - \log_3(3x + 2) + \log_3(x + 2) = \log_3 4$

15. Show: $\dfrac{\csc\theta}{\sec\theta - \tan\theta} - \dfrac{\csc\theta}{\sec\theta + \tan\theta} = 2\sec\theta$

16. Two cables are attached to a vertical tower from a point on the ground. The angle between the cables is 20°. The longer cable is 225 feet long and attached to the top of the tower. The shorter cable is attached to the tower 90 feet below the top of the tower. Find the length of the shorter cable.

17. Write the equation in standard form and graph the ellipse: $25x^2 + 4y^2 = 100$

18. The amount of substance initially present was 480 grams, and after 100 hours only 320 grams remained. Assume exponential decay. Write the exponential equation describing the amount of substance present as a function of time and determine the half life of the substance. Sketch the graph.

19. Find the twenty-sixth term of an arithmetic sequence whose first term is 12 and whose common difference is −4.

20. Write the first three terms of an arithmetic sequence in which the twenty-first term is 28 and the fiftieth term is −59.

Advanced Mathematics **by Saxon**

1. The urn contains 3 green marbles, 7 blue marbles, and 5 yellow marbles. Two marbles are randomly drawn. What is the probability that both are green (a) with replacement and (b) without replacement?

2. A pair of dice is rolled. What is the probability that the number rolled will be less than 8?

3. How soon after noon will the hands of the clock point in opposite directions?

4. Sketch the graph of $y = 2 - 3 \sin (x + 30°)$.

5. Solve $2 \cos^2 2\theta = 3 \sin 2\theta$ given that $0° \le \theta < 360°$.

6. Find the measure of the largest angle.

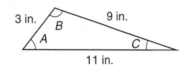

7. Given the hyperbola $x^2 - 16y^2 = 64$, write the equation in standard form and find the coordinates of the vertices and the equations of the asymptotes. Graph the hyperbola.

8. Use Cramer's Rule to solve for y: $\begin{cases} 3x - 4y = 1 \\ -2x + 5y = 5 \end{cases}$

9. Solve for x: $3^{11x-4} = 11^{3x+4}$

10. Find the distance from the point $(3, -1)$ to the line $y - 3x = 15$.

11. Simplify $\sin \left(\theta - \dfrac{\pi}{2} \right)$ by using the sum and difference identity. Use exact values.

12. Write the three third roots of 64 cis 180° in rectangular coordinates. Give exact answers.

13. Develop the identity for $\tan (A + B)$ by using the identities for $\sin (A + B)$ and $\cos (A + B)$.

14. Solve for x: $\dfrac{2}{3} \log_3 8 - \log_3 (x - 1) + \log_3 (3x + 5) = \log_3 28$

15. Show: $\dfrac{\sec \theta}{\csc \theta - \cot \theta} - \dfrac{\sec \theta}{\csc \theta + \cot \theta} = 2 \csc \theta$

16. Two cables are attached to a vertical tower from a point on the ground. The angle between the cables is 35°. The longer cable is 250 feet long and attached to the top of the tower. The shorter cable is attached to the tower 170 feet below the top of the tower. Find the length of the shorter cable.

17. Write the equation in standard form and graph the ellipse: $16y^2 + 9x^2 = 144$

18. The amount of substance initially present was 800 particles, and after 60 seconds only 200 particles remained. Assume exponential decay. Write the exponential equation describing the amount of substance present as a function of time and determine the half life of the substance. Sketch the graph.

19. Find the twenty-first term of an arithmetic sequence whose first term is 9 and whose common difference is -3.

20. Write the first three terms of an arithmetic sequence in which the twenty-ninth term is 92 and the forty-eighth term is 168.

Advanced Mathematics by Saxon

1. Given the hyperbola $16x^2 - 25y^2 = 400$, write the equation in standard form and find the coordinates of the vertices and the equations of the asymptotes. Graph the hyperbola.

2. An ellipse has vertices at $(0, \pm 5)$ and foci at $(0, \pm 3)$. Write the equation of the ellipse in standard form. Graph the ellipse.

3. Under the onslaught of the College Algebra second period class, the pile of homework problems decreased exponentially. They decreased from 1000 to 700 in only 30 minutes. How long would it take to have only 300 problems left?

4. Find three consecutive even integers such that the product of the first and third is 54 less than 15 times the second number.

5. (a) Find the fourth term of a geometric sequence whose first term is 4 and whose common ratio is -5.

   (b) Find the two geometric means between 3 and -24.

6. Sketch the graph of $y = 2 + \cos 2\left(x - \dfrac{\pi}{4}\right)$.

7. Solve for x: $16^{3x-2} = 64^{4-x}$

8. Write the four fourth roots of -16 in rectangular coordinates. Give exact answers.

9. Develop the identity for $\sin 2A$ using the identity for $\sin(A + B)$.

10. Find the nineteenth term of an arithmetic sequence whose first term is -52 and whose common difference is 6.

11. Write the first four terms of an arithmetic sequence whose ninth term is -51 and whose fourth term is -1.

12. The urn held 4 black marbles, 3 red marbles, and 6 white marbles. If three marbles are drawn randomly and the first marble drawn is white, what is the probability that the second marble is red and the third marble is black (a) with replacement and (b) without replacement?

13. It was 9:00 and the algebra quiz was about to begin. The students were told that they could only work on the quiz until the hands of the clock pointed in the same direction. How long did they have to work?

14. A card is drawn at random from a full deck of 52 cards. What is the probability that the card is either a queen or a red card?

15. Simplify: $3^{\log_3 9 - 2\log_3 6 + 4\log_3 2 - 2\log_3 \sqrt{3}}$

16. Solve the following equations given that $0° \le \theta < 360°$:

    (a) $2\tan^2 2\theta = 3\sec 2\theta$ (b) $\cot^2 \theta = 3$

17. Solve for x: $2\log(x + 2) - \log(x + 6) = \log 2 + \log(x - 1)$

18. Find: (a) $\text{antilog}_2 (-1)$ (b) $\text{antilog}_{1/2} (-1)$

19. Show:

    (a) $\dfrac{\sec^2 x}{\sec^2 x - 1} - 1 = \cot^2 x$ (b) $\dfrac{\cos^2 \theta - \sin^2 \theta}{\cos^4 \theta - \sin^4 \theta} = 1$

20. Solve this triangle for A and B.

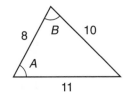

1. Given the hyperbola $9x^2 - 4y^2 = 900$, write the equation in standard form and find the coordinates of the vertices and the equations of the asymptotes. Graph the hyperbola.

2. An ellipse has vertices at $(0, \pm10)$ and foci at $(0, \pm6)$. Write the equation of the ellipse in standard form. Graph the ellipse.

3. Due to the students' hard work, the ignorance index in the classroom decreased exponentially. The index dropped from 30 to 25 in only 52 minutes. How much time will pass before the ignorance index is 20?

4. Find three consecutive odd integers such that the product of the first and the second is 26 less than 13 times the third number.

5. (a) Find the third term of a geometric sequence whose first term is 3 and whose common ratio is -3.

   (b) Find the two geometric means between 2 and -16.

6. Sketch the graph of $y = 3 + \sin 4\left(x + \dfrac{\pi}{4}\right)$.

7. Solve for x: $81^{x-3} = 9^{3-x}$

8. Write the four fourth roots of 16 in rectangular coordinates. Give exact answers.

9. Develop the identity for $\cos 2A$ using the identity for $\cos(A + B)$.

10. Find the seventeenth term of an arithmetic sequence whose first term is 12 and whose common difference is 3.

11. Write the first three terms of an arithmetic sequence whose fifth term is 8 and whose seventh term is 12.

12. The sock held 3 luminescent marbles, 6 white marbles, and 4 clear marbles. If three marbles are drawn randomly and the first marble drawn is white, what is the probability that the second marble is clear and the third marble is luminescent (a) with replacement and (b) without replacement?

13. It was high noon and the pie-eating contest was about to begin. The contestants were told that they could only eat until the hands of the clock were perpendicular to one another. When will they be stopped?

14. A card is drawn at random from a full deck of 52 cards. What is the probability that the card is either a king or a black card?

15. Simplify: $2^{\log_2 8 - 2\log_2 2 + 3\log_2 1 - 2\log_2 \sqrt{3}}$

16. Solve the following equations given that $0 \le \theta < 360°$:

   (a) $2\cot^2 2\theta = 3\csc 2\theta$ (b) $\tan^2 \theta = 3$

17. Solve for x: $2\ln(x + 5) - \ln(x + 2) = \ln 2 + \ln(x + 9)$

18. Find: (a) $\text{antilog}_3 (-1)$ (b) $\text{antilog}_{1/3} (-1)$

19. Show:

   (a) $\dfrac{\csc^2 x}{\csc^2 x - 1} - 1 = \tan^2 x$ (b) $\dfrac{\sec^2 \theta + \tan^2 \theta}{\sec^4 \theta - \tan^4 \theta} = 1$

20. Solve this triangle for A and B.

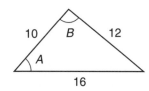

1. Develop the identity for tan 2A by using the identities for sin 2A and cos 2A.

2. Factor $x^2 + 7x + 19$ over the set of complex numbers.

3. Stacey observed that it took w women 10 days to do j jobs. Then, she calculated how long it would take n more women to do 28 more jobs. What was her answer?

4. A horizontal ellipse has a major axis of length 12 and a minor axis of length 6. If its center is at the origin, write the equation of the ellipse in standard form. Graph the ellipse.

5. Find the first three terms of the arithmetic sequence whose ninth term is 20 and whose fourteenth term is −10.

6. Find the four fourth roots of $5 + 2i$ and express the roots in polar coordinates.

7. Write the equations of these trigonometric functions:

(a)
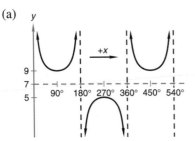

(b)
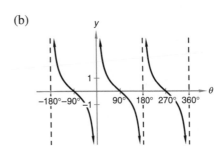

8. Graph: $y = \sec x$

9. Graph: $y = \tan x$

10. Solve this triangle for angle A and find the area.

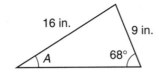

11. Solve this triangle for side c and find the area.

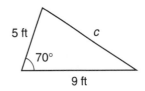

12. An urn contains 6 white balls and 5 black balls. Two of the white balls and one of the black balls are rough. What is the probability of drawing a ball that is either rough or white?

13. Solve $\tan^2 \theta - \sec \theta = -1$ given that $0° \leq \theta < 360°$.

14. A regular eight-sided polygon has a perimeter of 64 cm. What is the area of the polygon?

15. Find the distance from the point $(0, 0)$ to the line $y = -2x + 2$.

16. The athlete was afraid because the coach's anger increased exponentially. Only 20 minutes after practice began, the coach was twice as angry as when the practice began. How many times more angry will the coach be at the end of the three hour practice?

17. Sketch the graph of the function $y = -4 + 2 \sin \frac{2}{3}(x - 30°)$.

18. Solve for x: $10^{3x+1} = 14^{2x+1}$

19. Solve for x: $\log_5 (3x + 3) - \log_5 (x - 3) = \frac{2}{3} \log_5 27$

20. Show: $\dfrac{\cos \theta}{1 + \sin \theta} = \dfrac{1 - \sin \theta}{\cos \theta}$

Advanced Mathematics **by Saxon**

1. Develop the identity for tan 2A by using the identities for sin 2A and cos 2A.

2. Factor $x^2 - 4x + 5$ over the set of complex numbers.

3. Anastasia observed that it took w women 15 hours to do j jobs. Then, she calculated how long it would take 5 fewer women to perform twice as many jobs. What was her answer?

4. A horizontal ellipse has a major axis of length 14 and a minor axis of length 6. If its center is at the origin, write the equation of the ellipse in standard form. Graph the ellipse.

5. Find the first four terms of the arithmetic sequence whose eleventh term is 42 and whose sixteenth term is 57.

6. Find the three third roots of $2 + 3i$ and express the roots in polar coordinates.

7. Write the equations of these trigonometric functions:

(a)
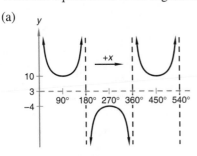

(b)
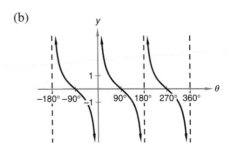

8. Graph: $y = \sec x$

9. Graph: $y = \tan x$

10. Solve this triangle for angle A and find the area.

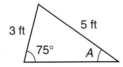

11. Solve this triangle for side c and find the area.

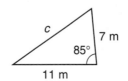

12. An urn contains 3 white balls and 7 black balls. One of the white balls and three of the black balls are hollow. What is the probability of drawing a ball that is either hollow or white?

13. Solve $\sec^2 \theta + \tan \theta = 1$ given that $0° \le \theta < 360°$.

14. A regular eight-sided polygon has a perimeter of 32 cm. What is the area of the polygon?

15. Find the distance from the point $(0, 1)$ to the line $y = \dfrac{3}{2}x - 3$.

16. The speed of the wind increased exponentially on the mesa. Ten minutes after sunrise, the windspeed was twice what it had been at sunrise. How many times faster will the wind be 15 minutes after sunrise?

17. Sketch the graph of the function $y = -5 + 8 \sin \dfrac{3}{2}(\theta - 60°)$.

18. Solve for x: $10^{2x+3} = 7^{x-1}$

19. Solve for x: $\log_5 \left(x - \dfrac{1}{2} \right) = \log_5 (x + 6) - \dfrac{1}{2} \log_5 4$

20. Show: $\dfrac{\cos \theta}{1 - \sin \theta} = \dfrac{1 + \sin \theta}{\cos \theta}$

Advanced Mathematics **by Saxon**

1. Christopher ran m miles at r miles per hour and arrived on time. Then the distance was increased 7 miles. How fast did he have to run to travel the new distance in the same amount of time?

2. Melanie bought t things for d dollars. If the price was increased k dollars per item, how many items could Melanie buy for 50 dollars?

3. Use a calculator to aid in finding: (a) $\log_5 13$ (b) $\log_7 63$

4. Simplify: $\left(\dfrac{1}{x+2}\right)7^{\log_7(x^2+5x+6) - \log_7(x+3)}$

5. Find the perimeter of the square which can be circumscribed about a circle whose radius is 11 inches.

6. Find both the arithmetic and geometric mean for 11 and 23.

7. A ball is dropped from a height of 162 feet. After each bounce, it rebounds two thirds of the distance if fell. How far does the ball fall on its fifth fall?

8. Mark working alone can do 2 jobs in m hours, and Bob working alone can do 2 jobs in b hours. How long will it take Mark and Bob to do one job if they work together?

9. Find the three cube roots of $-7 + 5i$ and express the roots in polar coordinates.

10. Sketch the graph of the following function: $y = 1 + \csc\theta$

11. A triangle has a 25° angle. A side adjacent to this angle has a length of 10, and the side opposite this angle has a length of 5. Draw the triangle(s) described and find the length(s) of the missing side(s) and angle(s).

12. When the meteor hit the earth, there were 600,000 dinosaurs alive. Thirty years later there were only 15,000. If they died exponentially, after how many years would there be only five dinosaurs left?

13. Find the fourth term of a geometric sequence whose first term is 2 and whose common ratio is 3.

14. The positive geometric mean of two numbers is 8, and the difference of the numbers is 30. Find the numbers.

15. Solve $2\sin^2 x = 13\cos x - 5$ given that $0 \le x < 2\pi$.

16. Compute $_{10}P_6$ and $_{10}C_6$.

17. An ellipse has foci at $(\pm 3, 0)$ and vertices at $(\pm 7, 0)$. Write the equation of the ellipse in standard form and find the lengths of the major and minor axes. Graph the ellipse.

18. Solve for x: $\log_2\left(\log_2 x\right) = 3$

19. Show: $\dfrac{2\sin^2 x + \cos 2x}{\sec x} = \cos x$

20. Which of the following graphs most resembles $f(x) = \sqrt{9 - x^2}$?

A.   B.   C.   D. 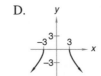   E.

Advanced Mathematics by Saxon

1. Ed hiked k kilometers at r kilometers per hour and arrived at camp on time. The next day he was to hike the same distance plus an additional 12 kilometers to reach camp. How fast did he have to hike the following morning to reach the new camp in the same amount of time?

2. Ms. Frese bought r new books for d dollars. The used books were each c dollars cheaper, how many used books could Ms. Frese buy for 20 dollars?

3. Use a calculator to aid in finding: (a) $\log_9 85$ (b) $\log_3 28$

4. Simplify: $\left(\dfrac{1}{x+6}\right)4^{\log_4(x^2+3x-18)-\log_4(x-3)}$

5. Find the perimeter of the square which can be circumscribed about a circle whose radius is 12 feet.

6. Find both the arithmetic and geometric mean for 23 and 41.

7. A ball is dropped from a height of 243 feet. After each bounce, it rebounds one third of the distance it fell. How far does the ball fall on its fifth fall?

8. Jennifer working alone can repair 2 sections of trail in r hours, and Kirsten working alone can repair one section in p hours. How long will it take Jennifer and Kirsten to repair a trail 6 sections long if they work together?

9. Find the three cube roots of $-6 + 3i$ and express the roots in polar coordinates.

10. Sketch the graph of the following function: $y = -2 + \csc\theta$

11. A triangle has a 50° angle. A side adjacent to this angle has a length of 5, and the side opposite this angle has a length of 4. Draw the triangle(s) described and find the length(s) of the missing side(s) and angle(s).

12. When the meteor hit the earth, there were 800,000 dinosaurs alive. Twenty-five years later there were only 20,000. If they died exponentially, after how many years would there be only one dinosaur left?

13. Find the fifth term of a geometric sequence whose first term is 4 and whose common ratio is –2.

14. The positive geometric mean of two numbers is 6, and the difference of the numbers is 5. Find the numbers.

15. Solve $2\cos^2 x = 13\sin x - 5$ given that $0 \le x < 2\pi$.

16. Compute $_{13}P_5$ and $_{13}C_5$.

17. An ellipse has foci at $(\pm5, 0)$ and vertices at $(\pm7, 0)$. Write the equation of the ellipse in standard form and find the lengths of the major and minor axes. Graph the ellipse.

18. Solve for x: $\log_3\left(\log_3 x\right) = 2$

19. Show: $\dfrac{2\sin^2 x + \cos 2x}{\csc x} = \sin x$

20. Which of the following graphs most resembles $f(x) = 3 - 3^{-x}$?

A. 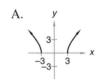   B.   C. 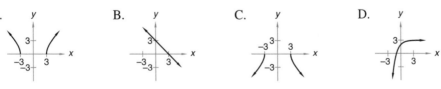   D.   E.

Advanced Mathematics **by Saxon**

1. A ball is dropped from a height of 250 feet. After each bounce, it rebounds three fifths of the distance it fell. How far does the ball fall on its fourth fall?

2. Evaluate: $\begin{vmatrix} 3 & 1 & 1 \\ 6 & 1 & 9 \\ 5 & 0 & 2 \end{vmatrix}$

3. Compute $_{10}P_6$ and $_{10}C_6$.

4. Write as a single logarithm: $2 \log \left(x^2 - 1\right) - 2 \log y - 3 \log (x + 1) + \log (y + xy)$

5. Use Cramer's rule to solve for x: $\begin{cases} 2x - 4y + z = 2 \\ 2y - 3z = -10 \\ -3x + 2y = -1 \end{cases}$

6. Use a calculator to aid in finding:

    (a) $\log_6 15$

    (b) $\log_{15} 6$

7. Find the exact value of $\sin 345°$ by using the identity for $\sin (A + B)$ and the fact that $345° = 120° + 225°$.

8. Solve for x: $\log_4 x = \sqrt{\log_4 x}$

9. Write the three cube roots of -27 in rectangular coordinates. Give exact answers.

10. (a) Find the pH of a liquid if the concentration of hydrogen ions $\left(H^+\right)$ is 7.9×10^{-9} mole per liter.

    (b) Find the concentration of hydrogen ions $\left(H^+\right)$ if the pH of the liquid is 3.2.

11. Sketch the graph of $y = -2 + 3 \cos \dfrac{1}{2}(\theta - 100°)$.

12. Find the fourth term of $\left(3x - 2y^2\right)^5$.

13. Develop the identity for $\cos x \cos y$.

14. A triangle has a 25° angle. A side adjacent to this angle is 10 units long and the side opposite this angle is 5 units long. Draw the triangle(s) and find the lengths of the missing side(s) and angle(s).

15. Solve $\sin 2x = \sin x$ given that $0 \le x < 2\pi$.

16. Show: $\dfrac{1 - 3 \sin x - 4 \sin^2 x}{\cos^2 x} = \dfrac{1 - 4 \sin x}{1 - \sin x}$

17. Expand as the sum of individual logarithms, each of whose argument is linear: $\log \left(\dfrac{xy^2}{z^4}\right)$

18. (a) Find the sum of the first 10 terms of the geometric series whose first term is -6 and whose common ratio is -2.

    (b) Find the sum of the first 10 terms of the arithmetic series whose first term is -6 and whose common difference is -2.

19. The onlookers gazed in excitement as the number of gremlins decreased exponentially. When they were first observed, there were 48, but in only 50 minutes they had decreased to 42. How long would it take before the gremlins decreased to 25?

20. Write the equations of these trigonometric functions:

    (a)

    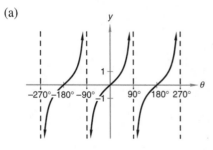

    (b)

    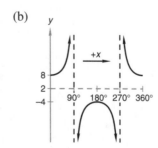

Advanced Mathematics by Saxon

1. A ball is dropped from a height of 50 feet. After each bounce, it rebounds two fifths of the distance it fell. How far does the ball fall on its third fall?

2. Evaluate: $\begin{vmatrix} 2 & 0 & 1 \\ 3 & 1 & 2 \\ 1 & 2 & 3 \end{vmatrix}$

3. Compute $_9P_3$ and $_9C_3$.

4. Write as a single logarithm: $\log\left(y^2 - 1\right) - 3\log x - 2\log(y + 1) + \log(x + xy)$

5. Use Cramer's rule to solve for x: $\begin{cases} x + 2y + z = 0 \\ 3x - y - z = 5 \\ 5x - 2y - 3z = 12 \end{cases}$

6. Use a calculator to aid in finding:

   (a) $\log_7 12$

   (b) $\log_{12} 7$

7. Find the exact value of $\sin 285°$ by using the identity for $\sin(A + B)$ and the fact that $285° = 150° + 135°$.

8. Solve for y: $\log_9 y = \sqrt{\log_9 y}$

9. Write the four fourth roots of -81 in rectangular coordinates. Give exact answers.

10. (a) Find the pH of a liquid if the concentration of hydrogen ions $\left(H^+\right)$ is 4.3×10^{-10} mole per liter.

    (b) Find the concentration of hydrogen ions $\left(H^+\right)$ if the pH of the liquid is 2.3.

11. Sketch the graph of $y = 2 + 2\cos\dfrac{1}{3}(\theta - 60°)$.

12. Find the third term of $\left(2x - 3y^2\right)^5$.

13. Develop the identity for $\sin x \sin y$.

14. A triangle has a 40° angle. A side adjacent to this angle is 9 units long and the side opposite this angle is 7 units long. Draw the triangle(s) and find the lengths of the missing side(s) and angle(s).

15. Solve $\sin 2x = \cos x$ given that $0 \le x < 2\pi$.

16. Show: $\dfrac{1 - 3\cos x - 4\cos^2 x}{\sin^2 x} = \dfrac{1 - 4\cos x}{1 - \cos x}$

17. Expand as the sum of individual logarithms, each of whose argument is linear: $\log\left(\dfrac{x^3 y}{z^2}\right)$

18. (a) Find the sum of the first 7 terms of the geometric series whose first term is 5 and whose common ratio is 3.

    (b) Find the sum of the first 7 terms of the arithmetic series whose first term is 5 and whose common difference is 3.

19. The onlookers gazed in excitement as the number of gremlins decreased exponentially. When they were first observed, there were 62, but in only 40 minutes they had decreased to 48. How long would it take before the gremlins decreased to 30?

20. Write the equations of these trigonometric functions:

(a)

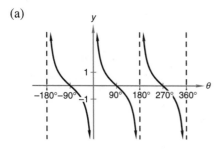

(b)

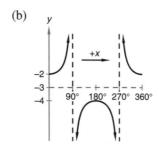

1. Beth could do p problems in 2 hours and Mollie could do x problems in h hours. How long would they have to work together to finish 400 problems?

2. Use cofactors to evaluate:

$$\begin{vmatrix} -3 & 2 & 4 \\ 0 & 1 & -2 \\ -1 & 7 & 0 \end{vmatrix}$$

3. Find the area of this triangle.

4. Find the four fourth roots of $-3 + 4i$ and express the roots in polar coordinates.

5. Express $\log_7 4$ in terms of natural logarithms. Do not find a numerical answer.

6. (a) Find the pH of a liquid if the concentration of H^+ is 4.1×10^{-5} mole per liter.

   (b) The pH of a solution is 3.7. What is the concentration of hydrogen ions (H^+) in moles per liter of the solution?

7. Find the middle term of $(3x^2 - 2y)^6$.

8. Use a calculator to compute: $\dfrac{\sqrt[4]{2300}\,\sqrt[3]{4800}}{\sqrt{5400}}$

9. Solve the following equations given that $0 \le x < 2\pi$:

   (a) $\cos^2 x - \sin^2 x = -1$

   (b) $1 + \sqrt{3}\tan 2x = 0$

10. The general form of the equation of an ellipse is $4x^2 + 9y^2 - 64x + 72y + 364 = 0$. Write the equation in standard form and give the coordinates of the center, the length of the major axis, and the length of the minor axis. Then graph the ellipse.

11. The general form of the equation of a hyperbola is $16x^2 - y^2 + 32x + 2y - 1 = 0$. Write the equation of this hyperbola in standard form and give the coordinates of the center, the coordinates of the vertices, and the equations of the asymptotes. Then graph the hyperbola.

12. Rene and Britta had \$500 to buy Buffalo Boys tickets. Goodey Tickets, Inc. was selling t tickets for d dollars. Since they arrived at the box office at 6 A.M. they got a discount of x dollars for each ticket. How many Buffalo Boys tickets could they buy?

13. Find $A + B$, $A - B$, and $2A$ where A and B are defined as follows: $A = \begin{bmatrix} 2 & 6 \\ 4 & 3 \end{bmatrix}$, $B = \begin{bmatrix} 1 & 0 \\ -3 & -4 \end{bmatrix}$

14. Expand as the sum of the individual logarithms, each of whose argument is linear: $\log_5\left(\dfrac{25\sqrt[3]{x^4 y^5}}{z^{-2}}\right)$

15. Find the sum of this infinite geometric series: $6 - \dfrac{6}{2} + \dfrac{6}{4} - \dfrac{6}{8} + \cdots$

16. Sketch the graph of each of the following: (a) $y = 2 + 2\sec\theta$ (b) $y = -1 + \cot\theta$

17. Solve for x: $\log(x + 3) - \log(2x - 3) = 2\log\sqrt{2}$

18. Show: $\dfrac{1 + \cos 2x}{\csc x \sin 2x} = \cos x$

19. Sketch the graph of $y = 2 + 3\sin\dfrac{1}{2}(x - \pi)$.

20. Write the equations of these trigonometric functions:

    (a)
    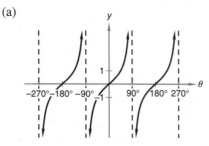

    (b)
    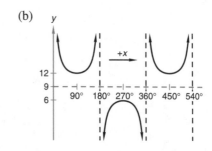

Advanced Mathematics by Saxon

1. Jessica could pin 4 wrestlers in 9 minutes, but her brother Jeremy could only pin 3 wrestlers in m minutes. Together, they had to pin 15 wrestlers. How many minutes would it take?

2. Use cofactors to evaluate:

$$\begin{vmatrix} 4 & 2 & -3 \\ -2 & 1 & 0 \\ -1 & 7 & 0 \end{vmatrix}$$

3. Find the area of this triangle.

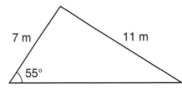

4. Find the four fourth roots of $-4 + 3i$ and express the roots in polar coordinates.

5. Express $\log_9 5$ in terms of natural logarithms. Do not find a numerical answer.

6. (a) Find the pH of a liquid if the concentration of H^+ is 2.6×10^{-2} mole per liter.

   (b) The pH of a solution is 11.6. What is the concentration of hydrogen ions (H^+) in moles per liter of the solution?

7. Find the middle term of $(2x - 4y^2)^4$.

8. Use a calculator to compute: $\dfrac{\sqrt[3]{1600}\sqrt[7]{20{,}000}}{\sqrt{2300}}$

9. Solve the following equations given that $0 \le x < 2\pi$:

   (a) $2\cos^2 x + \cos x - 1 = 0$

   (b) $1 - \sqrt{3}\tan 2x = 0$

10. The general form of the equation of an ellipse is $9x^2 + 4y^2 - 72x + 64y + 364 = 0$. Write the equation in standard form and give the coordinates of the center, the length of the major axis, and the length of the minor axis. Then graph the ellipse.

11. The general form of the equation of a hyperbola is $16y^2 - x^2 + 32y + 2x - 1 = 0$. Write the equation of this hyperbola in standard form and give the coordinates of the center, the coordinates of the vertices, and the equations of the asymptotes. Then graph the hyperbola.

12. Jason and Mr. Pham had $10 to buy food for their climbing trip. They could buy p packs of ramen noodles for c cents. When they arrived at the grocery store, they learned of a special on ramen noodles. They got a discount of d cents for every pack. How many packs of ramen noodles could they buy?

13. Find $A + B$, $A - B$, and $2B$ where A and B are defined as follows: $A = \begin{bmatrix} 2 & 2 \\ 2 & 0 \end{bmatrix}$, $B = \begin{bmatrix} 2 & 5 \\ 2 & 2 \end{bmatrix}$

14. Expand as the sum of the individual logarithms, each of whose argument is linear: $\log_6\left(\dfrac{36\sqrt[4]{x^2 y^9}}{z}\right)$

15. Find the sum of this infinite geometric series: $2 + \dfrac{1}{2} + \dfrac{1}{8} + \dfrac{1}{32} + \cdots$

16. Sketch the graph of each of the following: (a) $y = 3 + \sec\theta$ (b) $y = \cot\theta + 1$

17. Solve for x: $\log(x + 3) - \log x = 6\log\sqrt[3]{3}$

18. Show: $\dfrac{1 - \cos 2x}{\sec x \sin 2x} = \sin x$

19. Sketch the graph of $y = 1 + 2\sin\dfrac{1}{2}(x + \pi)$.

20. Write the equations of these trigonometric functions:

    (a)

    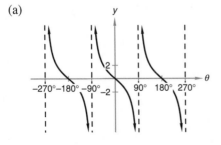

    (b)

    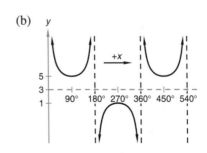

Advanced Mathematics by Saxon

1. The urn contained 5 red marbles and 4 blue marbles. John drew a marble at random and did not put it back. Then he randomly drew another marble. What is the probabilty that both marbles were blue?

2. Use Cramer's Rule to solve for y: $\begin{cases} 3x + 2y = 0 \\ x - 3z = 5 \\ x + y + z = -2 \end{cases}$

3. Use an infinite geometric series as an aid for expressing $0.0\overline{439}$ as a common fraction.

4. A ball is dropped from a height of 132 feet. After each bounce, the ball rebounds one fourth of the distance it fell. What is the total distance the ball will travel?

5. The first term of a geometric sequence is -4 and the common ratio is -3.
    (a) What is the tenth term of the sequence?
    (b) What is the sum of the first 10 terms?

6. (a) The pH of a solution is 11.8. What is the concentration of hydrogen ions in moles per liter of the solution?
    (b) Find the pH of a liquid if the concentration of H^+ is 3.25×10^{-8} mole per liter.

7. The general form of the equation of an ellipse is $x^2 + 9y^2 + 10x + 18y - 2 = 0$. Write the equation of the ellipse in standard form and give the coordinates of the center, the length of the major axis, and the length of the minor axis. Also, determine whether the major axis is horizontal or vertical and graph the ellipse.

8. The general form of the equation of a hyperbola is $4x^2 - y^2 - 24x + 2y - 1 = 0$. Write the equation of the hyperbola in standard form and give the coordinates of the center, the coordinates of the vertices, and the equations of the asymptotes. Then graph the hyperbola.

9. Simplify: $9^{\log_3 12 + 2\log_3 2 - \log_3 6}$

10. Solve for x: $\log_3 (x - 2) < 3$

11. The increase of aliens was exponential. After 5 hours the aliens numbered 120, and after 15 hours there were 400 of them. How many aliens were there after 25 hours?

12. Jim and Dot went to buy Eagles tickets which were selling at n tickets for d dollars. But they overslept and when they arrived they could only get tickets in row fifty behind a big post, which were discounted by \$10 each. Since they brought \$250 with them, they decided to buy some tickets. How many could they buy?

13. Solve for x: $\log \sqrt[4]{x^3} + \log \sqrt[4]{x^5} = \frac{2}{3} \log 27$

14. Use a calculator to compute: $\dfrac{\left(\sqrt[3]{406 \times 10^3}\right)^2}{\sqrt{807 \times 10^{17}}}$

15. Solve $\tan^2 2\theta = 1$ given that $0° \le \theta < 360°$.

16. Show: $\dfrac{2 \cot x}{\cot^2 x + 1} = \sin 2x$

17. Write the following as a single logarithm. Simplify your answer.

    $$-\log_3 (m + 1) + 2\log_3 m + \log_3 (m^2 - 1) - \log_3 (m^2 + m)$$

18. Find the fifth term in the expansion of $\left(2x - 3y^2\right)^{11}$.

19. Find the three cube roots of 1 in rectangular coordinates. Give exact answers.

20. Graph the relation $\theta = \arcsin x$. Indicate on the graph the portion that is the graph of the function $\theta = \text{Arcsin } x$. State the domain and range of $\theta = \text{Arcsin } x$. Then evaluate Arcsin x at $x = -\frac{\sqrt{2}}{2}$, $\frac{\sqrt{2}}{2}$, and -1.

1. The urn contained 6 green marbles and 5 yellow marbles. Clay drew a marble at random and did not put it back. Then he randomly drew another marble. What is the probability that both marbles are green?

2. Use Cramer's Rule to solve for y: $\begin{cases} 3x + 4y + z = 0 \\ y - 3z = -3 \\ x + y + z = 1 \end{cases}$

3. Use an infinite geometric series as an aid for expressing $0.0\overline{311}$ as a common fraction.

4. A ball is dropped from a height of 132 feet. After each bounce, the ball rebounds one third of the distance it fell. What is the total distance the ball will travel?

5. The first term of a geometric sequence is 5 and the common ratio is -2.
   (a) What is the ninth term of the sequence?
   (b) What is the sum of the first 9 terms?

6. (a) The pH of a solution is 4.3. What is the concentration of hydrogen ions in moles per liter of the solution?
   (b) Find the pH of a liquid if the concentration of H^+ is 7.94×10^{-12} mole per liter.

7. The general form of the equation of an ellipse is $x^2 + 4y^2 + 6x - 16y + 9 = 0$. Write the equation of the ellipse in standard form and give the coordinates of the center, the length of the major axis, and the length of the minor axis. Also, determine whether the major axis is horizontal or vertical and graph the ellipse.

8. The general form of the equation of a hyperbola is $x^2 - 9y^2 - 4x + 72y - 149 = 0$. Write the equation of the hyperbola in standard form and give the coordinates of the center, the coordinates of the vertices, and the equations of the asymptotes. Then graph the hyperbola.

9. Simplify: $4^{\log_2 3 + 2\log_2 2 - \log_2 5}$

10. Solve for x: $\log_2(x - 3) < 4$

11. The increase in UFO sightings was exponential. After 5 days the sightings numbered 70, and after 30 days there were 225 of them. How many sightings were there after 50 days?

12. Jemal wanted to buy the next issue of Z-MEN which was selling at x copies for y dollars. By the time Jemal got his paycheck, the price of the issue had been raised by \$5 per copy. Jemal decided to buy some copies anyway. How many copies could he buy with \$50?

13. Solve for x: $\log \sqrt[3]{x^7} + \log \sqrt[3]{x^2} = \dfrac{3}{4} \log 16$

14. Use a calculator to compute: $\dfrac{\left(\sqrt[3]{619 \times 10^5}\right)^2}{\sqrt{502 \times 10^{19}}}$

15. Solve $\sin^2 2\theta = 1$ given that $0° \le \theta < 360°$.

16. Show: $\dfrac{2\tan x}{\tan^2 x + 1} = \sin 2x$

17. Write the following as a single logarithm. Simplify your answer.
$$-\log_4(n + 2) + 3\log_4 n + \log_4(n^2 - 4) - \log_3(n^2 + n)$$

18. Find the fifth term in the expansion of $\left(2x^2 - 5y\right)^{10}$.

19. Find the three cube roots of i in rectangular coordinates. Give exact answers.

20. Graph the relation $\theta = \arccos x$. Indicate on the graph the portion that is the graph of the function $\theta = \text{Arccos } x$.
    State the domain and range of $\theta = \text{Arccos } x$. Then evaluate Arccos x at $x = -\dfrac{\sqrt{2}}{2}, \dfrac{\sqrt{2}}{2},$ and -1.

Advanced Mathematics by Saxon

1. A card was drawn from a full deck of 52 cards. What is the probability that the card was either a 3 or a heart or the 3 of hearts?

2. Use Cramer's rule to solve for x: $\begin{cases} 3x - 2y = 0 \\ x + 3z = 5 \\ -x + 2y - 5z = -7 \end{cases}$

3. Let $A = \begin{bmatrix} 2 & 0 \\ 2 & -3 \\ 4 & 1 \end{bmatrix}$ and $B = \begin{bmatrix} 1 & 3 \\ 2 & -5 \end{bmatrix}$. Find $A \cdot B$.

4. Graph the relation $\theta = \arccos x$. Indicate on the graph the portion that is the graph of the function $\theta = \text{Arccos } x$. State the domain and the range of $\theta = \text{Arccos } x$. Then evaluate Arccos x at $x = \frac{\sqrt{3}}{2}, -\frac{\sqrt{3}}{2}$, and 0.

5. Solve for x: $\log_4 (x - 2) > 2$

6. Find the eighth term of the expansion of $\left(2x^3 - y\right)^{12}$.

7. Use synthetic division to divide $x^3 - 5x^2 + x + 12$ by $x - 2$.

8. Sketch the graph of $y = \cot (x - \pi)$.

9. Show: $\dfrac{\sin^2 x}{1 - \cos x} = \dfrac{1 + \sec x}{\sec x}$

10. Sketch the graph of $f(x) = (x - 1)(x - 2)^2$.

11. Use synthetic division to see if 2 is a zero of $x^4 - 2x^3 + 5x - 10$.

12. Simplify: $(x + 3)6^{\log_6 \left(x^2 - 5x + 6\right) - \log_6 \left(x^2 - 9\right)}$

13. Find $\sin 105° + \sin 15°$ using the identity for $\sin x + \sin y$. Use exact values.

14. Use an infinite geometric series as an aid for expressing $4.\overline{13}$ as a common fraction.

15. Solve $\cos 2x - \sin x = 0$ given that $0 \le x < 2\pi$.

16. Write the following as a single logarithm. Simplify your answer.
$$\log (x - y) + 2 \log z - \log \left(x^2 z - y^2 z\right)$$

17. Use the remainder theorem to evaluate $2x^3 - 5x^2 + 2x + 5$ when $x = -2$.

18. The equation $9x^2 + 4y^2 + 54x - 8y + 49 = 0$ is the general form of the equation of an ellipse. Write the equation of the ellipse in standard form and give the coordinates of the center, the length of the major axis, and the length of the minor axis. Graph the ellipse.

19. Determine the radius of the "region of interest" for the polynomial function $y = x^3 - 2x + 1$. Then choose different x values within the region of interest and find corresponding y values. Sketch the graph.

20. Which of the following graphs most resembles the graph of $f(x) = (1 + x)(x - 3)(x - 2)$?

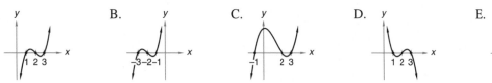

A.   B.   C.   D.   E.

1. A card was drawn from a poker deck of 52 cards. What is the probability that the card was either a 4 or a spade or the 4 of spades?

2. Use Cramer's rule to solve for x: $\begin{cases} 3x + 2y = 3 \\ 6z - 2x = -1 \\ x + 2y + 4z = -2 \end{cases}$

3. Let $A = \begin{bmatrix} 4 & 1 \\ 2 & -5 \\ 4 & 3 \end{bmatrix}$ and $B = \begin{bmatrix} -2 & -3 \\ 2 & 3 \end{bmatrix}$. Find $A \cdot B$.

4. Graph the relation $\theta = \arcsin x$. Indicate on the graph the portion that is the graph of the function $\theta = \text{Arcsin } x$. State the domain and the range of $\theta = \text{Arcsin } x$. Then evaluate $\text{Arcsin } x$ at $x = \frac{\sqrt{3}}{2}, -\frac{\sqrt{3}}{2}$, and 0.

5. Solve for x: $\log_3 (x - 1) > 2$

6. Find the third term of the expansion of $\left(2a^3 - b^2\right)^8$.

7. Use synthetic division to divide $x^5 - 7x^3 - 5x^2 + x - 12$ by $x - 3$.

8. Sketch the graph of $y = \tan (x - \pi)$.

9. Show: $\dfrac{\cos^2 x}{1 - \sin x} = \dfrac{1 + \csc x}{\csc x}$

10. Sketch the graph of $f(x) = (x + 2)(x - 1)^2$.

11. Use synthetic division to see if 3 is a zero of $2x^4 - 3x^3 - 5x^2 + 6x - 51$.

12. Simplify: $(x - 4)7^{\log_7 \left(x^2 - 3x - 28\right) - \log_7 \left(x^2 - 16\right)}$

13. Find $\cos 105° + \cos 15°$ using the identity for $\cos x + \cos y$. Use exact values.

14. Use an infinite geometric series as an aid for expressing $4.\overline{21}$ as a common fraction.

15. Solve $\cos 2x - \cos x = 0$ given that $0 \le x < 2\pi$.

16. Write the following as a single logarithm. Simplify your answer.
$$\ln (x + y) + 2 \ln z - \ln \left(y^2 z - x^2 z\right)$$

17. Use the remainder theorem to evaluate $3x^3 + 4x^2 + 5x + 6$ when $x = -3$.

18. The equation $9x^2 + 4y^2 - 54x - 16y + 61 = 0$ is the general form of the equation of an ellipse. Write the equation of the ellipse in standard form and give the coordinates of the center, the length of the major axis, and the length of the minor axis. Graph the ellipse.

19. Determine the radius of the "region of interest" for the polynomial function $y = 2x^3 - 3x + 2$. Then choose different x values within the region of interest and find corresponding y values. Sketch the graph.

20. Which of the following graphs most resembles the graph of $f(x) = x(x - 2)(x + 2)$?

A.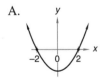

B.

C.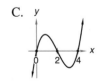

D.

E.

       Advanced Mathematics by Saxon

1. Are 153 and 42 relatively prime? If not, what common factor do both numbers share?

2. One root of $x^3 - 2x^2 - 9x + 18 = 0$ is 2. What are the other two roots?

3. Apply the rational roots theorem to list the possible rational roots of the equation $4x^7 + 5x^5 + 3x^2 + 3 = 0$.

4. For the polynomial function $y = x^3 - 4x^2 + x + 1$, determine the radius of the "region of interest." Then choose various x values within the region of interest and find the corresponding y values. Use the coordinates to sketch the graph.

5. Use the remainder theorem to evaluate $4x^3 + 2x^2 + 3x + 1$ when $x = -2$.

6. The half-life of zulus is 14 days and they decay exponentially. If Angela begins with 20 zulus, how long will it take until only 5 remain?

7. Let $A = \begin{bmatrix} 2 & 3 \\ 1 & 0 \\ 2 & 1 \end{bmatrix}$ and $B = \begin{bmatrix} -3 & 2 & 1 \\ 3 & 0 & 7 \end{bmatrix}$. Compute $A \cdot B$.

8. Find the inverse matrix of $\begin{bmatrix} 1 & 3 \\ 2 & 4 \end{bmatrix}$.

9. Expand as the sum of individual logarithms, each of whose argument is linear. Simplify your answer.

$$\log_3 \left(\frac{(x + 1)^3 \sqrt{y}}{\sqrt{y + 3}\,(x + 1)^2} \right)$$

10. Sketch the graph of $f(x) = \text{Arctan } x$. State the domain and range of the function. Then evaluate Arctan x at $x = 1$, -1, and $\sqrt{3}$.

11. Sketch the graph of the polynomial function $f(x) = x(x - 2)(x + 2)$. Indicate the locations where the graph intersects the x axis.

12. The equation of a hyperbola is $4x^2 - y^2 + 8x - 4y - 4 = 0$. Write the equation of the hyperbola in standard form and find the coordinates of the center, the coordinates of the vertices, and the equations of the asymptotes. Then graph the hyperbola.

13. Find the sixth term in the expansion $\left(3x^2 - \dfrac{1}{x} \right)^9$.

14. Solve for x: $4^{2x+3} = 8^{4x-1}$

15. Show: $\sin 2x + 2 \sin^2 x + \cos 2x = 1 + 2 \sin x \cos x$

16. Solve $2 \cot^2 x + 3 \csc x = 0$ given that $0 \le x < 2\pi$.

17. Use synthetic division with integers as divisors and the upper and lower bound theorem to find the upper and lower bounds for the real roots of the equation $y = x^3 + 2x^2 - x - 2$.

18. Write the three cube roots of $-i$. Express the roots in rectangular coordinates. Use exact values.

19. Use Descarte's rule of signs to determine the possible numbers of:

    (a) Positive real roots of $x^4 - x^3 - 3x^2 - x + 2 = 0$

    (b) Negative real roots of $x^4 - x^3 - 3x^2 - x + 2 = 0$

20. Torey's speed was 10 miles per hour less than Hannah's speed. Thus, Torey could travel 200 miles in half the time it took Hannah to travel 560 miles. Find the speed in miles per hour of Hannah.

Advanced Mathematics by Saxon

1. Are 51 and 340 relatively prime? If not, what common factor do both numbers share?

2. One root of $x^3 - 3x^2 - 4x + 12 = 0$ is 3. What are the other two roots?

3. Apply the rational roots theorem to list the possible rational roots of the equation $6x^6 + 3x^5 - x^3 - 2 = 0$.

4. For the polynomial function $y = x^3 - 4x^2 + 6x + 1$, determine the radius of the "region of interest." Then choose various x values within the region of interest and find the corresponding y values. Use the coordinates to sketch the graph.

5. Use the remainder theorem to evaluate $4x^3 - 2x^2 + 2x - 1$ when $x = -3$.

6. The half-life of zingers is 20 days and they decay exponentially. If Smith begins with 30 zingers, how long will it take until only 7 remain?

7. Let $A = \begin{bmatrix} 4 & 2 \\ 4 & 1 \\ 4 & 0 \end{bmatrix}$ and $B = \begin{bmatrix} 6 & 9 & 1 \\ 1 & 2 & 7 \end{bmatrix}$. Compute $A \cdot B$.

8. Find the inverse matrix of $\begin{bmatrix} 4 & 3 \\ 2 & 1 \end{bmatrix}$.

9. Expand as the sum of individual logarithms, each of whose argument is linear. Simplify your answer.

$$\log_4 \left(\frac{\sqrt[3]{y}\,(x-1)^2}{\sqrt{z+1}\,(x-1)^3} \right)$$

10. Sketch the graph of $f(x) = \text{Arctan } x$. State the domain and range of the function. Then evaluate Arctan x at $x = 1$, $-\sqrt{3}$, and $\frac{1}{\sqrt{3}}$.

11. Sketch the graph of the polynomial function $f(x) = x(x - 1)(x + 3)$. Indicate the locations where the graph intersects the x axis.

12. The equation of a hyperbola is $4y^2 - x^2 + 8y - 4x - 4 = 0$. Write the equation of the hyperbola in standard form and find the coordinates of the center, the coordinates of the vertices, and the equations of the asymptotes. Then graph the hyperbola.

13. Find the sixth term in the expansion $\left(2x^2 - \frac{1}{x} \right)^9$.

14. Solve for x: $4^{4x-1} = 8^{2x+3}$

15. Show: $(\cos x + \sin x)^2 - 1 = \sin 2x$

16. Solve $2 \cot^2 x - 3 \csc x = 0$ given that $0 \le x < 2\pi$.

17. Use synthetic division with integers as divisors and the upper and lower bound theorem to find the upper and lower bounds for the real roots of the equation $y = 3x^3 + x^2 - x + 1$.

18. Write the three cube roots of i. Express the roots in rectangular coordinates. Use exact values.

19. Use Descarte's rule of signs to determine the possible numbers of:
    (a) Positive real roots of $x^4 + x^3 - 3x^2 - x - 2 = 0$
    (b) Negative real roots of $x^4 + x^3 - 3x^2 - x - 2 = 0$

20. Climbing together Jason and Andy could climb the alpine face at a speed of 1 pitch per hour less than the Englishmen's speed. Thus, Jason and Andy could climb up 5 pitches in half the time it took the Englishmen to climb 12 pitches. Find the speed in pitches per hour of Jason and Andy.

Advanced Mathematics by Saxon

1. Hannah Rae walked k miles to town in only h hours, but still arrived one hour early. What should her speed have been to have arrived on time if the town were 3 miles further away?

2. Graph the piecewise function: $\begin{cases} y = 1 & \text{if } -\infty < x \le 0 \\ y = x & \text{if } 0 < x \le 2 \\ y = 2 - x & \text{if } 0 < x \le \infty \end{cases}$

3. Graph the hyperbola: $xy = 8$

4. Sketch the graph of $f(x) = [x] + 1$.

5. Find the roots of the polynomial equation $x^3 - 4x^2 + 6x - 4 = 0$.

6. Find the radius of a circle that circumscribes a regular hexagon whose perimeter is 24 inches.

7. Use Descarte's rule of signs to determine the possible number of:

   (a) Positive real roots of $4x^3 + 2x^2 + 7x + 9 = 0$ (b) Negative real roots of $4x^3 + 2x^2 + 7x + 9 = 0$

8. Write the equations for the function shown.

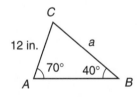

9. Sketch the graph of the following function showing clearly all x-intercepts, holes, and asymptotes.

$$y = \frac{x^2 - 3x}{(x + 1)(x - 2)(x - 3)}$$

10. Diana has an urn containing 6 blue marbles and 4 purple marbles. Two marbles are drawn at random. What is the probability that both are purple?

11. Solve this triangle for
    (a) angle C
    (b) side a
    (c) area

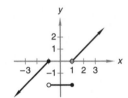

12. Listed below are the equations of conic sections, none of which are degenerate. Indicate whether each equation represents a circle, a parabola, an ellipse, or a hyperbola.

    (a) $x^2 - 4x + y^2 = 0$
    (b) $9x^2 + 4y^2 = 36$
    (c) $x^2 - 4y^2 = 4$
    (d) $x^2 + 4x - 4y - 2 = 0$
    (e) $x^2 + y^2 - 3x + 4y - 9 = 0$

13. Write equation (b) of problem 12 in standard form and graph the conic section that the equation represents.

14. Find the coordinates of the point that lies three fourths of the way between $(2, 4)$ and $(6, 6)$.

15. Determine the radius of the "region of interest" of the polynomial function $y = 2x^4 - 8x^2$. Determine the coordinates of some points on the graph and sketch the graph.

16. Solve for x: $\log_{1/3}(x - 2) > 2$ 17. Solve $\sin 2x - \cos x = 0$ given that $0 \le x < 2\pi$.

18. Show: $\cos 3x = 4\cos^3 x - 3\cos x$ $[\textit{Hint: } \cos 3x = \cos(2x + x)]$

19. One root of $x^4 - 3x^2 - 4 = 0$ is i. What are the other three roots?

20. Which of the following graphs most resembles the graph of $f(x) = x^2(x - 1)^2$?

A.   B.   C.   D.   E.

Advanced Mathematics by Saxon

1. The lab assistant calibrated t thermometers in h hours, but still got off work 3 hours late. What should her rate of calibration have been to get off work on time if she had to calibrate $t + 2$ thermometers?

2. Graph the piecewise function: $\begin{cases} y = 3 & \text{if } -\infty < x \leq 1 \\ y = x & \text{if } 1 < x \leq 3 \\ y = -x + 1 & \text{if } 3 < x < \infty \end{cases}$

3. Graph the hyperbola: $xy = 9$

4. Sketch the graph of $f(x) = [x] - 1$.

5. Find the roots of the polynomial equation $x^3 - 2x^2 + 2x - 15 = 0$.

6. Find the radius of a circle that circumscribes a regular hexagon whose perimeter is 30 inches.

7. Use Descarte's rule of signs to determine the possible number of :

    (a) Positive real roots of $6x^3 - 2x^2 - 3x + 7 = 0$ (b) Negative real roots of $6x^3 - 2x^2 - 3x + 7 = 0$

8. Write the equations for the function shown.

    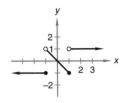

9. Sketch the graph of the following function showing clearly all x-intercepts, holes, and asymptotes.

    $$y = \frac{x^2 + 4x}{(x + 2)(x - 1)(x + 4)}$$

10. Jif has a bucket containing 5 red balls and 7 green balls. Two balls are drawn at random. What is the probability that both are green?

11. Solve this triangle for

    (a) angle C

    (b) side a

    (c) area

    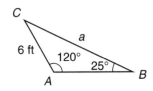

12. Listed below are the equations of conic sections, none of which are degenerate. Indicate whether each equation represents a circle, a parabola, an ellipse, or a hyperbola.

    (a) $x^2 - 4y^2 = 4$

    (b) $2x^2 - 4x + y^2 = 0$

    (c) $x^2 + y^2 - 6x + 4y + 9 = 0$

    (d) $xy = 8$

    (e) $x^2 + 4x - 4y - 2 = 0$

13. Write equation (c) of problem 12 in standard form and graph the conic section that the equation represents.

14. Find the coordinates of the point that lies two thirds of the way between $(1, 3)$ and $(7, 6)$.

15. Determine the radius of the "region of interest" of the polynomial function $y = 3x^3 - 9x$. Determine the coordinates of some points on the graph and sketch the graph.

16. Solve for x: $\log_{1/2}(x - 3) > 3$ 17. Solve $\sin 2x - \sin x = 0$ given that $0 \leq x < 2\pi$.

18. Show: $\sin 3x = 3 \sin x - 4 \sin^3 x$ [Hint: $\sin 3x = \sin(2x + x)$]

19. One root of $x^4 + 3x^2 - 4 = 0$ is $2i$. What are the other three roots?

20. Which of the following graphs most resembles the graph of $f(x) = x^2(x + 1)^2$?

Advanced Mathematics **by Saxon**